IF YOU THINK YOU'VE HEARD IT ALL, YOU PROBABLY HAVEN'T HEARD THIS . . .

Moroccan running machine Hicham El Guerrouj holds the mile record, setting a time of 3:43.13 in Rome, Italy, on July 7, 1999.

The male goliath bird-eater is the largest spider, weighing up to 6 ounces, with a legspan of 11 inches—big enough to cover a dinner plate.

The greatest distance over which anyone has traveled on a pogo stick while simultaneously juggling is 4 miles by Ashrita Furman, while visiting Easter Island, Chile, on January 28, 2010.

With a price tag of 10 million Chinese yuan or $1.5 million dollars, an 11-month-old red Tibetan mastiff became the world's most expensive dog when sold by breeder Lu Liang to a Chinese multi-millionaire in March 2011.

The youngest commercially published author is Dorothy Straight, of Washington, DC, who wrote *How the World Began* in 1962 at age four. It was published in August 1964 by Pantheon Books.

Accreditation

Guinness World Records Limited has a very thorough accreditation system for records verification. However, while every effort is made to ensure accuracy, Guinness World Records Limited cannot be held responsible for any errors contained in this work. Feedback from our readers on any point of accuracy is always welcomed.

Abbreviations & Measurements

Guinness World Records Limited uses both metric and imperial measurements. The sole exceptions are for some scientific data where metric measurements only are universally accepted, and for some sports data. Where a specific date is given, the exchange rate is calculated according to the currency values that were in operation at the time. Where only a year date is given, the exchange rate is calculated from December of that year. "One billion" is taken to mean one thousand million. "GDR" (the German Democratic Republic) refers to the East German state, which was unified with West Germany in 1990. The abbreviation is used for sports records broken before 1990. The USSR (Union of Soviet Socialist Republics) split into a number of parts in 1991, the largest of these being Russia. The CIS (Commonwealth of Independent States) replaced it and the abbreviation is used mainly for sporting records broken at the 1992 Olympic Games. Guinness World Records Limited does not claim to own any right, title or interest in the trademarks of others reproduced in this book.

General Warning

Attempting to break records or set new records can be dangerous. Appropriate advice should be taken first and all record attempts are undertaken at the participant's risk. In no circumstances will Guinness World Records Limited have any liability for death or injury suffered in any record attempt. Guinness World Records Limited has complete discretion over whether or not to include any particular records in the book. Being a Guinness World Records record holder does not guarantee you a place in the book.

GUINNESS WORLD RECORDS 2012

BANTAM BOOKS
NEW YORK

A 2012 Bantam Books Mass Market Edition

GUINNESS WORLD RECORDS™ 2012
Copyright © 2011 Guinness World Records Limited.
Published under license.

GUINNESS WORLD RECORDS™ is a trademark of Guinness World Records Limited and is reproduced under license by Bantam Books, an imprint of The Random House Publishing Group, a division of Random House, Inc., New York.

Revised American editions copyright © 2012, 2011, 2010, 2009, 2008, 2007, 2006, 2005, 2004, 2003, 2002, 2001, 2000, 1999, 1998, 1997, 1996, 1995, 1994, 1993, 1992, 1991, 1990, 1989, 1988, 1987, 1986, 1985, 1984, 1983, 1982, 1981, 1980, 1979, 1978, 1977, 1976, 1975, 1974, 1973, 1972, 1971, 1970, 1969, 1968, 1966, 1965, 1964, 1963, 1962, 1960 by Guinness World Records Ltd.

For more information address: Guinness World Records Ltd.

BANTAM BOOKS and the rooster colophon are registered trademarks of Random House, Inc.

ISBN: 978-0-345-53437-8

Printed in the United States of America

www.bantamdell.com

1 3 5 7 9 8 6 4 2

Bantam mass market edition: May 2012

GUINNESS WORLD RECORDS

RECORDS

EDITOR-IN-CHIEF
Craig Glenday

CONTENTS

RECORD BUBBLES: Popping up across the book you'll find these bubbles, each featuring another Guinness World Records feat. **Brand-new records** get a ●. Those that are **updates of existing records** get a ○.

122: Number of facts about your life listed in this book! At the top of most spreads you'll find this fact box, written by Tadg Farrington, author of *The Average Life of the Average Person*, based on the typical reader of Guinness World Records.

THIS IS YOUR LIFE: On average, how many times will you sneeze during your life? And how much will you sweat? Uncover a wealth of fun facts about yourself, courtesy of writer and researcher Tadg Farrington.

> These boxes give a cross-reference to a related feature on another page.

Guinness World Records takes you on a global tour of record-breaking with these bottom-of-the-page entries. Records on the left-hand page will be from a particular country, and will have a particular theme . . .

Q. WHAT ARE THESE BOXES FOR?

A. They're full of surprising, record-related teasers that will challenge what you think you know—rather like our "Mythconceptions" feature (see pp. xxxix–xliv).

. . . the theme is then picked up in a record listed here, at the bottom of the right-hand page. This record will be from a different country. On the following page you'll find another record from the same country. And so on, around the world!

INTRODUCTION

AIR

Farthest flight by a paper aircraft Stephen Krieger (U.S.A.) flew a paper aircraft 207 ft. 4 in. (63.19 m) in a hangar near Moses Lake, Washington, U.S.A., on September 6, 2003.

○ **GREATEST DISTANCE FLOWN IN A WING SUIT** Shinichi Ito (Japan) flew a horizontal, straight-line distance of 10.19 miles (16.4 km) after jumping from an airplane 33,430 ft. (10,550 m) above Yolo County, California, U.S.A. He flew for 4 min. 57 sec. on September 24, 2010, reaching a maximum speed of 178.3 mi./hr. (287 km/h) and deploying his parachute at an altitude of 3,050 ft. (929.6 m). During his record attempt, he wore a "Blade II" wing suit, manufactured by Birdman, Inc. (Finland).

THE LIGHT STUFF: The **least dense solid** is an aerogel made by Lawrence Livermore National Laboratory (U.S.A.). With a density of just 0.25 grains/in.^{3} (1 mg/cm^3), it is lighter than air.

7,248 Volume in gallons of intestinal gas you'll pass during your lifetime. In total, you'll contaminate the air around you by passing wind for the equivalent of 8.7 days nonstop! That's enough gas to demolish a small apartment building.

LARGEST BUBBLEGUM BUBBLE BLOWN

20 in. (50.8 cm), by Chad Fell (U.S.A.), Winston County, Alabama, U.S.A., April 24, 2004.

○LARGEST FREE-FLOATING SOAP BUBBLE

483 ft.^{3} (13.67 m^3), by Jarom Watts (U.S.A.), Spokane, Washington, U.S.A., February 21, 2009.

●LARGEST FROZEN SOAP BUBBLE

0.15 ft.^{3} (4,315.7 cm^3) by Sam "Samsam Bubbleman" Heath (UK), London, UK, June 28, 2010.

○MOST PEOPLE INSIDE A SOAP BUBBLE

94, by Hammou Bensalah (Algeria), Soltau, Germany, September 24, 2009.

●LONGEST-DURATION FLIGHT BY HELIUM BALLOONS Piloted by Jonathan Trappe (U.S.A.), the *Spirit Cluster* (made up of 57 balloons) flew for 13 hr. 36 min. 57 sec. across North Carolina, U.S.A., from April 10 to 11, 2010. In total, Jonathan covered 109 miles (175 km) during his flight and reached a peak altitude of 7,474 ft. (2,278 m).

Air guitar contests use a 6.0 scale for scoring—like figure skating.

Most aircraft flown in by one passenger Edwin A Shackleton (UK) had flown in a total of 841 different types of aircraft by January 2007.

MOST AIR GUITAR WORLD CHAMPIONSHIP WINS The Oulu Music Video Festival's Air Guitar World Championships, held in Oulu, Finland, have been won by Zac "The Magnet" Monro (UK, above) in 2001 and 2002, and by Ochi "Dainoji" Yosuke (Japan) in 2006 and 2007.

● **MOST MODELING BALLOON SCULPTURES MADE IN ONE MINUTE** John Cassidy (U.S.A.) made 13 balloon sculptures in one minute in New York City, U.S.A., on November 21, 2005. John sculpted a bone, bracelet, crocodile, dagger, dachshund, dog (no breed), dragonfly, elephant, fish, hat, honeybee, Indian headdress, and sword.

LARGEST WHOOPEE CUSHION Measuring 10 ft. (3.05 m) in diameter, the largest whoopee cushion ever was made by Steve Mesure (UK) on behalf of the Street Vibe music project for an event at The Scoop in London, UK, on June 14, 2008. Volunteers were encouraged to sit on the cushion to demonstrate how wind instruments work.

Farthest distance traveled by a human voice The normal intelligible outdoor range of the male human voice in still air is 590 ft. (180 m). *Silbo Gomero,* the whistled language of the Spanish-speaking inhabitants of the Canary Island of La Gomera, is intelligible under ideal conditions at 5 miles (8 km).

● **Longest-duration Malteser blowing** Dermot Whelan (Ireland) kept a Malteser suspended in the air for 3.18 seconds by blowing, in Dublin, Ireland, on September 16, 2008.

Air

78% nitrogen

21% oxygen

1% argon

less than 1% carbon dioxide, other gases and water vapor

WHAT IS AIR? Air is, in fact, a mixture of gases. The air pressing down on us—the atmosphere—is about 74 miles (120 km) thick and weighs 2,204.62 lb. (1 metric ton). We can't feel its weight because the air pressure inside our bodies is the same as that outside them. If it wasn't, we'd be crushed. The higher you go, the less air there is pressing down on you. If you climbed Mount Everest you would have gone through 70% of the atmosphere, so the weight pressing down on you would be less. The atmosphere thins further still until you reach outer space.

China is the country with the **highest consumption of cigarettes.** A breathtaking 1.69 trillion cigarettes are smoked in China each year, and one out of every three cigarettes smoked in the world is smoked there.

Most kites flown simultaneously by one person In Weifang City, China, 43 kites were flown at the same time by Ma Qinghua (China) on November 7, 2006.

EDITOR'S LETTER

No two words better sum up Guinness World Records than "Officially Amazing." As the global authority on superlative achievements, we process thousands of record applications from around the world each year, applying our expertise and experience to fully investigate each claim. And the result? An annual book bringing you the very best, most awe-inspiring, and entertaining accomplishments. . . .

Welcome to the new, fully updated edition of the world's **best-selling copyright book**. We've spent the last 12 months processing more claims than ever before, and the result is an unrivaled compendium of superlatives that will blow your mind. This year's book is full to bursting with the most thrilling, awesome, inspiring adventures from the world of record breaking—illustrated with some of the world's most amazing photos.

○ **LARGEST GA-GA-GATHERING** No, you're not hallucinating—here are some of the 121 fans of Lady Gaga who set a new world record on the red carpet at the 2011 Grammy Awards. Organizers E! Entertainment ensured that there were plenty of "Paparazzi" on hand. . . .

MAKE A CONNECTION: Here's the first of our record connections. We begin with China, followed by a related record from Austria on the right. Turn the page and you'll find another Austrian record, and a related record from somewhere else on the opposite page, and so on. . . .

Measured per capita, the world's **heaviest smokers** are the Austrians—36.3% of the population indulge in this habit regularly.

27,154 Number of record holders named in our archives. If you're one of them, congratulations—you're among an elite group that makes up just 0.00038% of the world's population!

NBA WEST: The ●**most three-pointers** made by a pair in one minute is 15, by Kevin Durant (left) and Dirk Nowitzki at the NBA All-Star weekend in Los Angeles on February 19, 2011.

●**MOST LANDMARKS ILLUMINATED** This year, we were proud to join Evelyn Lauder and Elizabeth Hurley in supporting the Estée Lauder Companies' Breast Cancer Awareness Campaign. Turn to p. 363 for details of their record-breaking campaign.

With the 2012 Olympics on the horizon—and, if certain astrologers are correct, the end of the world—then 2012 is going to be an explosive year! To mark London's record third time as the host of the Olympiad, we've compiled an extended Olympics feature (pp. 438–452). Sports fans will see that we've also completely restructured the Sports section (pp. 438–553)—you'll find all your favorite subjects as usual, but this year ordered by theme.

If you're intrigued by the idea that the world's going to end, as predicted by the Maya (see p. 99), then our pages on asteroids (p. 16) and killer climates (p. 51) might make you panic!

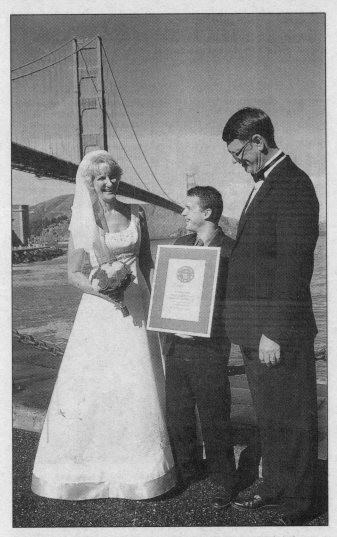

○TALLEST MARRIED COUPLE When Wayne fell head-over-heels in love with Laurie, he had a long way to tumble! After a short romance, the towering twosome married—and with a combined height of 13 ft. 4 in. (407.3 cm), Mr. and Mrs. Hallquist of California are now the tallest married couple on Earth!

2 Minutes per day that the average person spends reading reference books, compared with seven minutes of reading online. Hopefully this edition will inspire you to read for a bit longer each day—otherwise, you'll spend only four years of your life learning from books.

DOG MEET DOG: To celebrate the launch of GWR 2011, we brought together the world's tallest and shortest dogs in Central Park, New York. Find out more about our four-legged friends on pp. 263–271.

● **MOST PEOPLE IN A NURSERY RHYME RELAY** To gain first-hand experience of record breaking, and to understand the effort required, 154 delegates from the Jim Pattison Group—the company that owns Guinness World Records—took it in turns to recite the lines of various nursery rhymes in San Antonio, Texas, on March 12, 2011.

Austria has the world's **highest proportion of organic farming** with an amazing 10% of its entire land area dedicated to organic production.

GUTSY GRANDMA: Congratulations to Ernestine Shepherd (U.S.A., b. June 16, 1936) for her continuing success as the **oldest female bodybuilder.** The sturdy septuagenarian is still going strong despite turning 75 at her last birthday.

●**LARGEST GATHERING OF LEPRECHAUNS** We'd like to say a big thank you to Jay Leno and everyone at NBC's *The Tonight Show* for organizing this fantastic flock of 224 Irish imps in Burbank, California. The great green gathering took place as part of the St. Patrick's Day celebrations on March 17, 2011.

●**HIGHEST INSURED HAIR** He's famous for his luscious, lengthy locks, and now Troy Polamalu of the Pittsburgh Steelers has had his hair insured with Lloyd's of London for a record $1 million. Pictured here is Mike Janela presenting an official certificate to the NFL strong safety, who's sponsored—not surprisingly—by the Procter and Gamble shampoo brand Head & Shoulders!

The **largest consumers of organic food** are the Danish, who spend $350 million on organic produce every year—equivalent to $65.88 per person.

X GAMES Fans of extreme sports can find us each summer at the "Break Fest" area of the X Games. We offer everyone the opportunity to strap on some kneepads and have a go at BMX and skateboard records. Our adjudicators approved no less than 15 new world records at X Games 16 in Los Angeles—including the **most backside grinds on a skateboard in one minute (31)** by Annika Vrklan (U.S.A., pictured).

JERSEY SHORE Here's adjudicator Mike Janela with the cast of reality show *Jersey Shore* at MTV's *New Year Bash* in Times Square, New York, on December 31, 2010. The eight housemates formed part of a group of 5,726 people who set a new world record for the ●**most people fist pumping!**

BOOK 'EM: If novels are more your thing, you'll be excited to learn that we awarded two writers with new world records this year. *Goosebumps* creator R. L. Stine, the **biggest-selling author of children's horror,** and 27-year-old Christopher Paolini, the **youngest author of a best-selling book series** (*Inheritance Cycle*).

●**LARGEST HUMAN-MATTRESS DOMINOES** We had another record-breaking day on *Live! with Regis and Kelly,* as Stuart joined Kelly and fill-in host Anderson Cooper for a giant game of human-mattress dominoes. Congratulations to the 380 people who took part in the attempt, which was staged on the deck of New York City's Intrepid Sea, Air & Space Museum.

For those who think (probably rightly!) that the world *won't* end in 2012, there's always Alan Turing Year to look forward to. Turing was a major pioneer in the history of computing and code-breaking, and we celebrate the life of this important scientist with exciting new sections on Codes & Cryptography (p. 289) and Computing (p. 297) exploring the history of computer technology.

Indeed, history plays a big part in this year's book—we've dedicated an entire chapter to bringing you a superlative (if brief) history of the world (Time Tales, pp. 97–120).

○**MOST PEOPLE DRESSED AS SUPERHEROES** To celebrate the launch of the Dreamworks movie *Megamind* in October 2010, star Will Ferrell hosted a gathering of 1,580 costumed superheroes in Los Angeles. Our own superhero, Stuart Claxton, was on hand to award the giant certificate.

●MOST HAIRCUTS IN 8 HOURS (TEAM) And while we're in Jersey, well done to the cast of the Style Network's show *Jerseylicious* for 246 haircuts achieved in 8 hours by the Gatsby Salon team.

IT'S A RAP We turned up at MTV's first O Music Awards in Vegas in 2010 to recognize the record-breaking rapping of Chidera "Chiddy" Anamege (U.S.A.)—one-half of the hip-hop duo Chiddy Bang. He performed for an incredible 9 hr. 18 min. 22 sec.—setting records for the **●longest freestyle rap** and **●longest rap marathon.**

Talking of which, history was being made just as we went to press, with the UK's Prince William marrying Catherine Middleton, watched by a record online audience—YouTube's Royal Channel hosted 72 million streams during the nuptials, which is the **most live streams for a single event**. And with the fast-approaching diamond jubilee of Queen Elizabeth II (**longest reigning queen—living**), it seemed a good time to explore superlative sovereigns in our Royalty & Monarchies spread (p. 284).

Another special feature of this year's book is a unique series of photographs documenting some of the best of the recent adventuring world records. The brainchild of GWR's Picture Editor, Michael Whitty, Spirit of Adventure (pp. 205–206) is a visual celebration of young pioneers and proof—were it needed—that our planet continues to be a thrilling, challenging, and dangerous place to discover… and that you're never too young to achieve greatness!

●**LONGEST CAREER AS AN ENTERTAINMENT NEWS HOST** We'd like to thank Regis Philbin for helping us surprise showbiz host Mary Hart, who retired from her role as anchor at CBS's *Entertainment Tonight* after a record 28 years! Regis—himself a record holder for the **most hours on television** (an incredible 16,343 hours), stopped by the May 11 show to award the gossip queen her much-deserved certificate.

If you can't explore the world, then discovering *Guinness World Records 2012* is the next best thing. Visit the spectacular and endangered UNESCO World Heritage sites in World of Wonders and Water World (pp. 43–51) without leaving the comfort of your armchair; find out how to climb Mount Everest (p. 207), the **highest peak** on Earth; and if the world is not enough, you can explore our fully updated features on the *International Space Station* (p. 20) and Space Disasters (p. 24). Or perhaps you'd prefer to wile away the time with some record recreations such as Juggling (p. 195) or Collectible Card Gaming (p. 387).

We could be here all day listing the new features, so why not just jump right in now and see what you find? And remember—if you come across something you think you can do better, then let us know about it. You'll find out How to be a Record Breaker on p. xxxiv. Who knows—perhaps this time next year, you'll find your name listed alongside the new Olympic greats, the latest Oscar winners, and the rest of 2012's record-breaking community. Of course, that's assuming the world doesn't come to an end in December! Good luck!

Craig Glenday
Editor-in-Chief
twitter.com/craigglenday

GWR DAY

NOVEMBER 17

. . . is the date for Guinness World Records Day 2011. Each year, people worldwide try to set or break a Guinness World Record on this special day—as these photos from GWR Day 2010 show. Want to break a record of your own? Find out how at www.guinnessworldrecords.com!

● **LARGEST SCREW ARTWORK** Saimir Strati (Albania) used 235,500 metal screws in an artwork depicting the poet Homer in Tirana, Albania, unveiled specially on GWR Day.

○ **MOST HEADSPINS IN ONE MINUTE** Aichi Ono (Japan) performed a dizzying 135 headspins on the set of Mino Monta no Asazuba (TBS) for GWR Day 2010.

All this happened in just one day. For records that were achieved in just one hour, turn to p. 159.

The Danes can boast the world's ○ **oldest movie theater still in operation**. Denmark's Korsør Biograf Teater opened on August 7, 1908.

○ LARGEST MELODICA ENSEMBLE A group of 158 children from the Jyosei Elementary School in Hikone, Japan, played "Twinkle Twinkle Little Star."

○ MOST ARROWS CAUGHT IN TWO MINUTES Joe Alexander (Germany) caught 43 arrows by hand, from 26 ft. 3 in. (8 m) away, in Hamburg, Germany.

The **first operating movie theater** was the Cinématographe Lumière at the Salon Indien, 14 Boulevard de Capucines, Paris, France, which opened on December 28, 1895.

●FARTHEST DISTANCE TO RIDE A WATER SLIDE IN FOUR HOURS A mixed German team covered 199.27 miles (320.68 km) on a water slide in just four hours.

○MOST DOGS IN FANCY DRESS The Suncoast Animal League (U.S.A.) assembled 426 dressed-up dogs during their annual Dogtoberfest in Dunedin, Florida, U.S.A.

●MOST SIMULTANEOUS HIGH KICKS IN 30 SECONDS BY A CHORUS LINE Moulin Rouge cancan dancers performed 720 high kicks at the Moulin Rouge theater, Paris.

●MOST FLAMES BLOWN IN ONE MINUTE Hot, hot, hot! Fire-breather Preacher Muad'dib (Ireland) managed to blast out 69 fire torches in 60 seconds by London's iconic Tower Bridge.

ON THE SAME DAY

● Farthest distance static cycling in three minutes: 3.6 miles (5.8 km), by Miguel Angel Castro (Spain).

● Most jokes told in one minute: 17, shared by Ted Robbins, BBC Lancashire, and Ben Day, Touch FM (both UK).

● Tightrope walking—greatest distance in 24 hours: 9.74 miles (5.68 km), by Joey Kelly (Germany).

● Most rotations while juggling in one minute (five clubs): 735, by Mario Berousek (Czech Republic) at the Moulin Rouge in Paris, France.

● Heaviest shoes walked in: 323 lb. (146.5 kg), by Ashrita Furman (U.S.A.).

● Largest rice ball mosaic: 566.5 ft.² (52.63 m²), by 500 participants at the Gohanshoku Network Conference (Japan).

● Longest line of bunting: 8,982 ft. (2,737.72 m), by Malbank Secondary School and Sixth Form College (UK).

● Most capital cities named in a minute: 33, by James Way (UK).

● Most concrete blocks broken while holding a raw egg: 24, by Joe Alexander (Germany).

○ Most consecutive Double Dutch-style skips (team): 371, by Summerwind Skippers (U.S.A.).

● Most spinning splits in 30 seconds: 34, by Adonis Kosmadakis (Greece) and Nicolas Pihiliangegedera (France). Shared record.

○ Largest game of leapfrog: 1,348 students and visitors to the Canterbury Agricultural & Pastoral (A&P) Show in Christchurch, New Zealand.

● Most words spelled backward in a minute: 14, by Emma Britton (UK).

● Tallest tower of paper cups built in 30 seconds: 10.63 in. (27 cm), by Masato Kajiwara (Japan).

 ○ **OLDEST WING WALKER** Veteran wing walker Thomas Lackey (UK, b. May 22, 1920) took to the skies over Cirencester, Gloucestershire, UK, at the age of 90.

●LONGEST MARATHON SLICING MEAT Francisco Alonso (Spain) spent 24 hr. 54 min. 6 sec cutting ham in Tenerife, Spain, piling up 166 lb. 12 oz. (75.641 kg) of meat in total!

●LARGEST MAPLE LEAF In October 2010, Joseph Donato (Canada) discovered a maple leaf—Canada's national symbol—13.6 in. (34.61 cm) wide and 11.5 in. (29.21 cm) long.

●LARGEST GATHERING OF WIZARD OF OZ CHARACTERS Mile Oak Primary School, Brighton, UK, assembled 446 people dressed up as Oz folk.

 ●MOST BASKETBALL SLAM DUNKS WITH A TRAMPOLINE IN ONE MINUTE Norway's Team Kangaroos sank 28 trampoline-powered slam dunks in Marienlysthallen, Norway.

GWR DAY Guinness World Records Day 2010 was actively celebrated by over 250,000 people, in over 15 countries, breaking 56 records. We'd like to thank everyone who took part—you made it the best GWR Day yet!

 ●LARGEST TUG OF WAR TOURNAMENT A total of 1,290 students from Het Nieuwe Lyceum and De Werkplaats (both Netherlands) took the strain for GWR Day.

○LARGEST PAINTING BY NUMBERS The Ecole de Dessin in Lagos State, Nigeria, unveiled a 208-ft. 4-in. (63.5-m) x 161-ft. 9-in. (49.3-m) painting by numbers.

HOW TO BE A RECORD BREAKER

ARE YOU OFFICIALLY AMAZING?

There are now more ways than ever to earn yourself a much-coveted Guinness World Records certificate. Record breaking is free and open to everyone, so if you've got a special skill or a talented pet, tell us about it now! You can attempt a record at one of our live events, or make a star appearance on a global TV show . . . you might even get your name listed in the world's **best-selling copyright book!**

STEP 1—APPLY ONLINE
Your first step on the path to glory begins at the GWR website: www .guinnessworldrecords .com. Choose the "Break a Record" option and tell us as much as you can about the record you want to set or break. We want the Who, What, Where, When, and Why to help us decide if it really is worthy of the name Guinness World Records! Aim to do this about three weeks before your attempt.

Lucien Laurent's goal for France against Mexico on July 13, at the 1930 World Cup in Uruguay, was the **first FIFA World Cup goal**.

STEP 2—GET THE GUIDELINES
If we like your idea—or if you
want to try to break an existing
record—we'll send you the official
rules that you must follow when
attempting the record. (If we
reject your proposal, we'll tell
you why.) Everyone MUST follow
the same guidelines so that each
attempt can be fairly judged.

**STEP 3—ATTEMPT YOUR
RECORD** Now it's time to plan
and practice, practice, practice!
Be sure to video your efforts, and
get lots of witnesses and at least
two independent eyewitness
statements. Don't worry about
taking notes now—full instructions
are in the guidelines.

José Batista's (Uruguay) first-minute sending-off for fouling
Scotland's Gordon Strachan at Mexico '86 was the **fastest red
card in a World Cup finals match**. The game was played at the
Estadio Neza '86, Nezahualcoyotl, Mexico, on June 13, 1986.

How to Be a Record Breaker

STEP 4—SEND YOUR EVIDENCE Collate all your evidence as per the guidelines and post it to GWR HQ. There, our Records Management Team will sift through your clips, photos, witness statements, logbooks, and so on, and make a decision. If you're successful then you'll know about it when your official GWR certificate arrives in the post. This is the confirmation that you are **OFFICIALLY AMAZING!**

EXPERTS Pictured here are just a few of the dozens of consultants who advise us in every field of knowledge—from astronomy to zoology. They're always on the lookout for new world records, and, if we've got a query, these are the mavens we turn to.

MARCO PRONTO! Here's the Head of Records, Marco Frigatti, presenting a GWR certificate to Khagendra Thapa Magar, the world's **shortest man**. "It's only a world record when we say so," says Marco!

RECORDS MANAGEMENT Our team of multilingual Records Managers travels the world to adjudicate records. This team also writes the rules for record attempts and processes around 1,000 claims a week. You'll get to meet a member of this talented team if you apply for an onsite adjudicator.

DIGITAL Whether it's online, or via ebooks or iPad apps, GWR Digital provides the 24/7 face of record breaking. Check out the site, guinnessworldrecords.com, for record-breaking news, and search for some of your all-time favorite record holders. It's also your chance to make a claim or mail your attempt directly to our video channel. When you're there, sign up to our Facebook and Twitter feeds and meet the Challengers team, who'll help you realize your record-breaking dreams!

How to Be a Record Breaker

LIVE! Experience the heart-in-your-mouth thrill and excitement of attempting a Guinness World Records challenge LIVE and in front of a crowd of onlookers at one of the GWR LIVE! roadshow events. One minute you're an idle bystander and the next you're a record holder! It's so immediate, you won't know what's hit you! Our LIVE! helpers are there to make sure you get the most fun out of your experience, so visit guinnessworldrecords.com/live to find a LIVE! event near you. . . .

LIVE! ACTION These roadshow visitors became instant record-breakers when they built the ●**tallest coffee cup tower in three minutes**, measuring 6 ft. 10 in. (2.08 m), at the GWR LIVE! event in Barcelona, Spain, on May 14, 2010.

TV Only the most visually spectacular record attempts get picked for our TV shows. GWR TV is filmed and shown all around the world, and if you're lucky enough to be shortlisted, you could find yourself in China, India, Australia, Italy . . . just some of the locations in which we've filmed over the past 12 months!

MYTHCONCEPTIONS

PUT YOUR RECORD-BREAKING KNOWLEDGE TO THE TEST . . .

So, Everest is the tallest mountain, is it? And you can see the Great Wall of China from the Moon? And we all know that the Sahara is the largest desert, right? Wrong, wrong, and wrong again. Forget what you think you know and take our quirky quiz of common myths and misconceptions. . . .

Can you name the world's tallest mountain? No, not Mount Everest! At 29,029 ft. (8,848 m), Everest is the *highest* **mountain** on Earth—in that it reaches the highest altitude—but the *tallest* is actually Mauna Kea in Hawaii, U.S.A. You can see only 13,796 ft. (4,205 m) of it (the rest is underwater), but from its submarine base in the Hawaiian Trough, it reaches up for a total of 33,480 ft. (10,205 m).

57,782 Number of lies you will tell in your lifetime. A third of all adult conversations involve some kind of deception, and you'll tell two major fibs every day. And that's no word of a lie!

WHERE IS THE LARGEST POPULATION OF WILD CAMELS? There are up to one million wild camels living in—no, not Mongolia or Arabia—Australia! Imported there in the 19th century as a form of desert transportation, the camels escaped into the wild, where they now thrive.

With a total length of at least 2,150 miles (3,460 km), the Great Wall of China is the "longest wall in the world." But—contrary to popular belief—it is not visible from the surface of the Moon. This was confirmed by the *Apollo* astronauts who actually visited the Moon.

China's first taikonaut (or "yǔhángyuán"), Yang Liwei, admitted that he never saw the Great Wall during his maiden space flight in October 2003.

Things you *can* see from space—especially in low orbit—include cities, airports, major highway systems, bridges, and reservoirs.

The **largest revolving restaurant** is Bellini, located on the 45th floor of Mexico City's World Trade Center in Mexico. The restaurant has an area of 11,244.58 ft.² (1,044.66 m²).

WHO IS THE MOST PROLIFIC AUTHOR OF JAMES BOND NOVELS? Perhaps surprisingly, James Bond creator Ian Fleming was *not* the most prolific writer of Bond novels—between 1981 and 1996, John Gardner (UK) wrote 14 Bond novels and two screenplay adaptations, surpassing Fleming's output of 12 novels and two short-story collections.

LONGEST PREGNANCY? Not the elephant (22 months) or the blue whale (11.5 months) but the common frilled shark (*Chlamydoselachus anguineus*), whose young gestate for 42 months!

 To find the restaurant with the ●**largest menu** you will have to visit Hungary. The menu at the restaurant Mofarguru in the capital city, Budapest, features a whopping 1,810 different items.

TALLEST KNOWN MOUNTAIN? If you said Everest, then you'd be wrong by a factor of three—the tallest mountain known to man is Olympus Mons on the planet Mars at a whopping 15 miles (25 km)!

What is the most dangerous animal? The great white shark? The poison-dart frog? What about the huntsman spider? Yes, these creatures are extremely dangerous, but would you be surprised to hear that the answer is the mosquito? It may be just 0.12 in. (3 mm) long but mosquitoes of the genus *Anopheles*—and specifically its malarial parasites of the genus *Plasmodium*—have been responsible for approximately 50% of all human deaths since the Stone Age (excluding wars and accidents).

And what's the longest animal? Surprisingly, it's not the 90-ft.-long (27-m) blue whale or even the lengthy *praya dubia*—the jellyfish-like siphonophore that can reach 160 ft. (50 m) long. The **longest creature** is the bootlace worm (*Lineus longissimus*), a species of nemertean or ribbon worm inhabiting shallow waters of the North Sea. The longest known specimen, washed ashore in Fife, UK, in 1864, measured more than 180 ft. (55 m) long.

How do bats see? With their eyes, of course! Bats have the **most acute hearing of any non-aquatic animal**—some can hear frequencies as high as 250 kHz (compared with just 20 kHz for a human)—and they do use echolocation to find prey and communicate, but they're not blind. To be fair, many bat species have under-developed eyesight but not one of them is blind. Indeed, Old World fruit bats have relatively large eyes with decent light-gathering capacity. Bats are mostly active at night to avoid competition from other animals, so they need all the sensory input they can get.

Who were the first passengers in a hot-air balloon? The Montgolfier brothers? Good answer, but no. Joseph-Michel and Jacques-Etienne Montgolfier (France) did invent and build a hot-air balloon for a test in front of French royals Louis XVI and Marie Antoinette in 1783, but the effects of flight on a human were unknown, and it was decided to test the venture with a sheep (named Montauciel, or "Reach the Sky"), a duck, and a rooster—the **first living creatures to take flight in a man-made craft**.

Who was first to sail around the world? Ferdinand Magellan, you say? The man who gave his name to the Straits of Magellan, the Magellanic penguin, and the Magellanic cloud? Erm, no. The Portuguese explorer may have set off on the **first circumnavigation of the world** in 1519 but he never completed the journey. Instead, he was hacked to death in the Philippines in March 1521, leaving the Spanish navigator Juan Sebastian de Elcano to complete the trip. Theories abound of earlier circumnavigations by others, but these are impossible to date and verify accurately.

MOST TORNADO-HIT COUNTRY? By area, the Netherlands has more twisters than any country, with one for every 769 miles^2 (1,991 km^2) of land! The U.S.A. has one per 3,161 miles^2 (8,187 km^2).

In Antarctica—the largest arid expanse on earth—the average temperature is –4°F.

WHERE IS THE LARGEST DESERT? The Sahara in north Africa covers 3.5 million miles² (9.1 million km²) and is the largest *hot* desert. But a "desert" is simply an area that has no or very little rainfall, so by this definition the largest must be Antarctica (5.4 million miles²; 14 million km²), with about 2 in. (50 mm) of precipitation per year.

When a tourist in London bought what he *thought* was Tower Bridge, what did he end up buying instead? This story involves the record for the **farthest distance to move a bridge**—but it's not the apocryphal tale of the tourist who bought the *wrong* bridge. The story goes that a U.S. tourist in London bought what he thought was Tower Bridge and had it shipped back home—only to discover he'd bought the less iconic London Bridge. Only part of this tale is true. The American was Robert McCulloch, and in 1962 he *did* buy London Bridge—but he did so willingly, and had it rebuilt 5,300 miles (8,530 km) away at Lake Havasu City in Arizona, U.S.A., as a tourist attraction.

UNIVERSE

CONTENTS

STAR LIVES

LIFE CYCLE OF A STAR

Stars are born, have a life span, then die, and the stars we can see in the night sky are all at various different stages of this life cycle. Our star—the Sun—

was born about 4.57 billion years ago, and is expected to reach the ripe old age of 14 billion years. The life story of a star is shaped by its mass—smaller stars go down one avenue of evolution, and larger stars down another. . . .

A STAR IS BORN Stars are formed in nebulae. As clouds of dust and gas collapse under gravity, they start to spin and become hot in the center, finally forming nuclear furnaces. This stage, from the start of fusion to the state of equilibrium, is known as a star's "main sequence."

LARGEST LOCAL GALAXY Andromeda is the largest galaxy in the "Local Group," the cluster that includes Earth's own galaxy, the Milky Way. This composite image shows Andromeda's dust lanes in infrared and its X-ray binary star systems, which probably contain black holes or neutron stars. Containing about a trillion stars, and at a distance of around 2.5 million light-years, the Andromeda galaxy is the farthest object visible to the naked eye.

7,350: Apples you will eat in a lifetime. Just 6,000 of the 3 septillion stars in the universe can be seen by the naked eye, so you'll eat more apples than there are visible stars in the sky.

FROM SUN TO RED GIANT As the star reaches its middle age, it slowly uses up its fuel. The core begins to shrink, and the remaining hydrogen burns with a greater luminosity. When the Sun expands to a red giant it will engulf and destroy the inner planets.

PLANETARY NEBULA The dying star sheds its outer layers into space, illuminated by the remnant white dwarf in the center. The expanding shells of matter recycle the star's bulk back into the galaxy, where it can be recycled to form new stars. Most stars become planetary nebulae.

WHITE DWARF The star ends its life as an incredibly dense mass of carbon and oxygen at a fraction of its original size (scientists predict that our Sun will end up as small as Earth). Now out of fuel, this "white dwarf" will continue to cool. As it solidifies into pure carbon, white dwarfs crystallize into the **largest diamonds in the universe.**

The ● **largest serving of pastries** took place in Hungary on May 23, 2009 during the Életfa-Hosök tornája, when 10,000 were dished out at the Puskas Stadium in Budapest.

The yellow sun burns itself out into a red giant before its outer layers form a planetary nebula with a remnant white dwarf at its core.

MASSIVE STAR TO RED SUPERGIANT
Stars much more massive than the Sun "burn" through their hydrogen fuel much more quickly, and the main part of the star's life lasts just millions—as opposed to billions—of years. They are typically 200–800 times larger than our Sun.

SUPERNOVA When a massive star exhausts its hydrogen, it then fuses its helium into heavier elements. When this process reaches the element iron, fusion can no longer occur and the star's core collapses catastrophically, resulting in a titanic supernova explosion that can outshine an entire galaxy.

NEUTRON STARS The collapsed remnant of the star's core, a neutron star is the **smallest star** and one of the densest known objects in the universe, with the mass of the Sun squeezed into the size of a city. Compressing all of humanity into a sugar cube would yield the same density as a neutron star, some of which spin hundreds of times per second.

If big baking is your thing, head for Portugal. The **longest loaf of bread** measured 3,975 ft. (1,211.6 m) and was achieved at the Bread and Bakers' Party held in Vagos on July 10, 2005.

A massive star expands quickly as a supergiant before exploding in a supernova and ending up as a black hole or neutron star.

BLACK HOLE The densest objects in the universe, black holes are characterized by a region of space in which gravity is so strong that not even light can escape. At the center is the "singularity," where the mass of the dead star is compressed to a single point of zero size and infinite density.

Nearest planetary nebula The Helix Nebula (also known as NGC 7293), at a distance of around 400 light-years, is the closest planetary nebula to the Earth. It formed when a dying star threw off its outer layers, which are gradually expanding into space. They are called planetary nebulae because astronomers originally believed they were new planets, owing to their often spherical shapes.

The **youngest planetary nebula** is the Stingray Nebula in the southern constellation of Ara. It was observed as a star in the 1970s, but in the last 30 years its central star had heated up enough to make its surrounding ejected gas shells glow as a planetary nebula.

Nearest red supergiant Betelgeuse, in the constellation of Orion, lies just 427 light-years from the Solar System. Like all red supergiants, it is a massive star nearing the end of its relatively short life span of perhaps just a few million years in total. It has a mass of around 14 times that of the Sun and varies in size between around 400 and 600 times the Sun's diameter.

DEPTHS OF SPACE

○**Farthest object in the universe** In January 2011, NASA scientists announced that the Hubble Space Telescope had photographed a galaxy so old that its light has taken 13.2 billion years to reach us. The galaxy as we see it today was formed less than 480 million years after the Big Bang, and is the earliest known object to have formed in the universe.

The **largest firework display** consisted of 66,326 fireworks and was achieved by Macedo's Pirotecnia Lda. in Funchal, Madeira, Portugal, on December 31, 2006.

> In the time it takes you to read this sentence, *Voyager* 1 has traveled 31 miles (51 km).

○**Most distant black hole** In June 2007, astronomers announced that results from the Canada-France-Hawaii Telescope (CFHT) and the Gemini South 8m-class telescope had revealed a quasar containing a supermassive black hole with a redshift of 6.43. (A quasar is a very distant, old, and bright celestial object emitting high levels of electromagnetic radiation.) Named CFHQS J2329-0301, the quasar is in the constellation of Pisces and is estimated to be 2 million light-years farther away from Earth than the previous record holder. At just under 13 billion light-years' distance, it is only 0.7 billion years younger than the estimated age of the universe from the moment of the Big Bang.

○**Most distant observed supernova** Astronomers led by Jeff Cooke (U.S.A.) have found what is thought to be a Type IIn supernova—a massive exploding star—in a distant galaxy some 11 billion light-years from Earth. Using data from the CFHT, the astronomers noticed a galaxy that brightened momentarily, with a spectrum that is characterized by a very narrow color band of light emitted from burning hydrogen.

Study of this type of supernova could help scientists to discover more about the true size—and origins—of the universe. The results from the analysis of the data were announced in July 2009.

Fastest matter The fastest objects observed in the universe are blobs of superheated plasma, ejected from black holes in the cores of extremely active galaxies known as blazars. These blobs, with as much mass as the planet Jupiter, have been observed moving at 99.99% of the speed of light.

○**MOST REMOTE MAN-MADE OBJECT**
NASA's *Voyager 1*, launched on September 5, 1977, encountered Jupiter in March 1979, and then Saturn in November 1980. The flybys produced slingshot effects whereby *Voyager 1* was flung upward out of the plane of the Solar System. As of February 4, 2011, it was 10,791,000,000 miles (17,367,000,000 km) from the Sun.

The **largest chocolate firework** measured 9.8 ft. (3 m) in height and contained 132 lb. (60 kg) of Swiss Cailler chocolates. It was released at the Hechtplatz, Zürich, Switzerland, on December 31, 2002.

518: Weight in pounds of salt you will eat during your lifetime. If each individual grain weighs $2.06352677 \times 10^{-6}$ ounces, your 518 lb. contains 4,017,094,017 grains of salt. That's four grains for every star in the Milky Way.

○ **MOST DISTANT EXTRASOLAR PLANET OGLE-2005-BLG-390Lb** is 21,500 ± 3,300 light-years away from Earth, near the center of the Milky Way. It orbits a star located in the constellation of Scorpius (see artist's impression, left) at a distance that would put it somewhere in the region between Mars and Jupiter in our own solar system. It may be the most distant Earth-like planet yet found—that is, a planet with a rocky core and a shell atmosphere.

○ **MOST DISTANT OBJECT IN THE SOLAR SYSTEM** The dwarf planet Sedna has a highly elliptical orbit taking it 84 billion miles (130 billion km) from the Sun, which it takes around 10,500 years to orbit. Scientists at Mount Palomar Observatory, California, U.S.A., discovered it on November 14, 2003. The picture at left shows an artist's impression of a view of the Sun from the surface of Sedna.

The **fastest speed possible in the universe** is the speed of light, achieved only by light and other forms of electromagnetic radiation, such as radio waves, X-rays, or infrared radiation. The speed of light varies depending on what it passes through. It is fastest traveling in a vacuum, when its velocity is 983,571,056 ft./s. (299,792,458 m/s). This means that when you look at the Moon, you are actually seeing it as it was about 1.3 seconds ago, while you see the Sun as it was around 8.3 minutes in the past.

Fastest star in the galaxy On February 8, 2005, a team of astronomers from the Harvard-Smithsonian Center for Astrophysics in Cambridge, Massachusetts, U.S.A., announced their discovery of a star traveling at a speed of over 1.5 million mi./hr. (2.4 million km/h). The star, named SDSS J090745.0+24507, had probably been accelerated by an encounter with the supermassive black hole at the center of our Milky Way galaxy slightly less than 80 million years ago.

FARTHEST PLANET IN THE SOLAR SYSTEM Since the International Astronomical Union (IAU) demoted Pluto in 2006, Neptune is regarded as the farthest major planet from the Sun. It is 2.8 billion miles (4.5 billion km) from the Sun, which it orbits at 3.38 mi/s (5.45 km/s), taking 164.79 years to make one orbit. Neptune is also home to the **fastest winds in the Solar System**, measured at around 1,500 mi./hr. (2,400 km/h).

For record-breaking aviation, take off for p. 233.

Fastest-approaching galaxy Despite the overall expansion of the universe, a few galaxies are approaching our own. M86, a lenticular galaxy around 52 million light-years away in the Virgo Cluster, is moving toward our Milky Way at 260 mi/s (419 km/s).

Largest structure in the universe In October 2003, a team of astronomers led by Richard Gott III and Mario Juric (both U.S.A.) of Princeton University, New Jersey, U.S.A., announced the discovery of a huge wall of galaxies some 1.37 billion light-years long. They used data from the Sloan Digital Sky Survey, which is mapping 1 million galaxies in the universe.

Depths of Space   **9**

●BRIGHTEST RADIO SOURCE IN THE NIGHT SKY Lying in the Cassiopeia constellation, the supernova remnant Cassiopeia A is the brightest radio source seen from Earth. It is the result of a supernova explosion some 11,000 years ago. Light from the explosion (and the radio waves we see today) was thought to have reached Earth about 300 years ago, but interstellar dust may have made this hard to see at the time.

Greatest explosion Most astronomers now believe that the universe began about 13.7 billion years ago in a cataclysmic explosion we call the Big Bang. All of the matter and energy in the universe had its origins in this event, as did time itself.

At the very instant of the Big Bang, the universe is thought to have had infinite temperature (the **highest temperature ever**), as it existed as a single, infinitely small and infinitely dense point. Just 10^{-43} seconds later, the universe had expanded to a size of around 10^{-33}cm across and cooled to roughly 10^{32} kelvin ($0°C = 273.15$ kelvin).

Coldest place in the Milky Way The Boomerang Nebula is a cloud of dust and gases 5,000 light-years from Earth. It has a temperature of $-457.6°F$ ($-272°C$) and is formed by the rapid expansion of gas and dust flowing away from its central, aging star.

●Closest planetary binary system to Earth The term "binary system" refers to two objects in space that are close enough for their respective gravities to influence each other, causing the objects to orbit around a common point. The minor planet Pluto (716.44 miles, or 1,153 km, in diameter) and its moon Charon (375 miles, or 603.5 km, in diameter) form

Although first seen in 1846, Neptune's existence had been mathematically predicted beforehand.

The **largest ski lesson** was attended by 594 skiers who were instructed by Hansjürg Gredig (Switzerland) of the Swiss-Snowsport School at Sarn-Heinzenberg (Graubünden), Switzerland, on February 23, 2008.

the only true planetary binary system in the Solar System. Charon is so large in relation to Pluto that they orbit a common point in space above the surface of Pluto. For a normal moon orbiting a planet, the point in space about which they both orbit is near the center of the planet involved, and so produces only a small wobble in the planet's orbit. True binary systems orbit a point in space outside either body.

JUPITER

Planet with the shortest day Jupiter has the shortest day of all eight major planets in the Solar System, performing a full rotation on its axis once every 9 hr. 55 min. 29.69 sec.

●**Largest metallic hydrogen ocean** Inside Jupiter is an ocean of metallic hydrogen up to 34,175 miles (55,000 km) deep. Metallic hydrogen forms when liquid hydrogen is subjected to enormous pressures and becomes ionized. This gives the hydrogen metallic properties, thus turning it into an electrical conductor and creating the **strongest magnetic field in the Solar System** – around 19,000 times stronger than Earth's.

●**First Jupiter flyby** Launched in 1972, the unmanned NASA spacecraft *Pioneer 10* reached Jupiter on December 3, 1973. After becoming the first spacecraft to travel through the asteroid belt, it passed by the planet at a distance of 80,778 miles (130,000 km). The encounter yielded not only the first close-up images of the planet but also data on its magnetic field, and proved Jupiter to be a mostly liquid planet.

LARGEST RECORDED IMPACT IN THE SOLAR SYSTEM On July 16–22, 1994, fragments of the comet Shoemaker-Levy 9 collided with Jupiter. The greatest impact was of the "G" fragment (pictured), which exploded with the energy of roughly 6 million megatons of TNT (600 times the nuclear arsenal of the world). Jupiter has also taken the brunt of the ●**largest asteroid impact** in the Solar System. On June 3, 2010, amateur astronomer Anthony Wesley (Australia) observed an asteroid of around 26–43 ft. (8–13 m) across crashing into the planet.

The **largest indoor ski resort** is Ski Dubai in the United Arab Emirates. With a total area of 242,187 ft.^{2} (22,500 m^2) covered with 13 million lb (6,000 metric tons) of real snow all year around, it has room for 1,500 visitors.

LARGEST PLANET IN THE SOLAR SYSTEM With an equatorial diameter of 89,405 miles (143,884 km) and a polar diameter of 83,082 miles (133,708 km), Jupiter is the largest of the eight major planets. It has a mass 317.828 times, and a volume 1,323.3 times, that of the Earth. With its Sun-like composition, powerful magnetic field, and array of more than 60 moons, it is effectively a Solar System in miniature—indeed, it actually would be a star if it had sufficient mass to collapse in on itself and trigger a thermonuclear reaction.

●**Most spacecraft to visit an outer planet** Jupiter has been visited by eight spacecraft. After *Pioneer 10*'s visit in 1973, *Pioneer 11* performed a flyby in 1974, with *Voyagers 1* and *2* following in 1979. *Ulysses* made two long-distance flybys in 1992 and 2004, while *Galileo* orbited Jupiter between 1995 and 2003. *Cassini-Huygens* and *New Horizons* both used Jupiter as a slingshot on their journeys to Saturn in 2000 and Pluto in 2007, respectively.

 The **most expensive license plate**—the single digit "1"—was sold to Saeed Abdul Ghaffar Khouri (UAE) for Dh52.2 million ($14.2 million) during a special number plate auction in Abu Dhabi, UAE, on February 16, 2008.

Longest orbital survey of an outer planet NASA's *Galileo* space-craft was launched on October 18, 1989, and reached Jupiter on December 7, 1995, where it slowed to enter the planet's orbit and became the first probe to orbit a world in the outer Solar System. It lasted nearly eight years, ending on September 21, 2003, when *Galileo*'s power began to fail and the craft burned up in the atmosphere.

Largest anticyclone in the Solar System Jupiter's Great Red Spot is the largest known anticyclonic storm. Although it has varied in size since its discovery in 1664, it has been up to 24,800 miles (40,000 km) long and 8,700 miles (14,000 km) wide, and is as wide as three Earths. The storm rotates anticlockwise at around 270 mi./hr. (435 km/h) and its clouds tower some 5 miles (8 km) above the cloudscape.

All vehicles need a license plate, even the VH Valiant that pulled off the **longest ramp jump**. Driven by Ray Baumann (Australia), the automobile covered 237 ft. (72.23 m) at Ravenswood International Raceway in Perth, Australia, on August 23, 1998.

> **DIZZYING HEIGHTS** Boosaule Montes, on the moon Io, reaches up to 52,493 ft. (17,000 m) in height—taller than Earth's two biggest mountains, Everest and K2, put together.

JOVIAN MOONS Jupiter has 63 confirmed moons, comprising eight "regular" moons (including the four "Galilean" moons detailed below) and 55 "irregular" moons. The Galilean moons—so called because they were discovered by the Italian astronomer Galileo—account for 99.997% of the mass of Jupiter's satellites and ring system.

IO Jupiter's closest Galilean moon, Io is the **most volcanically active world in the Solar System**, pulled and squeezed by tidal interactions with Jupiter and Europa.

EUROPA With prominences of just a few hundred yards, this ice-covered moon has the **smoothest surface in the Solar System**; believed to have a subsurface sea of saltwater.

GANYMEDE At 3,273 miles (5,267 km) in diameter, Ganymede is the **largest satellite in the Solar System**, and bigger than the planet Mercury; it is also 2,017 times heavier than our own Moon.

CALLISTO The outermost of Jupiter's satellites, Callisto is the **most heavily cratered moon**, its surface entirely pitted with craters caused by meteorite impacts; its distance from Jupiter—and its geological stability—means that Callisto is a likely first target for future human exploration of the outer Solar System.

●**First discovery of extraterrestrial volcanic activity** Shortly after *Voyager 1*'s 1979 encounter with Jupiter, navigation engineer Linda Morabito (U.S.A.) discovered in a black-and-white image an anomalous crescent protruding from the moon Io. Although initially thought to be a moon behind Io, the crescent was soon confirmed to be a part of Io itself. What Morabito had discovered was the first active volcano on a world other than Earth.

28,745: How many sunsets there will be during the 78.7 orbits of the Sun you will make during your life. A tiny proportion compared to the 1,600,000,000,000 there have been in the 4.6-billion-year history of the Earth.

INSIDE THE GAS GIANT Jupiter has a mass 318 times greater than Earth—indeed, it has nearly three times the mass of all the other Solar System planets added together. Despite this, it's composed mostly of gases and liquids around a relatively small, solid core.

A. ATMOSPHERE Similar to the Sun: 86.1% hydrogen and 13.8% helium with traces of nearly all other elements (plus methane, ammonia, and water vapor).

B. MOLECULAR HYDROGEN Pressure and temperature compresses hydrogen gas in the atmposhere into an ever-thicker fog until it changes to the liquid form.

C. METALLIC HYDROGEN Increased pressure turns hydrogen into an electrically conducting metal; here, the planet's fast rotation generates an immense magnetic field many times more powerful than Earth's.

D. CORE Intense pressure (and 30,000 K temperatures) at the core is likely to have created a solid rock center one to two times the size of planet Earth.

Most powerful observed eruption In February 2001, Io's Surt volcano erupted with an estimated power output of 78,000 gigawatts (GW)—a huge force by comparison with the 1992 eruption of Mount Etna in Sicily, Italy, which had an output of just 12 GW. The observations were made with the WM Keck II Telescope in Hawaii, U.S.A., and published in the journal *Icarus* in November 2002.

Highest volcanic eruption On August 6, 2001, *Galileo* performed a flyby of Io at a distance of 120 miles (194 km) from the surface and passed through the top of a volcanic plume measuring around 310 miles (500 km) high. Originating at the Tvashtar volcano, near Io's North Pole, it is the highest volcanic eruption plume ever witnessed in the Solar System.

●Planet with the most trojan asteroids Trojan asteroids are clusters of small bodies that share the orbit of a planet, at positions 60° behind and ahead of the planet. As of January 2011, some 4,793 trojans have been discovered sharing Jupiter's orbit, with Neptune having seven and Mars

MOST POWERFUL AURORAE IN THE SOLAR SYSTEM The aurorae on Jupiter are around 1,000 times more powerful than Earth's. They are caused by energetic particles from the Sun being channeled on to the Jovian poles by Jupiter's magnetic field and causing atoms in its upper atmosphere to glow like the gas in a neon tube. They produce around 1 million megawatts (MW) of energy, enough to power 100 major cities on Earth. The bands and curtains of the Jovian aurorae can be as large as the Earth.

four. The asteroids are named after figures from the Trojan Wars—the first being 588 Achilles, discovered in 1906 by the astronomer Max Wolf (Germany)—and designated one of two "camps": Greek (for those 60° ahead of Jupiter) or Trojan (60° behind).

ASTEROIDS

Largest impact crater on Earth Of approximately 150 impact craters identified so far on Earth, the largest is the Vredefort crater, located near Johannesburg, South Africa, with an estimated diameter of 186 miles (300 km). This enormous, eroded structure was formed approximately 2 billion years ago, when an asteroid or comet collided with the Earth.

Greatest impact on Earth Most astronomers now believe that 4.5 billion years ago, a planet the size of Mars collided with the young Earth. Some of the debris from this cataclysm went into orbit around the Earth and collected together under its own gravity to form the Moon. The effect of this impact would have been absolutely devastating to the Earth. The entire crust of the planet would probably have been blasted off into space, leaving behind an Earth whose entire surface was an ocean of molten magma.

●**FIRST MATERIALS RETURNED FROM AN ASTEROID** On June 13, 2010, the unmanned spacecraft *Hayabusa*, built and operated by the Japanese space agency JAXA, landed on Earth with around 1,500 tiny solid grains of material collected mostly from the surface of the asteroid Itokawa. *Hayabusa* was the first spacecraft to lift off from an asteroid.

●**First triple asteroid** The potato-shaped asteroid 87 Sylvia was discovered in 1866 in the main asteroid belt. Its first moon was discovered
in 2004; subsequently, in 2005, it became the first asteroid known to have
two moons.

●**Closest triple asteroid to Earth** Asteroid 2001 SN263 is a near-
Earth asteroid—its orbit brings it close to the Earth, not to the main asteroid belt. Its closest approach to Earth is 6.9 million miles (11.2 million
km). In 2008, astronomers at the Arecibo radio observatory, Puerto Rico,
struck the asteroid with 500,000 watts of radar energy and discovered
from the reflections that it consists of three small asteroids orbiting each
other. They measure just 1.2 miles, 0.6 miles, and 0.2 miles (2 km, 1 km,
and 0.4 km) across respectively.

Largest concentration of asteroids Sitting between the orbits of Mars
and Jupiter is the largest gathering of asteroids in the Solar System—the
main asteroid belt. It contains between 700,000 and 1,700,000 asteroids
that are at least 0.3 miles (1 km) across, and many millions of smaller
bodies.

The **largest asteroid** within
the main asteroid belt is 1 Ceres,
which has an average diameter of
584.7 miles (941 km) and was discovered by Giuseppe Piazzi (Italy), a
Catholic priest, on January 1, 1801.

● **FIRST ACCURATELY PREDICTED
ASTEROID IMPACT** On October
6, 2008, astronomers discovered a
small asteroid, later named 2008
TC3. Analysis of the asteroid's orbit
indicated it would arrive at Earth
just 21 hours later. At 2:46 a.m.
(UTC) on October 7, 2008, it struck
the atmosphere at high speed,
causing it to explode some 23 miles
(37 km) above Sudan. The top
picture shows a NASA scientist with
debris from the explosion; the other
picture, below, shows the asteroid's
trail, distorted by high-altitude
winds.

TORINO SCALE

Professor Richard P Binzel of the Massachusetts Institute of Technology (MIT), U.S.A., devised this scale, which ranks the chances of an object in space colliding with Earth.

0	No hazard	No prospect of a meteor or asteroid colliding with Earth
1	Normal	The body will pass near Earth, but there is little danger
2	Meriting attention from astronomers	Close but safe approach. No cause for concern
3		Extremely small chance of collision and local damage
4		Small chance of collision and regional damage
5	Threatening	Serious but uncertain danger of impact. Astronomers to investigate
6		Serious but uncertain danger of impact from large object. Astronomers to investigate
7		Prospect of an impact by a large object. International studies and contingency planning needed
8	Certain collisions	Local destruction
9		Large-scale regional destruction
10		Certain impact. Possible climatic catastrophe worldwide. Occurs perhaps once every 100,000 years on average

First discovered in 1885, 253 Mathilde, like 1 Ceres, is found in the main asteroid belt. It measures 41 x 29 x 28 miles (66 x 48 x 46 km) and became the third and **largest asteroid visited by a spacecraft** in June 1997, when it was passed by NASA's *NEAR Shoemaker*.

●**First asteroid with a moon** While en route to Jupiter, NASA's *Galileo* spacecraft performed a flyby of the asteroid Ida in 1993. On February 17, 1994, scrutiny of the images from the flyby revealed that Ida, which is 33.3 miles (53.6 km) along its longest axis, has its own natural satellite.

●**FIRST NEAR-EARTH ASTEROID TO BE DISCOVERED**
433 Eros, discovered on August 13, 1898, by Carl Gustav Witt (Germany) and—independently—by Auguste Charlois (France)

The **most expensive cricket bat** was "The Don," used by Aussie cricket legend Sir Don Bradman in his debut Test in 1928. It sold for A$145,000 ($121,900) at Leski Auctions, Melbourne, Australia, on September 24, 2008.

700,000–1: The odds of you being killed by asteroid impact. In fact, asteroids with a diameter of up to 33 ft. enter the Earth's atmosphere around once a year, but usually explode harmlessly almost immediately.

Dactyl measures just 0.9 x 0.8 x 0.7 miles (1.6 x 1.4 x 1.2 km) in diameter and orbits Ida once every 20 hours.

Brightest asteroid Asteroid 4 Vesta was discovered on March 29, 1807, and is the only asteroid visible to the naked eye. This is due to a combination of the brightness of its surface, its size (357.9 miles, or 576 km across), and the fact that it approaches Earth to within 110 million miles (177 million km).

●**FIRST ASTEROID VISITED BY A SPACECRAFT** 951 Gaspra, visited by NASA's *Galileo* on October 29, 1991

Smallest asteroid There are several contenders for this record. Asteroid 1993KA2 was discovered on May 21, 1993, and has a diameter of around 16 ft. (5 m); 2000LG6, discovered on June 4, 2000, appears to have a similar diameter. The other candidates are 1991BA, 1991TU, 1991VG, and 1994ES1.

First asteroid landing The *NEAR Shoemaker* spacecraft touched down on asteroid 433 Eros on February 12, 2001. The craft transmitted 69 images of the surface of Eros during its descent, showing details of small rocks just centimeters across. Eros measures around 20.5 miles (33 km) across.

Largest object chaotically rotating Saturn's moon Hyperion measures 254 x 161 x 136 miles (410 x 260 x 220 km) and is the largest highly irregularly shaped body in the Solar System. It is one of only two bodies in the Solar System discovered to have completely chaotic rotation, essentially randomly tumbling in its orbit around Saturn. The other is asteroid 4179 Toutatis, which has an area of 2.7 x 1.5 x 1.1 miles (4.5 x 2.4 x 1.9 km).

●**FIRST ASTEROID WITH A TAIL** P/2010 A2, discovered in 2010 in the main asteroid belt between Mars and Jupiter

The **most valuable baseball bat** in the world once belonged to George Herman "Babe" Ruth. It was sold at an auction at Sotheby's, New York City, U.S.A., for $1,265,000 on December 2, 2004.

> "Near-earth objects": small objects whose orbits bring them close to earth

OLDEST CONFIRMED IMPACT
Around 3.47 billion years ago, an asteroid 12–19 miles (20–30 km) across crashed into the Earth, leaving deposits in Australia and South Africa that were discovered by U.S. scientists in 2002.

●**Slowest-rotating asteroid** The asteroid 288 Glauke was discovered by telescope in 1890. It measures around 20 miles (32 km) across but takes around 50 days to spin once on its axis. Of all the bodies in the Solar System, only the planets Mercury and Venus are known to spin more slowly.

Shortest-period asteroid Asteroid 2004 JG6 orbits the Sun in 184.46 days. It was discovered by Brian Skiff (U.S.A.) at the Lowell Observatory, Flagstaff, Arizona, U.S.A., and announced on May 13, 2004.

Most asteroids discovered The eminent astrogeologist Dr. Eugene Shoemaker (U.S.A., 1928–97) discovered 1,125 asteroids, many in partnership with his wife and fellow astronomer, Carolyn.

INTERNATIONAL SPACE STATION

●**Most visited space station** As of December 2010, the *ISS* had received 297 visitors. This represents 196 different people, as many astronauts and cosmonauts have traveled to the station more than once. For comparison, the Russian *Mir* space station (in operation from 1986 to 2001) had 137 visitors over its lifetime, representing 104 different people.

Most visits into space by a tourist The Hungarian-born software billionaire Charles Simonyi (U.S.A.) paid $25 million for his first trip on a Russian *Soyuz* rocket on April 7, 2007, the first stage of a 12-day visit to the *ISS*.

Two years later, at the age of 60, Simonyi paid a further $35 million for a second voyage to the *ISS*, the most expensive tourist trip, departing March 26, 2009, and returning April 9, 2009.

By 2012, assembly of the *International Space Station*—the most expensive object ever made by humans—will be complete. Join us in low Earth orbit as we survey the record-breaking research facility...

FUNCTIONAL CARGO BLOCK Aka *Zarya* (Russian for "dawn"), the ●oldest *ISS* module was launched on November 20, 1998. Pictured here is *Zarya* docking with *Unity* (the station's first docking) on December 6, 1998. In subsequent missions, the *Zvezda* service module and the *Rassvet* research module were added.

A. TRUSS STRUCTURE The station's 357.5-ft-long (109-m) backbone on which solar arrays and radiators are mounted.

B. COLUMBUS A European laboratory—the largest contribution to the *ISS* by ESA, the European Space Agency.

C. LABS AND NODES The *Unity* and *Harmony* nodes, plus the U.S. laboratory *Destiny* and Italy's *Leonardo* module.

D. PHOTOVOLTAIC ARRAYS Four wing pairs of cells provide power to the main body of the station.

E. ELC The ExPRESS Logistics Carrier (ExPRESS stands for "Expedites the Processing of Experiments to the Space Station") collects and handles experiment data.

F. ● LARGEST ARTIFICIAL SATELLITE At 357 x 167 x 65 ft. (109 x 51 x 20 m), the *ISS* is the largest man-made object to orbit the Earth, doing so once every 91 minutes. It can easily be seen from the ground with the naked eye during darkness.

G. Remote Manipulator System

H. Exposed Facility (EF)

$12.26: The average annual contribution you will pay as a taxpayer to fund the International Space Station once the total cost is shared between the citizens of participating nations.

UNITY (NODE 1) This U.S.-built module acts as a passageway to the living and working areas of the space station.
A. Axial dock for *Zvezda* module
B. *Zarya* module
C. Solar arrays

KIBO The Japanese Experiment Module *Kibo* ("Hope") is 36 ft. 8 in. (11.19 m) long with a diameter of 14 ft. 5 in. (4.39 m), and has a mass of 32,628 lb. (14,800 kg), making it the ● largest ISS module. Connected to the main module are pressurized and exposed research facilities.
A. Experimental Logistics Module (ELM)
B. Pressurized Module (PM)

CANADARM2 The largest robotic arm in space measures 57 ft. 8 in. (17.5 m) long and weighs 3,618 lb. (1,641 kg).

LARGEST WINDOW IN SPACE *Cupola*—a module attached to *Tranquility*—is a cluster of seven windows with an overall diameter of 9 ft. 7 in. (2.95 m). It was built by ESA and launched on February 8, 2010. Pictured is NASA's Tracy Caldwell Dyson (U.S.A.) looking down over Earth on September 11, 2010.
A. Fused silica and borosilicate glass

Blast-off To avoid a buildup of noxious flatulence on board space stations (where you can't open a window!), NASA once issued a "banned foods" list that included cabbages and beans!

According to the World Wealth Report's 2010 figures, the U.S.A. has 2,886,200 millionaires—making it the ○ **country with the most millionaires**. The number has dropped from 3,028,000 in 2008.

The *ISS* toilet cost a record $19 million!

ASTRO-NOUGHTS The European Space Agency claims that the *ISS* will cost €100,000,000,000 ($136 billion) to build and operate, making it the ●**most expensive object ever made.**

Fastest marathon in space The fastest time to complete a marathon in orbit was achieved by NASA astronaut Sunita Williams of Needham, Massachusetts, U.S.A., above Earth on board the *ISS*. Ms Williams, who ran the 26.2-mile (42-km) race strapped to a treadmill with bungee cord, competed as an official entrant of the 111th Boston Marathon (U.S.A.) on April 16, 2007, finishing in a time of 4 hr. 24 min.

MOST TIME IN SPACE Sergei Krikalev (Russia), commander of the *ISS* between April 14 and October 10 2005, has accumulated 803 days 9 hr. 39 min. in space.

●**FIRST RESIDENT CREW ON BOARD THE** *ISS* The crew of Expedition 1—Russia's Sergei Krikalev (left) and Yuri Pavlovich Gidzenko (center), and the U.S.A.'s William Shepherd—arrived at the *ISS* on November 2, 2000, and stayed for 136 days.

●**MOST WOMEN IN ORBIT** On April 5, 2010, Dorothy Metcalf-Lindenburger, Stephanie Wilson, and Naoko Yamazaki joined Tracy Caldwell Dyson on board the *ISS*—the most females in orbit at once.

The country with the ●**highest concentration of millionaires** (measured in U.S. dollars) is not the U.S.A. but Singapore. Here, an astonishing 8.5% of households had $1 million in assets under management as of 2009.

SPACE DISASTERS

●**Shortest manned Moon shot** An oxygen tank exploded on *Apollo 13*'s outward journey to the Moon in April 1970, forcing the U.S. crew to evacuate the command module and use the attached lunar module as a lifeboat. *Apollo 13* used a "free return trajectory" to return home, relying on the Moon's gravity to slingshot the spacecraft around it and back to Earth. All three crew members survived their five-day, 22-hour ordeal.

Worst ground-based space disaster In the greatest space disaster on the ground, 91 people were killed when an R-16 rocket exploded during fueling at the Baikonur Space Center, Kazakhstan, on October 24, 1960.

Most damaging spacecraft collision On June 25, 1997, an unmanned *Progress* supply vehicle, weighing 15,000 lb. (7 tonnes), collided with the Russian *Mir* space station. Cosmonauts had to work quickly to seal a breach in the hull of *Mir*'s *Spektr* module, while a U.S. astronaut prepared *Mir*'s *Soyuz* capsule for a possible evacuation. There were no fatalities, but *Mir* was left low on power and oxygen and temporarily tumbled out of control.

WORST DISASTER IN A MANNED SPACE FLIGHT Of the nearly 300 attempted manned space flights as of February 2011, two missions have each seen a record seven fatalities. On January 28, 1986, an explosion occurred 73 seconds after liftoff of the space shuttle *Challenger*'s STS-51L mission from the Kennedy Space Center, Florida, U.S.A., at a height of 46,000 ft. (14,020 m). Five men and two women (left) died. In 2003, tragedy struck again (see p. 27).

Far out! At 8:21 p.m. ET on April 14, 1970, the crew of *Apollo* 13 were at apocynthion (the farthest point from the Moon), 248,655 miles (400,171 km) above our planet's surface, the **greatest distance from Earth reached by humans.**

SPACE DEBRIS Many thousands of pieces of man-made debris orbit Earth, from tiny particles to defunct satellites. Around 20,000 of them are tracked by radar. Here is a selection.

A camera belonging to U.S. astronaut Suni Williams drifted away in June 2007 while she was working on the *International Space Station*.

In November 2007, a pair of needle-nosed pliers belonging to Scott Parazynski (U.S.A.) floated off while he was on a spacewalk to carry out work on a solar array.

A glove belonging to the first U.S. spacewalker, Ed White, waved goodbye in 1965. After orbiting the Earth for a month or so, it burned up in the atmosphere.

In 2006, while testing material that could be used to repair damaged heat shields, astronaut Piers Sellers (U.S., b. UK) lost a spatula on *Discovery*'s STS-121 flight.

A whole bag of tools belonging to Heide Stefanyshyn-Piper (U.S.A.) and worth about $100,000 drifted away while she was on a spacewalk in November 2008.

●**WORST UNCONTROLLED SPIN IN SPACE** In March 1968, during the first docking in space—between the *Gemini 8* craft flown by Neil Armstrong (left) and David Scott (both U.S.A.) and an unmanned *Agena* booster—the two spacecraft began an uncontrolled roll. After an emergency undocking, *Gemini 8* began to roll faster and the crew were close to g-forces that would have impaired their vision or made them black out. Armstrong stopped the roll using *Gemini 8*'s reentry thrusters and initiated a mission abort and emergency splashdown (below left).

●**First fire on a space station** On February 23, 1997, a fire broke out on the Russian space station *Mir*, caused by lithium perchlorate "candles" that supplied oxygen to the station. The fire was put out, but the crew had come close to abandoning *Mir* in their *Soyuz* "lifeboat."

●**First lightning strike during a space mission** Less than a minute after *Apollo 12* lifted off from Cape Canaveral, Florida, U.S.A., on November 14, 1969, the spacecraft suffered severe electrical anomalies, including the loss of the fuel cells that provided power to the command module, leaving it on battery power alone. Mission control and the crew were able to overcome these problems and stay on course for Earth orbit. It was found that *Apollo 12* had been struck twice by lightning at 36 seconds and 52 seconds after launch.

For explorations on planet earth itself, take off for p. 29.

Singapore is clearly a significant port of call for business. In 2009, a total of 1,040 billion lb. (472 million tonnes) of cargo passed through, making it the world's ○**busiest port**.

● MOST FATALITIES DURING REENTRY
On February 1, 2003, the space shuttle *Columbia* was lost with all seven crew during reentry into Earth's atmosphere after a successful 15-day mission in orbit. The resulting investigation determined that a piece of insulating foam from the external fuel tank had impacted the leading edge of a wing during launch. This made a hole that allowed heat to build up during reentry, causing the left wing of the orbiter to break apart, and the rest of the spacecraft to disintegrate.

 China's national railroad network carried 2.4 billion tons (2.178 billion tonnes) of freight during 2004, making it the world's **busiest rail network for cargo**, according to the International Union of Railways (UIC).

● **FIRST DEATH IN ORBIT** A dog named Laika (meaning "barker") became the first animal to orbit the Earth when she launched into space aboard the Soviet *Sputnik 2* spacecraft on November 3, 1957. In October 2002, it was revealed that she had died just a few hours after launch from stress and overheating.

● **First fatalities at a launch rehearsal** U.S. astronauts Virgil Ivan "Gus" Grissom, Edward Higgins White II, and Roger Bruce Chaffee were killed in a fire inside their *Apollo 1* capsule on January 27, 1967 during a launch rehearsal at Cape Canaveral, Florida, U.S.A. The fire was caused by a spark from an electrical fault in the capsule's artificial atmosphere of pure oxygen.

● **FIRST SPACE FLIGHT DEATH TOLL** By the end of the *Soyuz 11* mission, on June 30, 1971, Viktor Ivanovich Patsayev, Vladislav Nikolayevich Volkov (both Russia), and Georgy Timofeyevich Dobrovolsky (Ukraine) had spent three weeks on the Soviet *Salyut 1* space station. After undocking, a valve failed and exposed the crew, who were not wearing spacesuits, to the vacuum of space at an altitude of 104 miles (168 km). They were asphyxiated within seconds.

● **FIRST ASTRONAUT KILLED IN FLIGHT DURING TRAINING** Theodore ("Ted") Freeman (U.S.A.), pictured in training, died on October 31, 1964 when his T-38 trainer aircraft collided with a goose. Both engines flamed out and, while attempting an emergency landing away from buildings at Ellington Air Force Base, Freeman ejected too close to the ground to survive.

PLANET EARTH

CONTENTS

ANATOMY OF EARTH

OUR RECORD-BREAKING HOME

Earth is the ●**largest terrestrial planet**, the **densest**, the ●**most geologically active inner planet**, and the only body in the Solar System with significant liquid water on its surface. It is home to the only known life in the universe. We share the planet with at least 2 million species of animal that we know of, and maybe up to 100 million more. Our Moon—which is about as wide as Australia—is the **largest satellite relative to planet size**, and with it we revolve around our Sun at 18.5 mi/s (29.78 km/s). What an amazing world we live on!

WHAT A MOUTHFUL! The Earth's total mass is given as 1.32 x 10²⁵ lb., which can also be expressed as 13,200,000,000,000, 000,000,000,000 lb., or 5.972 septillion kg.

THE MOTHER OF ALL THUNDERSTORMS Supercells are powerful thunderstorms that form around a mesocyclone (a deep, rotating updraft). They can be several miles across and may last several hours, making them both the ●**longest-lasting** and ●**largest thunderstorms**. They often occur on the Great Plains of the U.S.A. and can spawn tornadoes. This supercell occurred in July 2010 in Montana, U.S.A., and was photographed by Sean Heavey. "It was around five-to-ten miles in diameter with hurling winds of around 85 miles an hour," he reported. "I'm not ashamed to admit that it scared the living daylights out of me."

2.01: Your share of the Earth in acres—i.e., the area of the world suitable for farming divided by the world's population. Barring fish, all your food comes from a piece of land the size of a soccer field.

ATMOSPHERE
Layer of gases, held to the Earth by gravity, that extends upwards for *c.* 62,000 miles (100,000 km), although the boundary with space is considered to be 62 miles (100 km), below which lies almost 100% of the atmosphere.
• Weighs 1.1×10^{19} lb.
• Divided by temperature into five major layers:
- Troposphere (0–11 miles)
- Stratosphere (11–30 miles)
- Mesosphere (30–50 miles)
- Thermosphere (50–430 miles)
- Exosphere (up to 62,000 miles)

CONTINENTAL CRUST
• Thin layer of minerals that forms the continents.
• Accounts for just 0.375% of the planet's mass.

OCEANIC CRUST
Thinnest layer of the Earth, forming the ocean floor; 0.099% of total mass.

DEPTH	TEMPERATURE
A. 3,200–3,963 miles	A. 11,000–13,000°F
B. 1,750–3,200 miles	B. 7,250–11,000°F
C. 400–1,750 miles	C. 4,350–5,450°F
D. 250–400 miles	D. 1,600°F

A. INNER CORE (1,517 MILES WIDE)
• Solid ball of mostly nickel and iron and largest crystal on Earth. • The fastest-rotating part of the Earth.

B. OUTER CORE (1,400 MILES THICK)
• Represents 29.3% of Earth's mass (and 16% of its volume). • Largest liquid body on Earth, comprising iron, nickel, sulfur, and oxygen.

C. LOWER MANTLE
• Flowing layer of silicon, magnesium, and oxygen. • Largest region of Earth's interior, accounting for 49.2% of the planet's mass.

D. UPPER MANTLE
• Mostly rigid layer that, along with the crust, forms the "lithosphere."
• Accounts for 10.3% of Earth's mass.

As of 2006, China is the **largest producer of energy**, with 1,749 Mtoe (million metric tons of oil equivalent). A "toe" is a unit of measurement representing the amount of energy released when 1.1 tons (1 metric ton) of crude oil is burned.

For a breakdown of air, turn to xvi.

THE OCEANS About 97% of the surface water on Earth is ocean. We identify and name up to seven different oceans, but they are connected to form one continuous body of water covering an area of approximately 139×10^6 miles^2 (3.6×10^8 km^2). The droplets of water pictured here show the relative volumes of the five major oceans; in reality, the oceans combined would form a drop of water 852 miles (1,371 km) wide— about the same length as the British Isles.

A. Pacific Ocean (50.1% by vol.)
• Area of Earth: 33.03%
• Volume: 160.7 million miles^3
• Average depth: 13,385 ft.

B. Atlantic Ocean (23.3% by vol.)
• Area of Earth: 16.69%
• Volume: 74.5 million miles^3
• Average depth: 11,962 ft.

C. Indian Ocean (19.8% by vol.)
• Area of Earth: 13.83%
• Volume: 63.3 million miles^3
• Average depth: 12,274 ft.

D. Southern Ocean (5.4% by vol.)
• Area of Earth: 4.3%
• Volume: 17.2 million miles^3
• Average depth: 10,728 ft.

E. Arctic Ocean (1.4% by vol.)
• Area of Earth: 3.05%
• Volume: 4.5 million miles^3
• Average depth: 3,953 ft.

Q. WHAT COLOR IS WATER?

A. It really *is* blue! But not because it reflects the blue sky. The main reason is because it absorbs light at the red end of the spectrum, so we see the opposite color: blue.

The country with the **largest consumption of energy per head** is Qatar, with an average energy consumption of 48,627 lb. (22,057 kg) of oil equivalent per person in 2006.

THE BLUE PLANET Earth is known as the Blue Planet because its surface is covered mostly in water. Liquid water hasn't been found in significant quantities on the surface of any other planet in our Solar System. The word "hydrosphere" describes all the water on, over, and inside a planet, but although 70.9% of Earth's surface is covered in water, the hydrosphere accounts for just 0.023% of the planet's mass.

The average depth of the ocean is 12,430 ft. (3,790 m)—roughly as deep as the Alps are tall—but the **deepest point in the ocean** is 35,797 ft. (10,911 m). If Mount Everest was dropped into the ocean at this point, it would disappear 1.2 miles (2 km) below the surface.

A. LAND (29.1% OF SURFACE)
Area: *c.* 57,506,000 miles^2
(*c.* 148,940,000 km^2)
All the land on Earth combined would form a perfectly round island 8,556 miles wide—large enough to stretch across the Pacific Ocean from Mexico to China with 620 miles to spare at either end!

B. WATER (70.9% OF SURFACE)
Area: *c.* 139.3 million miles^2
(*c.* 361.9 million km^2)
Of this, only 2.5% is fresh, comprising ice (1.6%), underground aquifers (0.6%), and lakes/rivers (0.36%). The rest is ocean and sea.

COMPOSITION OF THE EARTH
The Earth was formed from the same cloud of gas and dust as the Sun and the other planets. But the chemical composition of the Earth is very different from that of the universe as a whole, where hydrogen is the **most abundant element** (accounting for at least 90% of all matter). The ●**most abundant element on Earth** is iron, at around 36%.

Like the other elemental building blocks of our planet, pictured here in their raw form, most of the oxygen (which is highly reactive) on Earth is locked away in minerals—the crystalline solids from which rocks are formed. The ●**most abundant minerals on Earth** are the silicates (formed with silicon and oxygen), which account for about 95% of the planet's crust. This explains why oxygen (a colorless gas indicated by the jar in the picture above) forms such a large part—around 46%—of the mass of the crust.

A. Oxygen (O) 30.1%

B. Iron (Fe) 32.1%

C. Nickel (Ni) 1.8%

D. Aluminum (Al) 1.4%

E. Silicon (Si) 15.1%

F. Trace elements 1.2%

G. Calcium (Ca) 1.5%

H. Sulfur (S) 2.9%

I. Magnesium (Mg) 13.9%

Earth is a 4.6-billion-year-old oblate spheroid, meaning that its polar axis is shorter (by 26.7 miles) than its equatorial axis, giving it a bulge around the middle.

EARTH*

Mass (total)	1.32×10^{25} lb.
Mass (atmosphere)	1.1×10^{19} lb.
Mass (hydrosphere)	3.09×10^{21} lb.
Surface area (total)	196,939,900 miles^2
Surface area (water)	139,397,000 miles^2
Radius (equatorial)	3,963 miles
Radius (polar)	3,950 miles
Volume	2.6×10^{11} miles^3
Rotational period	23 hr. 56 min. 4.1 sec.
Average temperature	59°F (15°C)

EXTREMES

Highest point	29,029 ft. (Mount Everest, Nepal)
Lowest point (on land)	1,371 ft. (Dead Sea shore, Israel and Jordan)
Deepest point	35,797 ft. (Challenger Deep in the Marianas Trench)
Highest temperature recorded	136°F (58°C) at Al'Aziziyah in the Sahara Desert, Libya
Lowest temperature recorded	-128.6°F (-89.2°C) at Vostok, Antarctica

*Sources: NASA, National Geophysical Data Center; boundaries, and therefore data, vary depending upon agency.

POPULATIONS

○**Most densely populated country** With a disproportionately large population of 30,586 people and an area of just 0.75 miles^2 (1.95 km^2), the tiny sovereign state of Monaco manages to squeeze in a world record 40,624 people per mile^2 (15,685 per km^2).

●**Most densely populated territory** The Chinese territory of Macau is just as crowded, with an estimated 567,957 people sharing a landmass of 11.3 miles^2 (29.2 km^2)—that's a whopping 50,262 people for every mile^2 (19,450 per km^2)!

290: Number of people you know at any one time. In a lifetime, 1,981 people will pass through this group of friends, colleagues, and acquaintances, which means you will get to know 0.0000003% of the world's population.

Q. WHICH COUNTRY HAS THE LOWEST POPULATION DENSITY IN THE WORLD?

A. Mongolia—which borders the world's most populous nation, China—is a lonely place, with just 5.11 people per mile^2 (1.97 people per km^2).

●**LEAST COMMON LANGUAGE** Yaghan is an indigenous language of Tierra del Fuego, an archipelago on the southern tip of South America. The Yaghan numbered as many as 10,000 people before Argentina and Chile began exploring the islands in the late 19th century, but disease, relocation, and exploitation have since caused the population to collapse, to around 70 by 1930. Today, Cristina Calderón (born *c.* 1938), pictured, is the last native speaker.

○**LOWEST LIFE EXPECTANCY** Poor health care and a prevalence of diseases such as cholera mean that Angola's 13 million people can expect to live for an average of just 38.48 years. By 2010, females were living for 39.52 years, while males were surviving just 37.48 years.

○**Highest life expectancy** Monaco's wealthy inhabitants live for an average of 89.78 years, with males enjoying 85.81 years and females 93.9 years—2.5 times the life of an Angolan man!

●**Largest urban population north of the Arctic Circle** Despite its inhospitable location 2° north of the Arctic Circle, the northwest Russian seaport of Murmansk has a healthy population of around 311,000 people.

The **most money paid for a cell phone number** is 10 million QAR ($2.75 million), by an anonymous Qatari bidder for the number 666-6666 on May 23, 2006.

LARGEST MAN-MADE FLOATING REED ISLANDS Lake Titicaca (Peru/Bolivia) is famous for its unique population of several hundred Uros people, who live on its waters on a man-made archipelago of 42 islands. Knitted from mats of totora reed, the islands are constantly under construction, as they rot away over a three-month period. The largest is Taquile Island, which is around 0.6 miles (1 km) wide and 4 miles (7 km) long.

Most southerly inhabited place The hamlet of Puerto Toro on Navarino island, Chile, is the most southerly *permanent* human outpost, discounting Antarctic research stations. The 2002 census recorded a population of just 36 people.

●**Largest annual human migration** During the Lunar New Year celebrations in China, an estimated 1.3 billion city workers migrate back to their rural family homes. In 2010, *c.* 2.26 billion railroad journeys were made in China over this 40-day period.

The ○**fastest completion of a prescribed 160-character text message** is 34.65 seconds by Frode Ness (Norway) at the Oslo City shopping mall in Oslo, Østlandet, Norway, on November 13, 2010.

DISCOVER THE LARGEST POPULATIONS ON THE PLANET, WHERE ELBOW ROOM COMES AT A PREMIUM . . .

○ **City: Tokyo, Japan**

36 million people, making Greater Tokyo home to 28% of Japan's 126.8 million citizens.

○ **Island: Java, Indonesia**

136 million people, or an incredible 57% of the Indonesian population!

○ **Country: China**

1.330 billion people, ahead of India's 1.148 billion and the U.S.A.'s 303.8 million.

○ **Continent: Asia**

4 billion people, thanks largely to Chinese and Indian contributions.

● **HIGHEST-DWELLING ARBOREAL TRIBE:** The remote Korowai of Papua, Indonesia, are a tree-dwelling people who live in tree-houses as high as 100 ft. (30 m) above the ground.

● **Highest seasonal population change** The human population of Antarctica is not permanent, but exists in research stations across the continent. In the course of a year, its population swells by a factor of five, from around 1,000 in the winter to around 5,000 during the more forgiving summer months.

○ **HIGHEST FERTILITY RATE:** In Niger, 7.68 children are born to each woman on average. The West African state also has the highest population growth rate—3.66% per year.

SOCIAL CLIMBERS: Discovered in the early 20th century, the 3,000-strong Korowai people originally took to the trees to escape the dangers of flooding, animals, and other tribes, building tree-homes with tools of stone or bone.

● **HIGHEST CONCENTRATION OF UNCONTACTED TRIBES** According to the human rights organization Survival International, there are approximately 100 uncontacted tribes in the world today. More than half of these are believed to live in the Amazon rainforest (such as this tribe photographed in 2008 on the Peru–Brazil border), and many choose to have no contact with the outside world, sometimes exhibiting hostility to strangers.

○ **SMALLEST REPUBLIC:** The Pacific island of Nauru has an area of just 8.1 miles² (21 km²) and a population of 9,267, making it the world's smallest independent republic.

CONTINENTS

LARGEST CONTINENT EVER Have you noticed that some of the coastlines of the continents seem to fit together, rather like a jigsaw puzzle? Geologists believe that around 250 million years ago, the world's landmasses formed one huge supercontinent, which they named Pangea (meaning "entire Earth").

0.12: Inches per month by which your fingernails grow—the same rate at which the continents of North America and Europe are moving apart. In a lifetime, that's 6 ft. 8.7 in.

LONGEST CONTINENTAL MOUNTAIN RANGE The Andes mountain range is 4,700 miles (7,600 km) long and spans seven countries. More than 50 of its peaks exceed 20,000 ft. (6,000 m).

GREATEST DESERTIFICATION Two-thirds of Africa is now desert or dryland. Deforestation, overintensive farming, and human migration have all contributed to this condition.

WIDEST CONTINENTAL SHELF The world's widest continental shelf extends for 750 miles (1,210 km) off the coast of Siberia, Russia, into the Arctic Ocean.

●**LARGEST CRATON** Cratons are large parts of continental crust that are stable and that have remained relatively unmodified by plate tectonics since the end of the Precambrian era, 542 million years ago. They are normally located in the interior of continents and contain some of the oldest rocks on Earth. The North American craton is the largest, covering around 70% of the continent. It was formed around 2 billion years ago by the collision of several smaller microcontinents. Pictured is the Adirondack Mountains, an exposed part of the craton.

Located in Longyearbyen on the island of Svalbard, Norway, the Radisson SAS Polar Hotel is the world's **most northerly full-service hotel**, with just 828 miles (1,333 km) separating it from the North Pole.

THE CONTINENTS

The Earth has seven continents—although some authorities regard Europe and Asia as one landmass, termed Eurasia. In terms of their relative size, they are:

Continent	Area
Asia	17,226,000 miles^2 (44,614,000 km^2)
Africa	11,667,000 miles^2 (30,216,000 km^2)
North America	9,355,000 miles^2 (24,230,000 km^2)
South America	6,878,000 miles^2 (17,814,000 km^2)
Antarctica	5,500,000 miles^2 (14,245,000 km^2)
Europe	4,056,000 miles^2 (10,505,000 km^2)
Oceania	3,283,000 miles^2 (8,503,000 km^2)

●**LEAST-EXPLORED CONTINENT**
Antarctica's shoreline was first sighted in 1820 by sea captain William Smith (UK) and explorer Fabian Gottlieb von Bellingshausen (Russia). It was also the last continent to be discovered.

With an overall floor area of 570 ft.^{2} (53 m^2), the cosy Eh'hausl Hotel in Amberg, Germany, is the world's **smallest hotel**, capable of providing overnight accommodation for just two paying guests.

LAND FARTHEST FROM THE SEA The point on the Earth's surface at latitude 46º15.8'N, longitude 86º40.2'E—in the Dzungarian Basin in China's Xinjiang Uygur region—is 1,645 miles (2,648 km) from the nearest open sea.

FASTEST LANDMASS Over time, Earth's continental plates move, relative to each other. The greatest movement occurs at the Tonga microplate, near Samoa, which is moving steadily into the Pacific Ocean at a rate of 9.4 in. (24 cm) per year.

●**LEAST VOLCANICALLY ACTIVE CONTINENT** The continental landmass of mainland Australia has experienced no volcanic eruptions for more than 5,000 years. Geological processes other than recent volcanism therefore dominate the landscape. Wave Rock (pictured), more than 2.7 billion years old, is made from granite and has been shaped by chemical weathering. Australia has a mean elevation of just over 656 ft. (200 m) above sea level, making it the **flattest continental landmass**. The highest point on the mainland is the tip of Mount Kosciuszko, at 7,312 ft. (2,229 m) above sea level.

LARGEST VOLCANIC ZONE The Pacific Ring of Fire is a huge arc of concentrated earthquake and volcanic activity about 24,800 miles (40,000 km) long, located in the Pacific Ocean. It contains some 452 volcanoes and more than 75% of the active and dormant volcanoes in the world. Japan, for example, experiences 1,500 earthquakes each year and is home to 10% of the planet's volcanoes.

●**LONGEST TRANSCONTINENTAL ISTHMUS** The country of Panama is 420 miles (676 km) long—and 31 miles (50 km) wide at its narrowest point—and provides the only land connection between North and South America. Shipping passes between the Atlantic Ocean and Pacific Ocean through the Panama Canal.

WORLD OF WONDERS

●**Highest tropical mountain range** Huascarán National Park in the Cordillera Blanca mountain range, Peru, has its highest point at 22,204 ft. (6,768 m) above sea level. The protected area covers 840,158 acres (340,000 ha) and includes 33 peaks over 18,045 ft. (5,500 m) in height.

Largest geoglyphs Peru is also home to the Nazca Lines—as many as 70 giant animals, lines, and shapes etched into the Nazca desert some time between 300 B.C. and A.D. 540. Remarkably, these shapes and animals can only be discerned when viewed from the sky—they are too huge to be perceived as shapes when viewed on the ground.

Tallest mountain face The Rupal face of Nanga Parbat, in the western Himalayas, Pakistan, is a single rise of some 16,000 ft. (5,000 m) from the valley floor to the summit. With a peak at 26,656 ft. (8,125 m), Nanga Parbat is the world's eighth-highest mountain.

Fastest-rising mountain Nanga Parbat, in Pakistan, is growing taller at a rate of 0.27 in. (7 mm) per year. The mountain is part of the Himalayan Plateau, formed when India began colliding with the Eurasian continental plate between 30 and 50 million years ago.

●**HIGHEST DENSITY OF EOCENE WHALES:** Since 1905, some 379 fossil whales from the Eocene era (56–34 million years ago) have been found in Wadi Al-Hitan in Egypt's Western Desert.

Over the next four pages, Guinness World Records focuses on the rich diversity of our planet, from deserts to ice fields, volcanoes to submarine mountains. The photographs on these pages show animals or places that the United Nations Educational, Scientific, and Cultural Organization (UNESCO) has designated World Heritage Sites because they have great cultural significance.

TALLEST LIVING TREE
On August 25, 2006, a coast redwood (*Sequoia sempervirens*) was discovered by Chris Atkins and Michael Taylor (both U.S.A.) in the Redwood National Park in California, U.S.A. Dubbed "Hyperion," it reached 379 ft. 1 in. (115.54 m) tall—more than twice the height of the Statue of Liberty—when measured in September 2006. The park is part of California's Redwood National and State Parks, home to thousands of redwoods, including the world's tallest trees.

TREE-MENDOUS! Trees such as the coast redwood (see above) are exceptionally long lived. Some of those redwoods standing today were saplings around 2,000 years ago!

Karl Friedrich Benz of Karlsruhe, Germany, built the **first successful gasoline-driven automobile**, the three-wheeled Motorwagen. He tested it at Mannheim in late 1885.

BEARING UP! The giant panda population was in decline for years, but now the numbers seem to be steadying. The latest available figures, from 2004, suggest a global population of 1,600.

●**FIRST DISCOVERY OF PALEOLITHIC CAVE ART** In 1879, Don Marcelino Sanz de Sautuola, an amateur archeologist, and his daughter Maria (both Spain) discovered prehistoric paintings in the Altamira Cave, Cantabria, Spain. The artworks, which include animals and human handprints, have been dated to between 25,000 and 35,000 years old.

●**LARGEST GIANT PANDA HABITAT** The Sichuan Giant Panda Sanctuaries in the Qionglai and Jiajin Mountains of Sichuan Province, China, represent the largest contiguous habitat of the giant panda (*Ailuropoda melanoleuca*). More than 30% of the world panda population lives in this 3,569-mile^2 (9,245-km^2) network of nature reserves and scenic parks.

●**Largest mudflow from a volcano** The Osceola Mudflow occurred some 5,600 years ago and began on top of Mount Rainier in the U.S. Cascade Mountain range. The result of a volcanic eruption, it consisted of a debris flow of around 106,000 ft.^{3} (3 km^3) that hurtled down the mountain at around 56 mi./hr. (90 km/h). By the time it had reached the Puget Sound, more than 62 miles (100 km) away, the mudflow still had a thickness of around 98 ft. (30 m). After it had subsided, it had created 177 miles^2 (460 km^2) of new land on the coast.

Nowadays, automobiles are commonplace and nowhere more so than in Luxembourg, which has the **highest rate of automobile ownership** in the world, with 647 automobiles per 1,000 people.

1,005: Weight in pounds of the butter you'll eat in your lifetime. Your personal butter mountain is the size of 1.5 refrigerators. If Mount Everest was made of butter, it could supply the whole world for 1,348 years.

LARGEST BUDDHIST TEMPLE:
Borobudur, near Yogyakarta in Java, Indonesia, was built between A.D. 750 and 842. It is 113 ft. (34.5 m) tall, with a base measuring 403 x 403 ft. (123 x 123 m).

●**OLDEST REPTILE FOSSILS** The Joggins Fossil Cliffs are a 9.3-mile-long (15-km) stretch of cliffs on the Bay of Fundy, Canada, rich in fossils of the Carboniferous period (*c.* 354–290 million years ago). Fossil remains of 148 species have been found here, including those of *Hylonomus*—at *c.* 315 million years old, one of the oldest known reptiles.

Most active volcano Kilauea, in Hawaii, U.S.A., has been erupting continually since 1983. Lava is being discharged at a rate of 176 ft.³/s (5 m³/s).

Mount Stromboli, in the Tyrrhenian Sea off the Italian coast, has given off mild emissions of gas and lava since at least the 7th century B.C., making it the **longest continually erupting volcano**. The emissions—usually several every hour—have led it to be known as the "Lighthouse of the Mediterranean."

First "Dark Sky" Park The International Dark Sky Association has named Utah's Natural Bridges National Monument as the first Dark Sky Park—that is, an area in which the night sky can be viewed clearly, without any "light pollution."

The ●**largest restaurant wine list** is that of the Restaurant Chiggeri in Luxembourg City, Luxembourg. The list featured 1,746 wines when counted on December 31, 2008.

●Oldest wooden building The Hōryū-ji temple in Ikaruga, Nara Prefecture, Japan, was built in A.D. 607 and is one of 48 ancient buildings protected by UNESCO in the area. The temple includes a five-story building known as the Gojunoto.

Longest stone arch The longest natural arches in the world are both in Utah, U.S.A., and both span openings of equal width. Landscape Arch, in Arches National Park, and Kolob Arch, in Zion National Park, both stand over openings 310 ft. (94.5 m) wide. Landscape Arch is the more dramatic as it spans an open gully and narrows to only 16 ft. (5 m) thick, while Kolob Arch stands close to a high cliff face.

WATER WORLD

Largest hot spring The largest boiling river issues from alkaline hot springs at Deildartunguhver, north of Reykjavik, Iceland, at a rate of 65 gal. (245 liters) of boiling water per second.

Longest river The Nile is credited as the longest river in the world. Its main source is Lake Victoria in east central Africa. From its farthest stream in Burundi, it extends 4,160 miles (6,695 km) in length.

The **widest river**, however, is the Amazon River in South America. While not in flood, its main stretches (i.e., not its tidal reaches, where an estuary or delta can be much wider) can reach widths of up to 7 miles (11 km) at its widest points.

The Amazon also has the **greatest flow** of any river. It discharges an average of 7,100,000 ft.³/s. (200,000 m³/s) into the Atlantic Ocean, increasing to more than 12,000,000 ft.³/s. (340,000 m³/s.) in full flood. The flow of the Amazon is 60 times greater than that of the Nile.

●LARGEST CONCENTRATION OF GEYSERS: Located mostly in Wyoming, U.S.A., Yellowstone National Park boasts at least 300 geysers, two-thirds of the planet's total; 250 are active.

The **largest wine cellars** belong to the Koöperatiewe Wijnbouwers Vereniging, at Paarl in Cape Province, South Africa. They cover an area of 54 acres (22 ha) and have a capacity of 27 million gal. (121 million liters) of wine.

0.28: Gallons of urine the average person produces every day. Over a lifetime, this comes to 7,904 gal. It would take you 22 days to pee it all in one go and you would fill up 10 standard fire trucks.

●**Widest rapids** During the monsoon season, the Mekong River on the border between Cambodia and Laos increases in volume by a factor of 20, flooding the Sipandone wetlands and creating an area of turbulent rapids up to 8.5 miles (14 km) wide. The flow rate is twice that at Niagara Falls, with 2.2 million gal. (10 million liters) of water thundering its way through a maze of channels between the area's many islands every second.

Largest swamp Located principally in southwestern Brazil but encompassing small areas within neighboring Bolivia and Paraguay too, the Pantanal (which is Spanish for "marshland") covers a surface area of 57,915 miles^2 (150,000 km^2)—roughly that of the state of Georgia! During the rainy season (December–May), 80% of the Pantanal is flooded, and it contains the greatest diversity of water plants in the world.

Largest river island The island of Majuli in the Brahmaputra River in northeast India covers an area of around 340 miles^2 (880 km^2). Owing to the frequent flooding of the Brahmaputra, Majuli suffers heavy erosion, and in the last 30–40 years it is estimated that it has lost about one-third of its area. Majuli is currently home to some 160,000 people.

LARGEST SAND ISLAND: Fraser Island, off the coast of Queensland, Australia, has a sand dune 75 miles (120 km) long and covering approximately 402,750 acres (163,000 ha).

STEAM POWER: Geysers are hot springs of boiling water that erupt periodically into the air as the underground steam expands up to 1,500 times its normal volume.

The Republic of South Africa is the **country with the most official languages**, with 11. The most widely spoken language is isiZulu, followed (in order) by isiXhosa, Afrikaans, Sepedi, Setswana, English, Sesotho, Xitsonga, siSwati, Tshivenda, and isiNdebele.

●LARGEST NON-POLAR ICE FIELD Located in Yukon Territory, Canada, the 8,490-mile^2 (21,980-km^2) Kluane National Park and Reserve is home to the largest ice field outside the Poles. Around 8,200–9,800 ft. (2,500–3,000 m) high, it occupies more than half of the park and incorporates glaciers that stretch for 37 miles (60 km).

●LARGEST REEF IN THE NORTHERN HEMISPHERE The Belize Barrier Reef Reserve is a 372-mile^2 (963-km^2) coastal system of atolls, sand cays, mangrove forests, lagoons, and estuaries, and is home to the largest reef system in the northern hemisphere. The submarine shelf and barrier reef stretches from Mexico in the north to Guatemala in the south and is second in size only to the Great Barrier Reef of Australia. Pictured is the Great Blue Hole, a 407-ft.-deep (124-m) submarine sinkhole located off the Belize coast.

The **most common language** is Chinese, which is spoken by more than 1.1 billion people. The "common speech" (Pûtônghuà) is the standard form of Chinese, with a pronunciation based on that of Beijing.

●**LARGEST PROTECTED MARINE AREA** The Phoenix Islands Protected Area covers 157,630 miles^2 (408,250 km^2) within the Republic of Kiribati. It is home to around 500 species of fish, 200 species of coral, and 44 bird and 18 marine mammal species.

Thickest ice On January 4, 1975, a team of seismologists measured the depth of ice in Wilkes Land, in eastern Antarctica, to be 2.96 miles (4.77 km) deep. That's the equivalent of 10 Empire State Buildings piled one on top of another!

The Antarctic ice cap is the largest single body of freshwater, holding *c.* 7.25 million miles^3 (30 million km^3)—or around 70% of the world's total.

LARGEST MANGROVE FORESTS: The Sundarbans stretches for nearly 6,000 miles^2 (15,540 km^2) across India and Bangladesh. Its trees sometimes exceed 70 ft. (21 m) in height.

Longest submarine mountain range The Mid-Ocean Ridge extends 40,000 miles (65,000 km) from the Arctic Ocean to the Atlantic Ocean, around Africa, Asia, and Australia, and under the Pacific Ocean to the west coast of North America. It has a maximum height of 13,800 ft. (4,200 m) above the base ocean depth—nearly eight times the height of the CN Tower in Toronto, Canada.

Highest submarine mountain Mount Pico in the Azores Islands (Portugal) has a base-to-summit height of 27,719 ft. (8,449 m)—just fractionally shorter than Mount Everest—but it has a prominence of just 7,711 ft. (2,351 m) above the surface of the sea; beneath the waves, the mountain sinks 20,000 ft. (6,098 m) to its submarine base—giving it the largest underwater mountain face.

Highest waterfall The Salto Angel, or "Angel Falls"—located in Venezuela, on a branch of the Carrao River—has a total drop of 3,212 ft. (979 m). The longest single drop measures 2,648 ft. (807 m).

On the basis of average annual flow, the **greatest waterfall** is the Boyoma Falls in the Democratic Republic of the Congo (former Zaire), at 600,000 ft.³/sec. (17,000 m³/sec.).

KILLER CLIMATE

●**Longest-lasting tropical cyclone** Hurricane/Typhoon John formed on August 11, 1994 in the eastern Pacific Ocean, lasted for 31 days, and covered the ●**farthest distance recorded for a tropical cyclone**: 8,250 miles (13,280 km). It traveled from the eastern to the western Pacific; as the two regions use different labels for tropical cyclones, it is known as both a hurricane and a typhoon.

GREATEST MONTHLY RAINFALL For a calendar month, the record for rainfall is 366 in. (9,300 mm), at Cherrapunji, Meghalaya, India, in July 1861. Cherrapunji also saw the greatest rainfall in 12 months, with 1,041.75 in. (26,461 mm) from August 1, 1860, to July 31, 1861.

●**WIDEST TORNADO DAMAGE PATH:** On May 22, 2004, 56 tornadoes hit the Midwestern U.S.A. One, the Hallam Nebraska tornado, left a swathe of destruction up to 2.4 miles (4 km) wide.

●**Longest tornado path length** On March 18, 1925, a tornado traveled at least 218 miles (352 km) through the U.S. states of Missouri, Illinois, and Indiana. It killed 695 people, more than any other tornado in U.S. history. The tornado also lasted 3.5 hours, longer than any other in history.

●**Largest tropical cyclone** At its maximum strength on October 12, 1979, Typhoon Tip had a diameter of around 1,370 miles (2,200 km) in the Pacific Ocean. During this period, Tip's gale-force winds covered an area of around 1.2 million miles^2 (3.8 million km^2). Typhoon Tip was studied in detail by the U.S. Air Force, who flew some 60 research missions into the cyclone.

●**Highest sea-level rise** Since detailed records began in the mid-19th century, the global average sea level has risen by 7.87 in. (20 cm). The average rate for the 20th century was around 0.07 in. (1.7 mm) per year. Satellite observations have shown that, since 1993, the global sea level has been rising by around 0.12 in. (3 mm) per year.

The **earliest recorded use of paper currency** can be traced back to China during the Song dynasty (A.D. 960–1279). It was utilized by a group of wealthy merchants and businessmen in Sichuan, China, where the art of printing was invented.

●GREATEST CLIMATIC DISRUPTION TO AIR TRAVEL On April 14, 2010, the erupting Eyjafjallajökull volcano on Iceland began a highly explosive phase of activity, ejecting fine ash more than 5 miles (8 km) into the atmosphere. The ash cloud was carried by a jet stream (a fast-flowing air current) towards mainland Europe and—until April 21—313 airports were closed, about 100,000 flights were canceled, and 7 million people were stranded. The disruption is estimated to have cost the airline industry as much as $2.2 billion.

●**Worst damage to coral reef by a natural event** In 1998, around 16% of the world's coral reefs were destroyed or seriously damaged in a once-in-a-millennium event. The 1998 El Niño phenomenon may have triggered the disaster.

 Canada is home to the **largest coin**, which weighs 220 lb. 7 oz. (100 kg) and measures 19.6 in. (50 cm) in diameter and 1.1 in. (3 cm) in thickness. It has a face value of CAN$1 million ($900,375).

> **HAIL HERO:** This Herculean hailstone was found by Vivian resident Les Scott, who stored it in his freezer until its size could be validated. Its weight—despite some melting—was a whopping 1 lb. 15 oz. (0.87 kg).

HAILSTONES Pictured here is an 8-in.-wide (20.3-cm) hailstone that fell in Vivian, South Dakota, U.S.A., on July 23, 2010, during a 85-mi./hr. (135-km/h) tornado. The largest on record in the U.S.A., it pales somewhat when compared with the **largest ice fall** ever reported—a 20-ft.-long (6-m) mass (technically known as a "megacryometeor") that fell in Ord in Scotland, UK, on August 13, 1849. In both cases, the hailstone was composed of smaller pieces of ice or hail fused together.

The **heaviest hailstones** accurately recorded weighed up to 2 lb. (1 kg) and are reported to have killed 92 people in the Gopalganj area of Bangladesh on April 14, 1986.

A record 246 people died in a hailstorm in India in April 1888.

● HIGHEST CONCENTRATION OF LIGHTNING: An area near Kifuka in the Democratic Republic of the Congo receives 409 bolts per mile² (158 lightning bolts per km²) a year.

Greatest rainfall in 24 hours A record 73 in. (1,870 mm) of rain fell in 24 hours in Cilaos, Réunion, Indian Ocean, on March 15 and 16, 1952. This is equal to 8,327 tons (7,554 metric tons) of rain per acre.

For the **greatest number of rainy days**, you'd have to go to Hawaii. Located on the island of Kauai, Mount Wai'ale'ale has up to 350 rainy days per annum.

Worst damage toll for a snowstorm A total of $1.2 billion worth of damage was caused by a storm that traversed the entire east coast of the U.S.A. on March 12–13, 1993. In all, 500 people perished in this monumental winter storm, which has been described by one meteorologist as "a storm with the heart of a blizzard and the soul of a hurricane."

Lowest temperature for a permanently inhabited place The coldest inhabited place on Earth is the Siberian village of Oymyakon, which lies in the icy wastes of Russia at 63°16'N, 143°15'E. On February 6, 1933, the temperature there fell to -89.9°F (-67.7°C), which is the lowest ever seen outside Antarctica. Lying in second place is nearby Verkhoyansk (67°33'N, 133°23'E), which experienced -89.7°F (-67.6°C) on February 5 and 7, 1892.

Greatest temperature range Verkhoyansk is also subject to the world's greatest variations in temperature. Over the years, the temperature there has ranged an incredible 189°F (105°C) from the all-time low of -89.7°F (-67.6°C) in 1892 to a summer high of 99.1°F (37.3°C) in 1988.

●DEADLIEST HEATWAVE In the summer of 2010, the northern hemisphere suffered from a series of freak heatwaves. The most devastating effects were felt in Russia, where as many as 56,000 people perished from overheating, droughts, forest fires, and smog. An estimated 11,000 people died in Moscow alone.

On January 23–24, 1916, the town of Browning in Montana, U.S.A., experienced the **greatest temperature range recorded in a day** when an Arctic cold front caused the temperature to plummet 100°F (56°C) from 44°F (7°C) to -56°F (-49°C).

Highest recorded temperature The highest shade temperature ever recorded is 136°F (58°C), at Al'Aziziyah in the Sahara Desert, Libya, on September 13, 1922.

VARIETY OF LIFE

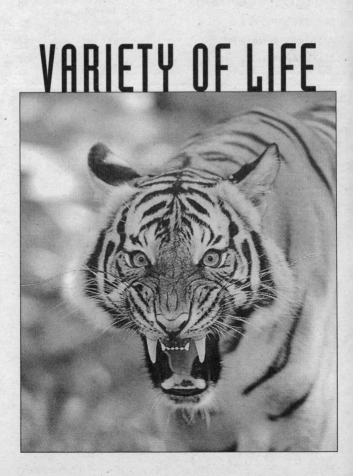

CONTENTS

CREEPY CRAWLIES

IT'S A BUG'S LIFE

Bugs are the most numerous—and diverse—forms of life on our planet. Here we present some of the titans of the bug world, and while some are gentle giants, others are ferocious predators, equipped with a lethal arsenal of stings, fangs, and even barbed hair.

LONGEST BEETLE South America's appropriately named titan beetle (*Titanus giganteus*) is a huge 6 in. (15 cm) long, not including its antennae. Bizarrely, adult titans don't eat, but instead fly around in search of a mate until they die.

ON THE DEFENSIVE: Given the considerable size of the goliath bird-eater's fangs, it may seem wise to stand behind, rather than in front, of it. However, the furry fiend has all angles covered, firing barbed hairs from its abdomen when threatened.

LARGEST SPIDER The male goliath bird-eater (*Theraphosa blondi*) weighs up to 6 oz. (170 g) and has a legspan of 11 in. (28 cm)—big enough to cover a dinner plate. This spider, however, is more predator than prey, and feeds on birds in the coastal rainforests of Suriname, Guyana, French Guiana, Brazil, and Venezuela.

For cuddlier creatures, turn to p. 267.

Canada is home to the world's **largest uninhabited island**. Devon Island is part of the Canadian archipelago in the Arctic Circle, to the north of Baffin Island, and has an area of 21,331 miles² (55,247 km²).

SNAP! Australian saltwater crocodiles can live to over 100 years of age and reach 23 ft. (7 m) long, while mature specimens may weigh over 1.1 tons (1 metric ton). They are apex predators (see p. 70) and can be very dangerous!

MOST VENOMOUS SPIDER Watch your step if you go walking in the rainforests of South America—venom from the aggressive Brazilian wandering spider (*Phoneutria* genus, which means "Murderess" in Greek) is so potent that just 0.00000021 oz. (0.006 mg) will kill a mouse, while larger doses can be lethal to humans.

HEAVIEST INSECT The goliath beetles (Scarabaeidae family) of Equatorial Africa are the heavyweights of the beetle world. The male, the larger of the two sexes, measures up to 4.33 in. (11 cm) from the tips of the frontal horns to the end of the abdomen, and weighs a hefty 2.5–3.5 oz. (70–100 g).

MOST VENOMOUS SCORPION The Tunisian fat-tailed scorpion (*Androctonus australis*) has a very nasty surprise in its tail—it's responsible for 80% of all stings and 90% of all deaths from scorpion stings across the whole of North Africa.

LARGEST WASP Native to the mountains of Japan, the Asian giant hornet (*Vespa mandarinia*) can grow to 2.2 in. (5.5 cm) in length, with a wingspan of 3 in. (7.6 cm). Unfortunately, it also has a 0.25-in. (0.6-cm) sting and can inject a venom so powerful that it dissolves human tissue. At least its size means you should see this angry critter coming. . . .

Discounting Australia, which is usually regarded as a continental landmass, the **largest island** overall is Greenland, with an area of about 840,000 miles² (2,175,600 km²).

100 TRILLION: Number of cells that you are made of. Although this sounds like a lot, your own cells are in fact outnumbered 10:1 by the hordes of bacteria—or microscopic creepy crawlies—hitching a ride on your body.

LARGEST CENTIPEDE
Measuring up to 10 in. (26 cm) long, the giant centipede (*Scolopendra gigantea*) of Central and South America is a fearsome predator with huge jaws that are capable of killing mice, frogs, lizards, and even bats.

LARGEST WETA With a length of 4.33 in (11 cm) and a legspan of 7 in. (17.5 cm), there is nothing little about the Little Barrier Island giant weta (*Deinacrida heteracantha*). Hailing from New Zealand, this cockroach-like cricket also weighs as much as 2.5 oz. (70 g)—three times the weight of a house mouse.

NEW SPECIES

NEWEST . . .

●**Bird of prey** The most recently discovered bird of prey is the Socotra buzzard (*Buteo socotraensis*), which was first formally described and named in 2010. The bird is native only to the Socotra archipelago, a group of tiny islands forming part of Yemen in the Arabian peninsula.

●**NEWEST MONITOR LIZARD Over 6 ft. 6 in. (2 m) long, the northern Sierra Madre forest monitor (*Varanus bitatawa*) was formally described and named in spring 2010. This yellow-and-black species is very unusual in that it is a fruit eater, making it only the third known species of frugivorous lizard.**

With its northernmost two-thirds covered in permafrost, Greenland is the world's **least populated territory**, with a density of 0.43 people per mile² (0.16 per km²).

●NEWEST MONGOOSE The semiaquatic Madagascan mongoose species Durrell's vontsira (*Salanoia durrelli*) first came to scientific attention in 2004, when a single specimen was encountered swimming in a remote lake. It was not formally recognized as a new, separate species until 2010. The mongoose shown here is being treated firmly but carefully by its handler. Mongooses can be aggressive.

Breed of cat Although the Sphynx cat was first bred successfully in 1996, it was not until 2002 that the breed became officially recognized. This feline species appears to be hairless, but in fact it has a covering of short, fine down.

Carnivore Environmental researchers are hoping to capture what some believe may be a new species of carnivore on Borneo—which, if correct, would be the first such discovery on the island since that of the Borneo ferret-badger in 1895. The animal looks like a cross between a cat and a fox and was photographed in the mountainous rainforests of the Kayan Mentarang National Park in 2003, but was kept unpublished as research continued.

Some researchers have suggested that it might be a viverrid—a family of animals that includes the civets—but this potential new species has not yet been confirmed. Indeed, the latest theory is that it may not be a carnivore at all, but actually a specimen of an already known species of giant flying squirrel.

●NEWEST APE: Discovered by scientists from the German Primate Centre (DPZ) in Göttingen, Germany, the northern buff-cheeked gibbon (*Nomascus annamensis*) was formally described and named in September 2010.

Because of its size, the Vatican City—an enclave within Rome, the Italian capital—has a relatively high population density. Even so, it is still the world's ○ **least populated country**, with just 821 inhabitants in 2007.

●**HUMAN TYPE** The newest type of fossil humans to have been discovered is Denisovan Man—a type whose existence was revealed in March 2010 following the discovery in Denisova Cave, Russia, of bone fragments from a juvenile human who had lived *c.* 41,000 years ago (pictured left is a tooth). Based upon mitochondrial DNA analysis, in December 2010 scientists revealed that this individual belonged to a previously unknown member of the hominin genus *Homo*, distinct from Neanderthals, with whom it coexisted, and modern humans.

Cetacean The most recently recognized species of cetacean is the Australian snubfin dolphin (*Orcaella heinsohni*), formally reclassified as a separate species in its own right in 2005. This shy, tricolored dolphin, with a very rounded, bulbous brow and a very small, stubby dorsal fin, has been sighted regularly in the shallow waters off the Great Barrier Reef, Australia, for many years, but until DNA evidence and other studies confirmed its distinct status it had always been classified as belonging to the same species as the Irrawaddy dolphin (*O. brevirostris*).

●**NEWEST LEMUR** So new that it doesn't even have a formal zoological name yet, this species of fork-marked lemur (genus *Phaner*) is the size of a squirrel. It is distinguished behaviorally from all other lemurs by its unique head-bobbing movement.

NOW YOU SEE IT . . . Spotted by primate expert Dr. Russell Mittermeier in 1995, this Madagascan lemur was not seen again until late 2010, when it was filmed by Dr. Mittermeier's scientific team and a BBC TV crew.

●NEWEST AMPHIBIANS On November 25, 2010, the discovery of three new amphibian species was announced. Native to the rainforests of Choco in western Colombia, and still awaiting formal scientific names and descriptions, they are a species of toad with ruby-colored eyes (left), a species of rocket frog characterized by bright red flashes on its legs (right), and a small toad with a long beak that hides in dead leaves.

○NEWEST MONKEY The Caquetá titi (*Callicebus caquetensis*) was scientifically described and named in 2010. It inhabits the Colombian Amazon region near the borders with Peru and Ecuador.

Crustacean In 1979, while diving in Lucayan Cavern, a water-filled cave beneath the island of Grand Bahama, American biologist Dr. Jill Yager encountered some tiny, wormlike crustaceans. These proved to be not only a new species—dubbed *Speleonectes lucayensis*—but also one so different from all others that, in 1981, an entirely new taxonomic class of crustaceans (Remipedia) was created in order to accommodate it.

Iguana Discoveries of large, conspicuously colored lizard species are very rare. In 2009, however, it was announced that a new species of iguana, rose-pink (rosada) in color and up to 5 ft. 8.8 in. (1.75 m) long, had been found living on a single volcanic mountain called Volcan Wolf on the island of Isabela in the Galápagos chain.

Genetic tests confirmed that it was a very distinctive species, dating back over 5 million years, and which had already branched off from the other, yellowish-brown species of iguana here while the Galápagos archipelago was still forming. Interestingly, park rangers first spotted the pink iguana, which has been named *Conolophus rosada*, on Isabela in 1986, although it was initially dismissed as nothing more than a freak color variety of the familiar yellow land iguana (*C. subcristatus*).

Tree Discovered accidentally by a picnicking family in a remote, hilly, wooded area of northwestern Madagascar in 2006, but only recognized as a dramatically new species and genus following DNA analysis a year later, the Tahina palm tree (*Tahina spectabilis*) was not officially named and described until January 2008. What makes this species' belated scientific discovery so surprising is its size—standing more than 58 ft. 6 in. (18 m) tall, with fanlike leaves 16 ft. (5 m) across—and its bizarre life cycle.

It takes decades for the tree to bloom, but when it does it produces an explosion of hundreds of nectar-rich flowers that tower above its crown, each of which develops into fruit. In doing so, however, the tree's nutrients become so depleted that once it has borne fruit it rapidly collapses and dies.

●**Wild cat** The newest species of wild cat is the Bornean clouded leopard (*Neofelis diardi*). In 2006, scientists officially recognized this species as being significantly different enough from the clouded leopard (*N. nebulosa*) for it to be elevated to a species in its own right.

ENDANGERED SPECIES

RAREST . . .

●**Boxwood** A shrub once found in Jamaica, Puerto Rico, and the US Virgin Islands, Vahl's boxwood (*Buxus vahlii*) is today threatened by habitat loss and is ranked as Critically Endangered by the IUCN. Two small populations survive in Puerto Rico, though these collectively number fewer than 50 specimens.

RAREST GROUP OF MAMMALS
The order Monotremata is a primitive group of mammals that lays eggs instead of producing live young. Its five living species include the platypus (left).

Vatican City is the **smallest independent country**. The enclave, which has an area of 0.17 miles² (0.44 km²), had its sovereignty recognized by the Italian government under the terms of the Lateran Treaty on February 11, 1929.

Chameleons change color according to their moods.

●**RAREST CHAMELEON** Classed as Critically Endangered by the IUCN, Smith's dwarf chameleon (*Bradypodion taeniabronchum*) is limited to an area of occupancy estimated at 154 miles² (400 km²), near Algoa Bay in South Africa.

●**RAREST BUMBLEBEE** Native to the U.S.A., Franklin's bumblebee (*Bombus franklini*) is classed as Critically Endangered by the International Union for Conservation of Nature (IUCN). In a 1998 survey, 94 specimens were found, at eight separate sites. During 2006, however, only one was found during extensive surveys of its limited distribution range in southern Oregon and northern California. It has the most limited range of any bumblebee.

●**Galago** The Rondo dwarf galago (*Galagoides rondoensis*) is Critically Endangered and labeled as one of the world's 25 most endangered primates by the IUCN. First described as recently as 1996, it is entirely confined to eight small, discrete, highly threatened forest patches—a total area of under 38 miles² (100 km²)—in coastal Tanzania.

The **largest landlocked country**, and the ninth largest overall, is Kazakhstan, which has an area of 1,052,100 miles² (2,724,900 km²).

●RAREST BIG CAT The Critically Endangered Amur or Manchurian leopard (*Panthera pardus orientalis*) is native to the forests on the border of northeastern China and the Russian Far East. Fewer than 35 individuals are believed to exist.

●**Civet** Once a very common species, today the Malabar large-spotted civet (*Viverra civettina*) is categorized by the IUCN as Critically Endangered. It is possible that fewer than 250 of these small mammals still exist in the wild in South Malabar, southern India.

●**Egg-laying mammal** The rarest species of monotreme (see p. 66) is Attenborough's long-beaked echidna (*Zaglossus attenboroughi*). Named after veteran British TV naturalist Sir David Attenborough, it is known from just a single specimen, found dead on a mountain peak in Irian Jaya, Indonesian New Guinea, in 1961. Local hunters claim to have seen living specimens, but none has been recorded to date.

●RAREST SLOTH Confined to Isla Escudo de Veraguas, a small island off the coast of Panama, the pygmy three-toed sloth (*Bradypus pygmaeus*) was scientifically described as a new species in 2001. Critically Endangered according to the IUCN, around 300 specimens are thought to exist. They live exclusively in red mangrove trees.

SO WHAT CAN WE DO? To find out more about the world's amazing animal and plant species—and how we can help them—visit the World Wide Fund for Nature (WWF) website at wwf.org.

The **most powerful rocket**—the N-1 booster of the former USSR—was first launched from the Baikonur Cosmodrome at Tyuratam, Kazakhstan, on February 21, 1969. It exploded 70 seconds after takeoff.

OUT OF FISH? Herons love a fish dish, but probably won't come across the world's **most endangered fish**. There are between 200 and 500 Devil's Hole pupfish (*Cyprinodon diabolis*) left.

●**RAREST HERON** Native to the foothills of the eastern Himalayas, the world's rarest species of heron is the white-bellied heron (*Ardea insignis*). Critically Endangered, this large gray-and-white heron has a total population size estimated at between 50 and 249 individuals.

Only one heron is larger—the goliath heron (ardea goliath).

●**Opossum** Scientifically described in 1981, Handley's slender opossum (*Marmosops handleyi*) is categorized as Critically Endangered by the IUCN. It is known only from two specimens collected in a tiny area of rainforest in Antioquia, Colombia, at an altitude of 4,590 ft. (1,400 m).

Reptile The Abingdon Island giant tortoise (*Geochelone elephantopus abingdoni*) is represented by a single living specimen, an aged male called Lonesome George, who is the world's rarest reptile. With little hope of discovering another specimen, this particular subspecies of Galápagos giant tortoise is effectively extinct while still alive, unless cloning techniques can generate future replicas of George.

Unsurprisingly, he also has the dubious distinction of being the world's **most endangered animal**.

For a taller and more successful rocket, you need to visit the U.S.A. The *Saturn* V—the world's **largest rocket**—was 363 ft. (110.6 m) tall with the *Apollo* spacecraft on top and weighed 6,400,000 lb. (2,903 metric tons) on the launchpad.

Snake There are thought to be fewer than 150 Antiguan racers (*Alsophis antiguae*) in existence, including those in captivity. The snake was once common in Antigua, but disappeared from the island following the introduction of nonindigenous predators—first black and brown rats (*Rattus rattus* and *R. norvegicus*) and then the Asian mongoose (*Herpestes javanicus*). Despite its recovering numbers, the species remains classified as Critically Endangered on the IUCN Red List.

●**Stickleback** The world's rarest stickleback is the Greek stickleback (*Pungitius hellenicus*). Critically Endangered, it is entirely limited to three localities in the Sperchios Valley, central Greece, yielding a total area of less than 3.8 miles^2 (10 km^2).

APEX PREDATORS

●**First apex predator** *Anomalocaris*—a large, superficially crustacean-like carnivorous invertebrate—inhabited shallow seas worldwide during the early to mid-Cambrian Period, 540–500 million years ago. Up to 3 ft. 3 in. (1 m) long, it was huge in size relative to all other animals alive at that time and is believed to have preyed upon trilobites and primitive shrimp-like organisms.

●**Largest skua** Skuas constitute a family of gull-related seabirds with no natural predators. They feed upon small mammals and fish, and often steal fish from other birds. The largest species is the 23-in.-long (60-cm) brown skua (*Stercorarius antarctica*), which is broad-winged and heavy-bodied.

LARGEST FELINE CARNIVORE: The male Siberian tiger (Panthera tigris altaica) averages 10 ft. 4 in. (3.15 m) from nose to tail. An adult male weighs the same as FOUR men!

An apex predator is a creature at the top of its food chain—as an adult, it has no predators of its own. . . .

Most successful predator African hunting dogs, also called Cape hunting dogs or hyena dogs (*Lycaon pictus*), are successful in 50–70% of their hunts, consistently the highest figure in the mammalian world.

●**Largest wild dog** Hayden's bone-crushing dog (*Epicyon haydeni*) was the largest wild dog of all time. Estimated to weigh up to 225 lb. (170 kg)—nearly six times larger than the average pet labrador—it existed during the mid-to-late Miocene epoch (14–23 million years ago) in North America.

LARGEST PREDATORY FISH At the top of the ocean's food chain is the great white shark (*Carcharodon carcharias*). Adult specimens of this rare shark average 14–15 ft. (4.3–4.6 m) in length—about three arm spans if you're a typical 10-year-old child—and can weigh up to 1,700 lb. (770 kg). There are many claims of huge specimens up to 33 ft. (10 m) in length, although—not surprisingly—few have been authenticated! Its prey includes fish (even other sharks) and marine mammals such as seals and sea lions.

Prey is surprised from beneath by a torpedo-like strike at 43.5 mi./hr.

LARGEST EAGLE Commanding the skies over the coastal regions of Russia—and parts of Japan and Korea—is Steller's sea eagle (*Haliaeetus pelagicus*). This avian assassin weighs 11–20 lb. (5–9 kg) and has a wingspan of 7 ft. 2 in.–8 ft. (2.2–2.45 m). Its main prey? Salmon, cod, and trout, although it will happily snack on other birds such as geese and ducks, and even the odd seal has fallen prey to this beautiful but deadly creature.

Highest-living predator on land The range of the snow leopard (*Uncia uncia*) extends across 12 countries in the mountainous regions of central and southern Asia. This rarely seen cat has been photographed by hidden cameras at an altitude of 19,000 ft. (5,800 m).

Most dangerous shark From 1900 to 1999, great white sharks (see p. 71) caused 251 out of the 1,860 confirmed unprovoked shark attacks on humans. Of these, 66 were fatal—the highest number for any shark. In the past four years, there has been an average of four fatal shark attacks per year.

MOST EFFICIENT SCAVENGER No animal makes such a meal of its prey as the spotted (aka laughing) hyena (*Crocuta crocuta*). Its jaw muscles and teeth are strong enough to crush the bones of large vertebrates such as zebras and wildebeest, and its powerful digestive system can break down the organic matter of bones, hooves, horns, and hides. In one extreme example, a group of 38 hyenas was once seen to dismember an adult zebra in less than 15 minutes!

With an endowment of $26 billion, Harvard University in Cambridge, Massachusetts, U.S.A., is the **richest university**.

LARGEST CROCODILIAN The saltwater (estuarine) crocodile of tropical Asia and the Pacific reach up to 33 ft. (10 m) in length—the size of a stretch limo!

LONGEST SNAKE FANGS One specimen of the venomous gaboon viper of tropical Africa had fangs 2 in. (50 mm) long—about as big as your thumb!

Largest land carnivore The largest of all the carnivores is the polar bear (*Ursus maritimus*). Adult males typically weigh 880–1,320 lb. (400–600 kg)and have a nose-to-tail length of 7 ft. 10 in–8 ft. 6 in. (2.4–2.6 m).

The male Kodiak bear (*Ursus arctos middendorffi*)—a subspecies of brown bear found on Kodiak Island and the adjacent Afognak and Shuyak islands in the Gulf of Alaska, U.S.A.—is usually shorter in length than its northerly relation but more robustly built.

●**Greatest ecological damage caused by an apex predator** Since its accidental transportation shortly after World War II to the island of Guam, far from its normal South Pacific homelands, the brown tree snake (*Boiga irregularis*) has wreaked unprecedented devastation as an invasive apex predator.

Following a population explosion caused by a lack of predators, the snake has wiped out most of Guam's native vertebrate species (including birds). It has also caused thousands of residential, commercial, and military power breakdowns, and preyed extensively upon pets and livestock. It has even invaded human habitation, resulting in widespread panic.

The title of **oldest university** belongs to the University of Karueein, founded in A.D. 859 in Fez, Morocco. It is the world's longest continually operating educational institution.

ANIMAL HOMES

●**Longest chalk reef** Stretching for over 20 miles (32 km) along the coast of Norfolk, England, UK, is a chalk reef consisting of a series of enormous arches and deep chasms. Approximately 300 million years old, it is home to numerous species of fish, sea slugs, sponges, and other marine life. It was discovered by diver Rob Spray and a team of 20 volunteer conservationists in 2010.

○**Largest single cobweb** The world's largest cobwebs, measuring up to 30.13 ft.^{2} (2.8 m^2), are woven by a newly discovered species of Madagascan spider known as Darwin's bark spider (*Caerostris darwini*). It weaves them over rivers so that they stretch from one bank to the other, using a mechanism as yet undocumented. These are also the world's ●**longest cobwebs**, at 82 ft. (25 m), and the ○**strongest webs**, with a tensile strength of up to 520 MJ/m^3 (megajoules per cubic meter)—twice as strong as any previously described silk and the ●**strongest known biomaterial**.

●**Oldest cobweb** Encased in amber formed approximately 140 million years ago during the Cretaceous Period, the oldest cobweb was found on a beach at Bexhill, East Sussex, UK, by amateur fossil hunters (and brothers) Jamie and Jonathan Hiscocks. Its silk is also the **oldest spider gossamer** (the fine, filamentous substance spun by spiders).

LARGEST MAMMAL TO BUILD A NEST Every day, gorillas (*Gorilla gorilla*) create a new ground nest from the surrounding vegetation. The nests are circular and measure about 3 ft. 3 in. (1 m) in diameter. This makes the gorilla—at 5 ft. 6 in.–6 ft. (1.7–1.8 m) tall and weighing 300–500 lb. (136–227 kg)—the largest of all the mammalian nest builders.

The Great Hassan II Mosque in Casablanca, Morocco, has the **tallest minaret**, measuring 656 ft. (200 m). The mosque can accommodate 105,000 worshippers and is the fifth largest in the world.

1,000 TRILLION: Number of bacteria living on your skin and in your gut. Your body's bacteria count is more than 160,000 times the human population of the planet. Worth pondering the next time (you think) you are alone.

Termite mounds can weigh more than 110 tons.

GREATEST INSECT BUILDER Mounds built by the termites (order *Isoptera*) in eastern Australia have measured up to 20 ft. (6 m) tall and 100 ft. (30.5 m) in circumference. These complex structures contain fungus gardens (for food), garrets, basements, and nurseries, and are honeycombed with ventilation shafts to regulate temperatures in the brooding chambers and in the royal palace, where the queen termite resides. Mounds are made by soldier termites mixing their saliva with particles of sand or clay.

TOWERING ACHIEVEMENT Termites are roughly 0.4 in. (1 cm) long, so their mounds are the largest structures built relative to body size. The human equivalent would be a tower 4,600 ft. (1,400 m) tall—nearly twice the size of the current tallest building.

 The Grand Mosque in Djenne, Mali, is the **largest mud building** in the world, measuring 328 ft. (100 m) long and 131 ft. (40 m) wide. The present structure was built in 1905, based on the design of an 11th-century mosque.

EAGER BEAVERS Beaver lodges typically take 20 days to build using 6,600 lb. (3 metric tons) of materials. A family of four beavers can build 4 ft. 11 in. (1.5 m) of dam wall per day.

LARGEST STRUCTURE BUILT BY A TERRESTRIAL ANIMAL Beavers (*Castor canadensis*, inset) of North America use mud, wood, vegetation, and stones to dam water and form a still pond in which they build a lodge for winter. The largest beaver lodge ever recorded was 40 ft. (12.1 m) across and 16 ft. (4.8 m) high, and the longest beaver dam ever measured stretched 0.9 miles (1.5 km).

●**LARGEST BOWERS** The male bowerbirds of Australia and New Guinea build and decorate courtship "bowers" in order to attract females. These elaborate, hutlike structures measure up to 5.25 ft. (1.6 m) across and 3.28 ft. (1 m) in height and include a "front lawn" several square yards in area. This "lawn" is cleared of forest debris then decorated with bright, shiny objects such as fruit, flowers, beetle wingcases, and colorful pieces of litter. This satin bowerbird collects blue plastic garbage in an attempt to attract a mate!

LARGEST BIRD NESTS Bald eagles (*Haliaeetus leucocephalus*, pictured) build the largest single bird nests. A pair of bald eagles—and perhaps their successors—built a nest near St. Petersburg, Florida, U.S.A., that measured 9 ft. 6 in. (2.9 m) wide and 20 ft. (6 m) deep. It was examined in 1963 and estimated to weigh 4,409 lb. (2 metric tons).

Largest burrowing mammal The wombat (*Vombatus ursinus*) of Australia and Tasmania is a squat, bearlike creature that can measure up to 4 ft. (1.2 m) and weigh up to 77 lb. (35 kg). Their backward-opening pouch, large paws, and strong claws assist them in digging burrows that can be up to 65 ft. (20 m) long and 6 ft. (2 m) below ground, with interconnecting tunnels.

Largest badger set The European badger (*Meles meles*) spends more than half of its life underground, and builds the largest sets of any badger species. The largest set on record was estimated to contain a tunnel network measuring 2,883 ft. (879 m) long, with 50 underground chambers and 178 entrances.

Deepest bat colony A colony of approximately 1,000 little brown bats (*Myotis lucifugus*)—the most abundant bat in North America—spends each winter in a zinc mine in New York at a depth of 3,805 ft. (1,160 m)—almost six times deeper than this species' normal roosting depth.

Largest arboreal mammal The largest tree-dwelling mammal is the orangutan, which lives in the canopy of tropical rainforests in Borneo and Sumatra. Bornean orangutan (*Pongo pygmaeus*) and Sumatran orangutan (*P. abelii*) males typically weigh 183 lb. (83 kg) and measure 5 ft. (1.5 m) tall. They have opposable toes on their feet and use their arm span of approximately 6 ft. (2 m) to swing between branches and feed off fruit, small leaves, and tree bark. Being lighter (81 lb.; 37 kg), females usually build nests in the trees, whereas the adult males sleep on the ground.

Largest communal bird nests The sociable weaver (*Philetairus socius*) of southwestern Africa builds a nest up to 26 ft. (8 m) long and 6 ft. 6 in. (2 m) high. Resembling a giant haystack that hangs from a tree or utility pole, it contains up to 300 individual nests. Not surprisingly, these nests can get so heavy that the tree on which they are built collapses under the weight!

●Most housebound animal The wild animal that spends the longest time in an inactive state inside its home is the eastern chipmunk (*Tamias striatus*) of North America. When food is scarce, it will retreat inside its burrow and live off its stores of nuts for up to one year at a time.

Largest wasp nest A wasp nest found on a farm at Waimaukau, New Zealand, in April 1963 measured 12 ft. 2 in. (3.7 m) long and 5.25 ft. (1.75 m) in diameter, and was approximately 18 ft. (5.5 m) in circumference. It was so heavy that it had fallen from the tree in which it had been hanging and had then split into two. It had probably been constructed by introduced German wasps (*Vespula germanica*).

MIGRATIONS & MOVEMENTS

Longest terrestrial animal migration Grant's caribou (*Rangifer tarandus*), which lives in Alaska and also Canada's Yukon Territory, migrates up to 2,982 miles (4,800 km) per year to more sheltered wintering grounds. That's more than 620 miles (1,000 km) greater than the distance from New York to Los Angeles!

MUNCHING EN MASSE Each night, billions of tiny zooplankton make a return from the depths of the sea to the surface to feed on microscopic phytoplankton in the **●largest animal migration in terms of numbers**.

2,342: Days of your life you will spend on vacation. However, 1,186 of those will be school vacations, so by the time you leave school you'll already have had more than half your lifetime of days off.

LONGEST INSECT MIGRATION
A tagged male monarch butterfly (*Danaus plexippus*), set free at Presqu'ile Provincial Park near Brighton, Ontario, Canada, on September 10, 1988, was recaptured in Austin, Texas, U.S.A., on April 8, 1989. Assuming that it overwintered in Mexico, the insect traveled at least 2,880 miles (4,635 km) and possibly double this distance.

●LARGEST MIGRANT Up to 88 ft. (27 m) long and weighing 352,000 lb. (160 metric tons), the blue whale (*Balaenoptera musculus*) is the largest animal (by weight) and the largest to migrate, traveling thousands of kilometers from its Arctic or Antarctic feeding grounds to the warmer winter breeding grounds in the tropics. The calves—born with just a thin layer of blubber—need warm waters to survive.

BIG BOVINE The ●largest migrant on land—and the **largest land animal in North America and Europe**—is the bison (genus Bison). It weighs nearly 2,200 lb. (1 metric ton), and is as much as 6 ft. 5 in. (2 m) tall at the shoulder.

WHY FLY? Groups of mountain quail (*Oreortyx pictus*), native to western North America, often walk up to 5,000 ft. (1,500 m) in winter to reach lower, warmer altitudes in the ●**longest bird migration on foot**.

●**GREATEST LAND MIGRATION** The last great land migration on Earth sees between 1 and 2 million wildebeest (*Connochaetus taurinus*) traveling a circuit between the Serengeti of Tanzania to Kenya and across the Mara River. Millions of other animals, such as zebras, impalas, and gazelles—plus their predators—join the wildebeest on their annual round trip in search of water.

Largest herd of mammals In the 19th century, vast herds of springbok (*Antidorcas marsupialis*) migrated across the plains of western parts of southern Africa. In 1849, John Fraser, the son of a local minister, observed a mass migration that took three days to pass through the town of Beaufort West, South Africa.

Every 60 years or so, the Dogon peoples of Mali celebrate the Sigui, a festival marking the handover of secrets to the next generation. The last Sigui ran from 1967 to 1973. Unsurprisingly, it is the **longest religious ceremony**.

●**LONGEST AMPHIBIAN MIGRATION**
Most amphibians do not migrate very far
due to their reliance on water, but two
species of European water frog—the pool
frog (*Rana lessonae*) and the green frog
(*R. esculenta*)—have been known to cover
distances of up to 9 miles (15 km).

●**Longest reptile migration** The leatherback sea turtle (*Dermochelys coriacea*), the world's **largest living turtle,** also holds the record for the longest migration by any reptile. Between 2006 and early 2008, a leatherback was tracked by satellite on a 12,774-mile (20,558-km) journey from its nesting site on the beaches of Papua, Indonesia, to feeding grounds off the coast of Oregon, U.S.A. The journey, to the other side of the planet, took 647 days.

●**Largest gathering of mammals**
Each October, between 5 and 10 million straw-colored fruit bats (*Eidolon helvum*) converge from all over Africa on Kasanka in Zambia for a six-week binge on ripened mangoes.

Shortest bird migration During the winter, North America's blue grouse (*Dendragapus obscurus*) inhabits mountainous pine forests. When nesting time commences in spring, it descends just 984 ft. (300 m) to deciduous woodlands in order to feed upon the early crop of seeds and fresh leaves.

LONGEST BIRD MIGRATION The Arctic tern (*Sterna paradisaea*) breeds north of the Arctic Circle, then flies south to the Antarctic for the northern winter and back again. This represents a round trip of approximately 50,000 miles (80,467 km).

Arctic terns spend most of their lives in the air.

Speaking of big parties, the annual carnival in Rio de Janeiro, Brazil, normally held during the first week of March, is the **largest carnival** in the world. It attracts approximately 2 million people each day.

●**HIGHEST MIGRANT** The bar-headed goose (*Anser indicus*) migrates over the Himalayas to overwinter in India, Pakistan, and Burma, a journey of around 1,000 miles (1,600 km). Its migration sees it regularly reach altitudes of 29,000 ft. (9,000 m), although it has been reported at 33,382 ft. (10,175 m).

●**First human-led bird migration** In 1993, two "artists turned naturalists," William Lishman and Joseph Duff (both U.S.A.), used two ultralight aircraft to guide 18 Canada geese 400 miles (644 km) from Ontario, Canada, to Virginia, U.S.A. The flight confirmed that the birds could be "taught" to follow safe migratory routes.

Longest mammal migration The humpback whale (*Megaptera novaeangliae*) swims up to 5,100 miles (8,200 km) back and forth between its warm breeding waters near the Equator and the colder, food-rich waters of the Arctic and Antarctic regions.

On September 21, 2001, a female humpback seen off the coast of Brazil in August 1999 was photographed 6,089 miles (9,800 km) away near the island of Madagascar. The whale, known as Antarctic Humpback Whale Catalogue No. 1363, had covered nearly a quarter of the globe in the ●**longest documented single journey ever undertaken by a mammal.**

●**Smallest migrant** Copepods (subphylum Crustacea) are planktonic organisms measuring 0.04–0.08 in. (1–2 mm) long on average and are the principal diet of many of the oceans' inhabitants, including whales. They live mainly at the bottom of the ocean to avoid predators, but make a nightly ascent to the surface to feed.

In 2005, Brazil had an estimated total forest cover of 1,844,400 miles² (477,698,000 ha), representing 57.2% of the state's total area, and making it the world's **most forested country**.

MICROSCOPIC LIFE

●**Smallest living organism** The smallest entity universally recognized as a living organism (not all scientists consider the slightly smaller nanobes to be alive) is *Nanoarchaeum equitans*. This minuscule microbe was discovered only in 2002, in a hydrothermal vent on the seafloor off the coast of Iceland, and its cells are only 400 nanometers across. (One nanometer is a billionth of a meter.)

●**EARLIEST FOSSIL CILIATE PROTOZOANS** Characterized by tiny hairlike structures (cilia) on their external surface, ciliate protozoans are microscopic single-celled organisms. Fossils of the species were formally documented in 2007. They were discovered within the Doushantuo Formation, a fossil-rich sedimentary deposit in China's Guizhou Province. Scientists have dated them to the Ediacaran Period, around 580 million years ago.

MOST DANGEROUS ANT The bulldog ant (*Myrmecia pyriformis*)—so called because of its ferocity and determination—is found in coastal regions of Australia. When attacking, the ant holds on to victims with its long mandibles while injecting deadly venom. Bulldog ants have caused at least three human fatalities since 1936, the latest a farmer in 1988.

This ant's sting can kill a person in just 15 minutes.

The **longest avenue of trees** is the 22-mile (35.41-km) Nikko Cryptomeria Avenue in Imaichi City, Tochigi Prefecture, Japan. Planted in 1628–48, more than 13,500 of its original 200,000 Japanese cedar (*Cryptomeria japonica*) trees survive.

24: Ounces of insect parts that make it into your meals every year. It's impossible to stop insects getting into food somewhere along the line. During a lifetime, you'll swallow 117 lb. of them.

LONGEST PARASITIC FASTS The soft tick (*Ornithodoros turicata*), which spreads the spirochaete bacteria that cause relapsing fever, can survive for five years without food. The common bedbug (*Cimex lectularius*, above), which feeds upon human blood, is able to survive without feeding for more than a year.

●**HARDIEST ANIMALS IN OUTER SPACE** In 2007, scientists sent two species of tardigrade (microscopic eight-limbed creatures) into orbit, where they were exposed both to the vacuum of space and to sufficient radiation to incinerate a human. When they were brought back, a third of the total number were still alive, making them the only animals native to Earth that are known to have survived extraterrestrial conditions unassisted.

Tardigrades are also known as "water bears."

●LARGEST TARDIGRADE
Echiniscoides sigismundi, a marine Eurasian species of tardigrade, can reach 0.05 in. (1.5 mm) long as a mature adult. Most other tardigrade species remain microscopic throughout their lives.

Smallest cell The brain cells in the cerebellum measure about 0.0001968 in. (0.005 mm), or 5 microns.

Smallest parasite *Pneumocystis jirovecii*, which causes pneumonia in humans, inhabits the lungs. It is 0.01–0.02 in. (0.5–1 mm) long.

●Smallest organism capable of independent reproduction *Mycoplasma genitalium*, a parasitic species of ultramicrobacterium that lives in the respiratory and genital tracts of primates, is the smallest creature that can reproduce independently and grow. It is approximately 200–300 nanometers in size.

LARGEST FAMILY OF SPIDERS
The largest zoological family of spiders is Salticidae, which includes jumping spiders. More than 4,400 species are known to science, and most live in the tropics. Jumping spiders hardly ever spin webs, catching their prey not by entrapment but by actively leaping at them.

If you like things on a small scale, take a close look at the atomic world on p.305.

MOST INSECTICIDE-RESISTANT INSECT The green peach aphid (*Myzus persicae*) has been documented as resistant to 71 different chemical pesticides. The aphids are approximately 0.09 in. (2.3 mm) long when fully grown and vary in color from green to pale yellow or pink.

Largest microbe In terms of volume, the largest known protozoans are the extinct calcareous foraminifera (Foraminiferida) of the genus *Nummulites*. Samples 6 in. (150 mm) wide were found in Middle Eocene Epoch rocks in Turkey. The Eocene Epoch was *c*. 55 million to 38 million years ago.

●**SMALLEST NEMATODES** The world's smallest nematodes, or round worms, have no common names and live in marine sediments. They are only 80 micrometers long (one micrometer is a millionth of a meter)—roughly the same as the width of an average human hair. Nematodes are the most abundant multi-celled creatures on Earth.

Most deadly bug The bacterium *Yersinia pestis* caused the death of around 25 million people in mid-14th-century Europe. Named after French scientist Alexandre Yersin, who identified it in 1894, it causes bubonic plague, which is transmitted by fleas and rats.

Oldest living bacteria In October 2000, U.S. scientists disclosed that they had revived and cultured bacteria that had been trapped in suspended animation inside salt crystals for 250 million years. Named Bacillus 2-9-3, it is 10 times older than the previous oldest revived bacteria.

Most radiation-resistant life form The red-colored bacterium *Deinococcus radiodurans* can resist 1.5 million rads of gamma radiation—about 3,000 times the amount that would kill a human.

AMAZING MENAGERIE

●**Largest population of white tigers** Nandankanan Zoo, in the state of Orissa, India, is home to more than 34 white tigers. This zoo has bred many white tigers over the years, and has sent them to other zoos all over the world.

●**RAREST GORILLA** Little Snowflake was a unique male albino western lowland gorilla (*Gorilla gorilla gorilla*) who lived at Barcelona Zoo from 1966 until his death from age-related ill health on November 24, 2003. Unlike full albinos, Little Snowflake had blue eyes, suggesting that he was a chinchilla albino, caused by a recessive mutant gene form named chinchilla (also responsible for white tigers).

WHY WHITE? Albinism affects all vertebrates, humans included. It is caused by the lack of a particular enzyme that is required to produce melanin—a pigment that provides color for eyes, hair, and skin.

●LARGEST WATER WALKER The South American basilisk lizard
(*Basiliscus basiliscus*) can run bipedally at a velocity of 5 ft./s (1.5 m/s) for
approximately 14 ft. 9 in. (4.5 m) before sinking. It can also "walk on water"
on all fours, which extends the distance that it can travel on the surface by
about 4 ft. 3 in. (1.3 m). Various small insects are also able to move across
the surface of water in ponds and lakes without sinking. A long tail helps the
lizard maintain its balance while skimming over water on two legs. Strong
legs propel the lizard across water at high speed. Flaps between the lizard's
toes increase the surface area of its feet and help trap pockets of air.

●MOST TENTACLED
OCTOPUS In
December 1998,
an extraordinary
specimen of common
octopus (*Octopus
vulgaris*) was
captured alive in
Matoya Bay, Japan.
Each of its eight
normal tentacles
had branched to
produce a profusion
of additional ones,
yielding an amazing
96 tentacles.

Population figures for 2009 reveal that in Japan, the median age—
that is, the age at which there are an equal number of people
above and below—is a record high of 44.7, giving Japan the
world's ○ **oldest population**.

13,807: Hen eggs you will consume in a lifetime. That's enough eggs to make an omelette with a 164-ft. diameter—the same distance as the length of an Olympic-sized swimming pool.

FASTEST MAMMALIAN EATER: Dr. Kenneth Catania (U.S.A.) has recorded the average food "handling time" of the star-nosed mole (*Condylura cristata*) at 230 milliseconds.

●**LARGEST HORN ON A BIRD** Also known as the unicorn bird, the South American horned screamer (Anhima cornuta) has a curved horn measuring up to 6 in. (15 cm) in length.

From high age to lofty heights: the Dutch are the world's **tallest citizens**, with the average Dutch male measuring 6 ft. (184 cm) tall.

●LAZIEST FRESHWATER TURTLE Native to the Mekong River in Cambodia, Cantor's giant soft-shelled turtle (*Pelochelys cantorii*) spends 95% of its life motionless in sand on the river bottom waiting for prey to approach. It comes up to the water surface to breathe air only twice each day.

●FURRIEST CRUSTACEAN The yeti lobster (*Kiwa hirsuta*) lives on hydrothermal vents on the seafloor in the South Pacific Ocean. Its long claws and shorter thoracic limbs are covered in long, silky, blond-colored filaments called setae. These very distinctive hairlike structures bear bacteria intertwined among them.

●**Largest collection of two-headed animals** Todd Ray (U.S.A.) owns the world's most impressive collection of two-headed, or dicephalic, animals. He has spent over $157,824 on acquisitions and now owns 22 different specimens. These include a two-headed albino hog-nosed snake, a two-headed goat, a two-headed terrapin, a two-headed king snake, a two-headed bearded dragon (a species of lizard) named Pancho and Lefty, plus the world's only living three-headed creature: a turtle named Myrtle, Squirtle, and Thirdle.

●**Oldest living species** Tadpole shrimps (*Triops cancriformis*) are thought to be the oldest pedigree of any living creature. Fossil evidence suggests that they have hardly changed in the 200 million years they have existed.

○**Shortest cow** Diana, a seven-year-old Vechur cow who was born and bred at the Vechur Conservation Centre, Kerala, India, measured 30 in. (77 cm) from the hoof to the withers (between the shoulder blades) on November 9, 2010.

●**Largest eardrum** The eardrum of the gorilla (*Gorilla gorilla*) measures about 0.15 in^2 (97 mm^2); our eardrums, by comparison, are just 0.096 in.^{2} (62 mm^2).

Fish with most eyes The six-eyed spookfish (*Bathylychnops exilis*) lives at depths of 300–3,000 ft. (91–910 m) in the northeastern Pacific. A slender 17-in.-long (45-cm) pikelike species, it has a pair of large principal eyes, but also a second, smaller pair, known as secondary globes, within the lower half of its principal eyes and pointing down. Each globe possesses its own lens and retina, and may help to increase the spookfish's sensitivity to light in its shadowy surroundings.

Behind the secondary globes is a third pair of eyes. These lack retinas, but divert incoming light into the fish's large principal eyes.

●**Camel with most humps** The Bactrian camel (*Camelus bactrianus*) normally has two humps, while the Arabian camel or dromedary (*C. dromedarius*) normally has just one. During the early 1970s, however, German zoologist Dr Bernhard Grzimek documented an apparently unique, freak dromedary that possessed no fewer than four distinct, fully formed humps.

●**Longest-surviving Janus cat** Caused by a protein called sonic hedgehog homolog (SHH), diprosopia is an extremely rare congenital condition in which part or all of an individual's face is duplicated on its head. This condition has been recorded in the domestic cat (*Felis catus*) and some of the resulting two-faced kittens have survived into adulthood. Mindful of Janus, the two-faced Roman god of gates and doorways, British zoologist Dr. Karl Shuker has dubbed these animals Janus cats. The longest-surviving Janus cat is Frank and Louie, from Millbury, Ohio, U.S.A., which had reached six years of age by July 2006.

Largest cat hybrid The liger (no scientific name) is the offspring of a male lion and a tigress. Ligers typically grow larger than either parent, reaching lengths of 10–12 ft. (3–3.6 m). Although these hybrids could occur in the wild, such crossbreeding usually happens in zoos or private menageries.

●**LARGEST CAPTIVE CROCODILE** The Australian saltwater crocodile (*Crocodylus porosus*) is the largest present-day species of crocodile. Cassius, seen here, is the largest specimen in captivity, at 18 ft. (5.5 m) in length, and the largest crocodile ever caught in Australia. He is currently housed in Marineland Melanesia wildlife zoo on Green Island, Australia.

PECULIAR PLANTS

●**First bioluminescent flower** In December 1999, Professor Chia Tet Fatt from Singapore's National Institute of Education produced the world's first successful bioluminescent flowers, using a white-petaled Dendrobium White Fairy #5 orchid. He transferred biologically active DNA containing the luciferase gene from fireflies into the orchid tissues and then propagated them, yielding orchids that retain the firefly gene. These orchids emit a constant greenish-white light from their petals, roots, stem, and leaves for up to five hours at a time.

Fastest-growing plant Certain species of the 45 genera of bamboo have been found to grow at a rate of up to 35 in. (91 cm) a day, or 0.00002 mi./hr. (0.00003 km/h). The ●**tallest bamboo**—the giant bamboo (*Dendrocalamus giganteus*) of tropical southeast Asia—can reach as high as 164 ft. (50 m).

○**Largest inflorescence** The puya (*Puya raimondii*) is a rare species of giant bromeliad that lives high in the Bolivian mountains. When it blooms, the panicle (vertical stalk) it produces can grow to 35 ft. (10.7 m) in height, with a diameter of up to 8 ft. (2.4 m), and bears around 8,000 small white flowers. This enormous inflorescence (flowering) is strong enough to support a human.

○**Tallest bloom** Louis Ricciardiellò (U.S.A.) grew a Titan arum (*Amorphophallus titanum*) that measured 10 ft. 2.25 in. (3.1 m) tall on June 18, 2010. It was displayed at Winnipesaukee Orchids in Gilford, New Hampshire, U.S.A.

●**LARGEST ALBINO PLANTS** There are between 25 and 60 albino coast redwood trees (*Sequoia sempervirens*) in California, U.S.A., some up to 69 ft. (21 m) tall. Lacking chlorophyll, they are a pale white color and are known as "everwhites."

● MOST DANGEROUS TREE The manchineel (*Hippomane mancinella*) of
the Florida Everglades and the Caribbean coast exudes a sap that can blister
human skin and, if it touches the eyes, can make a person blind. One bite of
its small, apple-like fruit causes blistering and severe pain and can be fatal.
If a manchineel is burned, the resulting smoke can cause blindness if it gets
into the eyes.

● LONGEST CONIFER CONES The longest cones of any species of conifer
belong to the sugar pine (*Pinus lambertiana*, see above), native to the
western U.S.A. and to Baja California in northwestern Mexico. They range in
size from 10 to 26 in. (25–66 cm) and have a diameter of 4–5 in. (10–13 cm).

●DESERT PLANT WITH THE LONGEST LEAVES The wonder plant (*Welwitschia mirabilis*) of the Namib Desert in Namibia and Angola produces only two leaves, but each grows 6 ft. 6 in.–13 ft. 1 in. (2–4 m) long. The leaves eventually split, or at least become shredded at their tips, owing to the arid desert winds and harsh living conditions.

The Netherlands has a total area of around 16,033 miles² (41,526 km²), around 27% of which actually lies below sea level, making it the world's **lowest country**.

158,000: Number of new plant species that will be discovered during your lifetime. That works out at 2,000 new plants per year, or more than five every day.

○**Most leaves on a clover** Shigeo Obara of Hanamaki City, Iwate, Japan, found a 56-leaf white clover (*Trifolium repens L.*) on May 10, 2009.

●**Smallest species of water lily** *Nymphaea thermarum*, also known as the thermal lily, has pads that measure 0.3–0.6 in. (10–20 mm) across.

The world's **largest water lily** is *Victoria amazonica*: its gigantic floating leaves measure up to 10 ft. (3 m) across, and are held in place by an underwater stalk 23–26 ft. (7–8 m) long.

●**FASTEST-GROWING TREE** The empress or foxglove tree (*Paulownia tomentosa*) can grow as much as 12 in. (30 cm) over three weeks, and 19 ft. 8 in. (6 m) during its first year. It is native to central and west China, but is naturalized now in the U.S.A.

Rising above the Netherlands, but only just, comes the Maldives, with a maximum elevation above sea level of 8 ft. (2.4 m). As the world's **flattest country**, the Maldives is now under threat from rising sea levels and coastal erosion.

●MOST ENDANGERED LOBELIA
Only eight plants of the species
Lobelia monostachya are known
to exist. They are confined to
the southern leeward Koolau
Mountains of Oahu, Hawaii.

●**Oldest-known human-planted tree** A 2,300-year-old sacred fig or bo-tree (*Ficus religiosa*) given the name Sri Maha Bodhiya stands in Anuradhapura, Sri Lanka. It was planted in 288 B.C. The mother tree from which this specimen was propagated was the famous Bodhi tree, under which the Lord Buddha, Siddhartha Gautama, was sitting for three days and three nights when he gained enlightenment.

Largest living tree In the Sequoia National Park in California, U.S.A., there is a giant sequoia (*Sequoiadendron giganteum*) known as General Sherman. An estimated 2,100 years old, it stands 271 ft. (82.6 m) tall and has a circumference of approximately 85 ft. (26 m). The trunk had a volume of 52,508 ft.^{3} (1,487 m^3) in 1980, when it was last measured accurately, but by 2004 it was thought to be almost 54,000 ft.^{3} (1,530 m^3)—that's enough wood to provide timber for building as many as 35 five-room houses.

TIME TALES

CONTENTS

BRIEF HISTORY OF TIME

IS THE END NIGH? The Maya used three interlocking calendars that created "Great Cycles" of time. The present cycle is due to end on December 23, 2012, at which time the Maya would expect not the end of the world but a spiritual "rebirth."

● **OLDEST PRE-COLUMBIAN CALENDAR STILL IN USE** Sacred round Mesoamerican calendars—that is, those devised by the pre-Columbian cultures of present-day Mexico and Central America—continue to be used in one form or another to the present day, having passed from the Olmecs (1500–400 B.C.) to the Maya (up to A.D. 900) and then to the Aztecs (up to the 1500s; pictured is an Aztec calendar at the Mexico Museum of Anthropology in Mexico City).

The ● **oldest calendar still in use** is the Jewish calendar, which has been in popular use since the 9th century B.C. It is based on biblical calculations that place the creation at 3761 B.C.

TIME ON YOUR HANDS Wristwatches were a natural progression from pocket watches, but men initially refused to wear them, preferring the more traditional timepiece. The ● **first wristwatch** was made for a woman, Countess Koscowicz of Hungary, by Patek Philippe (Switzerland) in 1868.

Turn to p. 137 for more old timers . . .

KEEPING TRACK OF TIME

Time is the measure by which we live our lives, and over the last 5,000 years we have developed ever more accurate ways of keeping track of it. Starting at 1 o'clock, work your way round the clock face to discover how we have harnessed the power of sunlight, water, fire, gravity, electricity, and even atoms, all just to tell the time. . . .

1. TIME STICK First used in Mesopotamia in *c.* 3500 B.C., the time (or shadow) stick was the ●**earliest form of clock**. Planted in the earth, it told the time by casting a shadow on the ground that changed length and position as the Sun "moved" overhead. Later, more sophisticated versions such as this 19th-century Tibetan example were created with multiple sides featuring timescales for different months.

2. OBELISK Around 2500–2000 B.C., the Egyptians developed the obelisk, a tall, four-sided pillar made from a single piece of stone. A monumental form of sundial, it worked in a similar way to the shadow stick, measuring time according to the relative position of the Sun overhead and the shadows it cast.

The country may be flat but the divorce rate in the Maldives is anything but—this beautiful island nation has the **highest divorce rate** in the world, with 10.97 divorces per 1,000 inhabitants per year.

3. WATER CLOCK As sundials depended on light, the Egyptians created water clocks in the 15th century B.C. to tell the time in all conditions, 24 hours a day. Essentially the ●**first all-weather clock**, the device, called a *clepsydra* ("water thief"), was a large pot that leaked water through a hole in the bottom at a steady, measurable rate.

4. SUNDIAL Sundials such as the one shown left were first developed in *c*. 300 B.C. A vertical pointer—called a *gnomon* (Greek for "one who knows")—cast a shadow on to a dial marked with the hours of the day. Special devices called "merkhets" could be placed over the sundial at night to measure the time by the stars.

5. CANDLE CLOCK Invented in *c*. A.D. 800, the candle clock was the ●**first practical indoor clock**. Markers on the stem indicated the passing of time as the candle burned down. In the late 9th century, King Alfred the Great of England created an intricate 24-hour clock made from six large candles, each of which was designed to burn for four hours.

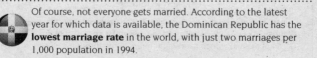

Of course, not everyone gets married. According to the latest year for which data is available, the Dominican Republic has the **lowest marriage rate** in the world, with just two marriages per 1,000 population in 1994.

78: Orbits you will make of the Sun in your lifetime—one for every year of your life. In celebration, you will receive a total of 1,450 birthday cards—18 per orbit.

●FIRST MECHANICAL CLOCK

The earliest mechanical clock—that is, one that features an escapement—was built in China in A.D. 725 by Yi Xing and Liang Lingzan (China).

6. WATER WHEEL CLOCK In _c._ 1088, the astronomer Su Sung (China) built a vast water clock for the Emperor, powered by an 11-ft. (3.3-m) water wheel (model, left). The complex device featured one of the earliest escapements—the mechanism by which continuous motion is converted into the uniform "tick-tick" of a mechanical clock.

OLDEST SURVIVING CLOCK

The faceless mechanical clock at Salisbury Cathedral, Wiltshire, UK, was built in around 1386. It was restored in 1956, having struck the hours for 498 years and ticked more than 500 million times.

7. HOURGLASS The ●first hourglass, or sand clock, measured time by the descent of sand from one glass bulb to another. It may have been invented by a French monk named Liutprand in the 8th century. However, concrete evidence of the device first appeared in European ship inventories from the 14th century. Arriving just in time for the "Age of Discovery," the hourglass was ideal for ocean travel because the bobbing waves didn't affect its accuracy.

LARGEST HOURGLASS

In 2000, Bob Ciscell (U.S.A.) built the world's largest hourglass. Standing 42 in. (1.06 m) tall and 15 in. (38 cm) across, it contains 65 lb. (29.4 kg) of sand, which takes eight hours to run through.

8. PENDULUM CLOCK The Italian scientist Galileo Galilei (1564–1642) was among the first to observe that the steady, predictable rate of a pendulum's swing made it ideal for use in timekeeping. Soon afterward, in 1656, the Dutch horologist Christiaan Huygens (1629–95) built the ●**first operational pendulum clock**, which was accurate to within a minute per day and represented a huge leap forward in timekeeping. Toward the end of the century, this margin of error had been reduced to just 0.5 seconds—accurate enough to warrant the introduction in the late 1690s of the first-ever second hand.

9. HARRISON'S H4 SEA CLOCK John Harrison (UK, 1693–1776) built the **first marine clock**, the H4, in response to a UK Government challenge to create a timekeeping device capable of calculating a ship's longitude to within 0.5° (two minutes of time). No bigger than a large pocket watch, the H4 was 5.11 in. (13 cm) across and weighed 3 lb. 3 oz. (1.45 kg). On its first trial, sailing to Jamaica on HMS *Deptford* from November 18, 1761, to January 9, 1762, the clock was found to be just 5.1 seconds slow, thus solving the "longitude problem" and revolutionizing long-distance navigation at sea.

10. ELECTRIC CLOCK The ●**first electric clock** was designed by the Scottish inventor Alexander Bain (1811–77) and patented in 1841. Although Bain employed a pendulum to measure time, he took the revolutionary step of powering it with an electric current rather than the traditional method of springs or weights. The clock pictured was a refinement of Bain's design, built by Frenchmen Marcel Moulin (1881–1914) and Maurice Favre-Bulle (1870–1954), who claimed it could run for 800 days on one battery.

11. QUARTZ CLOCK In *c.* 1880, scientists discovered that when an electric current passes through quartz crystals, it made the crystals vibrate with a regularity that was ideal for timekeeping. The first quartz clocks arrived in the 1920s, but were so large that they were confined to laboratories. By the late 1960s, technological refinements led to smaller, domestic models such as the popular Astro-Chron (above) as well as the first ever analog quartz wristwatches.

12. ATOMIC CLOCK Today, we live on atomic time, which is measured through the vibration of atoms to produce an unprecedented level of accuracy—1 second in millions of years. Although atomic clocks have existed since the 1930s, Louis Essen's (1908–97) Caesium I clock, built in 1955, was the first to keep time more precisely than pendulum and electric clocks. Since the 1980s invention of radio-controlled clocks such as the Space Timer (left), which synchronize with atomic clocks over the airwaves, we no longer have any excuse to be late.

MAPS

●**Oldest surviving map** In the 1920s, archeological excavations at Nuzi in northern Iraq turned up a series of clay tablets dating to 2300 B.C. that depict the Euphrates river and nearby hills, streams, and settlements. These ancient clay "maps" represent the earliest direct evidence of cartography.

First silk maps In 1973–74, archaeologists exploring a 2nd-century-B.C. tomb in Hunan, China, found a series of detailed silk maps depicting the topography of Hunan Province all the way down to the South China Sea.

Joaquín Balaguer (1907–2002) was president of the Dominican Republic three times, from 1960 to 1962, 1966 to 1978, and 1986 to 1996, by which time he was the world's **oldest president** at the age of 89.

●Oldest surviving map with distance measurements A brass map dating to the 4th century B.C. was discovered in Hebei, China, in the 1970s. Engraved with the words *Zhao Yu Tu* ("Map of the Mausoleum"), it maps the five mausoleums of Emperor Wang Cuo and is marked with numerals indicating distances.

●First road map Prolific road-builders, the Romans were also the first to map them, creating a huge circular map of the Empire's network engraved in stone near the Forum in Rome, Italy. Marcus Agrippa (63–12 B.C.), the son of Emperor Augustus Caesar, was the man charged with driving this mammoth project. In the course of 20 years, he oversaw the charting of the Empire's *cursus publicus* ("roads") for thousands of miles across Europe and as far afield as the Middle East. The finished map, known as the "Itinerarium," was used primarily to help administer the vast Empire, but it also stood as a symbol of Roman power.

●Most expensive map On December 3, 2010, a map of the U.S.A., the first to be printed in that country, sold at auction at Christie's, New York, U.S.A., for $2,098,500 including commissions. Created in 1784, the map came from the collection of the New Jersey Historical Society and is one of only seven such prints known to exist. It is also the first map printed in the U.S.A. to show the national flag and the first map to be copyrighted in the U.S.A.

●FIRST MAP OF THE NEW WORLD The first cartographer to compile a map of the New World was Martin Waldseemüller (Germany). His map, created in 1507, showed for the first time the new lands explored by Christopher Columbus and Amerigo Vespucci, while it also marked the first use of the name "America," which Waldseemüller coined in honor of Vespucci.

●FIRST GEOLOGICAL COUNTRY MAP William Smith's (UK) 1801 *Delineation of the Strata of England and Wales with part of Scotland* was the first countrywide map to illustrate the different rock layers found across the land. The "Father of English Geology," Smith had earlier created the **●first geological map**, of the area around Bath, UK, in 1799.

When it comes to staying power, few can compare to Fidel Castro (Cuba, b. August 13, 1927), who led Cuba from July 26, 1959, until his retirement on February 19, 2008—in total, 48 years 208 days— making him the world's **longest-serving nonroyal head of state**.

●OLDEST SURVIVING TERRESTRIAL GLOBE In 1491–92, Martin Behaim—a German cosmographer and explorer working for the Portuguese court—created the *Erdapfel* ("Earth Apple"), a metal sphere on which a world map was painted by Georg Glockendon (Germany). The map does not include the Americas as their discoverer, Christopher Columbus, did not return from his famous journey until 1493.

Largest map collection The Geography and Map Division of the U.S. Library of Congress, Washington, DC, U.S.A., has custody of the largest and most comprehensive cartographic collection in the world. In total, it holds over 4.5 million maps, including 60,000 atlases, 6,000 reference works, numerous globes and plastic relief models, and a large variety of cartographic material in other formats, including digital.

Largest atlas The huge Klencke atlas measures 5 ft. 10 in. (1.78 m) high, 3 ft. 5 in. (1.05 m) wide, and 4 in. (11 cm) thick. Presented to Charles II, King of England, by a Dutch merchant in around 1660, it contains 39 pages with 41 maps all dating from the first half of the 17th century.

●FIRST PUBLISHED WORLD ATLAS Created by the Flemish cartographer Abraham Ortelius, the *Theatrum Orbis Terrarum* ("Theater of the World") was published in 1570 by the notable Antwerp printer Gilles Coppens van Diest. The original was in Latin and featured 70 maps on 53 pages, but between 1570 and 1612, numerous updated editions followed, including versions in German, Dutch, French, Spanish, English, and Italian.

●MOST EXPENSIVE ATLAS A version of Ptolemy's *Cosmographia* dating from 1477 went under the hammer for a record £2,136,000 ($3,990,010) at Sotheby's auction rooms in London, UK, on October 10, 2006.

The **smallest bird** is the bee hummingbird (*Mellisuga helenae*) of Cuba's Isle of Youth. The male weighs 0.056 oz. (1.6 g) and measures 2.24 in. (57 mm) in length, half of which is taken up by the bill and tail.

113: Gallons of ice-cream you'll eat in a lifetime. If you were seized by an urge to turn this into handy tools for the study of geography, such an amount would produce 92 globes the size of soccer balls!

● **MOST POPULAR SAT-NAV VOICE** According to TomTom, the market-leading manufacturer of automobile satellite navigation systems, Homer Simpson, voiced by U.S. actor Dan Castellaneta, has been downloaded a record 128,500 times since 2009.

Largest online map Google Earth, owned by search engine Google, is a virtual 3D globe of the entire planet comprised of satellite data that can be browsed by home internet users.

Smallest map In 1992, Dr. H. Jonathon Mamin of IBM's laboratory in Zürich, Switzerland, used sudden electrical pulses to create a map of the Western Hemisphere from atoms. It has a diameter of 1 micron—just 100th of the diameter of a human hair.

● **First map for automobile drivers** For an automobile race held in the U.S.A. on Thanksgiving Day in 1895, the *Chicago Sun Herald* published a map of the 53.4-mile (86-km) course from Jackson Park, Illinois, to Waukegan, Illinois, and back again. Competitor Frank Duryea—the first American to build a successful commercial automobile—tore the map out of the newspaper and used it to drive to victory.

LARGEST REVOLVING GLOBE Old as it is, the *Erdapfel* (see p. 106, top) is tiny compared to the world's largest revolving globe, *Eartha*, which was built by GPS and digital map manufacturer DeLorme (U.S.A.) in 1998. The vast globe, which has a diameter of 41 ft. 18 in. (12.52 m) and weighs 5,600 lb (2,540 kg), occupies a three-story glass atrium at the company's headquarters in Maine, U.S.A. Powered by two computer-controlled electric motors, it revolves on a specially designed cantilever arm.

By contrast, the now-extinct elephant bird or vouron patra (*Aepyornis maximus*) is the **largest bird ever**. A flightless bird, it lived on the island of Madagascar and grew to around 10–11 ft. (3–3.3 m) tall and weighed about 1,100 lb. (500 kg).

PILGRIM'S PROGRESS In A.D. 330, a French pilgrim wrote the ●**first tourist guide**—the Itinerarium Burdigalense. In it, he described his route to Jerusalem, Israel, and gave details of hostels and watering points.

●**FIRST INTERACTIVE AUTOMOTIVE ROUTE PLANNER** **The modern sat-nav had an intriguing precedent in the Plus Fours Routefinder, created in 1920. This device took the form of a wristband that could be loaded with small scrolls featuring UK road maps. By rotating the rollers, the map on the scroll could be advanced, enabling a driver to navigate the route.**

Smallest-scale 3D map A representation of the 2dF survey of galaxies—the most detailed available—was created by Crystal Nebulae (UK) on a scale of 1 cm (0.39 in.): 1 billion light-years. Around 200,000 galaxies were laser-etched into a cube of just 0.37 in.^{3} (6 cm^3).

Oldest Moon map A series of 5,000-year-old carvings on a rock at Knowth in Ireland have been identified as the world's most ancient Moon map.

●**Oldest surviving star chart on manuscript** Dating to A.D. 649–684, the Dunhuang Chinese Sky star chart comprises a sequence of drawings of sky maps on rolls of manuscript. Discovered in 1907, it depicts the constellations visible from the Northern Hemisphere and includes 1,300 stars.

EARLY CIVILIZATIONS

○**First zoo** Archaeological discoveries made south of Luxor in Egypt in 2009 suggest the existence of a vast menagerie of animals—112 creatures in total, including elephants, wildcats, baboons, and hippos—dating back to 3500 B.C. The zoo—likely to have been privately owned, as the animals were buried in an elite cemetery—was unearthed during excavations of the ancient settlement of Hierakonpolis.

Madagascar is the world's **oldest island**. It split off from the Indian subcontinent around 80–100 million years ago and is now closer to the coast of Africa than it is to India.

OLDEST PYRAMIDS The Djoser Step Pyramid (top left) at Saqqâra, Egypt, was built *c*. 2750 B.C. and rose to a height of 204 ft. (62 m) and is the ● **first cut-stone pyramid.** Archaeologists later found that, *c*. 2700–2600 B.C., similar structures were built in the Peruvian city of Caral (bottom left), which featured up to 20 pyramids. It is impossible to say for certain which pyramids are the oldest.

●**First city** Dating back to *c*. 3200 B.C., Uruk, located in southern Mesopotamia (modern Iraq), was home to some 50,000 people. It was the largest settlement of its time, covering 1,112 acres (450 ha) and encircled by a 5.9-mile (9.5-km) city wall. Uruk thrived as a result of trade and agriculture and became a great artistic center.

●**Oldest royal cemetery** In 1922, British archaeologist Leonard Woolley excavated what is believed to be the first royal cemetery, at Ur in ancient Mesopotamia. He uncovered some 1,800 graves dating back as far as 2600 B.C., 16 of which were elaborate tombs with several rooms with spectacular artefacts. The tombs also included the remains of servants and members of the court.

●**FIRST PEOPLE TO RECORD HISTORY IN THE AMERICAS** The Maya were the first people in the Americas to keep historical records. Their writing (although not the first produced in the New World) used ideographic and phonetic elements on stone monuments. The Maya were also responsible for the ● **first written record of tobacco use.**

FIRST DOMESTICATION OF DOGS The oldest verifiable domestication of dogs (*Canis familiaris*) is thought to have been carried out by Paleolithic humans in east Asia, approximately 15,000 years ago, as they successfully bred aggression out of wolves (*Canis lupus*).

 The **largest volcanic island** is Iceland, formed from eruptions from the Mid-Atlantic Ridge. Measuring 39,768 miles^2 (103,000 km^2) in area, Iceland is essentially ocean floor exposed above the ocean surface.

· ·

28: Average life expectancy of a person living in ancient Greece or ancient Rome. Richer citizens often lived longer, unsurprisingly, while slaves often died at a younger age.

· ·

●**LARGEST GLADIATOR SCHOOL**
Protected only by basic armor, such as the helmet seen below left, gladiators were armed combatants who provided entertainment by fighting each other. The Ludus Magnus—the Great Gladiator School—was the largest of the four gladiator schools in ancient Rome; its arena could accommodate up to 3,000 spectators.

The **first gladiatorial games** took place in Rome in 264 B.C. and were staged by the sons of Junius Brutus Pera to mark his death. Other citizens were swift to offer their own (increasingly large) gladiatorial contests.

Oldest mummy Mummification dates from 2600 B.C. or the 4th dynasty of the Egyptian pharaohs. The oldest complete mummy is of Wati, a court musician of *c.* 2400 B.C. from the tomb of Nefer in Saqqâra, Egypt.

●**First horse race** Horsemanship was an important part of the Hittite culture of Anatolia, Turkey, dating from 1400 B.C. The 33rd ancient Olympic Games of 648 B.C. in Greece featured horse racing as an event.

●**First actor** Dionysian priest Thespis of ancient Greece was part of a chorus group that performed songs and dances based on Greek myths. In 534 B.C., at a performance in Athens, he is said to have leapt from the chorus to act out the roles of the characters that the group were singing about.

●**First permanent theater** Constructed in ancient Athens *c.* 500 B.C., the outdoor Theater of Dionysius was the world's first theater. It had an estimated capacity of up to 17,000 people.

●**OLDEST LEATHER SHOE** In 2008, archaeologists found a 5,500-year-old leather shoe in the Areni-1 cave in the southeastern Vayotoz Dzor province of Armenia.

KEY STAGES IN THE HISTORY OF MANKIND, FROM THE BEGINNING OF AGRICULTURE IN 8000 B.C. TO THE FOUNDING OF ISLAM IN *c.* A.D. 600.

8000 B.C.	Agriculture begins; wheat, oats, rye, and barley grown along the Tigris and Euphrates Rivers in Mesopotamia and in Egypt by the Nile River
5000 B.C.	Mesopotamia, "the cradle of civilization," comes into being; earliest system of laws, mathematics, and astronomy developed
3200 B.C.	World's **first city**, Uruk, established in southern Mesopotamia
c. 3000 B.C.	**ASTROLOGICAL TABLET** Clay tablet, c. 3000 B.C., inscribed in cuneiform with astrological data
1800 B.C.	According to Jewish tradition, Abraham, the first Jewish Patriarch, born in the city of Ur in Babylonia
1100 B.C.	Mesoamerican civilization begins with settlements in Mexico built by the Olmecs
1200–800 B.C.	**OLMEC SCULPTURE** Green jadeite ceremonial ax with "flaming eyebrows"
776 B.C.	First Olympic Games
c. 753 B.C.	Rome founded
600 B.C.	Buddhism started by Siddhartha Gautama, a prince who spurns wealth in favor of spiritual enlightenment **BUDDHA** Representation of Buddha in pure gold
500 B.C.	Western theater originates in Greece **THEATER MASK** Life-size terracotta mask from the Hellenistic period (5th century)
214 B.C.	Great Wall of China completed
4 B.C.	Jesus Christ is born, leading to founding of Christianity
A.D. 80	The Colosseum—the **largest Roman amphitheater**—first used for gladiator games **COLOSSEUM** Amphitheater in Rome, Italy, capable of seating 50,000 spectators
A.D. 476	The Western Roman Empire falls as Germanic leader Odoacer deposes Romulus Augustus
A.D. 570	Mohammad, founder of Islam, born in the Arabian city of Mecca

LARGEST BATTLE AT SEA IN ANCIENT TIMES The largest ancient naval battle was the Battle of Salamis, Greece, which took place in autumn 480 B.C. There were thought to be 800 vessels in the defeated Persian fleet and 380 in the victorious fleet of the Athenians and their allies. It is estimated that as many as 200,000 men were involved in the conflict.

●**Oldest seed germinated** A 2,000-year-old date-palm seed found in Masada, Israel, in the 1960s and replanted in 2005 by Dr. Sarah Sallon (Israel) and Dr. Elaine Soloway (U.S.A.) germinated after eight weeks. The seed was carbon-dated to the infamous siege of Masada by the Romans in A.D. 73, during which hundreds of Jewish zealots committed suicide.

Oldest novel Chariton's (Greece) *Chaireas and Callirhoe*, written in the 1st century A.D., narrates the adventures of a beautiful bride named Callirhoe.

Oldest castle The earliest known castle is in the old city of Sana'a, Yemen. Known as Gomdan or Gumdan Castle, it dates from before A.D. 200 and originally had 20 stories.

GREATEST EMPIRES

●**Largest empire by percentage of world population** By share of population, the largest empire was the Achaemenid Empire, better known as the Persian Empire, which accounted for approximately 49.4 million of

The **largest recorder**, constructed of specially treated stone pine and measuring 16 ft. 5 in. (5 m) long, was made in Iceland by Stefan Geir Karlsson in 1994. Each hole has a diameter of 3.3 in. (8.5 cm).

the world's 112.4 million people in around 480 B.C.—an astonishing 44%. Originating in modern-day Iran, the empire was first established by Cyrus the Great and included parts of Central Asia, the Mediterranean, North Africa, and European territories such as ancient Thrace and Macedonia.

Largest new world civilization The most successful and largest empire in the New World, before its discovery by European explorers, was that of the Inca, a tribe who founded the city of Cuzco around the year 1200. At their height, c. 1460, they ruled over 10 million people across an area of western South America similar in size to the Roman Empire.

●**FIRST EMPIRE** The Neo-Assyrian Empire originated in the late 10th century B.C. in Mesopotamia (modern Iraq). It reached the height of its power and influence in the 8th century B.C., when the territories under its control stretched from the Persian Gulf in the Near East to the Mediterranean Sea to the west. The empire fell in 612 B.C., when the capital city of Nineveh (modern Mosul) was destroyed by the Babylonians and their allies. Pictured is a relief of an Assyrian priest c. 721–705 B.C.

●**FIRST SENATE** The term "senate" comes from the Latin word "senex," meaning elder, old man, or council of elders. The Roman Senate dates back to the earliest days of Rome in the 8th century B.C. The early Senate was a deliberative body—it did not propose laws or vote on them. The Roman historian Livy said that it comprised 100 senators, whose duty was to advise the King of Rome.

Staying on a musical note, Rosario Varela (Spain) performed 1,274 flamenco taps on the set of the TV show *Guinness World Records* in Madrid, Spain, on January 23, 2009—the **most flamenco taps in a minute by a woman**.

●FIRST GLOBAL EMPIRE In the 15th century, Portugal established the first global maritime and commercial empire, under Henry the Navigator. In the 1440s, he sent key expeditions to Africa and Asia, and in the 16th and 17th centuries, Portugal set up colonies in Brazil, Africa, East Timor, India, and Macau. This 16th-century map shows two Portuguese claims in Africa—"Guine" (Guinea) and "Amina," meaning the Mina Coast, which was also known as the Portuguese Gold Coast and later just the Gold Coast (modern-day Ghana).

●Longest empire Most historians agree that the Roman Empire began in 27 B.C., when Octavian overthrew the Roman Republic to become Emperor Augustus. Rome later fell to the Barbarians in A.D. 476, but the ensuing Eastern (Byzantine) Empire based at Constantinople (modern-day Istanbul in Turkey) is widely regarded as a continuation. The fall of Constantinople in 1453 finally ended a period of dominance that had lasted for almost 1,500 years.

Largest palace The Imperial Palace in the center of Beijing, China, covers 3,150 x 2,460 ft. (960 x 750 m) over an area of 178 acres (72 ha). The outline survives from the construction under the third Ming Emperor, Yongle (1402–24), but owing to constant reconstruction most of the internal buildings are from the 18th century. By way of comparison, the Palace of Versailles, completed for Louis XIV in 1682, is 1,902 ft. (580 m) long.

●LARGEST EMPIRE (ABSOLUTE) Geographically, the British Empire was the largest in history. In 1922, it covered over 13 million miles^2 (34 million km^2), about a quarter of the world's landmass, and boasted territories on every continent except Antarctica. Pictured is a British soldier in India, and the stamp shows Britain's reach, giving credence to the saying, "The Sun never sets on the British Empire."

LARGEST EMPIRE (CONTIGUOUS) The Mongol Empire (1206–1367) was run by the Khan Dynasty. At its height in 1279 under Khubilai Khan (pictured), it encompassed 100 million people and 13.8 million miles² (35.7 million km²), including the present-day territories of China, Russia, Mongolia, Central Asia, the Middle East, and the Korean Peninsula.

KEY STAGES IN THE HISTORY OF MANKIND, FROM THE RISE OF THE TANG DYNASTY IN A.D. 618 TO COLUMBUS'S VOYAGE TO THE AMERICAS IN 1492.

A.D. 618	The rule of the Tang Dynasty begins. For nearly 300 years it will preside over the unification of China
A.D. 712	Muslim conquest of Spain is completed, after an eight-year campaign
c. A.D. 797	Irish monks create the Book of Kells, a masterfully illustrated version of the four Gospels of the Bible
A.D. 800	**BRONZE SCULPTURE** Sculpture from A.D. 814 depicting Charlemagne, who became Emperor of the Romans in A.D. 800
A.D. 871	Saxon king Alfred the Great begins his reign in England
1066	**TAPESTRY** William of Normandy becomes ruler of England, defeating Harold. Later celebrated in the Bayeux Tapestry
1095	Start of the First Crusade. It will last for four years
c. 1100	Statue-building begins on Easter Island · **MONGOL COINS** A dirham and dinar from the reign of Genghis Khan (ruled 1206–27)
1206	Mongol ruler Genghis Khan comes to power. Over the next 21 years he conquers parts of China and Persia, and advances toward the Caspian Sea, establishing the Mongol Empire
1299	Birth of the Ottoman Empire, which becomes the preeminent power in the Eastern Mediterranean
1325	Tenochtitlan (modern-day Mexico City) is founded by the Aztecs
c. 1350	The Black Death, the **worst pandemic**, kills 75 million worldwide · **BLACK DEATH** Woodcut of a plague victim being treated
c. 1400	Beginning of the "Little Ice Age" in Europe
1492	Christopher Columbus sets sail from Spain to the Americas

Greatest historical ransom Historically, the greatest ransom paid was that raised for Atahualpa, the last emperor of the Inca, and given to the Spanish conquistador Francisco Pizarro in 1532–33 at Cajamarca, Peru. The payment constituted a hall full of gold and silver, worth some $1.5 billion in today's terms. Atahualpa was later executed.

●**Largest empire by population** At the outbreak of World War I in 1914, the population of the British Empire stood at an estimated 400 million. By 1922, however, following the acquisition of additional territories in the wake of that war, this figure had grown to some 458 million. The population eventually peaked in 1938, on the eve of World War II, by which time the British Empire accounted for an incredible 531 million people, making it history's largest empire by population. Today, it is estimated that the British Commonwealth includes as many as 2 billion people within its 54 member states.

BRAVE NEW WORLD

Oldest mechanically printed book It is widely accepted that the first mechanically printed full-length book was the Gutenberg Bible, printed in Mainz, Germany, c. 1455 by Johann Henne zum Gensfleisch zur Laden, called zu Gutenberg (c. 1398–1468). The Chinese, however, may have invented movable type 600–700 years earlier.

●**First watch** The invention of a portable timekeeping device c. 1509 is attributed to Peter Henlein (Germany), designer of the "Nuremberg Egg"—a small, drum-shaped clock (with only an hour hand) that could be carried. References to a "pocket clock" have since been discovered that predate this invention by 40 years, but Henlein is credited with being the first person to manufacture such devices and introduce the concept of regular timekeeping—an essential tool for the "modern" world.

MOST EXPENSIVE MANUSCRIPT
The *Codex Leicester*, written by Leonardo da Vinci (Italy) in 1508–10, was bought by Bill Gates (U.S.A.) for a record $30,802,500 at Christie's, New York City, U.S.A., on November 11, 1994. This working journal was used by da Vinci to document his sketches of the submarine and the steam engine.

8.3: Weight in tons of all the potatoes you will eat. The world's favorite vegetable was discovered in the New World and is mildly poisonous: 8.3 tons contains enough neurotoxin to kill 3,750 people.

●**FIRST HELIOCENTRIC SOLAR-SYSTEM MODEL** Just before his death in 1543, Nicolaus Copernicus (Poland) published *On the Revolutions of the Celestial Spheres*, in which he outlined his revolutionary notion of heliocentrism—the idea that planets travel around the Sun. It took at least another 150 years for his idea to become widely accepted.

●**Oldest museum** The British Museum in London, UK, has stood on the same site since it was established in 1753; it opened for free entry to the public on January 15, 1759. The original set of exhibits was based on scientist Sir Hans Sloane's collection.

●**FIRST PHONOGRAPH** Thomas Alva Edison (U.S.A.) invented the "Tinfoil Phonograph" in 1877, initially to record and play back messages from another new communications device—the telephone. To record sound, Edison used some tinfoil that was wrapped around a cylinder.

FIRST HUMANS ON THE MOON Neil Alden Armstrong and Edwin Eugene "Buzz" Aldrin (both U.S.A.) became the first people to set foot on the Moon when they stepped out of the *Eagle* lunar module on to the Sea of Tranquillity on July 21, 1969.

FIRST CELL PHONE Martin Cooper (U.S.A.) of Motorola invented the first portable telephone handset, making the first call on April 3, 1973, to his rival, Joel Engel, head of research at Bell Labs. The first commercial cell phone network launched in Japan in 1979.

First manned flight Frenchman François Pilâtre de Rozier is regarded as the first human to have flown. On October 15, 1783, he rose 84 ft. (26 m) into the air in a tethered hot-air balloon built by French inventors Joseph and Jacques Montgolfier.

First telephone call On February 14, 1876, Alexander Graham Bell (UK) filed a patent for the telephone. In March 1876, in Boston, Massachusetts, U.S.A., Bell phoned his assistant in a nearby room to say, "Come here, Watson, I want you."

Pablo Picasso (Spain) was the **most prolific professional painter**. He produced an estimated 13,500 paintings and designs, 100,000 prints and engravings, 34,000 book illustrations, and 300 sculptures and ceramics.

First country to pass women's suffrage The 1893 Women's Suffrage Petition led to New Zealand becoming the first self-governing nation in the developing world to grant women the right to vote.

●**First industrial moving assembly line** In 1913, the Ford Motor Company introduced a moving assembly line in Highland Park near Detroit, Michigan, U.S.A. Assembly time for vehicles was cut from 12.5 hours to 1 hr. 33 min. Manufacture soared from 200,000 automobiles in 1913 to well over a million by 1920.

●**First skyscraper** The Home Insurance Building in Chicago, U.S.A., was erected in 1884–85. It was 10 stories high, peaking at 138 ft (42 m).

First hypertext browser In October 1990, Tim Berners-Lee (UK) started work on a global hypertext browser. The finished result—the world wide web—was made available on the internet for the first time in the summer of 1991.

HIGHEST DEATH TOLL There are thought to have been 56.4 million fatalities in World War II (1939–45), including battle deaths and civilians of all countries.

World War II was also the costliest war. Its overall expense of $1.5 trillion exceeds the cost of the rest of history's wars put together.

●**FIRST SETTLEMENT IN THE NEW WORLD** La Isabela, on the island of Hispaniola (in the present-day Dominican Republic), was built in 1493 by Christopher Columbus's crew on his second voyage to the Americas. The area—the first permanent European settlement in the New World—was created in order to exploit local reserves of precious metals, but was abandoned within five years following hurricanes, hunger, disease, mutiny, and constant clashes with the native Taíno people.

Arushi Bhatnagar (India, b. June 1, 2002) had her first solo exhibition at the Kalidasa Akademi in Ujjain, India, on May 11, 2003, when she was 344 days old—making her the **youngest professional artist**.

KEY STAGES IN THE HISTORY OF MANKIND, FROM MICHELANGELO'S PAINTINGS IN THE SISTINE CHAPEL TO THE BIRTH OF THE WORLD WIDE WEB.

1512	Michelangelo completes his epic frescoes for the ceiling of the Sistine Chapel in Vatican City
1588	An attempt to invade England by the Spanish Armada is foiled by the British fleet—and storms
1620	Puritan pilgrims set sail on the *Mayflower* from Plymouth, England, for the Americas
1682	Peter I ("the Great") becomes ruler of Russia, ushering in a period of major reform and modernization
1776	American colonies formally declare their secession from Britain, prompting the American War of Independence
c. 1826	Joseph Nicéphore Niépce takes the first permanent photograph
1829	End of the Spanish American Wars of Independence
1859	Publication of *On the Origin of Species* by Charles Darwin
1914	Beginning of World War I
1917	The Russian Revolution—a series of violent uprisings—brings down the Czar and gives rise to the Soviet Union
1939	Adolf Hitler begins invasion of Poland, leading to World War II, which goes on to affect 61 nations
1961	Russian cosmonaut Yuri Gagarin becomes the **first human in space**
1991	Debut of the world wide web, created by Tim Berners-Lee

SHAKESPEARE Print taken from a painting of the writer (1564–1616)

NAPOLEON Watercolor of the French emperor by Jean-Baptiste Isabey, dated 1812

VENEZUELAN CURRENCY Coin honoring South American revolutionary Simón Bolívar (1783–1830)

GAS MASK British fireman's mask from World War II

HUMAN BODY

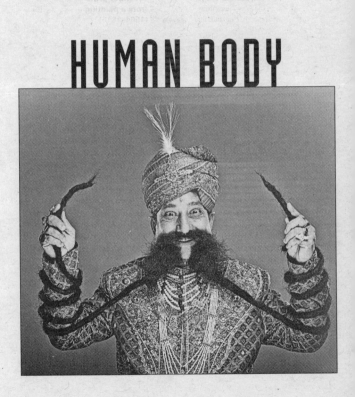

CONTENTS

BODY MODIFICATIONS

PUNCTURES, PIERCINGS, IMPLANTS, AND TATTOOS

Human beings have always sought to alter their looks. Otzi the iceman, who lived *c.* 5,300 years ago and was discovered preserved in ice in 1991, has at least 57 tattoos—the **oldest known tattoos** in the world. And even our Neanderthal cousins wore makeup. Here, then, is our selection of the most striking record-breaking transformations.

> "My first tattoo was like a little juggling club on my hip, but that was when I was nervous about what my Mom thought . . . "

MOST TATTOOED PERSON Having adorned his body with colorful designs from around the world, Lucky Diamond Rich (Australia, b. New Zealand) opted next for a 100% covering of black ink. He is now adding white designs over the black . . . and colored designs on top of those. With this layering of tattoos, he has over 200% skin coverage!

Total tattooing hours: 1,000 plus

LATE STARTER Isobel caught the tattooing bug at the age of 49 when she first visited a tattoo convention in London, UK. Her first tattoo followed shortly afterwards, and today, 93% of her body is covered in ink!

TATTOOING A tattoo is a permanent marking of the skin using pigments that are injected by needles deep into the dermis. In the healing process, the top layer of skin flakes away, leaving the deeper marks trapped beneath the surface. Here, illustrating the beauty of tattoos, is Isobel Varley (UK)—at 72 years old, the **most tattooed female senior citizen.**

TAT'S THE WAY TO DO IT! The **most tattooed senior citizen** is former most-tattooed man Tom Leppard. His body is 99.9% covered in a leopard-print pattern.

The **longest railroad platform** is located at Kharagpur Station in West Bengal, India, and measures 2,733 ft. (833 m) in length—as long as 12 jumbo jet planes end to end.

SCARIFICATION This permanent procedure involves taking a knife—or, more traditionally, stone or shards of glass or coconut shell—and etching or cutting the skin with a design. The deep wounds are often rubbed with toxic plant juices to promote (or encourage) raised scars or "keloids." This form of modification is still carried out by some Sudanese women belonging to the Nuer and Nubia-Kush tribes.

NECK STRETCHING The wearing of an increasingly long brass coil around the neck—as carried out by women of Burma's Padaung and Karenni tribes—results in a neck extension of up to 15.75 in. (40 cm). Only initial discomfort is reported after the coils are set, yet the distance from earlobe to collarbone lengthens to more than double the average.

COSMETIC SURGERY Going under the surgeon's knife remains a popular option for body modders, although figures are dropping as the economy falters—more than 1.5 million procedures took place in the U.S.A. in 2009, down 20% from 2000 figures. Continuing to lead the way with the **most cosmetic surgeries** is Cindy Jackson (U.S.A.), who has had 47 cosmetic procedures, including nine full-scale surgical operations, since 1988.

Sticking with rail records, the National Belgian Railroad Company (NMBS) built the **longest passenger train**. It measured 5,685 ft. 4 in. (1,732.9 m) and consisted of 70 cars pulled by one electric locomotive.

HUMAN PINCUSHION Since having her first piercing in 1997, Elaine Davidson (UK)—the **most pierced woman**—has had a record 4,225 pieces of metal attached to, and inside, her body.

LIP PLATING Necks are not the only body parts that can be stretched—earlobes are commonly elongated beyond their natural length, for example—but the most arresting example of this body art is lip stretching. Pictured is a female from Ethiopia's Mursi ethnic group, which practices the wearing of clay plates in the lower lip. Plates can reach 6 in. (15 cm) in diameter.

CORSETING Get that Victorian wasp-waisted look with years of perseverance in ever-tightening corsets. Epitomizing this retro look is Cathie Jung (U.S.A.), proud owner of the **smallest waist on a living person**—15 in. (38.1 cm).

PIERCING The practice of puncturing the skin with metal rings, studs, and other items of jewelry dates back at least 5,000 years—as confirmed by ancient mummified remains found wearing earrings. Piercings are no longer limited to ears—anything can be, and is, skewered and studded in the name of fashion. The ○**most pierced man**, for example, Rolf Buchholz, has 453 studs and rings all over his body.

WHAT A STUD! Rolf Buchholz, from Dortmund, Germany, has—among others—94 piercings in and around his lips, 25 in his eyebrows, 16 in his right ear, and eight in his nose.

BODY PARTS

Longest fingernails ever (female) The longest set of fingernails ever recorded belonged to Lee Redmond (U.S.A.), who started to grow them in 1979 and carefully manicured them to reach a total length of 28 ft. 4.5 in. (8.65 m), as confirmed on the set of *Lo Show dei Record* in Madrid, Spain, on February 23, 2008. Unfortunately, Lee lost her nails in an automobile accident in early 2009.

LONGEST LEGS (FEMALE) On July 8, 2003, the long, long legs of Svetlana Pankratova (Russia) were measured at 51.9 in. (132 cm) in Torremolinos, Spain.

LEGWORK Being a record breaker can present its own challenges! Svetlana has to have some clothes made for her, ducks through most doorways, and needs lots of legroom in automobiles and airplanes.

The Nemo 33 diving pool in Brussels, Belgium, is the world's **deepest pool**, sinking to 108 ft. (33 m) at its greatest depth.

The **longest fingernails for a man** belonged to Melvin Boothe (U.S.A.), whose nails had a combined length of 32 ft. 3.8 in. (9.85 m) when they were measured on May 30, 2009, in Troy, Michigan, U.S.A. Sadly, Melvin passed on in December 2009.

○**Largest hands on a living person** Sultan Kösen (Turkey)—the **tallest living man**—had hands measuring 11.22 in. (28.5 cm) from the wrist to the tip of the middle finger when last measured on February 8, 2011. He also has the **widest handspan** at 12 in. (30.48 cm).

The **largest hands ever**, though, still belong to Robert Pershing Wadlow (U.S.A., 1918–40), the **tallest man ever**, whose hands measured 12.75 in. (32.3 cm) from the wrist to the tip of his middle finger.

●**LONGEST TONGUE (FEMALE)** Chanel Tapper (U.S.A., left) has a tongue that measured 3.8 in. (9.75 cm), from tip to top lip, in California, U.S.A., on September 29, 2010. The outright **longest tongue** record, though, is held by Stephen Taylor (UK)—his lengthy licker measured 3.86 in. (9.8 cm) from tip to lip on February 11, 2009.

WIDEST TONGUE Measuring an amazing 3.1 in. (7.9 cm) across at its maximum is the tongue of Jay Sloot (Australia)—the widest in the world. The massive, mobile muscle was measured on the set of *Lo Show dei Record* in Rome, Italy, on March 18, 2010.

The **largest swimming pool** in the world is the San Alfonso del Mar seawater pool in Algarrobo, Chile. Completed in December 2006, it is 3,324 ft. (1,013 m) long and has an area of 19.77 acres (8 ha).

○**LONGEST FINGERNAILS** No woman has a longer set of fingernails than Chris "The Dutchess" Walton (U.S.A.). They come in at 10 ft. 2 in. (309.8 cm) for her left hand and 9 ft. 7 in. (292.1 cm) for her right—a total of 19 ft. 9 in. (601.9 cm). A rock singer and recording artist, The Dutchess had her record-breaking nails measured by Guinness World Records in Las Vegas, Nevada, U.S.A., on February 21, 2011.

"Rhinology" is the study of noses.

LONGEST NOSE ON A LIVING PERSON Mehmet Ozyurek (Turkey) has a remarkable nose that measured 3.46 in. (8.8 cm) long from the bridge to the tip on the set of *Lo Show dei Record* in Rome, Italy, on March 18, 2010.

Largest feet on a living person Excluding sufferers of elephantiasis, Sultan Kösen (Turkey) has the biggest feet. His 1-ft. 2-in. (36.5-cm) left foot and 1-ft. 1.98-in. (35.5-cm) right foot were measured in Ankara, Turkey, in 2009.

And the **largest feet ever**? You guessed it: the tallest man ever, Robert Pershing Wadlow, wore U.S. size 37AA shoes, equivalent to 18.5 in. (47 cm) long.

LONGEST TOOTH EXTRACTED:

1.26 in. (3.2 cm)—Loo Hui Jing (Singapore)

WIDEST TOOTH EXTRACTED:

0.6 in. (1.67 cm)—nine-year-old Shane Russell (Canada)

MOST TEETH AT BIRTH:

12—Sean Keaney (UK) on April 10, 1990

○ OLDEST PERSON TO GROW A NEW TOOTH:

Australian Brian Titford, 76, had two upper wisdom teeth erupt in March 2009.

Largest artery The aorta has a 1.18-in. (3-cm) diameter at the point where it leaves the heart. It ends with a diameter of 0.68 in. (1.75 cm) at the level of the fourth lumbar vertebra.

Slightly larger than the aorta is the inferior vena cava, which returns the blood from the lower half of the body to the heart. It is the **largest vein**.

Largest internal organ The adult liver can weigh 2 lb. 10 oz.–3 lb. 5 oz. (1.2–1.5 kg) and measure 8.6 in. (22 cm) long and 3.9 in. (10 cm) wide.

●**Largest kidney** On January 26, 2010, Dr. Abdul Rasheed Shaikh removed a kidney weighing 3 lb. 15 oz. (1.8 kg) and measuring 12 x 5 x 4 in. (30 x 13 x 10 cm) at the Chandka Medical College Hospital, Larkana Sindh, Pakistan. His patient was Waziran Malah (Pakistan).

Largest muscle The bulkiest of the body's 639 named muscles is usually the *gluteus maximus*, or buttock muscle, which extends to the thigh. However, in pregnancy the uterus (womb) can increase from about 1 oz. (30 g) to over 2 lb. 3 oz. (1 kg) in weight.

The **smallest muscle** in the body is the stapedius, which controls the stapes—the **smallest bone**, located in the ear. The muscle is less than 0.05 in. (0.127 cm) long.

Eye muscles move more than 100,000 times a day, making them the **most active muscles**.

LITTLE & LARGE

HEAVIEST MEN

Ever Jon Brower Minnoch (U.S.A., 1941–83) suffered from obesity since childhood. He reached his peak weight in March 1978—he was admitted to University Hospital in Seattle, U.S.A., where it was calculated that he must have weighed more than 1,400 lb. (100 st; 635 kg).

Living Manuel Uribe Garza (Mexico) weighed 917 lb. (65.5 st; 416 kg) during a weigh-in in December 2009.

For giants of the garden, see p. 254.

The Atacama Desert in Chile covers only 40,600 miles^2 (105,200 km^2) and is the world's **smallest desert**.

Human Body

○TALLEST MAN Sultan Kösen (Turkey)—the tallest living human—appears to have finally stopped growing at the height of 8 ft. 3 in. (251 cm). Revolutionary gamma-knife surgery on the tumor affecting his pituitary gland, provided by the University of Virginia (U.S.A.) in August 2010, has halted his production of growth hormone.

Twins (ever) Billy Leon and Benny Loyd McCrary, alias McGuire (both U.S.A.), were normal in size until the age of six. By November 1978, however, Billy and Benny weighed 743 lb. (53 st 1 lb.; 337 kg) and 723 lb.; 51 st 9 lb.; 328 kg) respectively, and each had a waist of 84 in. (2.13 m).

SHORTEST WOMEN

Ever "Princess" Pauline Musters (Netherlands, 1876–95) measured exactly 24 in. (61 cm) at the time of her death from pneumonia aged 19 years.

Living Madge Bester (South Africa) is 2 ft. 1.5 in. (65 cm) tall; she is confined to a wheelchair as a result of the skeletal disorder osteogenesis imperfecta.

○Living (mobile) Bridgette Jordan (see p. 135).

Living (teenager) Jyoti Amge (India, b. December 16, 1993) was measured by a team of physicians in Tokyo, Japan, for *Bikkuri Chojin 100 Special #2* (Fuji TV) and found to be 2 ft. (61.95 cm) tall on September 6, 2009. She is destined to become the new **shortest living woman (mobile)** if she remains this height on her 18th birthday in 2011.

Egypt's Nile Valley and Delta is the **largest oasis** on Earth, covering approximately 8,500 miles^2 (22,000 km^2). Without the Nile, Egypt would be entirely composed of desert.

TALLEST MAN EVER:

Robert Pershing Wadlow (U.S.A.): 8 ft. 11.1 in. (272 cm)

TALLEST WOMAN EVER:

Zeng Jinlian (China): 8 ft. 1.75 in. (248 cm)

TALLEST LIVING WOMAN:

Yao Defen (China): 7 ft.7 in. (233.3 cm)

TALLEST MARRIED COUPLE EVER:

Anna Hanen Swan (Canada): 7 ft. 5.5 in. (227 cm); Martin van Buren Bates (U.S.A.): 7 ft. 2.5 in. (220 cm). Combined height: 14 ft. 8 in. (447 cm).

SHORTEST MEN At the time of going to press, the ○ **shortest living man** was Khagendra Thapa Magar (Nepal, b. October 14, 1992, far left), who was measured by Guinness World Records at Fewa City Hospital in Pokhara, Nepal, on October 14, 2010, and found to be 2 ft. 2.41 in. (67.08 cm) tall.

In April 2011, however, an even shorter male came to our attention. Although Junrey Balawing (above right) of Zamboanga del Norte in the Philippines has yet to be measured by Guinness World Records, he is reportedly just 22 in. (55.8 cm) and, at the age of 17, unofficially the **shortest living teenager**. Once he turns 18, he will qualify as the **shortest living man**.

If the figures are confirmed, it would make Junrey shorter than Gul Mohammed (India, 1957–97), the **shortest adult ever** at 22.5 in. (57 cm).

TALL STORY The **tallest living teenager** is Brenden Adams (U.S.A., b. September 20, 1995), who is 7 ft. 4.6 in. (225.1 cm) in height. Brenden is taller than Robert Wadlow (see above) was at his age.

●**TALLEST PROFESSIONAL MODEL** Amazon Eve (U.S.A.) was 6 ft. 7.39 in. (201.66 cm) tall when measured in Beverly Hills, California, U.S.A., on February 25, 2011. Seen here with more diminutive model Qeyda Penate, the statuesque Amazon is also a wrestler and an actress. She credits her Dutch and German heritage with providing her record-breaking stature.

●**SHORTEST SIBLINGS** Bridgette and Brad Jordan (both U.S.A.) are 27.4 in. (69.5 cm) and 38.6 in. (98 cm) tall respectively. Their reduced height is caused by the condition Majewski osteodysplastic primordial dwarfism type II. Undeterred, they both have full and active lives—and Bridgette wants to become a model.

Bridgette's height makes her the ○**shortest living woman (mobile)**—a record she may only hold on to until December 2011, when Jyoti Amge (see main text) turns 18.

○HEAVIEST LIVING WOMAN Pauline Potter of Sacramento, California, U.S.A., weighed 643 lb. (291.6 kg) on May 13, 2010. Pauline leads the way in terms of large ladies, but she would be dwarfed by Rosalie Bradford (U.S.A.)—the **heaviest woman ever**—who peaked at 1,200 lb (85 st; 544 kg) in January 1987.

Lightest birth The lowest birth weight for a surviving infant of which there is evidence is 9.17 oz. (260 g). Rumaisa Rahman (U.S.A.) was born at Loyola University Medical Center, Maywood, Illinois, U.S.A., on September 19, 2004, after a gestation period of just 25 weeks 6 days.

●**Tallest living married couple** Wayne (6 ft. 10 in.; 209.3 cm) and Laurie (6 ft. 6 in.; 198 cm) Hallquist (U.S.A.) have a combined height of 13 ft. 4 in. (407.3 cm).

....

The **earliest known example of an alphabet** dates back to around 1900 B.C. and was found carved into limestone in Wadi el Hol near Luxor in Egypt.

....

LONG LIVES

○**Oldest living person** On May 13, 2011, Maria Gomez Valentim (b. July 9, 1896, p. 138) of Carangola, Brazil, was—at the age of 114 years 308 days—confirmed as the world's oldest living person.

Jeanne Louise Calment (February 21, 1875–August 4, 1997) of Arles, France, lived to be 122 years 164 days old, the **greatest age ever verified for a human being**.

○**Oldest living man** Jiroemon Kimura (Japan, b. April 19, 1897, pictured p. 138) became the oldest living man just five days before his 114th birthday. He is also the last living man born in the 19th century.

OLDEST MAN EVER Despite his fondness for smoking—a habit not generally associated with longevity—Thomas Peter Thorvald Kristian Ferdinand "Christian" Mortensen (Denmark, b. August 16, 1882) of San Ramon, California, U.S.A., lived to be the oldest man whose age has been satisfactorily verified. He died on April 25, 1998, aged 115 years 252 days.

Christian is the only Nordic person to have lived beyond the age of 113.

 The **language with the most letters** is Khmer (Cambodian), which has a total of 74 characters, including some that lack any current use.

3,019,107,744: Number of heartbeats in a lifetime. Your heart is slightly smaller than the size of your own clenched fist. It started beating eight months before you were born, when you were smaller than your thumb.

OLDEST LIVING PEOPLE

As of May 13, 2011, these are the world's 10 oldest people. When they were born, Queen Victoria was still alive and the Ford Motor Company did not yet exist.

	Holder	Age	Sex	Born
1	Maria Gomez Valentim (Brazil, below left)	114	Female	Jul. 9, 1896
2	Besse Cooper (U.S.A.)	114	Female	Aug. 26, 1896
3	Chiyono Hasegawa (Japan)	114	Female	Nov. 20, 1896
4	Venere Pizzinato-Papo (Italy)	114	Female	Nov. 23, 1896
5	Shige Hirooka (Japan)	114	Female	Jan. 16, 1897
6	Dina Manfredini (Italy/U.S.A.)	114	Female	Apr. 4, 1897
7	Jiroemon Kimura (Japan, below right)	114	Male	Apr. 19, 1897
8	Delma Kollar (U.S.A.)	113	Female	Oct. 31, 1897
9	Toshi Horiya (Japan)	113	Female	Nov. 8, 1897
10	Leila Denmark (U.S.A.)	113	Female	Feb. 1, 1898

LONG LIVE LADIES! Evidence suggests that if you plan to live to a ripe old age, it helps to be female! Of more than 75 people in history known to have reached the age of 114, only five have been men.

MOVIE MEMORIES Jeanne Calment, the **oldest woman ever**, was the last living person to have known the artist Vincent van Gogh. Aged 114, she played herself in the film *Vincent and Me* (Canada, 1990), making her the **oldest actress**.

○ **OLDEST LIVING TWINS (FEMALE)** At 101 years old, sisters Lily Millward (left) and Ena Pugh (née Thomas, right; both UK) are the oldest living twins. Farmers' daughters, they were born on January 4, 1910, in Llechach, Wales, UK.

○**Oldest living twins (mixed)** Benjamin Franklin Colvett and Rose Frances Bruce (both U.S.A.) were born near Alamo, Tennessee, U.S.A., on August 23, 1912.

Twins Glen and Dale Moyer (U.S.A.) each reached the age of 105, making them the **oldest male twins ever**. Born on June 20, 1895, they became the oldest living twins on January 23, 2000.

●**Oldest singleton twin ever** Mary Belle Murphy Crombie (U.S.A., 1890–2003) lived to the age of 113 years 78 days, while her twin sister Mabel Jean died in 1984 aged 94.

●**Highest combined age for four siblings** As of March 14, 2011, the four siblings of the Stepham family (UK) totaled 390 years 81 days: Clara Goldsmith (100 years 37 days), Belle Dell (98 years 344 days), Anne Goldsmith (96 years 119 days), and Jack Stepham (94 years 311 days).

Sadly, Jack passed away on March 14, 2011.

●**Oldest debut as a feature film director** Takeo Kimura (Japan, b. April 1, 1918) was aged 90 years 207 days when he made his directorial debut with *Dreaming Awake*, released on October 18, 2008.

○**Oldest ballerina** The oldest performing ballerina is Grete Brunvoll (Norway, b. July 27, 1930). She began dancing at the age of six and her first professional performance was at the Nathionalteater in 1945, when she was aged 15.

Travel back in time with our history features, from p. 108.

OLDEST IN THEIR FIELD

If you're lucky enough to enjoy good health into your old age, there's no reason why you can't stay active and even keep working. These people did just that. . . .

Oldest . . .	Name	Age/date achieved
○ Abseiler	Doris Cicely Long (UK)	96 years 11 days; May 29, 2010
○ Bungee jumper	Mohr Keet (South Africa)	96 years; April 10, 2010
● Doctor	Leila Denmark (U.S.A.)	Retired May 2001; 103 years
● Scuba diver (from shore)	Saul Moss (Australia)	85 years 14 days; August 1, 2009
Appointed prime minister	Morarji Ranchhodji Desai (India)	81 years; March 1977
Oscar winner (Best Actress)	Jessica Tandy (UK)	80 years 295 days; March 29, 1990
Oscar winner (Best Actor)	Henry Fonda (U.S.A.)	76 years 317 days; March 29, 1982
Ballet dancer	Frank Russell Galey (U.S.A.)	74 years 101 days; December 17, 2006

●**Oldest practicing physician** Dr. Walter "Papa Doc" Watson (U.S.A.), an obstetrician born in 1910, was still practicing at University Hospital in Augusta, Georgia, U.S.A., in May 2010 at the age of 100.

○**Oldest person to receive a doctorate** Emeritus Professor Dr. Heinz Wenderoth (Germany) was awarded the degree of Doctor of Science by the Gottfried Wilhelm Leibniz University of Hannover on September 29, 2008, at the age of 97 years 8 months 18 days. His dissertation was titled: *Cell Biological Studies in the Morphology and Physiology of Primitive Marine Placozoons Trichoplax Adhaerens*.

○**Oldest yoga teacher** The world's oldest yoga teacher was Gladys Morris (UK, b. January 31, 1921). At the age of 90, she was still teaching regular yoga classes at the Shaw Lifelong Learning Centre, Oldham, UK. She died in March 2011.

The **largest religious structure ever built** is Angkor Wat (City Temple), enclosing 401 acres (162.6 ha) in Cambodia. Dedicated to the Hindu god Vishnu, it was built by the Khmer king Suryavarman II between 1113 and 1150.

●**OLDEST CURLING PLAYER** Centenarian Stephen Gittus (Canada, b. February 17, 1910) continued to play in competitions on a regular basis at the Kamloops Curling Club in Kamloops, British Columbia, Canada, as of November 18, 2010. He first took up the sport when he turned 43.

HAIR

Hairiest child According to the Ferriman Gallwey score—which grades hair density on nine areas of the body from 0 (little) to 4 (heavy coverage)—the most hirsute child is Supatra Sasuphan (Thailand). She was assessed during a trip to Rome, Italy, on March 4, 2010.

●**Largest gathering of natural redheads** On July 17, 2010, Anne Lindsay (U.S.A.) organized for 890 redheads to meet at Skyline High School in Sammamish, Washington, U.S.A.

HAIR TODAY . . . We lose between 50 and 100 hairs every day. But don't worry! Replacement hairs are growing all the time.

A more modern construction, the **largest ice structure** is the Ice Hotel in Jukkasjärvi, Sweden, which has been rebuilt each December since 1990 and has a total floor area of 43,000–54,000 ft.^{2} (4,000–5,000 m^2).

LONGEST ARM HAIR:

5.75 in. (461 cm)—Justin Shaw (U.S.A.)

LONGEST BEARD (EVER):

17 ft. 6 in. (5.33 m)—Hans N Langseth (Norway)

LONGEST CHEST HAIR:

9 in. (22.8 cm)—Richard Condo (U.S.A.)

LONGEST EAR HAIR:

7.12 in. (18.1 cm)—Anthony Victor (India)

LONGEST EYEBROW HAIR:

7.01 in. (17.8 cm)—Toshie Kawakami (Japan)

LONGEST LEG HAIR:

6.5 in. (16.51 cm)—Wesley Pemberton (U.S.A.)

LONGEST NIPPLE HAIR:

5.07 in. (12.9 cm)—Douglas Williams (U.S.A.)

LONGEST BEARD ON A LIVING PERSON (FEMALE) Vivian Wheeler of Wood River, Illinois, U.S.A., started shaving at the age of seven and grew a full beard in 1990. The longest strand, from the follicle to the tip of hair, was measured at 11 in. (27.9 cm) in 2000. She is seen here with her son—who clearly likes beards too.

○**Largest gathering of mustachioed men** An event organized by KARE-1 TV at the Xcel Energy Center in St. Paul, Minnesota, U.S.A., on November 26, 2010, drew 1,131 men with 'taches.

LONGEST MUSTACHE Ram Singh Chauhan (India) is the owner of the world's longest mustache, which he has been growing since 1982. The phenomenal facial hair measured 14 ft. (4.29 m) in length on the set of *Lo Show dei Record* in Rome, Italy, on March 4, 2010. Ram was inspired by a previous GWR record holder for the longest mustache—Karna Bheel—who, like Ram, came from Rajasthan.

Ram grooms his mustache with coconut oil and mustard oil.

○**Tallest Mohican** It took four hours for stylists to erect Kazuhiro Watanabe's (Japan) 41.3-in.-tall (105-cm) mohican. The length was verified at the MACRO hair salon in Sapporo, Hokkaido, Japan, on January 10, 2011. The mohawk was an incredible 9.8 in. (25 cm) taller than that of the previous record-holder from Germany.

●**LARGEST AFRO** Aevin Dugas (U.S.A.) is the proud owner of a record-breaking afro. When measured in New Orleans, U.S.A., on October 4, 2010, it had a circumference of 4 ft. 4 in. (1.32 m). She trims her afro two or three times a year, and uses up to five conditioners at once when she washes it.

●**Most highly insured hair** The iconic locks of American footballer Troy Polamalu (U.S.A.) of the Pittsburgh Steelers (U.S.A.) were insured for $1 million with Lloyd's of London by shampoo brand Head & Shoulders on August 30, 2010.

○**Longest hair extensions** Sarina Russo (Australia) unveiled pink and blonde hair extensions measuring 966 ft. 2 in. (294.49 m) long at the Sydney Convention and Exhibitions Centre in Sydney, Australia, on June 13, 2010.

The world's **oldest surviving banknote** (banco-sedlar) is a five-daler note issued in Stockholm, Sweden, on December 6, 1662.

Highest hairstyle A hairdo measuring 8 ft. 8 in. (2.66 m) high was created by hairdressers from KLIPP unser Frisör in Wels, Austria, on June 21, 2009.

HAIRCUTTING

○**Most consecutive cuts in 24 hours (team)** Ten stylists from Pump Salon carried out 618 consecutive haircuts in 24 hours at Rookwood Commons & Pavilion in Cincinnati, Ohio, U.S.A., from September 24 to 25, 2010.

○**Most consecutive cuts in 24 hours (individual)** On May 20, 2009, Bharat L. Galoriya (India) cut 465 heads of hair in 24 hours at an event organized by Sunil Surani in Rajkot, India.

●**Most consecutive cuts in 12 hours (team)** Sport Clips Haircuts (U.S.A.) performed 329 consecutive haircuts in 12 hours in Nottingham, Maryland, U.S.A., on July 22, 2010.

○**HAIRIEST FAMILY**
Jesus Manuel Fajardo Aceves and Luisa Lilia De Lira Aceves (both Mexico) come from a family with the rare condition of Congenital Generalized Hypertrichosis, giving rise to excessive facial and torso hair. They are seen here with the ●hairiest car, a Fiat 500 owned by Maria Lucia Mugno (Italy), which is covered with 220 lb. (100 kg) of human hair.

The **smallest national bill ever issued** was the 10-bani note of the Ministry of Finance of Romania, which entered circulation in 1917. Its printed area measured 1.08 x 1.49 in. (27.5 x 38 mm).

○ **LONGEST BEARD ON A LIVING PERSON (MALE)** Sarwan Singh (Canada) has a world-beating beard that measured 7 ft. 9 in. (2.37 m) on the set of *Lo Show dei Record* in Rome, Italy, on March 4, 2010.

○**Fastest haircut** Ivan Zoot (U.S.A.) cut a full head of hair in 55 seconds at the Men's Grooming Center in Austin, Texas, U.S.A., on August 22, 2008. Those not in a rush could try the **most expensive haircut**—one customer paid Stuart Phillips (UK) £8,000 ($16,420) for a cut at his London, UK, salon on October 29, 2007.

●**Most people cutting hair** On November 9, 2010, 1,155 stylists cut hair at an event organized by United Dansk in Yokohama, Japan.

SKILLS & TALENTS

CONTENTS

BREAKING RECORDS WITH 3RUN On September 8, 2010, GWR spent a day record breaking with 3RUN—the UK-based freerunning team. As well as setting individual records (see below), a 3RUN team comprising Cane and Cole Armitage, Adam Brashaw, Scott Fidgett, Sam Parham, and James Stokes (all UK) completed the ●**most backflips off a wall in one minute**, with 55.

CHASE ARMITAGE UK, b. 08/02/85
●**Farthest backflip off a wall**
11 ft. 5 in. (3.48 m)
May 24, 2010

CANE ARMITAGE UK, b. 02/20/91
●**Longest standing jump between two objects**
9 ft. 4 in. (2.85 m)
September 8, 2010

> "It's about utilizing your environment as an obstacle course—tackling any objects that come in your way, both physical and psychological."
> **Sam Parham**

URBAN ACROBATS 3RUN is the UK's leading Parkour and Freerunning team. Parkour and Freerunning is a combination of disciplines and movement art forms in which practitioners adapt and overcome obstacles as they traverse their environment.

SAM PARHAM UK, b. 02/03/87
● **Longest distance vaulted between two objects**
7 ft. 8 in. (2.35 m)
September 8, 2010

MICHAEL WILSON UK, b. 02/02/82
● **Farthest distance wall running**
8 ft. 9 in. (2.69 m)
September 8, 2010

ADAM BRADSHAW UK, b. 10/15/84
● **Longest sideflip**
14 ft. 8 in. (4.48 m)
September 8, 2010

Made by Kwang Hua Industries, the **largest building made from paper** had a base measuring 49 ft. 9 in. x 58 ft. 8 in. (15.2 x 17.9 m) and was 21 ft. (6.4 m) tall. Unveiled in Bangkok, Thailand, in October 2003, it took the form of a traditional Thai house.

COLE ARMITAGE UK,
b. 10/07/87
● **Longest standing jump
from vault to handstand
7 ft. 9 in. (2.37 m)**
September 8, 2010

SCOTT FIDGETT UK, b. 09/17/88
● **Longest running vault-to-
vaulted handstand
7 ft. 3 in. (2.22 m)**
September 8, 2010

The **heaviest building** is the Palace of the Parliament in Bucharest, Romania. It is constructed from 1.5 billion lb. (700,000 metric tons) of steel and bronze, 35.3 million ft.^{2} (1 million m^2) of marble, 7.7 million lb. (3,500 metric tons) of crystal glass, and 31.7 million ft.^{2} (900,000 m^2) of wood.

MOST DANGEROUS

WHO DARES WINS

One of the questions most commonly asked of a GWR adjudicator is "What's the most dangerous record attempt you've ever witnessed?" As revealed here, we do monitor some records that are considered hazardous, even by the well-trained professionals who attempt them. Of course, these record attempts are strictly for professionals who plan carefully and have years of experience.

MOST SIMULTANEOUS FULL-BODY BURNS The greatest number of individuals carrying out full-body burns at one time is 17. The fiery feat was achieved during an event organized by Ted Batchelor and the Ohio Burn Unit (both U.S.A.) in South Russell, Ohio, U.S.A., on September 19, 2009. All participants remained alight for at least 43.9 seconds.

SWORD SWALLOWING There are many dangers associated with swords before you even *think* about sliding them into your throat! For years GWR declined to monitor such feats as world records, but following careful discussion with the sword-swallowing community we reconsidered our position and now accept claims from trained swallowers in conjunction with the Sword Swallowers Association International. Matt Henshaw (Australia, left), for example, has trained for years to achieve the record for the ⭕**most swords swallowed at once: 21.**

READ ME FIRST Before embarking upon any record attempt, please contact us first at www.guinnessworldrecords.com. We need to approve your idea and send you all the rules.

314: Number of visits you'll make to a physician in a lifetime. The average visit is 11.7 minutes—making a total of 61 hours, or 2.5 days. During your life, you will spend the equivalent of a long weekend with your physician.

LONGEST MOTORCYCLE RIDE THROUGH A TUNNEL OF FIRE On January 27, 2008, professional stunt rider Clint Ewing (U.S.A.) sped down a tunnel of fire 200 ft. (60.96 m) long on a motorcycle at Universal City, Los Angeles, U.S.A. The record was being attempted for the NBC TV Special *Guinness World Records Live—The Top 100*.

MOST CHAINSAWS JUGGLED Aaron Gregg (Canada) juggled three chainsaws, catching them 88 times, on the set of *El Show Olímpico* in Mexico City, Mexico, on July 28, 2008.

BANZAI! Heard of Banzai Skydiving? In this most extreme of sports, which originated in Japan, you fly to 10,000 ft. (3,000 m), throw your parachute out of the plane, wait two seconds, then throw yourself out. The aim? Grab that 'chute!

BREAKING BONES Motorcycle daredevil Evel Knievel (U.S.A., born Robert Craig Knievel) doesn't hold any records for his death-defying leaps, but he did set one record: **most bones broken in a lifetime!** Until his retirement in 1975, he endured a record 433 fractures (of the same 35 bones, including all of his ribs), plus 14 open surgeries and a total of 36 months in the hospital.

LOWEST DEATH-DIVE ESCAPE Robert Gallup (Australia) was leg-manacled, handcuffed, chained, tied into a secured mailbag, and then locked in a cage before being thrown from a C-123 plane 18,000 ft. (5,485 m) above the Mojave Desert in California, U.S.A. Less than a minute before impact—and traveling at 150 mi./hr. (240 km/h)—he escaped, deployed his parachute, and landed safely.

See chapter 7 for more folks who thrive on danger.

The **largest animal orchestra** is the 12-piece Thai Elephant Orchestra at the Thai Elephant Conservation Centre, Lampang, Thailand. The percussion- and wind-based orchestra was founded in 2000 to help conserve the Asiatic elephant species.

○MOST BUILDINGS CLIMBED UNASSISTED As of 2011, urban climber Alain "Spiderman" Robert (France) had climbed more than 100 towers, monuments, and skyscrapers without ropes, suction devices, or safety equipment. Amazingly, Alain suffers from vertigo.

IN A MINUTE

●**Most handcuffs unlocked** Merlin Cadogan (UK) unlocked six separate sets of handcuffs in a minute before a live studio audience on the set of ITV's *Magic Numbers* TV show in London, UK, on August 28, 2010.

●**Most gloves worn on one hand** On November 12, 2009, Alastair Galpin (NZ) pulled 10 gloves on to one hand in a minute at the Britomart Transport Centre, Auckland, New Zealand.

●**Most jokes told** The greatest number of jokes told in one minute is 17 and was achieved by Ted Robbins (UK) from BBC Radio Lancashire and Ben Day (UK) from Touch FM radio station on November 18, 2010, in celebration of Guinness World Records Day.

MOST JUICE TRODDEN FROM GRAPES Martina Servaty (Germany) extracted an impressive 1.19 gallons (5.4 liters) of juice from grapes in one minute by treading on them in Mesenich, Germany, on November 9, 2008. The feat took place in celebration of Guinness World Records Day.

The **smallest elephant** is the Borneo pygmy, which grows to 5 ft. 6 in.–8 ft. 6 in. (1.7–2.6 m) tall. It lives in the Malaysian states of Borneo.

●**MOST BALLOONS POPPED USING A POGO STICK** The most balloons popped using a pogo stick in one minute is 57 and was achieved by Mark Aldridge (UK) on the set of *Lo Show dei Record* in Rome, Italy, on April 1, 2010. Mark burst the balloons at a rate of nearly one per second.

○**Most champagne bottles sabered** On February 14, 2010, Andrew Duminy (South Africa) sabered 27 champagne bottles in one minute at the Bull Run Restaurant, Sandton, South Africa. The practice of using a saber to open a champagne bottle became popular during the reign of Napoleon Bonaparte.

●**Most coins balanced on the face** The most coins balanced on the face is 27. Marica Rosengård (Finland) achieved the feat in Stockholm, Sweden, on November 20, 2010.

●**Fewest pogo-stick jumps** A record sanctioned by the international governing body Pogopalooza, this feat requires that the participant not stall and not step off the stick at any time. As such, height per jump is optimal in achieving the best results. The fewest pogo-stick jumps in one minute is 39 by Biff Hutchison (U.S.A.) at Redstone Center in Park City, Utah, U.S.A., on August 20, 2010.

The first pogo sticks, patented in 1919, were made of wood.

> **DID YOU KNOW?** In a minute: the Earth rotates 17.3 miles (28 km) and is struck by lightning 6,000 times; light travels 11,176,943.82 miles (17,987,547.48 km); our hairs grow 0.00027 in. (0.00068 cm).

● **Most martial arts throws** Karipidis Konstantinos (Greece) carried out 51 martial arts throws in one minute at the indoor Central Stadium in Alexandroupolis, Greece, on June 26, 2010.

○ **Most custard pies thrown by a pair** Ashrita Furman received 56 custard pies in the face from Bipin Larkin (both U.S.A.) at the Sri Chinmoy Center in New York City, U.S.A., on April 7, 2010. Although 59 pies hit Ashrita, only 56 were full in the face as required.

● **Most beermats flipped and caught** David Cowling-Cass (UK) flipped and caught a total of 70 beermats in a minute at the World Trade Centre, Barcelona, Spain, on May 14, 2010.

● **Most soccer passes by a pair** On May 4, 2010, Shunsuke and Ryosuke Kaketani (both Japan) executed 79 soccer passes between them in a minute at Park Challenge/GWR Live! in Tokyo Midtown, Tokyo, Japan.

○ **Most kisses given** As part of World Aids Day, Rohit Timilsina (Nepal) set a new record for the most kisses given in one minute—116—in Kathmandu, Nepal, on December 1, 2009.

Q. WHAT WAS THE FIRST MAN-MADE OBJECT TO BREAK THE SOUND BARRIER?

A. Probably the whip. The "crack" is a mini sonic boom made by the end of the whip when it exceeds the speed of sound.

● **MOST PUSH-UPS ON THE BACKS OF HANDS WITH A 40-LB. PACK** Andre Turan (U.S.A.) carried out 40 push-ups using the back of his hands in one minute, while carrying a 40-lb. (18.2-kg) backpack, at Catskill Mountain Boot Camp in Sullivan County, New York, U.S.A., on November 15, 2008.

● **MOST WATERMELONS CHOPPED ON THE STOMACH** Jim Hunter chopped 25 watermelons on the stomach of Celia Curtis (both Australia) in one minute, using a machete, on the set of *Australia Smashes Guinness World Records* at Seven Network Studios, Sydney, New South Wales, Australia, on August 16, 2005.

MOST LASSO TEXAS SKIPS IN ONE MINUTE The most lasso Texas skips in a minute is 80 by Daniel Ledda (Spain) on the set of *Guinness World Records—El Show de los Records* in Madrid, Spain, on June 11, 2006. A Texas skip involves twirling a lasso in a vertical loop on one side of the body, then jumping sideways back and forth through the loop.

● **Most stairs climbed with books balanced on the head** On October 25, 2009, Ashrita Furman (U.S.A.) climbed 122 stairs while balancing books weighing 7 lb. 11.4 oz. (3.5 kg) on his head at the subway at Lexington Avenue and 63rd Street, New York City, U.S.A.

In a minute, 267 people are born and 108 die.

With a population of more than 22.5 million and a total of 336,000 admissions in 2003, Malaysia had the **lowest movie-theater attendance per capita** with 14.83 visits per 1,000 people (0.01483 visits per person).

○**MOST GRAPES CAUGHT IN THE MOUTH** On September 9, 2010, Ashrita Furman (U.S.A.) caught 85 grapes in his mouth in a minute at the Sri Chinmoy Marathon Team offices, New York City, U.S.A.

○**MOST KICKS TO THE HEAD** Walt Saine (Switzerland) administered 110 kicks to his own head in one minute in Lausanne, Switzerland, on October 30, 2010. Saine used both his left and right legs to kick himself in the forehead an average of 1.8 times per second.

○**Most eggs crushed with the head** Leo Mondello (Italy) crushed 130 eggs with his head in one minute in Patti, Messina, Italy, on April 24, 2010.

●**Most consecutive yo-yo inside loops** On July 6, 2010, Arron Sparks (UK) performed 151 consecutive yo-yo inside loops at Camden Town Hall, London, UK.

○**Most whip cracks with two whips** On August 7, 2010, Adam Winrich (U.S.A.) performed 513 whip cracks, using two whips, in one minute at the Bristol Renaissance Faire in Kenosha, Washington, U.S.A.

○**Most tap-dancing taps** Tony Adams (New Zealand) performed 1,056 tap-dancing taps in one minute live on Television New Zealand's *Good Morning Show* at Avalon TV Studios, Wellington, New Zealand, on June 19, 2009.

IN AN HOUR

○**Most cocktails mixed** Brilliant bartender Matthias Knorr (Germany) mixed 937 cocktails in an hour on the set of the television show *ZDF Fernsehgarten* in Mainz, Germany, on July 25, 2010.

A far bigger number for the big screen is The Panasonic IMAX Theatre at Darling Harbour, Sydney, Australia. Measuring 117 x 97 ft. (35.72 x 29.57 m), it is the **largest IMAX screen in the world**.

○GREATEST DISTANCE CYCLED WITHOUT USING HANDS Perfectly balanced Erik Skramstad (U.S.A.) cycled 23.25 miles (37.41 km) without the use of his hands in Las Vegas, U.S.A., on June 23, 2009.

○**Most pizzas made** Prolific pizzaiolo Brian Edler (U.S.A.) prepared 206 pizzas at the Domino's Pizza store on North Main Street, Findlay, Ohio, U.S.A., on December 9, 2010.

○**Most basketball free throws** Perry Dissmore (U.S.A.) sank a record 1,968 free throws on *Live! with Regis and Kelly* in New York, U.S.A., on September 14, 2010.

●**Most balloons blown up** On June 20, 2010, Brian Jackson (U.S.A.) inflated a lung-busting 335 balloons in an hour at Three Forks Harbor in Muskogee, Oklahoma, U.S.A.

Most legs waxed Susanne Baird (UK) waxed 40 pairs of legs in the name of beauty at Grange Cricket Club in Stockbridge, Edinburgh, Scotland, UK, on April 14, 2008.

○**Most haircuts** On August 22, 2008, Ivan Zoot (U.S.A.), the world's quickest clipper, treated 34 customers to new haircuts at the Men's Grooming Center in Austin, Texas, U.S.A.

●**Most escapes from handcuffs** On his way to a landmark 10,625 handcuff escapes in 24 hours, Zdeněk Bradáč (Czech Republic) set a new record of 627 escapes in an hour at the Liberec Film Club in Liberec, Czech Republic, on February 12, 2010.

○MOST VAULTS On September 5, 2009, the Blue Falcons Gymnastic Display Team leaped into the record books by performing 6,250 vaults at the Meadows Shopping Centre in Chelmsford, UK.

1,500,000: Skin cells you shed each hour. It sounds like an avalanche, but dead skin cells are tiny and very light. In a lifetime, it will amount to about 39 lb. 11 oz. (18 kg)—enough for a small snowman.

GIVE US A LIFT Mark Anglesea is also the proud holder of the record for the **most lifts of an automobile in an hour**, upending the rear end of a 1,785-lb. (810-kg) Mini Metro 580 times on October 3, 1998.

● **GREATEST DISTANCE CARRYING A CAR** In 60 breathless minutes, Mark Anglesea (UK) carried an 837-lb. (380-kg) automobile a record 1,337 ft. (407.7 m) at Herringthorpe Running Track, Rotherham, UK, on October 2, 2010.

● **MOST SANDCASTLES BUILT** On July 12, 2010, the staff, friends, family, and volunteers of Lewis-Manning Hospice (UK) built a miniature sand city on Southbanks Beach in Poole, UK, erecting 539 sandcastles in an hour and breaking the previous record of 520 set in 2007.

If shows of strength are your thing, turn to "tough guys" on p. 178.

●**MOST CUPS OF TEA MADE (12-MAN TEAM)** A team of 12 tea-lovers, led by Alex Loughlin (UK) and *X Factor* singer Olly Murs (UK, pictured here with Channel 4 TV host Miquita Oliver), brewed a record 491 cups of tea in 60 minutes on the set of *T4: Battlefront* at Witham Hall, Essex, UK, on January 17, 2010.

●**Most bungee jumps (cord of 5–10 m)** Using a 19-ft. 8-in. (6-m) bungee cord, James Field (UK) completed 42 bungee jumps in 60 minutes at an event organized by Extreme Element & UK Bungee Club at the London Rat Race (UK) on September 26, 2010.

●**MOST POTS THROWN** Master potter Mark Byles (UK) came out on top in the pot-throwing contest held at the Ceramics South East Potters Market at The Friars, Aylesford, UK, on June 28, 2009. Mark made 150 clay flowerpots in an hour, seeing off the challenge of nearest rival Mary Chapellhow (UK), who managed 118 pots of her own in the allotted time.

> **FLIGHT OF FANCY** An hour was more than enough time for pilot Steve Slade (UK) to perform a record 102 successive takeoffs and landings in his RANS S6 light aircraft at Kemble Airfield, UK, on July 27, 2002.

●**MOST BLUNT-TO-FAKIES** On September 18, 2010, 14-year-old Cohl Orebaugh (U.S.A.) performed a record 794 blunt-to-fakies (ollie blunts) in an hour at Liberty Lake, Washington, U.S.A., exceeding his own prediction of 500. The trick is carried out on a half-pipe and involves riding up and down each side and balancing the board on the lip of the ramp at the end of each run.

○**Greatest distance on a unicycle** Ken Looi (NZ) took an hour to cover 18.63 miles (29.993 km) on his unicycle at Victoria Park Oval, New South Wales, Australia, on August 18, 2009.

○**Greatest distance moonwalking** Krunoslav Budiselic (Croatia) performed a sole-destroying 3.54-mile (5.7-km) moonwalk in Zagreb, Croatia, on October 12, 2009.

●**Greatest distance pushing a mini scooter** Harald Hel (Austria) pushed a scooter 16.57 miles (26.66 km) in Vienna, Austria, on September 30, 2007.

○**Greatest distance static cycling** Literally going nowhere fast, Miguel Angel Castro (Spain) cycled 57.54 miles (92.6 km) at a sports center in Tenerife, Spain, on March 20, 2010.

PLANET DANCE

○**Most ballet dancers *en pointe*** On August 2, 2010, in an event organized by Ellen and Gene Schiavone (both U.S.A.), 230 ballet dancers stood *en pointe* (i.e., on the tips of their toes) in Central Park, New York City, U.S.A.

The invention of the windmill is credited to "Crazy Legs" of New York group the Rock Steady Crew.

○**MOST WINDMILLS IN 30 SECONDS** Mauro Peruzzi (Italy), also known as Cico, performed a total of 50 windmills in a break-dancing style in 30 seconds at the world finals of the Sony Ericsson UK B-Boy Championships in London, UK, on October 10, 2010.

Staying with the ballet, the ●most *grandes pirouettes à la seconde* **in 30 seconds by a woman** is 50 and was achieved by Alicia Clifton (U.S.A.) on the set of *Zheng Da Zong Yi—Guinness World Records Special* in Beijing, China, on December 19, 2010.

The ○**largest ballet class** involved 1,055 dancers in an event staged by Staatsoper Hannover (Germany) in Hanover, Germany, on June 13, 2010.

●**Most dance partners in 24 hours** On November 23–24, 2007, Michael Hull (Germany) danced with 1,068 partners in Osnabrück, Germany.

○**Most spins in a minute by a couple** Marina Femia (Italy) and Alexander Caicedo Sastoque (Colombia) made 195 dance spins in a minute for *Lo Show dei Record* in Rome, Italy, on March 27, 2010.

The Kalgoorlie Australian federal parliamentary constituency in Western Australia covers more than 1 million miles² (2.6 million km²)—an area greater than Western Europe—and is the world's **largest political constituency**.

137: Pairs of shoes that will get you through a lifetime of walking, running, and dancing. That's a new pair every six months. If each shopping trip takes one-and-a-half hours, that's eight-and-a-half days of your life spent buying footwear.

●LARGEST UMBRELLA DANCE On August 5, 2010, 322 dancers performed an umbrella dance in an event staged by Achariya World Class Educational Institutions (India) in Puducherry, India.

●LARGEST BHANGRA On November 11, 2010, 2,100 participants from the Art of Living Foundation (UK) danced a bhangra at the Punjab Agricultural University Campus, Ludhiana, India, in traditional bhangra costumes.

DANCE GAMING

●First full-body-motion dance game Released on September 25, 2007, for the Nintendo Wii, *Dance Dance Revolution Hottest Party* (Konami, 2007) was the first dance game to track players' upper and lower body movements.

Considered the world's **●largest democracy**, India holds the record for the **Omost votes cast in a national election**, with 59.7% of the population turning out to cast 417.2 million votes in five phases between April 16 and May 13, 2009.

She's now best known for her break-dancing skills, but B-Girl Roxy used to be a trampolinist.

●**MOST VIRGIN AIR FLARES IN A MINUTE** B-Boy Junior (France) made **39 break-dance virgin air flares in a minute at the world finals of the Sony Ericsson UK B-Boy Championships on October 10, 2010. At the same event, B-Girl Roxy (UK), aka Roxanna Milliner, performed the most consecutive headspins by a woman—25.**

●**Longest-running dance mat game series** A total of 11 years and 227 days elapsed between the release of *Dance Dance Revolution* (Konami, 1998) and the most recent game in the hit series, *Dance Dance Revolution X2* (Konami, 2010), which was released on July 7, 2010.

○**Largest dance mat routine** On July 2, 2010, a group of 120 dancers performed a dance mat routine together at an event staged by West Sussex West School Sport Partnership and Cyber Coach (both UK) at the Arena Sports Centre in Bognor Regis, UK. They danced to the "Disco Disco" game on the Webskape platform.

●**Longest marathon on a dance game** On October 23, 2010, Chris McGivern (UK) played *Dance Dance Revolution* for 13 hr. 33 min. 56 sec. at Funland in London, UK.

The **cheapest production automobile** is India's Tata Nano, a four-door, five-seater family automobile with a top speed of 43 mi./hr. (70 km/h). It went on sale in March 2009 for Rs 100,000 ($2,500).

> **DANCE ON! AND ON . . .** Fred Salter (UK, b. February 13, 1911) is the ○**oldest competitive ballroom dancer**. He passed his gold bar exams aged 99 years 3 months and 2 days on May 15, 2010.

LARGEST DANCES

●**Cancan** On September 13, 2009, 1,503 dancers did the cancan at Glasgow Green, Glasgow, UK, at an event organized by IRN-BRU.

○**Clog** A group of 2,605 people danced with clogs at an event staged by the Pella Historical Society (U.S.A.) in Pella, Iowa, U.S.A., on May 8, 2010.

●**Fandango** On November 30, 2009, a total of 1,146 people danced a fandango—originally an Andalusian folk dance—in an event organized by FUNDEV (Colombia) in Cereté, Cordoba, Colombia.

○**Hokey cokey** On September 3, 2010, 7,384 participants performed the hokey cokey at an event organized by FRY Fest (U.S.A.) at FRY Fest in Coralville, Iowa, U.S.A.

○**Macarena** On November 12, 2010, in celebration of Guinness World Records Day 2010, 1,861 people danced the Macarena in an event staged by Ancaster High School in Ancaster, Ontario, Canada. The dance was inspired by the 1995 Los del Rio hit "Macarena."

●**LARGEST TUCA TUCA DANCE** A group of 494 participants danced the Tuca Tuca at an event organized by (and staged in) the city of Bellaria Igea Marina, Italy, on August 7, 2010.

Nine people from Espoon Ammattioppilaitos (a Finnish technical school) took apart a five-door family saloon automobile in 35 minutes on November 28, 2001—the **fastest time to dismantle an automobile**.

If you're mad for music, jump to p. 404.

●LARGEST BAMBOO DANCE The government of Mizoram, in Aizawl, Mizoram, India, organized the largest bamboo dance (or Cheraw) on March 12, 2010. The event featured 10,736 dancers.

●Polonaise On September 12, 2010, at an event staged by the Polish Tourist Organization, 300 participants danced the polonaise in London, UK.

●Swing On July 11, 2009, a group of 291 people danced to swing music at an event organized by Øystein Ulen (Norway) and Dansefestivalen at Dansefestivalen, Norway. Swing, a type of jazz, emerged in the 1920s. The best-known style of swing dance is the energetic Lindy Hop.

○Tea dance A total of 306 couples took part in a tea dance in Glasgow, Scotland, UK, on September 12, 2010. To qualify as a tea dance, tea, cakes, and sandwiches must be served, and the music must be live; in this attempt, the Swing Sensation Big Band supplied the tunes.

○LONGEST DANCE BY AN INDIVIDUAL Kalamandalam Hemaletha (India) danced the traditional Indian Mohiniyattam for 123 hr. 15 min., from September 20 to 26, 2010, at the Kerala Sangeetha Nadaka Academy in Thrissur, Kerala, India.

● **LOWEST LIMBO (FEMALE)** Shemika Charles (U.S.A.) passed under a bar set at just 8.5 in. (21.59 cm) off the floor on the set of *Live! with Regis and Kelly* in New York City, U.S.A., on September 16, 2010.

INCREDIBLE CLOTHING

○ **Best-selling fashion brand** Nike had sales of $19 billion in the fiscal year ending May 31, 2010.

○ **Best-selling designer label** Designer clothing brand Ralph Lauren announced an annual revenue of over $4.9 billion as of April 3, 2010.

○ **Largest fashion franchise** The Benetton Group is present in more than 120 countries via 6,000 franchised stores and company-owned megastores. The group sells around 150 million garments annually, most under the casual "United Colors of Benetton" brand.

Most valuable tiara Decorated with 100-carat diamonds and set in yellow gold, a tiara designed by Gianni Versace (Italy) had an estimated retail value of $5 million.

○ **LARGEST T-SHIRT** The Qatar PetroChemical Company (QAPCO) unveiled a T-shirt 236 ft. 10.5 in. (72.2 m) long and 159 ft. 9 in. (48.7 m) wide at ASPIRE Park, Doha, Qatar, on November 23, 2010.

MODELS AND SHOWS

●**Most British *Vogue* covers** Kate Moss (UK) has appeared on the cover of British *Vogue* magazine 30 times. Her first cover was in March 1993 and her latest to date was for the September 2010 issue.

○**Oldest fashion model** Professional model Daphne Selfe (UK) celebrated her 82nd birthday in July 2010. Her career spans more than 60 years.

○**LONGEST LINE OF SOCKS** A line of socks measuring 7,624 ft. 11 in. (2,324.08 m) was created by the Erlebnispark Tripsdrill (Germany) in Cleebronn, Germany, on May 23, 2010.

○**LARGEST SHOE** The Nationaal Fonds Kinderhulp (Netherlands) unveiled a titanic shoe measuring 18 ft. (5.5 m) x 6 ft. 11 in. (2.11 m), and with a height of 9 ft. 6 in. (2.9 m), in Amsterdam, the Netherlands, on November 17, 2010, in celebration of Guinness World Records Day 2010. The shoe is an exact replica of a Converse Chuck Taylor All Star and is the equivalent of a U.S. size 846!

$56,825: Your total spending on clothes. A lifetime's supply of boiler suits and sensible shoes would cost $5,178. The extra $51,647 is the price you pay for a lifetime of fashion!

DESIGN OF THE TIMES Charles Frederick Worth, who died in 1895, was the first designer to sign his work with a label and show clothes on live models, thereby creating the **first designer label**.

○**MOST T-SHIRTS WORN AT ONCE** Krunoslav Budiselić (Croatia) successfully struggled into a phenomenal 245 T-shirts in Utrine, Zagreb, Croatia, on May 22, 2010. T-shirts ranging from size M to size 10XL were used for the attempt.

●**Most models on a runway** A total of 521 models paraded from end to end of a 492-ft.-long (150-m) runway at Galeries Lafayette in Paris, France, on September 30, 2010.

○**Highest annual earnings for a model** Gisele Bündchen (Brazil) earned $25 million in 2010, placing her at the top of the list of highest-paid supermodels. She has worked for famous brands such as Ralph Lauren, Dolce & Gabbana, and Versace.

●LARGEST LEDERHOSEN
The world's largest lederhosen measure 16 ft. 4 in. (5 m) tall and 12 ft. 3 in. (3.75 m) wide. They were created by Walter Sinnhofer (Austria) in Henndorf am Wallersee, Austria, on August 5, 2010. A total of 828.82 ft.² (77 m²) of cow suede was used to create the huge pants, which weigh 101 lb. 6.5 oz. (46 kg).

Heaviest model American model Teighlor (b. Debra Perkins) weighed 718 lb. 11 oz. (326.14 kg) in the early 1990s. She forged a successful career, appearing on greeting cards and in movies and advertisements.

Highest ever annual earnings for a fashion designer Giorgio Armani (Italy) earned $135 million in 1999, according to *Forbes* magazine.

The first lederhosen were made in the 6th century A.D.

"The Old Gentleman of Raahe," at the Museum of Raahe in Finland, is the ●**oldest surviving diving suit.** It was made from stitched calfskin and dates from the 18th century.

FASHION ITEMS

○**Most expensive bra** The Heavenly Star Bra, by U.S. lingerie retailer Victoria's Secret, was made in 2001 and has a $12.5-million price tag. It features 1,200 Sri Lankan pink sapphires and a 90-carat emerald-cut diamond worth $10.6 million.

○**Largest dirndl** The dirndl is a traditional Alpine peasant dress, the largest of which is 16 ft. (4.9 m) long and 12 ft. 4 in. (3.8 m) wide. It was presented by GDL-Handels-und Dienstleistungs GmbH in Bad Ischl, Austria, on July 17, 2010.

●**Largest knitted hat** The largest knitted hat measures 22 ft. 7 in. (6.9 m) high and 49 ft. 4 in. (15.05 m) in circumference. It was assembled by volunteers and presented in Puchheim, Germany, on October 5, 2008.

●**Largest straw hat** Created by Atalia Bis & Partners Company in Kozieglowy, Poland, the largest straw hat is 21 ft. 9 in. (6.65 m) in diameter and 8 ft. 6 in. (2.6 m) high. It was measured in August 2006.

●**Smallest tailored evening suit** Designed by John Richmond (UK), the smallest tailored evening suit comprised a jacket 8 in. (21 cm) long and trousers 1 ft. 6 in. (46 cm) in length. He Pingping (China)—then the world's **shortest man**—wore it on *Lo Show dei Record* on April 26, 2009.

●**LARGEST TURBAN** Major Singh (India), a Nihang Sikh, wears a turban made from 1,312 ft. (400 m) of cloth and featuring more than 100 hairpins and 51 religious symbols made out of metal. This style of round turban is known as a "dumaala" and is common to Nihang Sikhs.

The world's **deepest scuba-dive** was achieved by Nuno Gomes of South Africa. He dived to a depth of 1,044 ft. (318.25 m) in the Red Sea off Dahab, Egypt, on June 10, 2005.

MASS PARTICIPATION

●**Largest cycling race** Other sports-related mass gatherings include the Cape Argus Pick 'n Pay Cycle Tour, a grueling 68-mile (109-km) bike race in Cape Town, South Africa, that drew 42,614 entrants in 2004, including the five-times Tour de France winner Miguel Indurain (Spain).

●MOST PEOPLE WEARING RED NOSES On June 5, 2010, 15,956 people sported red noses at the Mega Pic-Nic 2010, arranged by Realizar Eventos Especiais and Modelo in Lisbon, Portugal.

○LARGEST SIMULTANEOUS BASKETBALL BOUNCE On July 22, 2010, a total of 7,556 people bounced basketballs in the air at the same time during an event organized by the United Nations Relief and Works Agency (UNRWA) in Rafah, Gaza Strip, Palestine.

UP IN THE AIR Talking of balls in the air, 1,062 students and footy fans played "keepy uppy" together in Yangi City, China, on July 10, 2010, breaking the record for the ○**most people keeping a soccer ball in the air.**

○**MOST NAKED RIDERS ON A THEME PARK RIDE The greatest number of people to bare all on a theme park ride is 102, a record set by enthusiastic members of the public on the *Green Scream* roller-coaster at Adventure Island, Southend-on-Sea, Essex, UK, on August 8, 2010.**

●**Largest game of dodgeball** On February 4, 2011, a record 2,012 competitors played the largest ever game of dodgeball, a sport made famous by the 2004 film of the same name. The game was organized by the University of Alberta at the Universiade Pavilion (Butterdome), in Edmonton, Alberta, Canada.

○**Longest human centipede** Staged by the Thai Beverage Marketing Co. and Have a Good Dream Co., a human centipede of 2,961 people linked up at Ratchaburi, Thailand, on June 16, 2010.

○**Longest human domino line** Sat in a line, 10,267 "human dominoes" formed a 4.5-mile (7.2-km) chain in Ordos City, China, on August 12, 2010.

Green Scream had to run three times to allow everyone to take part!

159,635: Number of people who will die on the same day as you. It might be more cheering to think of the 18,562,289 people around the world who share your birthday.

● **MOST ENTRIES IN A TWO-PERSON PANTOMIME ANIMAL RACE** In a contest organized by RSA, Have a Heart, and Action on Addiction, 37 two-man teams dressed as pantomime animals and raced one another at Goodwood Racecourse, UK, on June 24, 2010.

● **LARGEST GATHERING OF PEOPLE DRESSED AS SUMO WRESTLERS** On June 19, 2010, 205 people donned inflatable sumo suits to take part in the 3-mile (5-km) Sumo Run, a fancy-dress fun run organized annually by Gemin-i.org at Battersea Park in London, UK.

○ **MOST PEOPLE DRESSED AS SUPERHEROES** To promote the Dreamworks movie *Megamind*, 1,580 people donned superhero costumes in Los Angeles, U.S.A., on October 2, 2010, in an event staged by Paramount Studios (U.S.A.).

○ **MOST PEOPLE JUMPING ROPE** On February 1, 2010, 70,880 people from 294 schools jumped rope at an event staged by California Association for Health, Physical Education, Recreation & Dance (CAHPERD) and Jamba Juice in California, U.S.A.

DRESS TO EXCESS

In the bustling world of mass participation, there's nothing like a good costume for bringing people together in their hundreds and thousands! Check out this year's eclectic mix of fancy-dress get-togethers from all over the globe.

Category	People	Organizer	Location	Event date
○ Pirates	6,166	Roger Crouch (UK)	Hastings, East Sussex, UK	Aug. 6, 2010
● Peter Pan	5,206	Great Ormond Street Hospital Children's Charity (UK)	Schools across the UK	Apr. 30, 2010
● Wearing singlets	3,500	Deniliquin Ute Muster (Australia)	Deniliquin, NSW, Australia	Oct. 2, 2010
○ Gorillas	1,061	Mountain Gorilla Conservation Fund (U.S.A.)	Denver, Colorado, U.S.A.	Oct. 31, 2009
● Angels	1,039	Hauzenberg aktiv (Germany)	Hauzenberg, Lower Bavaria, Germany	Dec. 13, 2009
● *Flintstones* characters	905	Muckno Mania Festival (Ireland)	Co. Monaghan, Ireland	Jul. 16, 2010
● Wearing bobble hats	764	St Anne's Primary School (UK)	Belfast, Northern Ireland, UK	Nov. 18, 2010
○ Elvis	645	Nike Western Europe (U.S.A.)	Aria Hotel, Las Vegas, Nevada, U.S.A.	Nov. 23, 2010
○ *Star Trek* characters	543	Creation Entertainment (U.S.A.)	Hilton Hotel, Las Vegas, Nevada, U.S.A.	Aug. 7, 2010
● Regency costume	409	Jane Austen Festival (UK)	Bath, Somerset, UK	Sep. 19, 2009
○ Storybook characters	359	Higham Ferrers Junior School (UK)	Rushden, Northants., UK	Nov. 18, 2010
● Vampires	354	Loveland Road Runners (U.S.A.)	Loveland, Colorado, U.S.A.	Oct. 17, 2009
○ Superman	288	Cuchulainn Gaels (Ireland)	Omeath, County Louth, Ireland	Aug. 21, 2010
● Gandhi	255	AVB Matriculation Higher Secondary School (India)	Coimbatore, India	Jun. 13, 2010

●**LARGEST HUMAN CROSS** A group of 935 red-robed people formed a human cross under the guidance of the Oslo Red Cross (Norway) at the Oslo Opera House in Oslo, Norway, on May 7, 2010.

●**Largest human smiley** On September 22, 2010, 551 people formed a smiley face in a stunt orchestrated by Igors Puntuss (Latvia) in Riga, Latvia.

TOUGH GUYS

○**Most push-ups in 24 hours** On April 24–25, 1993, Charles Servizio (U.S.A.) completed 46,001 push-ups in 24 hours at Fontana City Hall in Fontana, California, U.S.A.

○**Most consecutive martial arts bouts** Paddy Doyle (UK) carried out 141 consecutive martial arts bouts at St. Benedict's School Sports Centre, Cheltenham, UK, on November 19, 2005.

●**LONGEST DURATION HOLDING WEIGHT WITH OUTSTRETCHED ARMS** On March 4, 2010, Tomi Lotta (Finland) held a weight (minimum 44 lb.; 20 kg) suspended with outstretched arms for 1 min. 16.63 sec. on the set of *Lo Show dei Record* in Rome, Italy.

 The Salt River Morgue in Cape Town, South Africa, handled more than 30,000 cadavers in 1998, making it the **busiest morgue**. Almost 4,000 of these bodies had untraceable identities and were likely to have been the victims of violent crime.

**A MINUTE MAY NOT SOUND LIKE A VERY LONG TIME,
BUT IT'S ENOUGH TO . . .**

- ● Smash 11 pumpkins (Ben Shephard, UK)

- ● Smash 88 alarm clocks using only your feet (Jay Wheddon, UK)

- ● Break 55 baseball bats or ○ 111 coconuts using only your hands
(both Muhamed Kahrimanovic, Germany)

- ○ Smash 40 watermelons with your head (John Allwood, Australia)

- ○ Perform 805 full-contact punch strikes (Robert Ardito, Australia)

- ● Deadlift 3,864 lb. (1,752.68 kg) (Thienna Ho, Vietnam)

○ MOST WATERMELONS SMASHED WITH A PUNCH IN ONE MINUTE
Davide Cenciarelli (Italy) smashed 70 watermelons with his fist in one minute
for *Lo Show dei Record* in Rome, Italy, on March 18, 2010.
   The ● fastest time to crush 10 watermelons with the head is 16
seconds, by Leonardo D'Andrea (Italy) on the set of *Zheng Da Zong Yi—
Guinness World Records Special* in Beijing, China, on December 17, 2006.

 An estimated 10.2 million people filled the 20-mile (32-km) route
to Tehran's Behesht-e Zahra cemetery, Iran, for the funeral of
Ayatollah Ruhollah Khomeini, the Iranian religious leader, on
June 11, 1989, making it the world's **largest funeral**.

296: Gallons of blood you'll lose in a lifetime, along with 557 gallons of sweat and 16 gallons of tears—enough blood for 10 baths, enough sweat for a five-hour shower, and enough tears to wash eight tracksuits!

THAT'S TORN IT! The ●**most telephone directories torn behind the back in three minutes** is six, by Alexander Muromskiy (Russia) on October 17, 2009, at the Moscow Center of Martial Arts, Russia.

●**MOST AUTOMOBILE WINDOWS SMASHED** Kevin Taylor (U.S.A.) smashed 20 automobile door windows using only his fists on the set of *Lo Show dei Record* in Rome, Italy, on February 25, 2010. The task took him just 1 min. 35 sec..

RUN FOR IT! Cristina Borra (Italy) ran a lung-bursting 13 marathons from February 16 to 28, 2010, in Turin, Italy—the ○**most marathons run on consecutive days by a woman**.

The Iranian/American businesswoman Anousheh Ansari became the **first female space tourist** on September 18, 2006.

> Chokeslam: grasp opponent's neck and slam him (or her) down

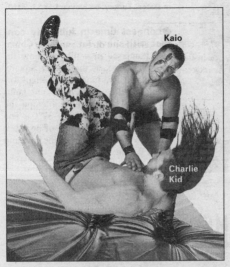

Kaio

Charlie Kid

MOST CHOKESLAMS IN ONE MINUTE Nury Ayachi (aka Kaio), Carlo Lenzoni (aka Charlie Kid), and Mariel Shehi (all Italy) performed 34 chokeslams in one minute on the set of *Lo Show dei Record* in Rome, Italy, on February 25, 2010.

○**Most chin-ups in one hour** On June 2, 2010, Stephen Hyland (UK) performed 968 chin-ups in an hour in Stoneleigh, Surrey, UK.

●**Heaviest house pulled** Kevin Fast (Canada) pulled a 79,145-lb. (35.9-tonne) house for 39 ft. 2.47 in. (11.95 m) in Cobourg, Ontario, Canada, on September 18, 2010.

○**Fastest time to bend an iron bar into a suitcase** Alexander Muromskiy (Russia) bent a 19-ft. 7-in.-long (6-m) iron bar and fitted it into a suitcase in 25 seconds in St. Petersburg, Russia, on November 9, 2008.

○**Longest time to hold one's breath voluntarily (male)** On April 1, 2010, Stig Åvall Severinsen (Denmark) held his breath for 20 min. 10 sec. in the shark tank at Kattegat Centre, Grenaa, Denmark.

Tourists visiting Planet Earth might like to use the world's **first official UFO landing pad**, built in the small Canadian prairie town of St. Paul in Alberta, Canada, and formally opened on June 3, 1967.

○**MOST CONCRETE BLOCKS BROKEN IN ONE MINUTE** Ali Bahçetepe (Turkey) broke 1,145 concrete blocks in one minute at the Taekwondo Sport Centre in Datça, Turkey, on November 17, 2010.

●**Longest time in full-body contact with snow** Jin Songhao (China) was immersed in a pile of snow for 46 min. 7 sec. at the Center Square, A'ershan City, Inner Mongolian Autonomous Region, China, on January 17, 2011. During the attempt, the temperature was -34.6°F (-37°C). The snow pile had a diameter of approximately 5 ft. 6 in. (1.7 m) at the base and was 2 ft. 3 in. (0.7 m) tall.

IN THE HOME

THE MOST FUN YOU CAN HAVE WITH A PAIR OF UNDERPANTS—OR TWO . . .

○**Most underpants worn at once:** 231, by Taro Yabe (Japan) on August 29, 2010.

○**Most underpants pulled on in a minute:** 22, by Sheena Reyes (Australia) on March 27, 2010.

●**Most underpants jumped into in an hour:** 234, by Kevin Velaiden (UK) on March 27, 2009.

●**Most underpants somersaulted into in 90 seconds:** 94, by Team Spektaculer (Germany), a troupe of 12 gymnasts, on January 20, 2000.

Trever McGhee (Canada) completed the **longest firewalk** when he hotfooted it 597 ft. (181.9 m) over embers with a temperature of up to 1,307°F (853.33°C) at Symons Valley Rodeo Grounds in Calgary, Canada, on November 9, 2007.

THE CRYING GAME Bob Blumer (Canada) fought back the tears to peel 31 onions in 2 min. 39 sec. on July 18, 2010, slicing his way to the record for the ●**fastest time to peel 50 lb. (22 kg) of onions**.

○**MOST SOCKS SORTED IN ONE MINUTE Super-quick** sock-sorter John Harrold (UK) managed to ball a world record 34 socks into 17 pairs in the space of a minute. John claimed his new sock-sorting record at a GWR Live! event held at the World Trade Centre in Barcelona, Spain, on May 14, 2010.

○**Fastest time to place six eggs in egg cups using one's feet** On February 16, 2008, nimble-toed Tatiana Dudzan (Ukraine) slotted half a dozen eggs into egg cups using only her feet in a time of 42.60 seconds on the set of *Lo Show dei Record*, in Madrid, Spain.

●**Fastest time to balance a dozen eggs** Prolific record breaker Ashrita Furman (U.S.A.) turned his talents to eggs on September 22, 2009, when he balanced 12 of them upright on a table in a record 1 min. 36 sec. in the kitchen of the Sri Chinmoy Centre, Jamaica, New York, U.S.A.

●**Fastest time to butter 10 slices of bread** Hungry New Zealander Alastair Galpin buttered 10 slices of bread in a swift 52.42 seconds in Pt. Chevalier, Auckland, New Zealand, on December 3, 2009.

Fastest time to boil water with electricity conducted through the body With electricity passing through his body, Slavisa Pajkic "Biba" (Yugoslavia) heated a 0.5-fl.-oz. (15-ml) cup of water from 77°F to 206°F (25°C to 97°C) in 1 min. 37 sec. on the set of *Guinness Rekord TV*, Stockholm, Sweden, on November 24, 2001.

The **largest bonfire** was built by ŠKD mladi Boštanj, and lit on April 30, 2007, in Boštanj, Slovenia. The enormous fire had an overall volume of 60,589 ft.³ (1,715.7 m³).

○**LONGEST IRONING MARATHON** In return for a small charity donation, Daniel Peetz (Germany) ironed the clothes of strangers nonstop for a record 58 hours exactly in Rheinberg, Germany, on June 17–19, 2010.

3.5: Washing machines you will own in a lifetime. You will spend 11 minutes a day on laundry, which equates to 219 days of your life—the same as an average person in 1900, when people wore fewer clothes and washed them less often.

● **MOST ITEMS WASHED UP IN EIGHT HOURS** On January 10, 2011, the soap suds flew as Louise Dooey (UK) donned her rubber gloves and embarked on an eight-hour washing-up marathon that left an incredible 2,250 plates, bowls, pans, and cutlery items sparkling! Louise achieved the feat at the Guinness World Records head office in London, UK.

● **Fastest time laying carpet** On August 7, 2008, on the set of ITV's *60 Minute Makeover* (UK), Stephen Dineley (UK) took a record 6 min. 20.18 sec. to lay a carpet measuring 129.2 ft.^{2} (12 m^2).

Fastest time to make a bed (team) Since November 26, 1993, nobody has managed to beat the bed-making masterclass performed by Charge Nurse Sharon Stringer and Nurse Michelle Benkel of the Royal Masonic Hospital, London, UK. The duo dressed a bed with a blanket, two sheets, an undersheet, an uncased pillow, a pillowcase, and a bedspread in just 14 seconds—and still had time for the hospital corners!

DO TRY THIS AT HOME! Damiano Falcioni (Italy) holds the record for the ○**longest time to spin a fry pan on one finger**, notching up 17 min. 47 sec. with his dynamic digit on March 24, 2010.

○ **FASTEST WINDOW CLEANER** Terry Burrows (UK) took just 9.14 seconds to clean three standard office windows (45 x 45 in.; 114.3 x 114.3 cm) with an 11.75-in. (300-mm) squeegee and 2 gal (9 liters) of water at the National Window Cleaning Competition held in Blackpool, UK, on October 9, 2009.

Fastest time to burst three hot-water bottles Brian Jackson (U.S.A.) blew up three standard hot-water bottles to bursting point in a record- and lung-busting 1 min. 8 sec. on the set of *Lo Show dei Record*, in Milan, Italy, on April 19, 2009.

○ **Most socks worn on one foot** On November 13, 2010, Croatian Krunoslav Budiselic adorned his right foot with a record-breaking 150 socks at City Centar One in Zagreb, Croatia. Budiselic used socks provided by local supplier Jadran Hosiery and needed 45 minutes to pull them all on to his foot.

○ **Most clothes retrieved from a washing line by a dog** On November 29, 2009, Gustl, a terrier cross owned by Heidi Deml (Germany), fetched 13 laundry items from a washing line in a minute at the Vienna Congress Centre, Vienna, Austria. The clever canine can perform more than 50 commands.

● **Most eggs cracked in one hour** Proving that you can't make an omelette without cracking some eggs, Canadian Bob Blumer broke open 2,069 eggs one-handed in an hour at the Festival de l'Omelette Géante in Granby, Québec, Canada, on June 24, 2010.

● **Most orange juice extracted in a minute** Ulaş Baş (Turkey) squeezed into the record books by extracting 0.19 gal. (880 ml) of juice from oranges at the GWR Live! Roadshow at Forum Mersin, in Mersin, Turkey, on June 20, 2010.

OUT OF THE ORDINARY

MOST . . .

●**Tops spun at the same time** Steve Faulkner (UK) spun 22 tops simultaneously at the Substance offices in London, UK, on November 30, 2010.

○**Golf balls held in one hand** Guillaume Doyon (Canada) held 24 golf balls in one hand for 10 seconds at Collège Saint-Alexandre in Gatineau, Quebec, Canada, on November 30, 2009. This record was equaled by Rohit Timilsina (Nepal) in Dharmasthali, Kathmandu, Nepal, on May 15, 2010.

●**Leapfrog jumps in 30 seconds by a pair** Haruka Nakano and Asuka Ogawa (both Japan) performed 25 leapfrog jumps in 30 seconds at Park Challenge GWR Live! in Tokyo Midtown, Tokyo, Japan, on May 5, 2010.

●**Mousetraps released on the tongue in one minute** Joshuah Hoover, aka "Sweet Pepper Klopek" (Canada), became a record breaker by releasing 40 mousetraps on his tongue in one minute on the set of *Lo Show dei Record* in Milan, Italy, on April 14, 2011.

●**FASTEST MILE BALANCING A SOCCER BALL ON THE HEAD** Yee Ming Low (Malaysia) completed a mile in 8 min. 35 sec, while balancing a soccer ball on his head, at MPSJ Athletics Stadium in Selangor, Malaysia, on March 20, 2010.

COOL HEADED The ●**longest journey with a refrigerator** covered 1,025.26 miles (1,650 km) and was achieved by comedian Tony Hawks (UK), who hitchhiked across Ireland between May 6 and 30, 1997.

FASTEST 100 M HURDLES WEARING FLIPPERS Christopher Irmscher (Germany) completed the 100 m hurdles wearing flippers in 14.82 seconds on the set of *Guinness World Records: Die Größten Weltrekorde* in Cologne, Germany, on September 13, 2008.

Veronica Torr (New Zealand) achieved the same feat in 18.523 seconds for *Zheng Da Zong Yi—Guinness World Records Special* in Beijing, China, on December 8, 2010, the ○fastest 100 m hurdles wearing flippers by a woman.

●**MOST TIMES TO PASS THROUGH A TENNIS RACKET IN THREE MINUTES** Skye Broberg (Australia) passed her body through a tennis racket seven times in three minutes on the set of *Lo Show dei Record* in Rome, Italy, on February 25, 2010. Skye honed her serpentine skills as a circus act and street theater artist: as well as contortion, her acts include performing with the hula hoop, aerial hoop, and neck hoop. One of her trademark specialities involves cramming her entire body into a small glass box!

Vrtoglavica (meaning "vertigo") is an unbroken vertical shaft 1,978 ft. 4 in. (603 m) deep in Monte Kanin, Slovenia. The **deepest naturally occurring shaft**, it could comfortably accommodate two Eiffel Towers (984 ft.; 300 m).

437,292,000: Words spoken in a lifetime. Our favorite topics of conversation are the weather, work, family, hobbies, and television.

FARTHEST DISTANCE TO . . .

○**Flick a coin** 39 ft. 8 in. (12.11 m), by Alastair Galpin (New Zealand), at the Britomart Transport Centre, Auckland, New Zealand, on November 12, 2009.

○**Blow a coin** 16 ft. 2.76 in. (4.947 m), by Ashrita Furman (U.S.A.), at the Jamaica YMCA in Jamaica, New York City, U.S.A., on October 9, 2010.

○**Throw a dry cowpat** 266 ft. (81.1 m), by Steve Urner (U.S.A.), at the Mountain Festival, Tehachapi, California, U.S.A., on August 14, 1981.

○**MOST SPEARS CAUGHT FROM A SPEARGUN IN ONE MINUTE** Joe Alexander (Germany) caught seven spears shot from a speargun underwater from a distance of 6 ft. 6 in. (2 m) in one minute on the live TV show *ZDF Fernsehgarten* in Mainz, Germany, on September 6, 2009.

○**Rubber bands stretched on the face** Shay Horay, better known as "Rubberband Boy" (NZ), had 78 rubber bands stretched over his face on the set of *Lo Show dei Record* in Milan, Italy, on April 8, 2011.

○**Eggs thrown and caught in one minute by a pair** Ashrita Furman and Bipin Larkin (both U.S.A.) threw and caught 75 eggs across 16 ft. 4 in. (5 m) in Felvonulasi Square in Budapest, Hungary, on May 14, 2010.

From great depths to soaring heights, the ●**highest cell phone call** was made from the summit of Mount Everest, Nepal—29,029 ft. (8,848 m), or 29.5 Eiffel Towers, above sea level—by Rod Baber (UK) on May 21, 2007.

●**Consecutive one-handed claps** The greatest number of consecutive one-handed claps performed by an individual is 310, by Abhinav Upadhyaya (India) at Pranav Studios in Bangalore, Karnataka, India, on May 16, 2010.

●**Handcuff escapes in 24 hours** Zdeněk Bradáč (Czech Republic) made 10,625 handcuff escapes in Liberec, Czech Republic, on February 12–13, 2010.

On September 9, 2009, he also set the ○**fastest time to escape from three sets of handcuffs underwater**: 38.69 seconds, in Jablonec nad Nisou, Czech Republic.

FASTEST TIME TO . . .

●**Halve 10 matches with an ax** Bipin Larkin (U.S.A.) took just 3.59 seconds to halve 10 matches with an ax at the Sri Chinmoy Center in New York, U.S.A., on October 20, 2010.

○**Type the alphabet** Sudhakar Raju (India) typed the alphabet in 3.52 seconds at Press Club in Anantapur, India, on February 13, 2011.

●**MOST SUGAR-GLASS BOTTLES BROKEN ON THE HEAD IN 30 SECONDS**
Mariana Arnaut (Moldavia) broke 56 sugar-glass bottles on her head in 30 seconds for *Lo Show dei Record* in Rome, Italy, on March 4, 2010. Sugar glass is a fake glass used in movies and on television.

Escape a straitjacket Jackson Rayne (U.S.A.) escaped a straitjacket in 7.26 seconds at the Las Vegas Convention Center, Las Vegas, Nevada, U.S.A., on November 17, 2009.

●**Pass through a toilet seat three times** Ilker Çevik (Turkey) wriggled his entire body through a toilet seat three times in just 28.14 seconds at the GWR Live! Roadshow at Forum Bornova in Izmir, Turkey, on May 25, 2010.

●**Dress a female mannequin** Nuran Ozdemir (Turkey) dressed a female dummy in 28.57 seconds at the GWR Live! Roadshow at Forum Trabzon in Trabzon, Turkey, on June 4, 2010.

●**Duct-tape a person to a wall** Hendrik Leschke duct-taped Kai Otte (both Germany) to a wall on the set of *Guinness World Records—Wir holen den Rekord nach Deutschland* in 55.03 seconds in Berlin, Germany, on April 2, 2011.

●**Fastest 4 x 100 m relay in high heels** The Pinkettes—Brittney McGlone, Jessica Penney, Laura Juliff, and Casey Case (all Australia)—ran a 4 x 100 m relay in 1 min. 4.19 sec. in Sydney, Australia, on September 28, 2010.

○**Complete a game of hopscotch** On November 9, 2010, Ashrita Furman (U.S.A.) finished a hopscotch game in 1 min. 1.97 sec. in New York City, U.S.A. Furman made just one errant throw, needing two tosses of the rock to land it in the "3" square.

●**Blow up a balloon with a 100 m fire hose** Ding Zhaohai (China) inflated a balloon using a 100-m-long (328-ft.) fire hose in 7 min. 49 sec. in Xitai City, Shandong Province, China, on November 21, 2010, for the TV show *Zheng Da Zong Yi*.

AT THE CIRCUS

●**MOST RABBITS PULLED OUT OF A HAT** Piero Ustignani, aka Jabba, and Walter Rolfo (both Italy) pulled 300 rabbits out of a magician's hat in less than 30 minutes. This variation on a classic magic trick took place during the Magic Congress in Saint-Vincent, Aosta, Italy, on May 17, 2008.

○**MOST DOGS SKIPPING ON THE SAME ROPE** A total of 13 dogs from Uchida Geinousha's Super Wan Wan Circus (Japan) skipped on one rope in Tochigi, Japan, on October 27, 2009, for *Bikkuri Chojin Special #3* (Fuji TV).

●**Oldest touring circus** The celebrated Circo Atayde opened on August 26, 1888 in the Plaza de Toros, Mazatlán, Mexico. It has been run continuously by the Atayde family ever since.

●**Farthest distance on a tightrope in 24 hours** Joey Kelly (Germany) walked 9.74 miles (15.68 km) along a tightrope over a period of 24 hours on the set of *RTL Spendenmarathon* at MMC studios in Hürth, Germany, on November 18–19, 2010 in celebration of Guinness World Records Day 2010. The wire was 36 ft. 1.07 in. (11 m) long and hung 36 ft. 1.07 in. (11 m) above the ground.

Fastest motorcycle wheelie on a tightrope Johann Traber (Germany) pulled off a daring 33-mi./hr. (53-km/h) motorcycle wheelie while riding along a tightrope at the Tummelum Festival in Flensburg, Germany, on August 13, 2005.

MILESTONES AT THE CIRCUS:

First three-ring circus
Presented by "Lord" George Sanger (UK), 1860

First human arrow
Tony Zedoras (U.S.A.), aka "Alar," Barnum & Bailey Circus, 1896

First loop-the-loop trick cycling
A member of the Ancillotti Troupe, Barnum & Bailey Circus, 1904

Deepak Sharma Bajagain (Nepal) licked 70 postage stamps in one minute at Hindu Vidya Peeth-Nepal in Balkumari, Lalitpur, Nepal, on August 6, 2010, giving him the record for the ●**most stamps licked in a minute**.

1,344,290: Number of times you will laugh throughout your life. According to German psychologist Dr Michael Titze, the average person spends six minutes a day laughing—12 minutes less than we did in the 1960s.

HIGHEST JUMP THROUGH A HOOP
Qiu Jiangning (China), of the China National Acrobatic Troupe, jumped 10 ft. 2 in. (3.12 m) through a hoop on the set of *Zheng Da Zong Yi—Guinness World Records Special* in Beijing, China, on June 17, 2009.

MOST OPEN UMBRELLAS BALANCED SIMULTANEOUSLY Liu Lina (China) balanced eight open umbrellas at the same time on the set of *Zheng Da Zong Yi—Guinness World Records Special* in Beijing, China, on June 21, 2009.

●**Fastest mile on stilts** Ashrita Furman (U.S.A.) covered a mile (1.6 km) on stilts in 12 min. 23 sec. at the Queens College running track in Flushing, New York City, U.S.A., on August 29, 2008.

Ashrita also ran the ●**fastest 100 m on spring-loaded stilts**, in a time of 19.78 seconds, at the Piazza dei Miracoli, Pisa, Italy, on March 27, 2010.

Finally, he also recorded the ●**greatest vertical height walked on stilts**—2,848 ft. (868 m)—when he climbed to the summit of Mount Equinox in Manchester, Vermont, U.S.A., on September 23, 2008.

Stamping his name into our record book, Christian Schäfer (Germany) claimed the ●**fastest time to blow a stamp 100 m**, with a time of 3 min. 3 sec. at ASV Dachau in Dachau, Germany, on October 3, 2010.

FIRST FLYING-RETURN TRAPEZE ACT Jules Léotard (France) in Paris, France, on November 12, 1859.

FIRST HUMAN CANNONBALL "Zazel," whose debut came in 1877 when she was shot about 30 ft. (6.1 m) at Westminster Aquarium, London, UK.

○**Highest flame blown by a fire breather** Antonio Restivo (U.S.A.) blew a flame 26 ft. 5 in. (8.05 m) into the air at a warehouse in Las Vegas, Nevada, U.S.A., on January 11, 2011.

○**Most candles extinguished by a whip in one minute** On November 11, 2008, Adam Winrich (U.S.A.) extinguished 50 candles in one minute by cracking a whip—without touching the candle wax—on the set of *Zheng Da Zong Yi—Guinness World Records Special* in Beijing, China.

●**Most axes thrown around a human target in 30 seconds** Wang Shengli (China) hurled a total of 12 axes at a revolving human target in 30 seconds on the set of *Zheng Da Zong Yi—Guinness World Records Special* in Beijing, China, on December 20, 2010.

Fastest throwing of 10 knives around a human target Dr. David R. Adamovich, aka "The Great Throwdini" (U.S.A.), threw ten 14-in. (35.5-cm) throwing knives around his partner, "Target Girl" Tina Nagy, in 4.29 seconds on July 29, 2008.

● **HEAVIEST STILTS WALKED WITH** Doug
Hunt (Canada) took an amazing 29 steps
unaided on a pair of stilts with a collective
weight of 137 lb. (62.1 kg), and 50 ft. 9 in.
(15.56 m) tall, on September 14, 2002.

● **Most swords swallowed underwater** On March 24, 2010, Dan Meyer
(U.S.A.) swallowed two swords underwater on the set of *Lo Show dei Record* in
Rome, Italy.

○ **Heaviest weight dangled from a
sword** Thomas Blackthorne (UK) dangled a weight of 55 lb. 1 oz. (25 kg) from
a swallowed sword on the set of *Lo Show
dei Record* in Italy on April 19, 2009.

● **Largest curve for a swallowed sword** On September 12, 2009,
Dai Andrews (U.S.A.) successfully swallowed a sword with a curvature
of 120° at the Blue Thunder Festival at Pimlico Racetrack, Baltimore,
Maryland, U.S.A.

JUGGLING

MOST OBJECTS JUGGLED

Balls: In the early 1900s, three performers were said to have succeeded
in juggling a record 10 balls: Frank Le Dent (U.S.A.), Jenny Jaeger (Rus-
sia/Germany), and Enrico Rastelli (Italy), who is still acclaimed as one
of the world's greatest jugglers. Yet history does not accurately record
whether they were able to do what is now called a "qualifying" run of at
least 20 catches, or only managed a "flash"—that is, making a single cycle
of the objects, attaining 10 catches. The only person to succeed in qualifying 10-ball juggling has been Bruce Sarafian (U.S.A.), who, in 1996, was
documented making 23 catches.

○ **Clubs**: Anthony Gatto (U.S.A., b. Anthony Commarota) juggled a record eight clubs on August 30, 2006, making 16 catches.

• **Flaming torches**: Anthony Gatto (U.S.A.) juggled seven flaming
torches in 1989.

• **Plates**: Enrico Rastelli reputedly kept eight plates aloft in the 1920s.

• **Rings**: At least three people have each been reported to have juggled
11 rings—Albert Petrovski in 1963, Eugene Belaur in 1968, and Sergei Ig-
natov in 1973 (all USSR)—but there is no verification that the attempts

qualified with the required 22 catches. The highest number of rings to be authenticated is 10 by Anthony Gatto (U.S.A.), who made 47 catches in 2005.

Greatest combined weight juggled Milan Roskopf (Slovakia) juggled three shot puts weighing a total of 57 lb. (25.86 kg) for 40.44 seconds in Starnberg, Germany, on November 7, 2004.

Most juggling catches in one minute (three balls) Zdeněk Bradáč (Czech Republic) achieved a record 339 catches of three balls in one minute at the Prinzenraub Festival in Altenburg, Germany, on July 12, 2009.

●**Longest time to juggle three objects blindfolded** Zdeněk Bradáč (Czech Republic) juggled three balls blindfolded for 25.30 seconds at the Flying Teapots Circus Club in Sheffield, UK, on February 25, 2009.

Flip to p. 509 for more aerial artistry.

○**MOST CONSECUTIVE FOOT-JUGGLING FLIPS** Hou Yanan and Jiang Tiantian (both China), from the Wuqiao County Acrobatic Group, performed 90 foot-juggling flips in a row in Beijing, China, on September 19, 2007.

WHY "JOGGLING"? Bill Giduz (U.S.A.) devised this hybrid of juggling and jogging in 1979. As a runner and a juggler, he saw that the two activities fitted well together: a runner's arms naturally make a juggling motion.

MOST SOCCER BALLS JUGGLED
Professional soccer freestyler Victor Rubilar (Argentina) juggled five regulation-size soccer balls for the required minimum of 10 seconds at the Gallerian shopping mall in Stockholm, Sweden, on November 4, 2006.

●**Most clubs passed by a duo** Wes Peden (U.S.A.) and Patrik Elmnert (Sweden) passed 13 clubs between them in 2009—a total of 26 catches. The ●**most clubs flashed** by a duo is 14, when Peter Kaseman and Darin Marriott (both U.S.A.) attempted a flash of 14-club passing in 2004.

●**Longest time to juggle five basketballs** Pedro Elis (Spain) was filmed juggling five basketballs for 37.46 seconds on the *Guinness World Records* TV show in Madrid, Spain, on January 30, 2009.

Most balls bounce-juggled Bounce juggling allows for balls to be bounced off the ground before returning to the hands. The most balls bounce-juggled at any one time is 11, by Tim Nolan (U.S.A.) at the Old Dominion University Fieldhouse in Norfolk, Virginia, U.S.A., on March 11, 2006.

THREE-BALL JOGGLING

Juggling + jogging = joggling! Sounds easy enough, but not when taken to these extremes. . . .

Distance	Time	Holder	Date
100 m (male)	11.68	Owen Morse (U.S.A.)	1989
100 m (female)	17.20	Sandy Brown (U.S.A.)	Jul. 22, 1990
1 mile (male)	4:43	Kirk Swenson (U.S.A.)	1986
1 mile (female)	6:17	Kathy Glynn (U.S.A.)	Jul. 22, 1989
○ 10 km (6.2 miles)	36:27	Michal Kapral (Canada)	Sep. 10, 2006
Marathon (26 miles; 42 km)	2:50.12	Michal Kapral (Canada)	Sep. 30, 2007
● 50 miles (80.5 km)	8:23.52	Perry Romanowski (U.S.A.)	Oct. 27, 2007

2: Number of hours it takes to teach the average person how to juggle. Record-breaking juggler David Slick was able to juggle four objects continuously for longer (2 hr. 23 min.) than that . . .

○LONGEST TIME TO JUGGLE THREE OBJECTS WHILE SUSPENDED Hanging from gravity boots, Erik Kloeker (U.S.A.) juggled three objects for 5 min. 45 sec. in Beijing, China, on May 23, 2010.

FASTEST 100 M JOGGLING WITH FIVE OBJECTS Owen Morse (U.S.) ran 100 m while juggling five objects in a time of 13.8 seconds in 1988.

FLASHING A "flash" is a single cycle of juggling in which you make one catch for each object; a true "juggle" involves at least two catches. The **most balls or beanbags flashed** is 12, achieved by Alex Barron (UK) with 13 beanbags in 2010.

In 2009, Germans spent $81 billion while on holiday in foreign countries according to the World Tourism Organization (UNWTO), giving them the record for the **○highest-spending tourists**.

Françoise juggles her batons like clubs, but baton twirlers spin theirs in the air.

MOST BATONS JUGGLED Françoise Rochais of Les Sables-d'Olonne, France, juggled seven batons at once while performing with the After Cloudy Company in Japan in 1999.

●**LONGEST TIME TO JUGGLE THREE OBJECTS UNDERWATER (NO AIR SUPPLY)** A submerged Merlin Cadogan (UK) juggled three objects underwater while holding his breath for 1 min. 20 sec. in Potters Fields Park, London, UK, on November 18, 2010.

●**GREATEST DISTANCE JUGGLING ON A POGO STICK** The greatest distance over which anyone has traveled on a pogo stick while simultaneously juggling is 4 miles (6 km) by Ashrita Furman (U.S.A.), while visiting Easter Island, Chile, on January 28, 2010.

The **most popular country for tourists to visit** is France. According to UNWTO, France saw 74.2 million visitors in 2009.

●**Fastest mile bounce-juggling** Ashrita Furman (U.S.A.) took just 7 min. 42 sec. to cover the distance of 1 mile (1.6 km) while bounce-juggling three objects at Jamaica High School in New York, U.S.A., on October 21, 2009.

WHEEL SKILLS

BICYCLE

●**Most candles extinguished with a trial bicycle in one minute** Benito Ros Charral (Spain) managed to put out 22 candles with a trial bicycle in just a minute in Beijing, China, on December 18, 2010.

LONGEST JUMP WITH BACKFLIP ON A MINIMOTO Spain's Ricardo Piedras produced a 41-ft. 9-in. (12.72-m) backflip on a minimoto bike on the set of *Lo Show dei Record* in Milan, Italy, on April 11, 2009.

●**HIGHEST INLINE SKATE DROP INTO A HALF-PIPE** The record for the highest inline skate drop into a half pipe was 41 ft. (12.5 m), achieved by Taïg Khris (France) during the M6 Mobile Mega Jump event in Paris, France, on May 29, 2010.

1.9: Average number of legs per person. Why? Average = number of legs ÷ number of people. If just one person has one leg, the average is less than two. Because of unicycles, the average cycle has 1.9 wheels.

1956: date of the first official artistic cycling contest

●**MOST ARTISTIC CYCLING ROUNDS WITH A PERSON ON THE SHOULDERS** Carla and Henriette Hochdorfer (both Germany) carried out four consecutive artistic cycling rounds in the raiser head tube reverse/shoulder stand position on the set of *Lo Show dei Record* in Rome, Italy, on March 18, 2010.

●**Highest backflip** Ben Wallace (UK) performed a bicycle backflip 9 ft. 2.23 in. (2.8 m) high on *Zheng Da Zong Yi—Guinness World Records Special* in Beijing, China, on December 9, 2010.

●**Longest 180 flip** On November 18, 2008, Jim Dechamp (U.S.A.) carried out a 10-ft. (3-m) 180° flip on a mountain bike at Miller Motorsports Park in Tooele, Utah, U.S.A., for the MTV show *Nitro Circus*. Jim also holds 10 other GWR cycling records.

○**Fastest 100 m wheelie** Austen Nunes (U.S.A.) covered 100 m on the back wheel of his bicycle in 14.05 seconds in Manteca, California, U.S.A., on March 15, 2010.

●**Longest wheelie in one hour** Aaron Stannage (UK) rode a sustained bicycle wheelie for a cumulative distance of 8.17 miles (13.15 km) in an hour at the John Charles Sport Stadium in Leeds, UK, on January 17, 2010. The course measured 454 ft. 8.6 in. (138.6 m) long and at no time did his front wheel touch the ground.

●**Most wheelies in one minute** On August 1, 2010, at X Games 16 in Los Angeles, California, U.S.A., Guadalupe Alvarez (U.S.A.) did 167 wheelies in a minute.

○**MOST STEPS CLIMBED BY BICYCLE** On December 31, 2007, Zhang Jincheng (China), Xavi Casas (Andorra), and Javier Zapata (Colombia) climbed all 88 stories of the Jin Mao Tower in Shanghai, China, by bicycle, covering 2,008 steps in all. The number 2,008 was symbolic: the feat took place on New Year's Eve and was in recognition of the 2008 Beijing Olympic Games.

To achieve the **fastest circumnavigational flight** under the Fédération Aéronautique Internationale (FAI) rules, Air France Concorde flight AF1995 traveled from JFK airport in New York, U.S.A., eastbound on August 15 and 16, 1995, in 31 hr. 27 min. 49 sec.

SKATEBOARD

○ **Most kick flips in one minute** On May 15, 2010, Zach Kral (U.S.A.) performed a total of 29 skateboard kick flips in one minute in Waterford, Wisconsin, U.S.A.

● **Fastest time to slalom 100 cones** Janis Kuzmins (Latvia) slalomed through 100 cones in 20.77 seconds at Meza Park in Riga, Latvia, on September 12, 2010. Each cone was placed 5 ft. 3 in. (1.6 m) apart from the next.

● **Most axle stalls in 30 seconds** Alex Sorgente (U.S.A.) made 15 axle stalls on a skateboard in 30 seconds at X Games 16 in Los Angeles, California, U.S.A., on July 30, 2010.

● **Most backside grinds in one minute** On August 1, 2010, Annika Vrklan (U.S.A.) produced 31 backside grinds on a skateboard in one minute at X Games 16 in Los Angeles, California, U.S.A.

● **HIGHEST TIGHTROPE CROSSING BY BICYCLE** Nik Wallenda (U.S.A.) rode a bicycle across a tightrope suspended at a height of 238 ft. (72.5 m) between the Royal Towers of the Atlantis Paradise Island hotel in Nassau, The Bahamas, on August 28, 2010.

Nik comes from a famous family of circus daredevils: the Flying Wallendas

 Frederick W. Finn (UK) made an incredible 718 Atlantic crossings by Concorde—the **most supersonic journeys by a passenger**—before the aircraft was retired in 2003.

○ **LONGEST WHEELIE ON FRONT WHEEL WITH FEET OFF PEDALS** On January 28, 2010, Shane Badman (Australia) performed a wheelie over 617 ft. 9 in. (188.3 m) on the front wheel of a BMX without touching the pedals. The feat took place on the set of *Australia Smashes Guinness World Records*, in Sydney, Australia.

● **Most ollie 180s in one minute** Gray Mesa (U.S.A.) racked up 17 ollie 180s on a skateboard in a minute at X Games 16 in Los Angeles, California, U.S.A., on July 30, 2010.

SPIRIT OF
ADVENTURE

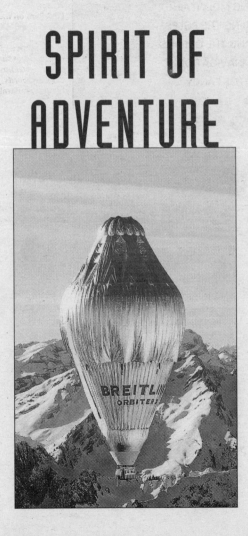

CONTENTS

GOING THE DISTANCE During his daredevil high-walk, Freddy also attempted the longest cable walk—5,249 ft. (1,600 m) along the full length of the cable to the Murtèl station. However, the onset of fog and the threat of ice on the wire forced him to abandon the bid—so watch this space!

●HIGHEST CABLE WALK On January 29, 2011, Swiss high-wire artist Freddy Nock braved high winds and temperatures of 5°F (-15°C) to perform a death-defying aerial walk 10,836 ft. (3,303 m) above the Silvaplana ski resort near St. Moritz, Switzerland. Despite the harsh conditions, Freddy performed his stunt without a harness or safety net and covered a distance of 1,876 ft. (572 m) under the watchful eyes of Guinness World Records adjudicators and photographers.

MOUNT EVEREST

GLOBAL WARNING Apa Sherpa (see p. 210) has talked passionately about how Everest has changed over the past 20 years—the warming planet has made the peak increasingly difficult to climb, he believes.

"Geneva Spur" — A steep spur of rock, snow, and ice (2 hr)

Climbers must clip on to the fixed main line when climbing Lhotse Face to avoid tumbling to their deaths

Fall here and it's a 1,000-ft (300-m) drop with no recovery!

Rock-hard blue ice

"Yellow Band" — A challenging 200-ft (60-m) strip of smooth limestone at 30-45° (3 hr)

"Khumbu Icefall" — A 2,000-ft (600-m) climb up a constantly shifting glacier with deep crevasses and teetering seracs; deadliest part of the climb

Death zone — Above 26,246 ft (8,000 m), your body uses up oxygen faster than it can take it in

A.

B. 4-6 hr

C. 2-3 hr

D. 3-6 hr

E.

F. 8-12 hr

G.

H.

I.

J. ~6 hr

K. ~5 hr

L.

THE FIVE-MILE-HIGH CLUB

Illustrated here is a typical route—one of many—to the top of the highest mountain on Earth. If you take this route via the southeast ridge, put aside about 60 days—and around $62,000. You could be on your way to the top of the world!

A. BASE CAMP 17,700 ft. (5,380 m) Acclimatize here for two weeks. When you're ready, begin your hike to Camp I at 3 a.m., before dawn, when the ice is at its most solid.

B. CAMP I 19,900 ft. (6,056 m) Garden stepladders are used to cross deep crevasses in the Khumbu Icefall; if you survive the treacherous terrain, Camp I will provide much-needed relief.

C. CAMP II 21,300 ft. (6,500 m) Temperatures between Camps I and II can get blisteringly hot; beware of thin snow bridges spanning 100-ft. (30-m) drops.

D. CAMP III 24,500 ft. (7,470 m) A fixed-rope climb leads to a small ridge and Camp III; high risk of avalanche here; and beware of traffic jams with other climbers!

E. LHOTSE FACE

F. WEST RIDGE

G. NUPTSE 25,790 ft. (7,861 m) Seven-peaked ridge along the Lhotse–Nuptse massif to the west-southwest of Everest.

H. LHOTSE 27,940 ft. (8,516 m) Fourth highest peak on Earth; the western flank (Lhotse Face) is a 3,700-ft. (1,125-m) wall of ice at pitches of 40–80°.

I. CAMP IV 26,000 ft. (7,920 m) It might be time to crack open the bottled oxygen after conquering the "Yellow Band" and "Geneva Spur"—the two energy-sapping barriers between Camp III and IV.

J. SOUTHEAST RIDGE and **SOUTH COL**

K. SOUTH SUMMIT 28,500 ft. (8,690 m) You will see your first proper view of the top from this rest point; it may be only a mile (1.5 km) away, but it can take a further 12 hours to get there.

L. EVEREST SUMMIT 29,029 ft. (8,848 m) Beyond the "Balcony" you tackle the "Hillary Step" and the "Summit Ridge" . . . then you've made it—the highest point on Earth.

● **FIRST BLIND MAN TO CONQUER EVEREST** Erik Weihenmayer (Hong Kong) was born with retinoschisis, an eye condition that left him totally blind by the age of 13. Despite this, on May 25, 2001, he reached the summit of Mount Everest. Pictured above left is Erik and his team traversing the South Col.

MOST DEATHS ON EVEREST IN A DAY On May 10, 1996, a severe blizzard on Mount Everest claimed the lives of eight climbers and caused serious injuries to more than 20 others. The climbers, from the U.S.A., India, Japan, and New Zealand, were surprised by 90 mi./hr. (145 km/h) winds that sent temperatures plummeting to -40°F (-40°C).

Pictured left is Dr. Seaborn "Beck" Weathers (U.S.A.), who was trapped on the South Col for 16 hours and who lost his right hand, part of his left hand, and his nose to frostbite.

○ **MOST CONQUESTS OF MOUNT EVEREST** Apa Sherpa (Nepal, b. Lhakpa Tenzing Sherpa) reached the summit of Everest for the 20th time on May 21, 2010, the most times anyone has ever successfully climbed the world's highest mountain. His first successful ascent was on May 10, 1990, as part of an international expedition alongside Peter and Edmund Hillary, sons of the mountain's first conqueror, Edmund Hillary (see p. 212).

The **first female Beefeater** was Moira Cameron (UK), who was appointed as Yeoman Warder of Her Majesty's Royal Palace and Fortress, the Tower of London, UK, in January 2007. Beefeaters are all retired members of the armed forces.

Spirit of Adventure

114: Length in miles of toilet roll you'll use in a lifetime—enough, when unraveled, to reach the top of Everest and back 10 times . . . plenty of paper for your 270 days of round-the-clock toilet sitting!

GODDESS OF THE SKY

STATS

Name	English: Mount Everest; Tibetan: Chomolungma ("Goddess Mother of Mountains"); Nepalese: Sagarmatha ("Goddess of the Sky")
Elevation	29,029 ft. (8,848 m) above sea level
Location	Himalayas, Nepal–China border
Coordinates	27°58'60N, 86°55'60E
Summit temperature	-4°F to -31°F (-20°C to -35°C)
Summit wind speed	Up to 174 mi./hr. (280 km/h); average of one hurricane every four days

COLONEL SIR GEORGE EVEREST (UK, 1790–1866) Surveyor-General of India after whom the mountain is named (pronounced EVE-rest). Prior to this, the peak was known to the Brits simply as PEAK XV.

THEODOLITE This large, unwieldy measuring device was used to assess Everest's height in 1856. It gave a reading documented as 29,002 ft. (8,840 m).

Another first for a fighting female, Sabiha Gökçen, an adopted daughter of the first president of Turkey, enrolled in the Military Aviation Academy in Eskişehir in 1936. She flew fighter and bomber planes, becoming the world's **first female combat pilot**.

EDMUND HILLARY & TENZING NORGAY
The New Zealand climber and Nepalese Sherpa were confirmed as the first people to reach the summit of Everest, on May 29, 1953. The expedition was led by Colonel Henry Cecil John Hunt (UK).

JUNKO TABEI (JAPAN, B. SEP. 22, 1939) The first woman to summit Everest, on May 16, 1975, and the first female to reach the peak of the highest points on each continent (the Seven Summits). See pp. 217–218 for more Seven Summits achievements.

GEORGE MALLORY (UK, 1886–1924) Why climb Mount Everest? "Because it's there," said this English mountaineer famously. Part of the first three British attempts to scale Everest in the 1920s, Mallory was last seen alive close to the summit. Did he make it and die on the descent? We may never know. . . .

FANTASTIC VOYAGES

○**Most completed journeys from Land's End to John O'Groats**
The greatest number of journeys from Land's End to John O'Groats (and vice versa) is 20, by John Taylor (Australia)—cycling, driving, or on foot—from January 14, 1980, to May 18, 2009.

The **largest consumers of bread per capita** are the Turks, who eat 440 lb. (199.6 kg) of it each year—more than three times their own body weight.

FASTEST JOURNEYS

John O'Groats to Land's End on foot Andrew Rivett (UK) ran between Great Britain's most extreme points in 9 days 2 hr. 26 min. from May 4 to 13, 2002.

The ●**fastest confirmed journey from Land's End to John O'Groats on foot by a woman** is 12 days 15 hr. 46 min. 35 sec., by Marina Anderson (UK) from July 16 to 28, 2008.

Crossing America on foot Frank Giannino, Jr. (U.S.A.) ran 3,100 miles (4,989 km) from San Francisco to New York City (both U.S.A.) in 46 days 8 hr. 36 min. from September 1 to October 17, 1980.

The **fastest time to cross America on foot by a woman** is 69 days 2 hr. 40 min. by Mavis Hutchinson (South Africa) from March 12 to May 21, 1978.

Cycling the length of South America Giampietro Marion (Italy) cycled the South American portion of the Pan-American Highway, from Chigorodo, Colombia, to Ushuaia, Argentina, in 59 days between September 17 and November 15, 2000.

Crossing Canada on foot From June 21 to September 1, 1991, Al Howie (UK) ran from St John's, Newfoundland, to Victoria, British Columbia—4,533.2 miles (7,295.5 km)—in 72 days 10 hr. 23 min.

Ann Keane (Canada) ran across Canada from St John's, Newfoundland, to Tofino, British Columbia, in 143 days from April 17 to September 8, 2002, the **fastest crossing of Canada on foot by a woman**. She covered 4,866 miles (7,831 km) and ran for all but three of the days.

●GREATEST DISTANCE BY CANOE/KAYAK IN 24 HOURS ON FLOWING WATER (FEMALE) Katherine Pfefferkorn (U.S.A.) paddled 192.1 miles (309.1 km) down the Missouri River, U.S.A., in 24 hours on May 29–30, 2010. It took Katherine just 9.5 hours to beat the previous record.

Sticking with bread, the ●**longest baguette** measured 354 ft. (111 m) and was baked at the Big C Supercenter in the Bình Tân district of Ho Chi Minh City, Vietnam, on August 22, 2009.

ROYAL LAUNCH The ●**first royal in space** was Prince Abdulaziz al-Saud, a nephew of King Fahd of Saudi Arabia. The Prince flew as part of the crew of the *Discovery* on flight STS 51G in 1985.

●**FASTEST TIME FROM PERTH TO SYDNEY BY HANDCYCLE (RELAY)** Thomas Bechter, Philipp Bonadimann, Jürgen Egle, and Wolfgang Wimmer (all Austria) traveled across Australia by handcycle, in relay, from Perth to Sydney in 6 days 10 hr. 42 min. The feat took place between October 16 and 23, 2010, in the Race Across Australia (RAAUS) charity event.

The four cyclists covered 2,505 miles (4,031 km) in all.

●**FIRST PERSON TO WALK THE LENGTH OF THE AMAZON** On August 9, 2010, Edward Stafford (UK) finished his walk along the length of the Amazon river in South America. The trip took him 2 years, 4 months, and 8 days (860 days in total).

RIDE OF A LIFETIME Rob's record-breaking skate was just a small part of a 12,427-mile (20,000-km) multi-leg trip he made from Switzerland to China by bike, raft, sailboat, and train!

LONGEST JOURNEY BY SKATEBOARD Rob Thomson (New Zealand) traveled 7,555 miles (12,159 km) on his skateboard, starting in Leysin, Switzerland, on June 24, 2007, and finishing in Shanghai, China, on September 28, 2008.

Crossing Australia on foot Donnie Maclurcan (Australia) ran across the Australian continental mainland from Cottesloe Beach, Perth, Western Australia, to Bondi Beach, Sydney, New South Wales, in 67 days 2 hr. 57 min. between January 5 and March 13, 2002.

FARTHEST JOURNEYS

By bus Between November 6, 1988, and December 3, 1989, Hughie Thompson, John Weston, and Richard Steel (all UK) covered 54,289 miles (87,367 km) and a total of 18 countries in the "World Bus," a red London Routemaster double-decker.

○**By automobile** Emil and Liliana Schmid (Switzerland) have covered 407,618 miles (656,000 km) in their Toyota Land Cruiser since October 16, 1984, crossing 169 countries and territories in the process.

●FARTHEST DISTANCE NORDIC WALKING IN 24 HOURS Walter Geckle (Austria) covered 108 miles (175 km) while Nordic walking in Unzmarkt, Austria, on August 14–15, 2010. Helpfully, he is a former world champion in the sport.

●**By airboat** Bill Fadeley and Eugene Hajtovik (both U.S.A.) completed a 1,100-mile (1,770.28-km), 13-day trip by airboat along the Intracoastal Waterway from Jacksonville, Florida, to the Statue of Liberty in New York, U.S.A., on July 3, 1986. They made their "Ride to Liberty" on the 16-ft. (5-m), 350-hp *Miss Jacksonville* and reached the iconic statue in time to celebrate its restoration and centennial.

●**By dragon boat** Team Beauties & Barnacles (U.S.A.) sailed 294 nautical miles (339 miles; 545 km) down the Missouri River by Chinese dragon boat, starting at Kaw Point, Kansas City, and ending in St. Charles, Missouri, U.S.A., on August 24–25, 2010.

●**By kite-ski (24 hours)** On June 5, 2010, Eric McNair-Landry (Canada) and Sebastian Copeland (U.S.A./France) kite-skied 370 miles (595 km) in 24 hours during their 43-day expedition to cross the 1,429-mile-long (2,300-km) Greenland icecap from Narsarsuaq in the south to Qaanaaq in the north. They reached speeds of 46 mi./hr. (60 km/h), beating the previous record of 315 miles (507.5 km) by Hugo Rolf Hansen and Bjørn Einar Bjartnes (both Norway), set on July 2, 2009.

By lawnmower Gary Hatter (U.S.A.) covered 14,594.5 miles (23,487.5 km) in 260 consecutive days on the back of his Kubota BX2200-60 lawnmower. He started in Portland, Maine, on May 31, 2000, and passed through all 48 contiguous U.S. states, as well as Canada and Mexico, before arriving in Daytona Beach, Florida, on February 14, 2001.

By motorcycle Between 1985 and 1995, Emilio Scotto (Argentina) made a 457,000-mile (735,000-km) trip by motorcycle, taking in 214 countries.

The ●**largest ceramic mosaic** has an area of 16,901 ft.^{2} (1,570.2 m^2) and was constructed by Nguyen Thu Thuy (Vietnam), with the help of 35 artists, on the walls of the Red River Dyke in Hanoi, Vietnam, on October 5, 2010.

●By motorcycle in a single country The longest continual motorbike ride within one country is 10,095 miles (16,240 km) by Ryan and Colin Pyle (both Canada), who toured China between August 16 and October 17, 2010. The brothers started and finished their expedition in Shanghai.

●By paddleboard From May 19 to 27, 2007, Wyatt Werneth (U.S.A.) traveled up the coast of Florida, U.S.A., on a paddleboard for a distance of 345 miles (555 km).

CLIMBING MOUNTAINS

●Fastest time to climb the highest peaks in all African countries Five years after he set out to climb the greatest peaks in each African country, Eamon "Ginge" Fullen (UK) completed his feat when he reached the Bikku Bitti Peak, Libya, on December 25, 2005.

○Oldest man to climb Mount Kilimanjaro On July 14, 2010, George Solt (UK, b. September 28, 1927) reached the summit of Mount Kilimanjaro, Tanzania, aged 82 years 289 days. He made the journey with his son, daughter-in-law, and three grandchildren. It took him from July 9 to 14 to reach the summit, after which he descended to the starting gate on July 16.

First ascent of K2 On July 31, 1954, Italians Achille Compagnoni and Lino Lacedelli completed the earliest ascent of K2, which at 28,251 ft. (8,611 m) is the world's second-highest mountain. They were part of an Italian expedition led by Ardito Desio. K2 is situated in the Karakoram range on the border between Pakistan and China.

FASTEST TIME TO CLIMB THE SEVEN SUMMITS Henrik Kristiansen (Denmark) climbed the highest peak on each of the seven continents in a record time of 136 days, between January 21, 2008, when he ascended Mount Vinson in Antarctica, and June 5, 2008, when he conquered Mount McKinley in Alaska, U.S.A.

The **●largest marble mosaic** measured 27 ft. 2.77 in (8.3 m) high and 17 ft. 4.66 in (5.3 m) wide. It was an image of His Majesty Sultan Qaboos bin Said of Oman, produced by Sablat Oman (Oman) in collaboration with more than 40 artists.

Wanda Rutkiewicz (Poland) became the **first woman to climb K2**, on June 23, 1986.

First person to climb all 8,000 m peaks

Reinhold Messner (Italy) became the first person to climb the world's 14 peaks above 8,000 m (26,246 ft.) when he summited Lhotse (27,890 ft.; 8,501 m), on the Nepal/Tibet border, on October 16, 1986. His quest had started in June 1970, and the difficulty of his achievement is illustrated by the fact that, 20 years later, only 12 people had achieved it.

Messner was also the **first person to climb Mount Everest solo**, reaching the summit on August 20, 1980. It took him three days to make the ascent from his base camp at 21,325 ft. (6,500 m). The climb was made all the more difficult by the fact that he did not use bottled oxygen.

YOUNGEST FEMALE TO CLIMB THE SEVEN SUMMITS Samantha Larson (U.S.A., b. October 7, 1988) is the youngest female to have climbed all seven summits (see left). She reached the seventh and final peak, the Carstensz Pyramid, on August 4, 2007, aged 18 years 301 days.

TIP-TOP POP Samantha climbed the Seven Summits alongside her dad David, which makes them the first father-and-daughter team to do so. Samantha also became the youngest non-Nepalese female to conquer Everest.

THE SEVEN SUMMITS

The highest peak on each of the seven continents according to alpinist Reinhold Messner . . .

Africa: Mount Kilimanjaro, Tanzania—19,340 ft. (5,894 m)

Antarctica: Vinson Massif, Ellesworth Land—16,863 ft. (5,140 m)

Asia: Mount Everest, Nepal/China—29,029 ft. (8,848 m)

Europe: Mount Elbrus, Russia—18,510 ft. (5,642 m)

North/Central America: Mount McKinley, U.S.A.—20,320 ft. (6,194 m)

Oceania: Carstensz Pyramid (Puncak Jaya), Indonesia—16,024 ft. (4,884 m)

South America: Cerro Aconcagua, Argentina—22,834 ft. (6,960 m)

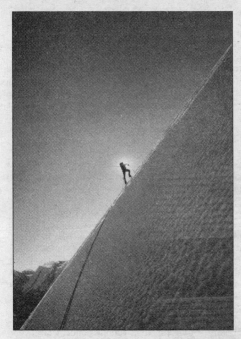

DEADLIEST MOUNTAIN TO CLIMB Annapurna I (pictured), in the 34-mile-long (55-km) Annapurna massif, has been climbed by 130 people, 53 of whom died along the way, giving the peak a 41% mortality rate. On October 28, 2007, Tomaz Humar (Slovenia) became the first person to climb Annapurna I solo. He climbed a new route along the right side of the south face in pure "alpine" style—i.e., he carried all his equipment and food with him.

Accompanied by Peter Habeler (Austria), Messner also completed the **first oxygen-less ascent of Mount Everest**, on May 8, 1978.

Oldest person to climb Mount Everest According to the Senior Citizen Mount Everest Expedition (SECEE), Min Bahadur Sherchan (Nepal, b. June 20, 1931) reached the highest point on Earth on May 25, 2008, at the age of 76 years 340 days.

First married couple to climb Mount Everest Phil and Susan Ershler (U.S.A.) reached the summit of Mount Everest on May 16, 2002—the same day that a record 54 people (including the Ershlers) reached the top. The couple have also scaled the highest peaks on every one of the world's seven continents.

UP UNDER The Seven Summits are the highest points on each continent (see list at left). If Australia is considered a continent, Mount Kosciuszko is listed instead of Carstensz—despite being only 7,310 ft. (2,228 m).

2.4: Annual growth in inches of Mount Everest. The geological processes that built Everest are still going on, so in your lifetime the highest peak in the world will become 15.8 ft. higher.

First explorers' grand slam Young-Seok Park (South Korea) reached the North Pole on foot on April 30, 2005, becoming the first person to achieve the explorers' grand slam. This feat involves climbing the highest peaks on all seven continents (the Seven Summits), the 14 peaks over 8,000 m (26,246 ft.), and reaching the North and South Poles on foot. His quest began when he summited Mount Everest on May 16, 1993.

First adventurers' grand slam The adventurers' grand slam involves climbing the highest peak on every continent and trekking to all four poles (magnetic and geographical). David Hempleman-Adams (UK) began this challenge in 1980 by climbing Mount McKinley in Alaska, U.S.A. He completed the feat 18 years later when he and Rune Gjeldnes (Norway) walked to the North Pole from March to May 1998.

Most ascents of Mount Everest by a woman Lakpa Sherpa (Nepal) reached the summit of Everest for a record fifth time on June 2, 2005, completing the climb alongside her husband, George Demarescu (U.S.A.), who was making his seventh ascent of the world's **highest mountain**. Lakpa made her first ascent in 2000, and her second in 2001. In 2003, she climbed with her sister Ming Kipa Sherpa, who was just 15 at the time. Her 2004 summit was her first with her husband.

Fastest ascents of Mount Everest Hans Kammerlander (Italy) completed the **fastest ascent of Mount Everest on the north side**, making the climb from base camp to the summit in 16 hr. 45 min. on May 23–24, 1996.

Pemba Dorje Sherpa (Nepal) climbed from base camp to the summit of Everest on the south side in 8 hr. 10 min. on May 21, 2004. This is the **fastest ascent of Mount Everest** by any route.

●**LARGEST CLEAR-UP ON MOUNT EVEREST** Since 2008, the Nepali Eco Everest Expeditions have seen annual trips to the world's highest mountain to clear away garbage from previous climbs, removing 26,450 lb. (12,000 kg) of ropes, tents, food packaging, oxygen bottles, gas canisters, and other discarded gear. The 2008 expedition saw the removal of 2,120 lb. (965 kg) of refuse. A record 13,225 lb. (6,000 kg)—including 1,540 lb. (700 kg) of debris from a helicopter that had crashed in 1973 and 253 lb. (115 kg) of human waste—was cleared in 2009, and 11,020 lb. (5,000 kg) of garbage was removed in 2010. This latest cleanup expedition was led by Apa Sherpa (Nepal).

●**OLDEST PERSON TO CLIMB THE SEVEN SUMMITS** On April 22, 2007, at the age of 73 years 357 days, Ramón Blanco (Spain) reached the tip of the Carstensz Pyramid in Indonesia, making him the oldest person to climb the highest peaks on each of the seven continents. The project took Ramón 31 years 114 days to complete.

First person to climb the Seven Summits The first person to reach the highest points on each of the seven continents was Richard "Dick" Bass (U.S.A.), who did so on April 30, 1985. The "Bass List," as it is known, counts Mount Kosciuszko as the highest point in Australasia; however, Reinhold Messner suggested that Puncak Jaya (aka the Carstensz Pyramid) in Indonesia should be climbed, in which case the "first" record goes to Patrick Morrow (Canada), who completed Messner's list on August 5, 1986.

●**Oldest female to climb the Seven Summits** Caroline (Kay) LeClaire (U.S.A., b. March 8, 1949) completed her last Seven Summit climb when she reached the summit of Mount Everest on May 23, 2009, aged 60 years 77 days. A nurse, competitive ballroom dancer, and mother, Kay did not take up climbing until she was 51 years old.

●**Youngest person to climb the Seven Summits** John Carl "Johnny" Collison (U.S.A., b. March 29, 1992) took exactly one year to climb the Seven Summits, reaching his seventh peak—the Vinson Massif in Antarctica—on January 18, 2010, at the age of just 17 years 295 days.

The youngest person to climb the Seven Summits *plus* Mount Kosciuszko in Australia is Robert "R. C." Scull II (U.S.A., b. March 16, 1987), who was 21 years 292 days old when he summited the Carstensz Pyramid.

EXPLORING THE POLES

First undisputed overland journey to the North Pole The earliest indisputable attainment of the North Pole over the sea ice took place at 3 p.m. (Central Standard Time) on April 19, 1968. Ralph Plaisted (U:S.A.) led an expedition that reached the Pole after a 42-day trek in snowmobiles.

Why "undisputed"? The issue of the first person to reach the North Pole has long been a matter of controversy and debate between two American explorers and their supporters. Robert Peary, traveling with Matt Henson, indicated he had reached the North Pole on April 6, 1909; however, Frederick Cook claimed that he had done so a year earlier, on April 21, 1908. Despite investigations into the claims, neither can be unquestionably proven.

OLDEST PERSON TO VISIT THE NORTH POLE
Dorothy Davenhill Hirsch (U.S.A., b. May 11, 1915) reached the North Pole aboard the Russian nuclear icebreaker *Yamal* on August 28, 2004, aged 89 years and 109 days.

First solo expedition to the North Pole

Naomi Uemura (Japan) became the first person to reach the North Pole solo at 4:45 a.m. GMT on May 1, 1978, after a trek across the Arctic sea ice. He had traveled 450 miles (725 km), setting out on March 7 from Cape Edward on Ellesmere Island in northern Canada.

Erling Kagge (Norway) completed the **first solo expedition to the South Pole** on January 7, 1993. His 870-mile (1,400-km) journey from Berkner Island took 50 days.

Fastest solo unsupported trek to the North Pole Børge Ousland (Norway) skied his way to the North Pole from the Severnaya Zemlya archipelago in the Russian Federation without any external assistance, motorized transport, or parafoil kites in a time of 52 days, from March 2 to April 23, 1994.

First person to visit both Poles Dr. Albert Paddock Crary (U.S.A.) reached the North Pole in a Dakota aircraft on May 3, 1952. He arrived at the South Pole by Sno-Cat as part of a scientific traverse party on February 12, 1961.

The **first person to walk to both the North and the South Poles**, however, was Robert Swan (UK). He led the three-man "In the Footsteps of Scott" expedition, which reached the South Pole on January 11, 1986. Three years later, he headed the eight-man "Icewalk" trip, which arrived at the North Pole on May 14, 1989.

○**FASTEST SOLO JOURNEY TO THE SOUTH POLE (UNSUPPORTED AND UNASSISTED)**
On January 13, 2011, Christian Eide (Norway) completed a solo unsupported trek to the South Pole in 24 days 1 hr. 13 min. He skied an average of 29 miles (47 km) per day—although managed 56 miles (90 km) on the last day—smashing Todd Carmichael's (U.S.A.) 39-day record and setting a benchmark that many polar explorers consider near-impossible to beat. Pictured is Eide's self-portrait, reflected in the sphere of the Ceremonial South Pole.

The **longest distance driven on a motorcycle in 24 hours** is 1,321 miles (2,127 km), by Omar Hilal Al-Mamari (Oman) on a sealed-off road between Marmool and Thamrait in Oman between August 18 and 19, 2009.

4.4: Weight in tons of the frozen food you'll eat during your life. Freezers keep food at 1.4°F, the point where the natural processes of ripening and rotting are put on hold. It's also the average temperature of the North Pole.

HEADING SOUTH At 11 a.m. on December 14, 1911, Captain Roald Amundsen (Norway), leading a five-man party, became the **first person to reach the South Pole** after a 53-day march with dog sleds.

Fastest time to reach both Poles unsupported Married couple Thomas and Tina Sjögren (both Sweden) reached the South Pole on February 1, 2002, and the North Pole 117 days later, on May 29, 2002—the shortest time taken to walk between Poles.

●First female to complete the Three Poles Challenge Tina Sjögren's success at the Poles (above) also constitutes the first completion by a female of the Three Poles Challenge—the conquest of the North and South Poles plus Mount Everest (regarded as a "pole" owing to its inaccessibility). Prior to her polar expeditions, Tina had summited Everest on May 26, 1999.

FASTEST OVERLAND JOURNEY TO THE SOUTH POLE Using a modified 6x6 vehicle, a team of five drivers—Jason De Carteret, Andrew Regan, Richard Griffiths, Andrew Moon (all UK), and Gunni Eglisson (Iceland)—completed an overland journey to the South Pole from Patriot Hills on the Antarctic coastline in 69 hr. 21 min., from December 9 to 12, 2005.

 Manrique Saenz Cruz (Colombia) performed the **longest nonstop motorcycle ride with no hands**, driving his Honda 125 XL—without a break and without touching the handlebars—for 132 miles (213 km) on February 25, 2001.

● **LONGEST ARCTIC SNOW-KITING EXPEDITION (UNSUPPORTED)** UAE-based adventurer Adrian Hayes (UK) and adventurers Devon McDiarmid and Derek Crowe (both Canada) achieved a straight-line vertical crossing of the Greenland ice cap by snow kite—a distance of 1,938.67 miles (3,120 km)—in 67 days from May 20 to July 25, 2009.

Fastest completion of the Three Poles Challenge Adrian Hayes (UK) summited Mount Everest on May 25, 2006, reached the North Pole on April 25, 2007 (from Ward Hunt Island, Canada), and made it to the South Pole on December 28, 2007 (from the Hercules Inlet). The feat took 1 year 217 days to complete.

Oldest person to trek to the South Pole unsupported At the age of 63 years 309 days, Simon Murray (UK, b. March 25, 1940) completed a trek to the South Pole. He left from the Antarctic coastline near Hercules Inlet on December 2, 2003, and arrived at the Pole with his trekking partner, Pen Hadow, on January 28, 2004.

Oldest person to ski to both Poles On January 18, 2007, Norbert H. Kern (Germany, b. July 26, 1940) skied to the South Pole. On April 27, 2007, he also skied to the North Pole, which he reached when he was 66 years 275 days old.

Oldest person to visit both Poles On April 9, 1990, Major Will Lacy (b. July 17, 1907) of Whitby, UK, journeyed to the North Pole at the age of 82 and, on December 20, 1991, the South Pole at the age of 84. On both trips, he arrived and left by light aircraft.

Q. HOW MANY POLES DOES EARTH HAVE?

A. More than you'd think! As well as the geographic North and South Poles, there are also the magnetic and geomagnetic North and South Poles, which move around as the Earth's magnetic field varies, and the "Poles of Inaccessibility"—those points on land or sea farthest from geographical features.

Created in December 2003 by Nelson Jimenez Florez (Colombia), the **largest sandal** measures 21 ft. 7 in. (6.6 m) long, 6 ft. 6 in. (2 m) wide, and 11 ft. 5 in. (3.5 m) high and was designed for Diseños Ruddy of Bucaramanga, Colombia.

Cecilie reached the North Pole in a record time of 48 days 22 hr.

●**FASTEST COMPLETION OF THE THREE POLES CHALLENGE (FEMALE)** Cecilie Skog (Norway) conquered Mount Everest, the North Pole, and the South Pole in 1 year 336 days. She topped Mount Everest on May 23, 2004, reached the South Pole on December 27, 2005, and finally claimed the North Pole on April 24, 2006.

Youngest person to visit both Poles Jonathan Silverman (U.S.A., b. June 13, 1990) reached the North Pole on July 25, 1999 and the South Pole on January 10, 2002, aged 11 years 211 days.

Youngest person to visit the North Pole Alicia Hempleman-Adams (UK, b. November 8, 1989) stood at the geographic North Pole at the age of 8 years 173 days on May 1, 1998, the youngest person ever to have done so. She flew to the Pole to meet her father, the well-known adventurer David Hempleman-Adams (UK), at the end of his successful trek to the Pole.

Youngest person to trek to the South Pole The youngest person to trek overland to the South Pole without the use of dogs or motorized vehicles is Sarah Ann McNair-Landry (Canada, b. May 9, 1986), who was 18 when she arrived at the Pole on January 11, 2005. Remarkably, she had made the 684-mile (1,100-km) kite-assisted trip as part of an unsupported expedition led by her mother Matty McNair, a professional polar-trekking guide. The expedition also featured her brother Eric (U.S.A./Canada), who was 20 years old at the time.

No sandals for Wim Hof (Netherlands), who completed the **fastest half marathon while barefoot on ice or snow** in Oulu, Finland, in 2 hr. 16 min. 34 sec. on January 26, 2007.

CROSSING THE OCEANS

●**Longest distance rowed in an ocean-rowing career** Between 1974 and 1996, ocean rower Peter Bird (UK) racked up a cumulative total of 18,487 nautical miles (21,275 miles; 34,238 km) rowing the Atlantic east to west, the Pacific east to west, and the Pacific west to east.

●**First female to row oceans three times** U.S. Paralympic rower Angela Madsen crossed her first ocean with Frenchman Franck Festor during the 2007 Atlantic Rowing Race from the Canary Islands to Antigua. Following this, she became the ●**first woman to row the Indian Ocean**, alongside Helen Taylor (UK) in the eight-man *Aud Eamus*, crossing from Australia to Mauritius between April 28 and June 25, 2009. For her third crossing, she returned to the Atlantic in the 16-man *Big Blue*, traveling from Morocco to Barbados in the West Indies from January 15 to March 4, 2011.

●**First female to row the Indian Ocean solo** In 2009, Sarah Outen (UK, b. May 6, 1985) became the first woman to row the Indian Ocean single-handed, making her journey on the *Serendipity* from Fremantle, Australia, to Mauritius in 124 days 14 hr. 9 min. from April 1 to August 3, 2009. Aged 23 years 310 days at the outset, Sarah is also the **youngest person to row the Indian Ocean solo**.

YOUNGEST MALE TO ROW ANY OCEAN SOLO Aged just 23 years 175 days at the outset, Oliver Hicks (UK, b. December 3, 1981) rowed *Miss Olive, Virgin Atlantic* across the Atlantic Ocean west to east solo and unsupported between May 27 and September 28, 2005. His journey took 123 days 22 hr. 8 min. and covered 3,967 miles (6,384 km) from Atlantic Highlands, New Jersey, U.S.A., to St. Mary's, Scilly Isles, UK.

BORN ADVENTURER Following his Atlantic exploits, Oliver Hicks aimed to become the first oarsman to row round Antarctica, on his custom vessel *The Flying Carrot* (pictured), but treacherous conditions in the Southern Ocean forced him to abort the journey after 95 days at sea, on April 30, 2009.

31: Gallons of vomit you will throw up in your lifetime—enough to fill 280 of those waxed paper sick bags available from the back of the seat in front of you on board ships and aircraft the world over.

FASTEST CROSSING OF THE PACIFIC OCEAN BY SOLAR POWER In his solar-powered boat, *Malt's Mermaid*, Kenichi Horie (Japan) traveled 10,000 miles (16,092 km) from Salinas, Ecuador, to Tokyo, Japan, in a record time of 148 days between March 20 and August 5, 1996. The boat was built from recycled aluminum and powered by 130 ft.² (12 m²) of solar panels.

●**Youngest person to row any ocean solo** On March 14, 2010, Katie Spotz (U.S.A., b. April 18, 1987) rowed across the Atlantic from Senegal to Guyana. She had set off on January 3, 2010, aged just 22 years 260 days.

●**Fastest Atlantic row in a multihull** On board the trimaran *Hallin Marine*, David Hosking, Chris Covey, Paddy Thomas, Naomi Hoogesteger, Justin Johanneson, and Jack Stonehouse (all UK) rowed the Atlantic east to west on the "Trade Winds I" route from San Miguel, Tenerife, to Barbados, West Indies, in a record 31 days 23 hr. 31 min. between January 6 and February 7, 2011. The crew covered 2,563 nautical miles (2,949.45 miles; 4,746.67 km) at an average overall speed of 3.34 knots (3.84 mi./hr.; 6.19 km/h).

●**FIRST PERSON TO ROW THREE OCEANS** Erden Eruç (Turkey) became the first oarsman to conquer three different oceans when he completed his crossing of the Indian Ocean from Australia to Madagascar on November 26, 2010, after 136 days 12 hr. at sea. Erden had previously crossed the Atlantic from the Canary Islands to Guadeloupe (January 29 to May 5, 2006) and the Pacific from California, U.S.A., to New Guinea (July 10, 2007, to May 17, 2008).

LONGEST OCEAN SWIM The farthest distance ever swum in the open sea without flippers is 139.8 miles (225 km) by Veljko Rogošić (Croatia), who swam across the Adriatic Sea from Grado to Riccione (both Italy) in 50 hr. 10 min. between August 29 and 31, 2006.

During her two crossings, Roz completed around 3.8 million oarstrokes.

●**FIRST FEMALE TO ROW TWO OCEANS SOLO** British rower Roz Savage is the first woman to cross two oceans—the Atlantic and the Pacific—under her own power. On November 30, 2005, she set out across the Atlantic from the Canary Islands, arriving in Antigua, West Indies, on March 13, 2006. She started the longer Pacific crossing on May 25, 2008, and rowed in three stages from California, U.S.A., to Madang, Papua New Guinea, arriving on June 3, 2010, after nearly 250 days at sea.

SAVAGE SEAS Roz Savage's transpacific journey, via Hawaii and Kiribati, made her the ●**first solo female to row the Pacific**. However, Roz was no stranger to the ocean—her first attempt to cross it, in 2007, ended when storms capsized her three times in 24 hours.

●**Fastest Atlantic row in a monohull** The fastest east–west transatlantic crossing via the "Trade Winds I" route was achieved by the six crew of the *Sara G*—Matt Craughwell, Graham Carlin (both UK), Thomas Cremona (Malta), Rob Byrne, Adam Burke (both Ireland), and Fiann Paul (Iceland)—who rowed 2,753 nautical miles (3,168 miles; 5,099 km) from Tarfaya, Morocco, to Barbados, West Indies, in 33 days 21 hr. 46 min. from January 5 to February 8, 2011, at an average overall speed of 3.38 knots (3.9 mi./hr.; 6.3 km/h).

Dennis Storm (Netherlands) holds the record for the ○**most bras unhooked in one minute using one hand**. Dennis detached 69 bras on the set of *Try Before You Die* in Amsterdam, the Netherlands, on August 17, 2008.

○**Fastest team to row the Atlantic west to east ("from U.S.A., New York area")** After 114 years, the longest-standing record in the history of ocean rowing finally fell in 2010, when Leven Brown, Don Lennox (both UK), Ray Carroll (Ireland), and Livar Nysted (Faroe Islands) rowed *Artemis Investments* from New York, U.S.A., to St. Mary's, Scilly Isles, UK, in 43 days 21 hr. 26 min. 48 sec. Traveling from June 17 to July 31, 2010, they beat the previous record, set in 1896, by over 11 days.

○**Oldest female to row any ocean** Suzanne Pinto (U.S.A., b. February 3, 1954) was 57 years 325 days old when she helped row the $126,800 12-man vessel *Britannia III* across the Atlantic east to west from Gran Canaria in the Canary Islands to Barbados in the West Indies between January 31 and March 15, 2011.

○**Oldest person to row any ocean** Suzanne Pinto's senior by nearly a decade, Swiss/Canadian oarsman Thomas Butscher (b. June 11, 1944) was 67 years 210 days old when he joined the 16-man crew of the ocean catamaran *Big Blue* and successfully rowed the Atlantic east to west from Tarfaya in Morocco to Barbados, West Indies, in 52 days between January 15 and March 4, 2011.

●**First team of 16 to row any ocean** Thomas Butscher and Angela Madsen were joined on board *Big Blue* by skipper David Davlianidze (Georgia), Ernst Fiby (Austria), Ryan Worth, Elizabeth Koenig, Aleksandra Klimas-Mikalauskas, Louise Graff (all U.S.A.), Liam Flynn (UK), Steve Roedde, Nigel Roedde, Dylan White, Zach Scher, Charles Wilkins, Sylvain Croteau (all Canada), and Margaret Bowling (Australia). The largest crew to cross the Atlantic, they completed the trip in a speedy 47 days 18 hr.

CIRCUMNAVIGATION

FASTEST BY MICROLIGHT In 2000, Colin Bodill rounded the globe in his Mainair Blade 912 Flexwing microlight, flying alongside Jennifer Murray, who was making a solo helicopter circumnavigation attempt (see p. 230). The pair covered approximately 21,750 miles (35,000 km), starting and finishing together at Brooklands Airfield, Surrey, UK.

The ○**longest bra chain** consisted of 166,625 bras and measured 101.7 miles (163.77 km). It was created by volunteers raising money for the breast cancer charity Citizens Who Care (Australia) at the Bundaberg Show Grounds, Australia, on August 9, 2009.

Turn to p. 212 for more epic adventures.

BY AIR

Fastest by scheduled flights, six continents Michael Quandt (Germany), travel editor of the *Bild am Sonntag* newspaper, flew around the world aboard scheduled flights in 66 hr. 31 min. from July 6 to 8, 2004. The speedy journey began and ended in Singapore and went via Sydney (Australia), Los Angeles (U.S.A.), Houston (U.S.A.), Caracas (Venezuela), London (UK), Cairo (Egypt), and Kuala Lumpur (Malaysia).

Quandt's journey was five days faster than the **first solo circumnavigation by aircraft**, in a Lockheed Vega named *Winnie Mae* piloted by Wiley Post (U.S.A.) from July 15 to 22, 1933.

First by helicopter via both Poles Flying out of Fort Worth, Texas, U.S.A., Jennifer Murray and Colin Bodill (both UK) piloted a Bell 407 helicopter around the globe, taking in the spectacle of the North and South Poles, in 170 days 22 hr. 47 min. 17 sec. from December 5, 2006, to May 23, 2007. In doing so, Murray added to her record for the **fastest helicopter circumnavigation by a solo female**—99 days from May 31 to September 6, 2000.

First by balloon Brian Jones (UK) and Bertrand Piccard (Switzerland) completed a nonstop circuit of the globe in March 1999, piloting their *Breitling Orbiter 3* balloon from Château d'Oex, Switzerland, to Mauritania in North Africa. The **first solo circumnavigation by balloon** was by Steve Fossett (U.S.A.), who flew his *Bud Light Spirit of Freedom* from Western Australia to Queensland, Australia, in 13 days 8 hr. 33 min. from June 19 to July 2, 2002.

FIRST BY AIRCRAFT Two U.S. Army Douglas DWC seaplanes—the *Chicago*, piloted by Lt. Lowell H. Smith, and the *New Orleans* (left), flown by Leslie P. Arnold—flew around the world in 57 "hops" from April 6 to September 28, 1924, beginning and ending in Seattle, Washington, U.S.A.

The **most livestock killed by a single bolt of lightning** is 68 Jersey cows zapped at Warwick Marks's (Australia) dairy farm near Dorrigo, New South Wales, Australia, on October 31, 2005.

74,565: Length in miles of all the blood vessels in your body. If you connected all your veins, arteries, and capillaries end to end, you'd be long enough to travel round the world three times.

BY SEA

Most consecutively Jon Sanders (Australia) completed a series of three consecutive nonstop solo circumnavigations in his 44-ft. (13.9-m) sloop *Parry Endeavour* in 657 days from May 25, 1986, to March 13, 1988. Starting and finishing in Fremantle, Western Australia, he made one journey west and two east, covering 81,732 miles (131,535 km)—the ●**longest distance sailed nonstop by any vessel**.

Fastest solo Francis Joyon (France) sailed solo and nonstop around the world in 57 days 13 hr. 34 min. 6 sec. from November 23, 2007, to January 20, 2008, in the 97-ft. (29.5-m) maxi-trimaran *IDEC II*. Joyon, who began and ended his 24,170-mile (38,900-km) journey in Brest, France, beat the previous record, set by Ellen MacArthur (UK), by around 14 days.

○**FASTEST POWERED-BOAT CIRCUMNAVIGATION:** Crewed by volunteers, Earthrace circled the world in 60 days 23 hr. 49 min. from April 27 to June 27, 2008, starting out from Sagunto, Spain.

BY LAND

First on foot The first man reputed to have walked around the planet was George Matthew Schilling (U.S.A.), from 1897 to 1904. However, the first verified effort was David Kunst's (U.S.A.) 14,450-mile (23,250-km) trek across four continents between June 20, 1970, and October 5, 1974.

The **worst lightning strike disaster** killed 91 people when LANSA Flight 508 was struck over Peru by a lightning bolt and then smashed into the Amazon rainforest on December 24, 1971. Incredibly, one passenger survived.

First over land via both Poles Relying only on land and sea transport, Charles Burton and Ranulph Fiennes (UK) circled the world on its polar axis in three years from September 2, 1979, to August 29, 1982. Traveling southward from London, UK, the pair covered 35,000 miles (56,000 km) and twice had to brave the dangers of polar exploration.

● **LONGEST JOURNEY BY FIRE ENGINE** Between July 18, 2010, and April 10, 2011, Stephen Moore (UK) traveled 31,663 miles (50,957 km) around the globe in a 16-year-old Mercedes 1124 AF fire engine nicknamed "Martha" and donated by Dorset Fire and Rescue (UK). Accompanied by volunteers, Stephen visited 28 countries on five continents, beginning and ending his journey in London, UK. He received his certificate at GWR's London offices (above right).

ROUGH RIDE Vincent's record ride was no picnic. Along the way, he braved floods, storms, snowdrifts, and earthquakes as well as 13 punctures, dysentry in Libya, and two arrests, in Egypt and Indonesia.

○ **FASTEST CIRCUMNAVIGATION BY BICYCLE (MALE)** Vincent Cox (UK) completed the fastest round-the-world trip by pedal power in 163 days 6 hr. 58 min. from February 7 to August 1, 2010. Starting and finishing in London, UK, he cycled a distance of 18,226 miles (29,331 km) and traveled a total of 36,860 miles (59,321 km) including transfers.

Vincent cycled through over 20 countries on six continents.

Fastest by car The record for the first and fastest man and woman to have circumnavigated the Earth by car covering six continents under the rules applicable in 1989 and 1991 embracing more than an equator's length of driving (24,901 road miles; 40,075 km), is held by Saloo Choudhury and his wife Neena Choudhury (both India). The journey took 69 days 19 hours 5 minutes from September 9 to November 17, 1989. The couple drove a 1989 Hindustan "Contessa Classic" starting and finishing in Delhi, India.

FLIGHTS OF FANCY

Closest Calypso Pass A "Calypso Pass" is an aerial maneuver in which two planes fly back-to-back at high speeds. The closest pass was performed by two 71,000-hp Lockheed-Martin F-16 Falcons from the U.S. Air Force Thunderbirds display team at the Aviation Nation Air Show 2005 held in Las Vegas, U.S.A. Flying at a speed of 760 mi./hr. (1,223 km/h), the planes closed to within 18 in. (45 cm) of each other.

Longest human-powered flight Kanellos Kanellopoulos (Greece) pedaled his *Daedalus 88* aircraft 71.52 miles (115.11 km) from Heraklion, Crete, to the Greek island of Santorini on April 23, 1988. His heroic flight lasted 3 hr. 54 min. 59 sec. before strong winds broke off the plane's tail and caused it to crash into the sea just a short distance from the shore.

Longest flight in a hang glider On July 17, 2001, pilot Manfred Ruhmer (Austria) steered his hang glider a record distance of 435.33 miles (700.6 km) from Zapata to Lamesa, Texas, U.S.A., powered by nothing but the wind.

Highest flight by a hot-air balloon On November 26, 2005, Vijaypat Singhania (India), a 67-year-old business tycoon and part-time adventurer, achieved the hot-air balloon altitude record in a Cameron Z-1600. In a pressurized cabin attached to a balloon the height of a 22-story building, he rose 68,986 ft. (21,027 m) over Mumbai, India—twice the cruising altitude of a commercial airliner.

○**OLDEST WING WALKER** At the spritely age of 90 years 177 days, fearless Thomas Lackey (UK, b. May 22, 1920) donned his goggles to complete a wing walk over Cirencester, Gloucestershire, UK, on November 15, 2010, for Guinness World Records Day.

129,354: The number of dreams you'll dream in a lifetime. Although many of these will be about flying—one of the most common and exhilarating types of dream—just as many will be about falling, so brace yourself!

FIRST SUPERSONIC FLIGHT On October 14, 1947, Captain (later Brigadier General) Charles "Chuck" Elwood Yeager (U.S.A.) became the first man to fly faster than the speed of sound, reaching Mach 1.015 (670 mi./hr.; 1,078 km/h) in his Bell XS-1 rocket aircraft at an altitude of 42,000 ft. (12,800 m) over Lake Muroc, California, U.S.A.

First hot-air balloon flights over the poles Ivan André Trifonov (Austria) flew a one-man Thunder and Colt Cloudhopper balloon 0.6 miles (1 km) over the geographic North Pole on April 20, 1996. Four years later, he followed this feat with the first balloon flight over the geographic South Pole, piloting a Cameron AX-60 EC-HDB into the record books alongside his two Spanish crew members.

YOUNGEST PERSON TO FLY SOLO AROUND THE WORLD From March 23 to June 27, 2007, 23-year-old Barrington Irving (Jamaica/U.S.A., b. November 11, 1983) braved snow, storms, and monsoon rains to circumnavigate the globe in his single-engine plane *Inspiration*, becoming the youngest person, and first black pilot, to achieve the feat.

INSPIRATION When Barrington found that nobody would lend him an aircraft for his journey, he had one built instead. The Columbia 400 he flew was made entirely from donated parts and assembled for free by the Columbia Aircraft Manufacturing Company.

The **largest roll of toilet paper** was 5 ft. 7 in. (1.7 m) in diameter and was created by Kimberly-Clark Perú, in Lima, Peru, on June 7, 2008. With its 602,779 ft.^{2} (56,000 m^2) of surface area, it had enough paper to last the average human 100 years.

FIRST SOLO CIRCUMNAVIGATION BY AIRCRAFT WITHOUT REFUELING From March 1 to 3, 2005, Steve Fossett (U.S.A.) flew around the world nonstop without refueling in 67 hr. 1 min. in the Virgin Atlantic *GlobalFlyer*, starting and finishing at Salina, Kansas, U.S.A. The aircraft, built by Scaled Composites (U.S.A.), carried nearly 5.5 tons (5 metric tons) of fuel.

●**Fastest speed in a hot-air balloon** The greatest speed ever reached in a manned balloon is 200.23 mi./hr. (322.25 km/h), by Steve Fossett (U.S.A.) in his *Bud Light Spirit of Freedom* on July 1, 2002. Fossett achieved the record during his successful solo circumnavigation of the world, a feat that also saw him claim the record for the **longest solo balloon flight**, with a distance of 20,627 miles (33,195.1 km).

First aircraft circumnavigation by aircraft without refueling Richard G. Rutan and Jeana Yeager (both U.S.A.) traveled westward around the world from Edwards Air Force Base in California, U.S.A., in 9 days 3 min. 44 sec., from December 14 to 23, 1986. The duo's plane, *Voyager*, was designed and built by the same man behind Virgin's *GlobalFlyer:* Rutan's brother Burt, of Scaled Composites.

First jet wing flight across the English Channel On September 26, 2008, Yves Rossy, a Swiss pilot and inventor known as "Jet Man," became the first person to fly across the English Channel using a jet-powered fixed wing strapped to his back. He completed the flight in 9 min. 7 sec., reaching a top speed of 186 mi./hr. (300 km/h) propelled by four kerosene-burning jet turbines.

FASTEST SPEED IN A NON-SPACESHIP AIRCRAFT On October 3, 1967, U.S. Air Force pilot Major William J. Knight (U.S.A.) hit Mach 6.7 (4,520 mi./hr.; 7,270 km/h) in the North American Aviation X-15A-2 over the Mojave Desert, U.S.A. In doing so, he set an absolute human speed record that stood unbroken until exceeded by the Space Shuttle in the 1980s.

Created by jeweler Lam Sai-wing in 2001, the world's **most expensive bathroom** is located in his store in Hong Kong, China—it is made out of 24-karat gold and jewels worth HK$27 million ($3.5 million).

SKY'S THE LIMIT On April 3, 1933, RAF pilots in two aircraft—one Houston-Westland and one Westland-Wallace—completed the **first flights over Mount Everest** (29,029 ft; 8,848 m), the highest mountain in the world, scraping over it by just 100 ft. (30.5 m).

The balloon of the *Breitling Orbiter* 3 stood 180 ft. (55 m) tall when fully inflated.

LONGEST FLIGHT IN A HOT-AIR BALLOON Between March 1 and 23, 1999, Brian Jones (UK) and Bertrand Piccard (Switzerland) undertook the longest balloon flight in history, in terms of both distance and duration. Lifting off from Chateau d'Oex, Switzerland, aboard the *Breitling Orbiter 3,* they traveled nonstop for 477 hr. 47 min. and covered 25,361 miles (40,814 km) on an epic journey that saw them circumnavigate the globe.

First flight across Antarctica by single-engine aircraft RAF Squadron Leader John Lewis (UK) and three crew flew a single-engined Otter XL 710 from South Ice to Scott Base in 10 hr. 58 min. on January 6–7, 1958.

First flight over the North Pole On May 12, 1926, Arctic explorers Roald Amundsen (Norway) and Umberto Nobile (Italy) led a crew of 16 men in the world's first flight over the North Pole, achieving the feat in three days aboard a 348-ft. (106-m) airship designed by Nobile himself.

First midair rescue Dolly Shepherd and Louie May (both UK) were part of a performing troupe who leapt from hot-air balloons wearing parachutes. However, on June 9, 1908, Louie's ripcord jammed during a jump 11,000 ft. (3,352 m) above Longton, UK, and Dolly had to save her by sharing her own parachute.

SOCIETY

CONTENTS

VILLAGE EARTH

CROWDED PLANET

According to the United Nations, the world's population will reach 7 billion on August 26, 2011—just 12 years after the 6-billion mark was passed in 1999. Although slowing down, population growth is still heading upward, and is estimated to reach 8 billion by 2030.

Below is a map projection showing the actual landmass (left), then the same map distorted to show where the population is distributed—if we all had a fair share of the Earth, this is how our nations would have to change to accommodate us. The largest area on the map is China, which currently has the **largest population** at 1.33 billion.

○COUNTRY WITH THE HIGHEST POPULATION China has the world's largest population, with 1.33 billion people and counting by 2010. As global population numbers continue to rise, our planet is set to become more crowded than ever. The UN estimates that by the end of 2011, there will be 7 billion of us, rising to 9 billion by 2045—a far cry from the 2 billion people who walked the Earth in 1930, just eight decades ago.

LARGEST POOL PARTY? On July 4, 2010, hundreds of residents of Suining, Sichuan province, China, enjoyed perhaps the largest pool party ever, when they crowded into the local pool to escape scorching summer temperatures of over 95°F (35°C).

A HUNDRED HUMANS
Demographics is the study of human populations. Attempting to comprehend numbers—and populations—in their billions can be difficult, so here we've reduced the planet to a village of just 100 people that best represent the mix of human life on Earth. This makes the demographics easier to grasp and helps paint a picture of how our population is composed. *Sources: UN, CIA, World Bank, Population Media Center*

SEX
51 are men
49 are women

EMPLOYMENT
63 work in the service sector
30 work in industry
5 work in farming
2 are unemployed

EDUCATION
17 cannot read or write

INTERNET
15 have a computer
30 have internet access

RELIGION
30 are Christian
21 are Muslim
15 are nonreligious
14 are Buddhist/Eastern
12 are Hindu

FIRST LANGUAGES
13 speak Chinese
5 speak Spanish
5 speak English
3 speak Arabic
3 speak Hindi
3 speak Bengali
3 speak Portuguese
2 speak Russian
2 speak Japanese
2 speak German
2 speak Javanese

TELEPHONES
18 have a telephone line
59 have a cell phone

AGES
29 are under 15
11 are over 60

MOST POPULATED CITY
While it's difficult to get global agreement on the populations (and even definitions) of cities, Tokyo (left) currently tops most lists. According to the *CIA Factbook*, 36.5 million people live in Tokyo's metropolitan area.

In terms of the population of a city's core and inner districts, the most populous is Shanghai, with 13.831 million urbanites.

1,465: Number of gallons of milk you'll drink. And to produce it, you'd need at least one cow eating 88 lb. of grass a day for the whole of your life.

HEAD COUNT It took from the dawn of mankind until *c.* 1800 for the population to reach 1 billion; to reach 2 billion took just over 100 years, and 3 billion took about 90 years. To go from 6 to 7 billion took a mere 13 years.

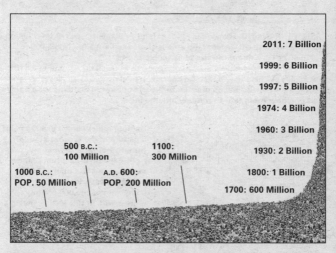

2011: 7 Billion

1999: 6 Billion

1997: 5 Billion

1974: 4 Billion

1960: 3 Billion

1930: 2 Billion

1800: 1 Billion

1700: 600 Million

500 B.C.:
100 Million

1100:
300 Million

1000 B.C.:
POP. 50 Million

A.D. 600:
POP. 200 Million

BOOMING POPULATION The graph creeping up the page charts world population against time. There are now more than twice as many people on Earth as there were 50 years ago. There's room on our planet for all these people (see p. 242), but we tend to concentrate ourselves into relatively small areas: there are 21 cities with more than 10 million inhabitants, and some cities are 40 times more populated today than they were 50 years ago.

100–1 This gathering of 100 people mirrors—as closely as possible—the demographics (age, sex, ethnicity, etc.) of the world today. It is only representative, however, given that half of the world lives in poverty. The real image would be somewhat different.

Skye, 639 miles²

ISLE OF MANKIND The average plot of land available to each of the 7 billion people on Earth—if surface land area is shared out equally—is 226,000 ft.² (21,500 m²) . . . about the size of 82 tennis courts.

But what's the smallest space we'd need to fit us all in? Assuming 2.5 ft.² (0.23 m²) per person—the typical space you're allocated in an elevator—you could squeeze all 7 billion of us on to the Isle of Skye in Scotland with a tiny bit of elbow room too! Everybody breathe in!

Demographics can be used to paint a picture of the ●most typical human being: a 28-year-old, right-handed, urban, Han Chinese male earning less than $12,000 (£7,480) a year. Pictured is a composite of 200,000 photographs of men who fit this profile, giving a face to the average human being.

On June 28, 2008, Zhao Danyang (Hong Kong) paid $2.1 million for the world's **most expensive lunch date sold at auction**, with the famous U.S. investor Warren Buffett at Smith & Wollensky's steakhouse in New York, U.S.A.

HIGHEST POPULATION DENSITY

The ⭕ **densest territory** is Macau, a Special Administrative Region of China, with 50,262 people per mile^2 (19,450 per km^2). But it's a small region—the true extent of Earth's overcrowding is told by looking at the top 10 most densely packed countries with a population over 50 million:

Country	Population	Area (miles^2)	Density (per miles^2)
Bangladesh	162,221,000	55,600	2,918
India	1,210,193,422	1,269,210	954
Japan	127,387,000	145,900	873
Philippines	92,226,600	115,860	796
Vietnam	85,789,573	128,066	670
UK	62,041,708	94,058	660
Germany	81,757,600	137,846	593
Pakistan	175,730,000	310,403	566
Italy	60,200,060	116,340	518
Nigeria	154,729,000	356,669	433

CRIME & PUNISHMENT

⭕**Most homicides per capita** According to figures from the United Nations Office on Drugs and Crime, Honduras is the most dangerous country on the planet, with 60.87 homicides per 100,000 people in 2008.

⚫**Most juvenile executions** Amnesty International has reported that in Iran in 2009 there were seven executions of juveniles—a person under the age of 18 at the time of their crime. This followed eight such executions in 2008, while today a further 133 juveniles remain at risk.

⭕**Largest DNA database** Between 1994 and April 2010, the FBI's (U.S.A.) National DNA Index System collected over 8.2 million offender profiles.

....

 On November 14, 2003, another kind of buffet lunch was held in Surin Province, Thailand. During the annual elephant parade, 269 Asian elephants chomped through 110,000 lb. (50 metric tons) of fruits and vegetables, making it the **largest elephant buffet**.

....

38,710,000: Homicides that will occur in the world during your lifetime. That's 490,000 every year or one every minute and is the equivalent of nearly the entire population of Kenya.

○ **MOST WANTED MAN** Following the death of Osama bin Laden in May 2011, *Forbes* identifies Mexican drug lord Joaquín 'El Chapo' Guzmán as the new most wanted man.

○ **Largest drugs haul by weight** On June 9, 2008, coalition forces in Afghanistan turned up a cannabis cache worth $443.2 million and weighing 261 tons (237 metric tons)—the equivalent of 30 double-decker buses. Found in trenches covering an area the size of two soccer pitches, the drugs were destroyed by Harrier fighter jets. In 2010, coalition forces went on to make the ○ **largest seizure of heroin**, which weighed 6.28 tons (5.7 metric tons).

● **Largest supplier of cannabis** Afghanistan produces up to 3,850 tons (3,500 metric tons) of cannabis each year, with up to 59,300 acres (24,000 ha) of land devoted to its production across 17 of the country's 34 provinces.

● **FIRST CAPTURED "NARCO SUB"** On July 2, 2010, Ecuadorian police seized a 102-ft.-long (31-m) diesel-electric submarine from drug smugglers in a mangrove swamp just south of the Colombian border. Although smugglers had been using semisubmersible subs for 17 years, this was the first time a long-range, fully submersible vessel had been captured. It was capable of transporting 7.7–11 tons (7–10 metric tons) of cocaine with an estimated value of $100 million.

In October 2008, the world's **longest tunnel aquarium** opened in Chiang Mai, in northern Thailand. It measures 436 ft. (133 m) long, 218 ft. (66.5 m) wide and houses 8,000 aquatic animals belonging to 250 different species.

●**WORST KLEPTOCRAT** President Suharto, president of Indonesia from 1967 until his regime was overthrown in 1998, looted more riches from his own country than any other government official in history, making him the world's biggest kleptocrat. In a 2004 report, Transparency International estimated that during his three decades in power he had stolen up to $35 billion. Suharto died in 2008, having never been brought to justice.

○**MOST LIFE SENTENCES** Terry Lynn Nichols (U.S.A.) is serving 161 consecutive life terms without the possibility of parole for his part in the 1995 bombing of a federal building in Oklahoma, U.S.A., in which 168 people, including 19 children, were killed.

○**LONGEST-SERVING PRISONER ON DEATH ROW** Now 75, Iwao Hakamada (Japan) has been on death row in Japan for 42 years, convicted of murdering a family in Shizuoka in 1968.

●**Longest-serving political prisoner** On May 1, 2009, Nael Barghouthi, a Palestinian sentenced to life in jail, became the longest-serving political prisoner. He began his sentence on April 4, 1978, and has now served more than 32 years in an Israeli jail. Incarcerated at the age of 21, Barghouthi has now been in jail for a decade longer than he was previously free.

●**Longest jail term** On December 23, 1994, American Charles Scott Robinson was sentenced in Oklahoma City, U.S.A., to 30,000 years, the jury having recommended 5,000 years for each of the six counts against him.

Lowest prison rate According to the current edition of the World Prison Population List, San Marino's 12-man prison had just a single occupier as of 2008.

A truly towering architectural achievement, the Burj Khalifa in Dubai, UAE, holds the record for the **building with the most floors**, with a staggering 160 stories. Make sure you use the elevator!

DOUBLE TROUBLE In 2010, policeman Andy Flitton (UK) handed out a traffic ticket to a motorist in his adopted New Zealand only to discover that the offender was the same man he had fined in 2008 while still living in the UK.

○**MOST HOSTAGES TAKEN BY PIRATES** According to the International Maritime Bureau, there were 445 pirate attacks globally in 2010, with 53 vessels and a record 1,181 hostages taken. Of these hostages, 638 were the crews of the 28 vessels remaining in Somali hands at the close of the year, representing ransoms of more than $10 million.

●**Oldest living judge** Born on June 22, 1907, in Kansas, U.S.A., Judge Wesley E. Brown is still presiding over courtrooms at the age of 103. If he continues for another year, he'll become the oldest federal judge in U.S. history.

Longest-serving executioner William Calcraft (UK) presided over nearly every hanging carried out at Newgate Prison in London, UK, for 45 years between 1829 and 1874.

●**HIGHEST NUMBER OF POLICE OFFICERS PER CAPITA** According to the British news and international affairs publication *The Economist*, the State of Brunei has more police officers per capita than any other country in the world. For every 100,000 citizens, it has 1,074 policemen.

●LARGEST SUPPLIER OF COCAINE
Colombia produces 70% of the global
cocaine supply, with much coming
through the Revolutionary Armed
Forces of Colombia (FARC), one of
the world's most powerful guerrilla
armies. By 2007, Colombia had
412,666 acres (167,000 ha) in coca
production, producing a potential
590 tons (535 metric tons) of pure
cocaine.

●FIRST COUNTRY TO USE IRIS
SCANS ON ID CARDS Mexico
introduced iris-scanning to ID cards
on January 24, 2011. The government
says the system, which identifies a
person by their unique iris pattern
using a camera, is 99% reliable and is
slated for full rollout by 2013. The ID
card will include fingerprints and an
image of the cardholder's eye.

Fastest police car On the road at least, the Italian police has the edge
over most criminals, with a fleet of 192-mi/h (309-km/h) Lamborghini
Gallardos.

○**Highest ransom paid for a ship** In November 2010, a ransom of
$9.5 million was paid to release the *Samho Dream*, a South Korean tanker
hijacked near the Gulf of Aden on April 4, 2010, carrying $170 million
of crude oil.

MODERN CONFLICT

○**Largest military budget** According to the Stockholm International
Peace Research Institute, the world spent $1,531 billion in total on de-
fense in 2009, with the U.S.A. alone accounting for $661 billion—over
43%. The U.S. figure is set to rise to some $739 billion by 2012.

●MOST SOPHISTICATED CYBER WEAPON
ATTACK In 2010, a software "worm"
named Stuxnet attacked computers
running software called WinCC, which
runs on Microsoft Windows. Because of
its complexity, experts suspect it was the
work of a government agency. Around
60% of the attacks centered on Iran and its
nuclear facilities (left).

●**LONGEST AFGHAN WAR** On November 27, 2010, NATO forces exceeded the nine years and 51 days the Russians spent in Afghanistan during the 1980s. NATO forces arrived on October 7, 2001, and have now been there for nine years and 236 days to the end of May 2011. The Russians sought to prop up a communist regime facing an uprising, whereas the U.S.A. and its allies entered Afghanistan to subdue the Taliban and destroy the terrorist organization Al Qaeda.

●**Largest military budget by GDP** Although China has the most troops and the U.S.A. has the biggest defense budget, the country that spends the most on its armed forces as a proportion of gross domestic product is the Middle East state of Oman—it invests 11.4% in its military might.

●**Largest supplier of fighter aircraft** The U.S.A. and Russia are the largest providers of combat aircraft to the world's air forces, with the U.S.A. supplying 341 planes, and Russia 219, between 2005 and 2009. India, Israel, and the UAE were the main customers.

●**Longest-running reparations bill** On October 3, 2010, nearly 92 years after the end of World War I (1914–1918), Germany paid the final $94-million portion of its war reparations, compensation for the costs incurred by the Allies and the damage suffered by France and Belgium.

●**LARGEST SPY-SWAP SINCE THE COLD WAR** On June 27, 2010, a group of 10 Russian "sleeper" agents were arrested in New York, U.S.A., put on trial and later deported to Russia on July 8, 2010. The most notable agent, Anna Chapman (left), has subsequently gone on to become a TV celebrity in Russia.

Opened in 2008, the **largest shopping mall** is the Dubai Mall, located within Downtown Dubai, UAE. Consisting of four levels with over 1,360 retail, food, and drink outlets, it has an internal floor area of 5.9 million ft.² (548,127 m²).

248   Society

12,646: Gallons of water you need to drink in a lifetime to stay alive. Water covers 70% of our planet, but drinking water is scarce in some parts of the world and it is likely that the wars of the future will be fought over it.

● **DEADLIEST YEAR IN THE WAR IN AFGHANISTAN** Of the 2,228 deaths among coalition forces in Afghanistan between October 2001 and January 2011, a record 711, or 32%, were killed in 2010 alone. Added to the 2,412 civilian deaths, this makes 2010 the deadliest year of the war so far.

LUCKIEST SOLDIER? In Afghanistan in 2010, Guardsman Ben Ralph (UK) was shot five times in one battle. His armor stopped two rounds, his ammo pouches stopped two more, and the fifth tore through his pants!

 Still with shopping, the **largest department store** is the Shinsegae Centumcity in Busan, South Korea. The store covers an area of 3.16 million ft.² (293,905 m²) and even contains an impressive 60-tee golf driving range!

●**LONGEST CEASEFIRE WITHOUT A PEACE TREATY** The Korean War between the communist North and democratic South started with the invasion of the South on June 25, 1950. After three years of fighting, a ceasefire was agreed on July 27, 1953. However, with relations worsening and no treaty in sight, the two sides are technically still at war.

●**Most deaths in the war on drugs** In 2006, Mexican president Felipe Calderón initiated a military crackdown on the drugs trade. According to the Attorney General, Arturo Chavez, over 30,000 soldiers, police, civilians, and gangsters have been killed since.

●**First modern-day climate-change war** In Darfur, Sudan, the dramatic reduction in rainfall in the last 50 years and the southward advance of the Sahara Desert have caused the province's northern Muslims and its southern Christian/Animists to arm themselves and begin fighting for land and water.

●**Most endangered food supply** According to the Food Security Risk Index 2010, Afghanistan's ability to feed itself is threatened by war, poverty, poor infrastructure, drought, and flooding. All of the other nine nations in the top 10 are in Africa.

●**Most foreign troops deployed in one country** By December 2010, there were 131,730 troops from 48 different nations deployed under the auspices of NATO's International Security Assistance Force (ISAF) in Afghanistan to deal with the Taliban insurgency and other problems in that country. The top contributor is the U.S.A. with 90,000 personnel, which represents just over 68% of the total force.

Longest sniper kill British sniper Craig Harrison killed two Taliban fighters from a distance of 8,120 ft. (2,474 m) in November 2009. The bullets took nearly three seconds to hit their targets.

●**Most IEDs defused** During a six-month tour in Afghanistan in 2010, bomb-disposal expert Sergeant Major Karl Ley (UK) made safe 139 improvised explosive devices (IEDs) planted by the Taliban—including 42 in one day. He was awarded the George Medal on his return. The ●**worst year for IED attacks in Afghanistan** was 2009, with 7,228 incidents—up 120% over 2008.

The ○**largest snowball fight** involved 5,387 participants at the 17th Mount Taebaek Snow Festival, Gangwon-do, South Korea, on January 22, 2010.

● OLDEST CONTINUOUSLY OPERATING INTELLIGENCE AGENCY Publicly acknowledged for the first time in 1994, the British Secret Intelligence Service was founded in 1909. Headquartered in London (left), it is popularly referred to as MI6—Military Intelligence 6—a cover name used in World War II.

First use of military robots in combat Robots were first deployed in combat in Afghanistan in July 2002. "Hermes," a wheeled robot fitted with cameras, a grenade launcher, and a shotgun, was used by U.S. troops to search a network of caves in Qiqay for enemy personnel and weaponry.

●Newest spy agency As head of the Coalition Provisional Authority in Iraq, U.S. diplomat Paul Bremer signed Authority No. 69 in April 2004, which brought into existence the Iraqi National Intelligence Agency with the aim of preventing terrorism and protecting the country's national security.

GARDEN GIANTS

⭘ HEAVIEST POTATO Peter Glazebrook (UK) is a 10-time Guinness World Record breaker and the current holder of three giant vegetable records. In 2010, he presented a potato at the Shepton Mallet big veg competition in Somerset, UK, that tipped the scales at 8 lb. 4 oz. (3.76 kg)—the weight of a newborn baby!

The snow petrel is the **most southerly bird**, nesting up to 150 miles (240 km) inland on the continent of Antarctica.

HEAVIEST FRUIT & VEG This selection of garden produce illustrates the heaviest specimens ever grown. The actual produce is, of course, *much* bigger than what you see here—the ◯ **heaviest pumpkin** ever recorded, for example, which was grown in 2010 by Chris Stevens (U.S.A.), weighed a whopping 1,810 lb. 8 oz. (821.23 kg) and measured 15 ft. 6 in. (4.73 m) around the middle—but we'd never fit them all on one page!

1. PINEAPPLE
17 lb. 12 oz. (8.06 kg)
E Kamuk, West New Britain
Province, Papua New Guinea, 1994

2. BANANAS (BUNCH)
473 bananas weighing 287 lb.
(130 kg)
Kabana SA and Tecorone SL, Canary
Islands, Spain, 2001

3. LEEK
17 lb. 13 oz. (8.1 kg)
Fred Charlton, Somerset, UK, 2002

4. CABBAGE
127 lb. (57.61 kg)
Steven Hubacek, Alaska, U.S.A.,
2009

5. SQUASH
1,236 lb. (560.64 kg)
John Vincent and Brian McGill,
Stroud, Ontario, Canada, 2009

6. GRAPEFRUIT
7 lb. 12 oz. (3.21 kg)
Cloy Dias Dutra, Niteroi, Brazil, 2006

7. BEETROOT
156 lb. 10 oz. (71.050 kg)
Piet de Goede, the Netherlands,
2005

8. MANGO
7.5 lb. (3.43 kg)
Sergio and Maria Socorro
Bodiongan, Cagayan de Oro City,
the Philippines, 2009

9. CAULIFLOWER
54 lb. 3 oz. (24.6 kg)
Alan Hattersley, Ecclesfield village,
Sheffield, UK, 1999

10. CELERY
63 lb. 4.8 oz. (28.7 kg)
Scott and Mardie Robb, Alaska,
U.S.A., 2003

11. ONION
16 lb. 8 oz. (7.495 kg)
John Sifford, West Midlands, UK,
2005

12. CUCUMBER
27 lb. 5 oz. (12.4 kg)
Alfred J Cobb, Somerset, UK, 2003

13. RED CABBAGE
42 lb. (19.05 kg)
R Straw, Derbyshire, UK, 1925

14. BROCCOLI
35 lb. (15.87 kg) John and Mary
Evans, Palmer, Alaska, U.S.A., 1993

13.5: Tons of vegetables you will eat—equal in weight to five medium-sized carrots a day. If all 13.5 tons were made into five giant carrots, each would be the size of a stretch limousine!

15. ROCKMELON
23 lb. 2 oz. (10.5 kg)
Ned Katich, Upper Swan, Western Australia, 1982

16. PEACH
25.6 oz. (725 g)
Paul Friday, Coloma, Michigan, U.S.A., 2002

17. ZUCCHINI
64 lb. 8 oz. (29.25 kg).
Bernard Lavery, Rhondda Cynon Taff, Wales, UK, in 1990

18. CARROT
18 lb. 13 oz. (8.61 kg) John Evans, Alaska, U.S.A., 1998

19. ●BELL PEPPER
0.63 lb. (0.29 kg)
Edward Curry, Arizona, U.S.A., 2009

20. POMEGRANATE
4.08 lb. (1.85 kg)
Aiguo village, Sichuan, China, 2009

21. PARSNIP
13 lb. (5.90 kg)
Peter Glazebrook, Somerset, UK, 2009

22. LEMON
11 lb. 9.7 oz. (5.26 kg)
Aharon Shemoel, Kefar Zeitim, Israel, 2003

23. NECTARINE
12.69 oz. (360 g)
Tony Slattery, Whangamata, NZ, 1998

24. TURNIP
39 lb. 3 oz. (17.7 kg)
Scott and Mardie Robb, Alaska, U.S.A., 2004

25. SWEET POTATO
81 lb. 9 oz. (37 kg)
Manuel Pérez Pérez, Lanzarote, Spain, 2004

26. AVOCADO
4.83 lb. (2.19 kg)
Ramirez Nahim, Caracas, Venezuela, 2009

27. ○POTATO
8 lb. 4 oz. (3.76 kg) Peter Glazebrook, Somerset, UK, 2010 (see p. 251)

28. GARLIC
2 lb. 10 oz. (1.19 kg)
Robert Kirkpatrick, California, U.S.A., 1985

29. TOMATO
7 lb. 12 oz. (3.51 kg)
G Graham, Oklahoma, U.S.A., 1986

30. CHERRY
0.76 oz. (21.69 g)
Gerardo Maggipinto, Sammichele di Bari, Italy, 2003

31. BRUSSELS SPROUT
18 lb. 3 oz. (8.3 kg)
Bernard Lavery, Rhondda Cynon Taff, Wales, UK, 1992

32. STRAWBERRY
8.14 oz. (231 g)
G Andersen, Kent, UK, 1983

33. RADISH
68 lb. 9 oz. (31.1 kg)
Manabu Oono, Kagoshima, Japan, 2003

34. APPLE
4 lb. 1 oz. (1.84 kg) Chisato Iwasaki, Hirosaki City, Japan, 2005

35. BLUEBERRY
0.4 oz. (11.28 g)
Polana SP. Zo.o, Parczew, Poland, 2008

OH MY GOURD! Chris Stevens's **heaviest pumpkin** or "gourd" (see p. 252) weighed almost the same as an entire Premier League soccer team! It was later carved into the world's **largest jack o'-lantern**.

○**MOST TOMATOES FROM ONE PLANT** Graham Tranter of Bridgnorth in Shropshire, UK, grew a single tomato stem (or "truss") that yielded a record 488 tomatoes when counted during the October 2010 harvest. Green-fingered Graham beat his own record, set the previous year at 304 tomatoes.

BIG FOOD

LARGEST . . .

○**Bowl of porridge** A bowl containing 1,388 lb. 14 oz. (630 kg) of porridge was prepared by Cupar Round Table in association with Scott's Porage Oats (both UK) during the Cupar Highland Games in Cupar, Scotland, UK, on July 4, 2010.

●**Burrito** A vast burrito prepared by CANIRAC La Paz in Baja California Sur, Mexico, on November 3, 2010, measured 1.5 miles (2.4 km) long and weighed a record 12,785 lb. (5,799 kg). Despite translating from the Spanish as "little donkey," the burrito contained the typical ingredients of fish, onions, chilis, and beans.

The **fastest, first, solo, and unaided crossing of the Antarctic continent** was made by the Norwegian Børge Ousland, who completed the 1,675-mile (2,690-km) trek on January 18, 1997, after 64 days.

○**LARGEST SERVING OF CURRYWURST** A currywurst—a pork sausage flavored with curry powder—weighing 386 lb. 4 oz. (175.2 kg) and 1,049 ft. 10 in. (320 m) in length was made by kitchen technologists MKN (Germany) in Wolfenbüttel, Germany, on April 30, 2010.

●**LARGEST ICE-CREAM CONE** An ice-cream cone measuring 9 ft. 2.6 in. (2.81 m) tall was created over a period of 30 hours by Mirco Della Vecchia and Andrea Andrighetti (both Italy) at the Rimini Fair in Rimini, Italy, on January 21–22, 2011.

○**Chocolate bar** On September 10, 2010, the Grand Candy Company of Yerevan, Armenia, unveiled a 9,722-lb. (4,410-kg) chocolate bar—enough chocolate to make a solid cube with sides 5 ft. (1.5 m) long!

○**Cocktail** Imagine a cocktail large enough to swim in. This is what Ricardo's Mexican Restaurant and Rosangel Tequila (both U.S.A.) created in Las Vegas, Nevada, U.S.A., with their 6,350-gal. (28,871-liter) margarita on October 15, 2010—enough to fill a bathtub every day for a year.

○**Hamburger** The largest commercially available hamburger weighs 300 lb. 4 oz. (136.2 kg). It was available for 150,000 yen ($1,780.59) at the Phoenix Seagaia Resort in Miyazaki, Japan, as of July 4, 2009. This is the cooked-weight equivalent of a gut-busting 796 quarterpounders!

The **first person to walk on skis to both Poles solo and unsupported** was Marek Kaminski (Poland), who reached the North Pole from Ward Hunt Island on May 23, 1995 (in 72 days) and the South Pole from Berkner Island on December 27, 1995 (in 53 days).

750: Milliliters of saliva you produce every day—enough to fill a wine bottle. You need saliva to lubricate the swallowing process. A lifetime's worth of food will be accompanied by 25,348 bottles of spit!

· ·

HAVE A PIZZA THAT! Too vast even for Big Mama's and Papa's Pizzeria, the **largest pizza** ever baked was 122 ft. 8 in. (37.4 m) across and weighed over 13 tons (12 tonnes). It was made at Norwood Hypermarket in Norwood, South Africa, on December 8, 1990.

○**Meatball** A meatball weighing 749 lb. 9 oz. (340 kg) and with a diameter of 5 ft. 3 in. (1.6 m) was prepared by Spieckermann BAU GmbH (Germany) during a staff picnic at their premises in Essen-Dellwig, Germany, on May 29, 2010.

●**Open sandwich** A bun weighing 1,337 lb. (606.45 kg) was prepared by Moore's BBQ (U.S.A.) in New Bern, North Carolina, U.S.A., on July 4, 2010. The sandwich, made to celebrate Moore's 300th anniversary, measured 8 ft. 9 in. (2.6 m) x 7 ft. 9 in. (2.37 m) and contained 586 lb. (265.81 kg) of pork.

○**LARGEST PIZZA COMMERCIALLY AVAILABLE** Available on the menu at Big Mama's and Papa's Pizzeria in Los Angeles, California, U.S.A., is a 4-ft.-6-in.-wide (1.37-m-wide) enormous square pizza. Retailing at $199.99 (£124) plus tax, this mammoth meal can feed up to 100 people and can be ordered for delivery—as long as you give the pizzeria 24 hours notice!

COOKIE AUCTION The colossal Custard Cream took 11 hours to make and was inspired by Simon's cookie-loving children Jack, Sam, and Olivia. It was auctioned for charity, raising £410 ($646) for Children in Need.

○ **LARGEST CREAM-FILLED COOKIE** The largest cream-filled cookie (aka Custard Cream) measures 1 ft. 11.2 in. x 1 ft. 3.3 in. x 2.5 in. (59 x 39 x 6.5 cm) and weighs 34 lb. 10.8 oz. (15.7 kg). It was crafted by Executive Chef Paul Thacker (above) and amateur biscuit master Simon Morgan (both UK) in the Chino Latino's restaurant in Park Plaza, Nottingham, UK, on November 18, 2010, for Guinness World Records Day 2010.

Custard creams are the most dangerous cookies, say insurance companies.

● **Pot of beans** A pot filled with 841 gal. (3,825.7 liters) of baked beans—or more than 9,000 regular cans—was prepared at the Alabama Butterbean Festival in Pinson, Alabama, U.S.A., on September 4, 2010.

○ **Salad** A serving of Greek salad measuring 82 ft. (25 m) in length was prepared by KEDI, the Public Benefit Municipal Enterprise of Ierapetra, on the Greek island of Crete on June 19, 2010. This super-sized salad weighed a record 29,579 lb. (13,417 kg).

See below for more record-breaking food fun.

●FALAFEL Chef Ramzi Choueiri (pictured) and students of Al-Kafaat University (all Lebanon) produced the ●largest serving of falafel—a total weight of 11,404 lb. 8 oz. (5,173 kg)—in Beirut, Lebanon, on May 9, 2010.

The ●largest falafel ball, however, was prepared two weeks later by the Jewish Community Relations Council of New York and the Olympic Pita Restaurant (both U.S.A.) and weighed 24 lb. (10.89 kg)!

●LARGEST OMELETTE A 9,702-lb. 8-oz. (4.4–ton) omelette made from 110,000 eggs was served by Yum-Bir (the Turkish Egg Producers Association) and the Pruva Neta tourist agency (both Turkey) at the Cepa shopping mall in Ankara, Turkey, on October 8, 2010.

○**Smoothie** To celebrate the quality of their home-grown produce, the Dairy Farmers of Canada blended a 219.9-gal. (1,000-liter) smoothie at the Bust-A-Record Dairy Day in Toronto, Ontario, Canada, on July 8, 2010. The ingredients included 661 lb. (300 kg) of blueberries.

FOOD FEATS

MOST . . .

○**Cocktails available** The menu of Pench's Cocktail Bar in Varna, Bulgaria, listed 1,244 separate cocktails as of September 23, 2010. Also on the list, but not included in the record count, are 44 nonalcoholic cocktails.

Measuring 3,314 ft. 6.7 in. (1,010.28 m) in length, the ○**longest pizza** was cooked by a team of chefs organized by MAKRO Cash and Carry Polska S.A. and Magillo restaurant (both Poland) in Krakow, Poland, on August 29, 2010.

○**LARGEST TOAST MOSAIC** Laura Hadland (UK) and 27 friends made a 1,387.31-ft.² (121.05-m²) mosaic from toast at Parr Hall in The Pyramid Centre, Warrington, UK, on October 17, 2010. It depicts Sandra Whitfield, Laura's mother-in-law.

○**Eggs balanced** Ashrita Furman (U.S.A.) balanced 888 eggs on their ends at York College in New York City, U.S.A., on June 12, 2010.

●**Pizzas made in 24 hours (team)** A team from Domino's Pizza #8209, including owners Bob and Tina Leikam (all U.S.A.), made 6,838 pizzas in a day in Taft, California, U.S.A., on October 22–23, 2010.

○**People in a pie fight** On November 11, 2010, 1,541 chocolate mousse pies were thrown in a fight between 671 people on the grounds of Lawrenceville School in New Jersey, U.S.A.

FAST FEEDERS

○**Hamburgers (3 min.)** Takeru Kobayashi (Japan) scoffed 10 burgers in three minutes in Madison Square, New York City, U.S.A., on August 29, 2010.

○**Rice grains (3 min)** Bob Blumer (Canada) ate 134 rice grains—one at a time, with chopsticks—in three minutes in Taipei, Taiwan, on August 30, 2010.

○**Chicken nuggets (3 min.)** Jordan Ryan (UK) ate 10.16 oz. (287.9 g, or 17 pieces) of McDonald's chicken nuggets in three minutes at Barclay House in Manchester, UK, on November 19, 2010.

 New Zealander Josh Anderson ate a 12-inch (30-cm) pizza in 1 min. 45.37 sec. in Wellington, New Zealand, on March 22, 2008—the **fastest time to eat a 12" pizza**.

EXTREME BARTENDING Flair bartending—aka "extreme bartending" or "flairtending"—was first contested in the TGI Friday's in Marina del Rey, California, U.S.A., in the mid-1980s.

● **COCKTAIL FLAIRING** When it comes to cocktail flairing—in which bartenders prepare drinks with dynamic, quickfire actions to entertain customers—world champion Tom Dyer (UK) is a real mover and shaker. On January 25, 2011, Tom performed the ● most consecutive bottle bumps on the elbow—29—and the ● most hand stalls in one minute—108—both in London, UK. He even has his own bartending school.

For art of a more conventional nature, see p. 431.

● **MOST EXPENSIVE HOT DOG** The Foot-Long Haute Dog sells for $69 at Serendipity 3 in New York City, U.S.A. Introduced on July 23, 2010—U.S. National Hot Dog Day—this fantastic frankfurter is served in a pretzel bun topped with foie gras and black truffles. The record-breaking snack also comes with specially prepared premium condiments.

A. Caramelized Vidalia onions
B. Truffled Dijon mustard
C. Heirloom tomato ketchup
D. Pretzel bun toasted with white-truffle butter
E. 100% beef sausage
F. Duck foie gras medallions

OLD-FASHIONED The **earliest known cocktail** was a concoction of honey, apple juice, tartaric acid, and barley found in a 5,000-year-old earthenware jug on the banks of the Tigris between Iran and Iraq in 2005.

GWR PRESENTS THE WORLD OF CRAZY COOKERY:

● **Longest cooking marathon (individual)**
24 hr. 30 min. 12 sec., by Dr. Chef K. Damodaran (India) at the Savera hotel in Chennai, India, on December 22, 2010.

○ **Largest cookery lesson**
440 participants, organized by Stichting Helioskoop in Beverijk, the Netherlands, on March 30, 2009.

● **Most people cooking simultaneously**
105, by Maison Malesan (France) in Salon de l'Escale, Yachts de Paris, Paris, France, on September 25, 2010.

● **FASTEST TIME TO EAT TWO BAGS OF WATERCRESS** Sam Batho (UK) scoffed two 3-oz. (85-g) bags of watercress in 49.69 seconds at the Watercress Festival 2010 in Alresford, UK, on May 16, 2010. His winning technique? Swallowing one bag at a time, with large gulps of water.

● **Mars bars (1 min.)** Pat Bertoletti and Joe Chestnut (both U.S.A.) each ate three Mars bars in a minute at the Tin Fish Restaurant in San Diego, California, U.S.A., on July 22, 2010.

○ **After Eights (1 min.)** Jim Lyngvilds (Denmark) ate nine After Eight thin mint chocolates—without using his hands—on the set of the TV show *Go'aften Danmark* in Copenhagen, Denmark, on October 1, 2010.

FASTEST TIME TO . . .

○ **Carve a face into a pumpkin** David Finkle (UK) cut the likeness of a face into a pumpkin in 20.1 seconds for the BBC's *Countryfile* program, in Colchester, UK, on October 7, 2010.

The ○ **fastest time to carve one metric ton (1.1 tons) of pumpkins** is 3 hr. 33 min. 49 sec., achieved by Stephen Clarke (U.S.A.) at Harrah's Casino Resort, Atlantic City, New Jersey, U.S.A., on October 29, 2008.

HIGH-FLYING FOOD The ○**highest pancake toss** measured 30 ft. 1 in. (9.17 m) and was thrown by Dominic Cuzzacrea (U.S.A.) at the Palace Theater in Lockport, New York, U.S.A., on June 22, 2010.

●**LARGEST CHEESE PLATTER** On November 24, 2010, a 40-cheese platter weighing 2,474 lb. 11 oz. (1,122.5 kg) was prepared at the World Cheese Awards at the NEC in Birmingham, UK.

○**Make one liter of ice cream** On June 6, 2010, Andrew Ross (UK) made a liter (just over one quart) of ice-cream in 10.34 seconds in Sheffield, South Yorkshire, UK. The ingredients included cream, vanilla, sugar, and liquid nitrogen.

●**Peel and eat three oranges** In just 1 min. 16 sec., Tekiner Sonkurt (Turkey) peeled and ate three oranges at the GWR Live! Roadshow at Forum Mersin, in Mersin, Turkey, on June 20, 2010.

●**Shell a boiled egg** Serial record breaker Alastair Galpin (New Zealand) took 18.95 seconds to shell one unpricked boiled egg at the Trusts Stadium in Waitakere, Auckland, New Zealand, on November 14, 2009.

LARGEST . . .

○**Mentos and soda fountain** Perfetti Van Melle (Philippines) organized for 2,865 Mentos and soda fountains to be launched at the SM Mall of Asia Complex in Manila, the Philippines, on October 17, 2010.

●**Serving of fried chicken** The Canoefest Fryers Club (U.S.A.) dished up 1,645 lb. (746.16 kg) of fried chicken in Brookville, Indiana, U.S.A., on July 2, 2010.

●**Serving of parmigiana** On August 7, 2010, Nuova Solidarietà (Italy) served up 833 lb. 5 oz. (378 kg) of the Italian dish parmigiana in Reggio Calabria, Italy.

....

The ○**largest game of leapfrog** involved 1,348 schoolchildren in an event organized at the Canterbury A&P Show (New Zealand) in Christchurch, New Zealand, on November 11, 2010.

....

●**Sushi mosaic** Featuring 8,374 pieces of sushi, and using 264 lb. 8 oz. (120 kg) of rice and 143 lb. 4 oz. (65 kg) of salmon, cod, mackerel, and prawns, the largest sushi mosaic is 216.67 ft.^{2} (20.13 m^2) in area. It was created by the Norwegian Seafood Export Council (Norway) with the help of the student chefs from Zhonghua Vocational School in Shanghai (China) at the 2010 World Expo Shanghai China, on October 15, 2010.

DOGS

Largest litter On November 29, 2004, Tia, a Neopolitan mastiff owned by Damian Ward (UK) and Anne Kellegher (Ireland), gave birth to a record litter of 24 puppies. Most survived, but one puppy was stillborn and three others died in the first week.

○**Oldest dog (living)** Pusuke, a male cross owned by Shigeo Nagai (Japan), was born on April 1, 1985 and is still enjoying life today at over 25 years of age. The **oldest dog ever** was an Australian cattle-dog named Bluey, who was obtained as a pup in 1910 and worked with cattle and sheep for almost 20 years before his death on November 14, 1939, at the ripe old age of 29 years 5 months.

○**Longest dog (living)** At a whopping 7 ft. 9 in. (2.37 m) from nose to tail, the longest dog alive is Farrell, an Irish wolfhound owned by Robert and Kate Fandetti (U.S.A.).

Smallest dog by length (living) At 6 in. (15.2 cm) long—just half the length of a standard ruler—Paulette Keller's (U.S.A.) diminutive dog Brandy is, from nose to tail tip, the shortest canine on the planet.

SMALLEST DOG BY HEIGHT (LIVING) Measuring just 4 in. (10.16 cm) tall on May 12, 2007, a female long-haired chihuahua called Boo Boo is the world's most vertically challenged dog. Owned by Lana Elswick of Kentucky, U.S.A., she is tiny enough to fit in the palm of a hand.

From leapfrog to real frogs. The **smelliest species of frog** is the Venezuelan skunk frog (*Aromobates nocturnus*); its vile-smelling skin secretion is released as a defense.

DOG-EARED Harbor is only beaten in the ear stakes by Tigger the bloodhound. Prior to his death in October 2009, Tigger sported a left ear of 13.5 in. (34.2 cm) and a right ear of 13.75 in. (34.9 cm)—the **longest dog ears ever**!

○**LONGEST DOG EARS (LIVING)** A black and tan coonhound named Harbor has the longest ears of any living dog, with measurements of 12.25 in. (31.1 cm) for the left ear and 13.5 in. (34.3 cm) for the right, as of June 8, 2010. Traditionally a hunting dog, the breed is well known for its droopy ears, which it uses to sweep up scents from the ground, but Harbor, owned by Jennifer Wert of Colorado, U.S.A., is way ahead of the pack!

A 2009 study says collies are the cleverest dogs, while Harbor's breed comes 44th!

●**Smallest working dog** Momo, a seven-year-old chihuahua weighing 6.6 lb. (3 kg), saw off competition from German shepherds to win a place in the search-and-rescue team of the Japanese police force in November 2010. Her size allows her to reach places other dogs can't.

The **longest bird beak** in relation to overall body length is that of the sword-billed hummingbird, found in the Andes from Venezuela to Bolivia. The beak measures 4 in. (10.2 cm)—longer than the bird's actual body.

3,326: Hours you will spend walking your dog in its lifetime. Regular walkies make dog owners slightly healthier than average. On the downside, there will be 15,308 separate pieces of dog poop to deal with.

●**MOST EXPENSIVE DOG** With a price tag of 10 million Chinese yuan or $1,513,417 (£945,000), an 11-month-old red Tibetan mastiff became the world's costliest canine when sold by breeder Lu Liang to a Chinese multimillionaire in March 2011. Weighing 180 lb (82 kg), Big Splash enjoys a diet of chicken and beef.

FASTEST TIME TO POP 100 BALLOONS Under the watchful eye of owner Doree Sitterly (U.S.A.), determined Jack Russell terrier Anastasia popped 100 balloons in just 44.49 sec. on the set of *Live! with Regis and Kelly* in Los Angeles, U.S.A., on February 24, 2008.

Loudest bark On June 15, 2009, Daz, a German shepherd belonging to Peter Lucken (UK), produced a "woof" measuring 108 dB—the most deafening ever registered by one dog.

Not to be outdone, a chorus of 76 hounds on the other side of the Atlantic produced the ○**loudest bark by a group**, hitting a record 124 dB in an event staged by Petmate in Colorado, U.S.A., on November 7, 2009.

Longest solid object swallowed by a dog Kyle, a collie–Staffordshire bull terrier cross, who was 18 in. (45.7 cm) long at the time, had to have a 15-in. (38.1-cm) bread knife removed from his stomach after swallowing it handle-first in December 2000.

Longest journey home by a lost dog In 1979, a labrador–boxer cross named Jimpa turned up at his old home in Victoria, Australia, after walking 2,000 miles (3,218 km) across the country from Nyabing, Western Australia. His owner, Warren Dumesney (Australia), had moved to Nyabing 14 months earlier for work, but had later lost his pet. During the epic trek, Jimpa negotiated the almost waterless Nullarbor Plain, which stretches 684 miles (1,100 km) east to west.

During Birdwatch Kenya 86, held on November 29–30, 1986, twitchers Terry Stevenson, John Fanshawe, and Andy Roberts (all Kenya) claimed the record for the **most bird species spotted in 24 hours**, sighting 342 different types of bird.

● **HIGHEST MAN-AND-DOG PARACHUTE DEPLOYMENT** Mike Forsythe (U.S.A.) and his working dog Cara dived from an aircraft and deployed a parachute at a record altitude of 30,100 ft. (9,174 m). Cara was strapped to Forsythe, a trainer for U.S. Special Operations Units, in a K9 Storm aerial insertion vest, a harness specially designed for dogs of war deployed on aerial missions.

A. Cara with oxygen supply
B. Alloy steel buckles and v-rings
C. Double Kevlar exterior for stab protection
D. ID patch

TALLEST DOG The aptly named Giant George is not only the tallest dog alive, but also the **tallest dog ever**. Owned by David Nasser of Tucson, Arizona, U.S.A., the huge great dane registered a height of 43 in. (1.092 m) on February 15, 2010.

● **Most knots untied by a dog in three minutes** Ben, a pug–springer spaniel cross owned by Claudia Neumann (Germany), managed to untie a record 14 knots in three minutes at the Vienna Recordia event in Vienna, Austria, on September 26, 2010.

BREAKING RECORDS WAS A WALK IN THE PARK FOR THESE FURRY FRIENDS:

○ **Largest dog walk:**
18,113 dogs (178 breeds), in the Great North Dog Walk in South Shields, UK, on June 13, 2010.

● **Largest dog walk (single breed):**
700 labradors, in a 3-mile (5-km) charity walk in Warsaw, Poland, on August 29, 2010.

○ **Most dogs walked by an individual:**
27 dogs, by Melissa Crispin Piche (Canada) in Alberta, Canada, on September 13, 2008. Although 31 dogs began the walk, one escaped and three retired!

Hardiest dog On April 15, 2003, 10-month-old mongrel Dosha escaped from her home in California, U.S.A., only to be run over by a car and then shot in the head by police, who were trying to put her out of her misery. Subsequently sealed in a bag and placed in a freezer at an animal center, she was discovered by staff two hours later, alive and sitting upright! All three potentially fatal events occurred in a 24-hour period, making Dosha the world's most resilient dog.

●**Most catches of a frisbee by a dog in three minutes** Ciaki caught a frisbee thrown by owner Nicola Ratti (Italy) 11 times on the set of *Lo Show dei Record* in Rome, Italy, on February 25, 2010.

CATS

First domesticated cats The oldest evidence of the domestication of the cat dates back 9,500 years. The bones of a cat were discovered in the neolithic village of Shillourokambos in Cyprus by a team of French scientists, and the find announced in the journal *Science* in April 2004.

Oldest cat ever Creme Puff was born on August 3, 1967, and lived until August 6, 2005, a total of 38 years 3 days. She lived with her owner, Jake Perry, in Austin, Texas, U.S.A.

Smallest cat ever A male blue point Himalayan-Persian named Tinker Toy measured only 2.75 in. (7 cm) tall and 7.5 in. (19 cm) long when full-grown (aged 2.5 years). The unusually tiny cat was owned by Katrina and Scott Forbes (U.S.A.).

Largest litter by a domestic cat On August 7, 1970, a Burmese–Siamese cat belonging to V. Gane of Kingham, Oxfordshire, UK, gave birth to 19 kittens. Four of the kittens in the litter were stillborn.

Most prolific cat A tabby cat named Dusty, born in 1935, who lived in Bonham, Texas, U.S.A., produced a total of 420 kittens during her breeding life. She gave birth to her last litter, a single kitten, on June 12, 1952.

> **PAWS FOR THOUGHT** The **cat with the most toes** is Jake, a male ginger tabby from Bonfield in Ontario, Canada, who has 28 toes—seven on each paw. Each toe has its own claw, pad, and bone structure.

● **FIRST ORCHESTRAL WORK WRITTEN FOR CAT AND PIANO** "Catcerto" is a four-minute piano concerto for chamber orchestra and cat composed by Mindaugas Piečaitis (Lithuania). The piece—in which an orchestra accompanies a video of a cat pawing at notes on a piano—debuted at the Klaipeda Concert Hall in Klaipeda, Lithuania, on June 5, 2009, with Nora the cat at the piano.

○ **LONGEST DOMESTIC CAT** At 48.5 in. (123 cm) long, Mymains Stewart Gilligan (aka Stewie) is the world's longest domestic cat. The five-year-old feline is owned by Robin Hendrickson and Erik Brandsness (U.S.A.) and was measured on August 28, 2010. He also has the ○ **longest domestic cat tail** at 16.34 in. (41.5 cm).

Longest cat whiskers The longest recorded whiskers on a cat measured 7.5 in. (19 cm) and belong to Missi, a Maine coon who lives with her owner, Kaija Kyllönen (Finland). The world-beating whiskers were measured in Iisvesi, Finland, on December 22, 2005.

Lake Turkana in Kenya has a surface area of 2,472 miles² (6,405 km²), making it the **largest desert lake** in the world.

0.44: Number of pets you can expect to own at any one time. It's most likely to be 0.44 of a cat or a dog. In its lifetime, the average dog will cost its owners $10,943, the average cat $8,029.

○ **SMALLEST LIVING DOMESTIC CAT** The shortest living cat is Fizz Girl, a two-year-old female munchkin cat who measured 6 in. (15.24 cm) from the floor to the shoulder on July 23, 2010. The pint-sized puss weighs just 4 lb. 2.3 oz. (2.09 kg) and is owned by Tiffani Kjeldergaard (U.S.A.).

Fizz Girl lives on a ranch with horses, dogs, and parrots.

● **LARGEST CAT SANCTUARY** The 30-acre (12-ha) Caboodle Ranch houses 500 cats in a sanctuary the size of 22 American football fields. It was founded in Lee, Florida, U.S.A., in 2003 by Craig Grant (U.S.A.), who has erected scale buildings for his feline guests.

HOUSE CAT Cats may have been the first (and perhaps only) animals to have chosen to be domesticated. They preyed on the rodents found in human communities, but also thrived on the food and company provided by people.

 At around 60 miles (100 km) by 18 miles (30 km) in extent, and 1,656 ft. (505 m) deep at its deepest point, Lake Toba in the Indonesian island of Sumatra is the **largest crater lake**.

●**FIRST ANIMAL WITH TWO BIONIC LEG IMPLANTS** Oscar the cat lost his legs in an accident in late 2009 and was not expected to survive. In June 2010, vet Noel Fitzpatrick and his team drilled holes into what remained of Oscar's legs and inserted metal implants into his ankle bones—making him the ●**first animal to receive implants into moving joints**. Skin and bone have grown over the implants, which have now become part of his body.

Most air flights by a pet A domestic cat called Smarty made her 79th flight on June 28, 2005. All the flights were trips between Cairo, Egypt, and Larnaca, Cyprus, with her owners Peter and Carole Godfrey (UK).

Wealthiest cat When Ben Rea (UK) died in May 1988, he bequeathed his $12.5-million (£7-million) fortune to Blackie, the last surviving of 15 cats.

Most expensive cat A Californian spangled cat was bought for $24,000 in January 1987.

Greatest mouser Towser (b. April 21, 1963), a female tortoiseshell cat owned by Glenturret Distillery near Crieff in Perth and Kinross, Scotland, UK, notched up an estimated 28,900 murine victims (i.e., dead mice). She averaged 3.3 rodents a day until her death on March 20, 1987.

COLLECTIONS

○**Cats** Carmen de Aldana (Guatemala) has 21,321 cat-related items, as of March 14, 2011. She has been collecting them since 1954.

Chickens As of June 2006, Cecil and Joann Dixon (both U.S.A.) had 6,505 chicken-themed items.

Dalmatians Karen Ferrier (UK) had 1,117 different Dalmatian-related objects as of February 3, 2009, including a car and items that had belonged to Dodie Smith, author of *The Hundred and One Dalmatians*.

○**Donald Duck memorabilia** As of March 2011, Mary Brooks (U.S.A.) had 1,411 objects relating to Donald Duck. Oddly, her husband's name was Donald and his school nickname was "Duck."

●**Donkeys** Since 1976, Delores DeJohn (U.S.A.) has amassed 690 donkey-related items.

Dragons Charlene Leatherman (U.S.A.) has a 793-strong dragon collection. European dragons are usually depicted with wings and most often pictured fighting knights, while Chinese dragons are usually shown as long and lean, holding a pearl jewel.

●**CRABS As of March 9, 2011, Darren Martin (UK) had created a collection of 441 crab-related items, which he had been putting together for over 10 years.**

○**COWS** Denise Tubangui (U.S.A.) had a collection of 2,429 cow-related items as of March 2011. Denise started collecting in 1990, when she saw a cow figurine in her mother's kitchen. Her favorite item is the life-sized calf that her neighbors gave her as a present.

Elephants As of April 8, 2008, Janet Mallernee-Briley (U.S.A.) had 5,779 items relating to elephants. She received her first elephant from an uncle when she was 16.

○**Frogs** Sheila Crown (UK) has 10,502 frog items that she has been collecting since 1979. Her collection was displayed at the FrogsGalore Museum, Malborough, UK, on May 12, 2002.

Giraffes Susa Forster (Germany) has collected 2,443 separate giraffe items since 1974. These include a 15-ft.-1-in.-tall (4.6-m) giraffe that stands in her living room.

○**LIONS** Reinhard Stöckl (Austria) had 1,761 different lion-related items as of March 27, 2010, a collection that he has been building since 1998.

Q. WHERE DO PENGUINS LIVE IN THE WILD?

A. Penguins are largely associated with Antarctica, of course, but they also live wild in Australia, New Zéaland, Africa, and South America. Even the Equator is home to penguins—the Galápagos penguin can be found living in Ecuador!

○**PENGUINS** As of March 14, 2011, Birgit Berends (Germany) had amassed a collection of 11,062 different penguin-related items. Birgit started her collection at the age of 18, inspired by the animated series *Pingu*, although her very first penguin dates back to her days in elementary school.

○**Hedgehogs** Bengt W. Johansson (Sweden) had 495 different hedgehog-related items as of March 2011, including a hedgehog clock from his wife.

Ladybirds Carine Roosen (Belgium) has amassed 3,531 ladybird items over a period of more than 10 years. One of her favorite items is a ladybird toilet seat.

●**Mice and rats** Christa Behmenburg (Germany) has a total of 27,623 objects related to mice and rats, including cigarette cards and money.

Mickey Mouse memorabilia As of December 2008, Janet Esteves (U.S.A.) had amassed 2,760 different Mickey Mouse items.

Monkeys Since 1970, Wang Lingxian (China) has collected 5,680 monkey-themed items. Fittingly, both she and her husband were born in the Chinese Year of the Monkey.

Owls Dianne Turner (U.S.A.) owned a collection of 18,055 owl-themed objects, which she completed in 2002, aged 55.

○**Pandas** As of March 2011, Miranda Kessler (U.S.A.) had a collection of 1,225 different panda items. She was given her first stuffed panda bear from her father when she was three years old.

○**Pigs** Anne Langton of Alfreton, Derbyshire, UK, has amassed a total of 11,505 pig items, which she has been collecting for over 20 years.

○**Rabbits** Husband and wife Steve Lubanski and Candace Frazee (both U.S.A.) had 28,423 bunny-themed collectibles as of March 2011, displayed in their own Bunny Museum in Pasadena, California.

Rubber ducks As of February 10, 2010, Charlotte Lee (U.S.A.) had 5,249 different rubber ducks, which she has been collecting since 1996. All her rubber ducks are kept in glass showcases on the four walls of her dedicated duck room.

Snails A. G. Straver (Netherlands) has 457 items relating to snails. In his village, many people share the same name, and each family has a nickname; that of his wife's family was "the snail." In 1993, he gave her a ceramic snail for her birthday, and then began his collection.

The ●**longest open saltwater scuba-dive** lasted 48 hr. 8 min. 17 sec. and was performed by William Goodman (UK) at Blue Marlin Dive, Lombok, Indonesia, from January 7 to 9, 2010.

○**Teddy bears** Jackie Miley (U.S.A.) had 7,106 different teddy bears as of March 11, 2011, having begun collecting in 2002. She now keeps the bears in a little house of their own, called Teddy Bear Town, located across the street from her own apartment.

●**Tortoises and turtles** Connie and Danny Tan (both Singapore) have built up a collection of 3,456 items relating to tortoises and turtles, including more than 1,000 live specimens. They keep their collection in the Live Turtle and Tortoise Museum, Singapore.

●**Chocolate bars** Chocolate-lover Bob Brown (U.S.A.) has the world's largest personal collection of chocolate bars, with 770 unique items. His tempting cache was put on display at the Castleton Square Mall in Indianapolis, U.S.A., on October 29, 2010.

○**"DO NOT DISTURB" SIGNS** Since 1985, Jean-François Vernetti (Switzerland), a frequent business traveler, has collected an extraordinary 11,111 different "Do Not Disturb" signs during his visits to hotels in 189 countries across the globe. Sssshhh . . .

For the ●**longest open saltwater scuba-dive in cold water** you have to go to the Republic of Ireland, where Declan Devane (Ireland) performed an 11-hr. 42-min. dive in Little Killary, Co. Galway, Ireland, on October 10, 2009.

COOKING UP A STORM Maria Coyne (U.S.A.) isn't short of a recipe or two, being the owner of the ●**largest collection of cookbooks**. With 1,070 collected since 1965, the only problem is finding a kitchen large enough to store them all.

●**DALEKS** Although not a fan of the sci-fi show *Doctor Who* (BBC, UK), Rob Hull (UK) is nevertheless the world's biggest fan of the Doctor's arch nemeses, the Daleks. As of March 25, 2011, Rob's Dalek collection runs to over 571 examples and includes several rare pieces as well as a full-size working model, which, at the press of a button, issues the famously menacing war cry: "Exterminate!"

●**Olive oil bottles** By April 2010, Ronald Popeil (U.S.A.) had collected 1,221 different olive oil bottles. Ronald started the unusual collection the year he began working on his invention, an electric automatic pasta maker, a device that requires a healthy supply of olive oil.

●**Mushroom-related items** If it features a mushroom, Shara Hoffman (U.S.A.) will buy it—since 2000, she has accumulated 263 mushroom-related items, ranging from clocks, pots, and pans to fabrics and even furniture.

The **longest dance party** was staged by Unique Events Limited (Ireland). It began on October 27, 2006, at 12:00 p.m. with 40 dancers, 31 of whom completed the marathon after 55 hours, at the Quay Front, Wexford, Ireland, on October 29, 2006.

●CLOWNS Clown-lover Ortrud Kastaun (Germany) has been collecting clown-related items since 1995 and had amassed a record 1,610 different pieces up to June 3, 2010. Over the years, Ortrud's flat became too small to accommodate her growing collection, so in 2001 she moved to a larger place and set up her own private clown museum, located in Essen, Germany.

●Salt and pepper shakers LaVerne Tish (U.S.A.) owns 6,971 pairs of salt and pepper shakers, collected between 1984 and January 2011.

○Sugar packets By June 11, 2010, sweet-toothed Ralf Schröder (Germany) had collected 6,991 different sugar packets.

●Coca-cola memorabilia Since 2005, Rebecca Flores (U.S.A.) has put together a colorful array of 945 Coke-related collectibles.

> **NO PLACE LIKE GNOME** Like Ortrud, another collector forced to set up a special home for her growing collection is Ann Atkin (UK), whose record 2,042 gnomes and pixies live at her Gnome Reserve in Devon, UK.

 From dance marathons to video games marathons, the **longest nonstop LAN party** lasted 40 hours and was completed by 274 gamers during Cyber Fusion 2009 at the Multimedia University in Cyberjaya, Malaysia, on April 11–12, 2009.

●**SUPER MARIO MEMORABILIA**
Mitsugu Kikai (Japan) is the proud owner of the world's largest collection of Super Mario memorabilia. Counted in Tokyo, Japan, on July 15, 2010, the collection contains 5,400 unique items relating to the famous Italian plumber from the popular Nintendo video game series.

●**Stamps featuring images of popes** Magnus Andersson (Sweden) has a philatelic collection with a twist, boasting 1,119 postage stamps featuring the faces of various pontiffs from over the years.

○**Pooh and friends memorabilia** At the last count on May 1, 2010, Pooh Bear fan Deb Hoffman (U.S.A.) had accumulated a record 4,805 different pieces of memorabilia from the popular children's story about a toy bear and his many animal friends.

●**Mr. Men memorabilia** Despite only beginning her collection in 2001, Joanne Black (UK) has wasted no time in putting together a collection of 2,225 Mr. Men toys, books, and other items.

○**Pokémon memorabilia** As of October 14, 2010, Lisa Courtney (UK) had amassed a record 14,410 Pokémon items, picked up in the UK, U.S.A., France, and Japan.

●**Charlie's Angels memorabilia** Since 1976, Jack Condon (U.S.A.) has collected 1,460 items related to the hit 1970s TV crime show.

Magic artifacts David Copperfield's (U.S.A.) International Museum and Library of the Conjuring Arts, founded in 1991 in Nevada, U.S.A., contains 150,000 props, books, posters, and other historical ephemera related to magic and conjuring, of which 90,000 are on display.

○**Playing cards** Liu Fuchang (China) is the real deal when it comes to collecting playing cards. His record-breaking collection, verified in 2007, features 11,087 different sets, themed on subjects ranging from art and literature to travel, television, and the military.

Model airplanes The largest collection of handmade aircraft belongs to John Kalusa (U.S.A.), who has created 5,737 wooden planes since 1936. The collection is currently housed in the library of Embry-Riddle Aeronautical University in Arizona, U.S.A.

○**Model buses** Classic car fan Geoff Price (UK) also has a passion for model four-wheelers. Among his vast collection of 10,955 buses, as of April 2011, he also has the ●**largest model tram collection**, with 830 amassed since 1959.

○**Telephones** Rita Zimmermann (Switzerland) must have ringing in her ears, due to her 771-strong collection of telephones, amassed from 1990 to July 10, 2010.

●**Men's neckties** Derryl Ogden (U.S.A.) is the undisputed king of grabatology—the collecting of neckties—with 16,055 accumulated since 1934.

○**Brooches** As of May 2011, Adam Wide (UK) has 4,061 brooches. Each one is themed on the festive season, making this also the ○**largest collection of Christmas brooches**.

●**Personal scrapbooks** U.S. media mogul Hugh Hefner has put together a record 2,396 personal scrapbooks during his colorful 85-year life.

TOYS & GAMES

●**LONGEST RAMP JUMP BY A REMOTE-CONTROL CAR** An HPI Vorza, controlled by Jason Bradbury (UK), completed a record leap of 85 ft. 10.7 in (26.18 m) on the set of *The Gadget Show* in Birmingham, UK, on March 25, 2010.

○**MOST GAMES OF CHESS PLAYED SIMULTANEOUSLY IN ONE LOCATION**
On December 24, 2010, an incredible 20,017 budding chess players from schools across the state of Gujarat, India, competed against 1,024 chess masters in 20,480 games of chess. Well prepared for their clash with the experts, the schoolchildren had been coached in preparation for the record attempt by the reigning World Chess Champion, Viswanathan Anand (India).

●**Most dominoes toppled in a minute** On August 7, 2010, Gemma Hansen (UK) stacked then toppled a line of 75 dominoes in the space of one minute at Butlins holiday park in Minehead, Somerset, UK.

●**Longest plastic toy train track** Built by Mattel Inc. and Hit Entertainment (both Australia), a toy train track measuring 6,902 ft. (2,104 m) was laid at the Workshops Rail Museum in Queensland, Australia, on November 4, 2010. A toy train took 2 hr. 52 min. 23 sec. to complete the epic journey.

○**LARGEST COMMERCIALLY AVAILABLE JIGSAW** Fans of the jigsaw will have their work cut out with this September 2010 offering from German manufacturer Ravensburger AG. Players must puzzle out a mind-boggling 32,256 pieces to complete the image, which measures 17 ft. 8 in. x 6 ft. 3 in. (5.4 x 1.9 m).

. . . .

The world's **largest butterfly farm** is on the Malaysian island of Penang. Opened in March 1986, and occupying 1.98 acres (0.8 ha), it contains over 4,000 living specimens belonging to more than 50 different species.

. . . .

●**Largest treasure hunt game** To mark the relaunch of the Kinder Surprise egg, 250 children took part in the world's largest treasure hunt in Bucharest, Romania, on September 4, 2010.

●**FASTEST REMOTE-CONTROL JET-POWERED MODEL AIRCRAFT** Axel Haché (Dominican Republic) and David Shulman's (U.S.A.) jet reached a speed of 293 knots (337.24 mi/h or 542.64 km/h) at Hobbyland Airfield in the Dominican Republic on January 18, 2010.

UP, UP, AND AWAY On May 3, 2008, a squadron of 99 remote-control planes took to the skies over Georgia, U.S.A., and flew into the record books as the ●**most model aircraft airborne simultaneously**.

 A prize catch for any butterfly farm would be the Queen Alexandra's birdwing (*Ornithoptera alexandrae*) of Papua New Guinea—the **largest known butterfly**. Females can weigh more than 0.9 oz. (25 g) and have a wingspan exceeding 11 in. (28 cm).

RUBIK'S REKORDS!

From Cubes to Clocks and everything in between, discover who has the fastest fingers in Rubik history. *Correct at March 31, 2011.*

Category	Holder	Time	Competition	Date
○ 3x3 Cube	Feliks Zemdegs (Australia)	0:06.65	Melbourne Summer 11	Jan. 29, 2011
● 4x4 Cube	Feliks Zemdegs (Australia)	0:31.97	Melbourne Cube Day	Nov. 13, 2010
● 5x5 Cube	Feliks Zemdegs (Australia)	1:01.59	Melbourne Summer 11	Sep. 19, 2010
● 7x7 Cube	Michal Halczuk (Poland)	3:25.91	Pabianice Open	Sep. 26, 2010
● Rubik's Clock	Sebastián Pino Castillo (Chile)	0:05.05	Bicentenario Open	Aug. 29, 2010
● 3x3 (one hand)	Piotr Alexandrowicz (Poland)	0:11.19	Polish Nationals	Nov. 7, 2009
● Rubik's Magic	Yuxuan Wang (China)	0:00.71	Beijing No Cubes	Nov. 28, 2010
● Megaminx	Simon Westlund (Sweden)	0:46.81	Helsinki Open	Jan. 23, 2011
● Pyraminx	Oscar Roth Andersen (Denmark)	0:02.40	Fredericia Open	Jan. 30, 2011

○ **LARGEST RUBIK'S CUBE MOSAIC** Depicting Michelangelo's *The Creation of Adam* (*c.* 1511) in the Sistine Chapel (The Vatican), the largest Rubik's Cube mosaic measured 28 ft. 10 in. (8.78 m) wide by 14 ft. 7 in. (4.44 m) tall and was created using 12,090 individual cubes by Cube Works Studio (Canada) in September 2010.

○**MOST YO-YOS SPUN SIMULTANEOUSLY** Australian yo-yo champion Ben McPhee got 16 yo-yos spinning at the same time at the Toy Fair, held in London, UK, on January 26, 2010. Ben mounted 10 spinning yo-yos on hooks, then hung two from his ears, two from his mouth, and a final pair, somewhat more conventionally, from his fingers.

●**Most people playing Monopoly simultaneously** On August 27, 2008, a record 2,918 people at 21 locations worldwide and online played Monopoly® at the same time in an event organized by the manufacturer Hasbro (U.S.A.).

○**Fastest game of operation** With nerves of steel and a steady hand, Maharoof Decibels (India) took just 21.87 seconds to extract every troublesome body part in the electronic surgery game Operation on November 28, 2008.

○**Largest Tetris game** On September 15, 2010, *The Gadget Show* (UK) created a fully working Tetris® game of 1,138.71 ft.^{2} (105.79 m^2) by projecting LED lights on to a grid of cardboard boxes.

●**Most simultaneous games of international checkers (Individual)** Dutch international checkers player Jos Stokkel took on 251 opponents at the same time in Hengelo, the Netherlands, on November 6–7, 2010. He won 174 games, drew 62, and lost just 15 in 18 hours of play.

●**Smallest remote-control helicopter** The Air Hogs Pocket Copter by Spin Master Ltd (Canada) is in fact pocket-sized, measuring just 3.94 in. (10 cm) from nose to tail on July 28, 2010. The mini-copter, which flies beautifully, achieved a flight of 3 min. 50 sec. on the day.

○**Tallest structure made with connecting plastic bricks** In an event organized by LEGO® Norway, children and adults joined forces to build a LEGO tower 99 ft. 1 in. (30.22 m) high in Oslo, Norway, on April 24, 2010.

○**Largest published crossword** It took Ara Hovhannisian of Armenia almost a year, from November 2007 to October 2008, to compile an enormous crossword consisting of 132,020 squares and featuring 12,842 clues across and 13,128 clues down. Measuring 61.14 ft.^{2} (5.68 m^2), it was published in a special edition of *Russiky Crossword*.

ROYALTY & MONARCHIES

For more on kings and queens, discover the age of empires on p. 112.

Shortest reign of a monarch In 1830, Louis XIX of France abdicated within 20 minutes of being crowned, making his reign the joint shortest in history. He shares the record with the unfortunate Prince Luis Filipe of Portugal, who technically became king for the same brief period on February 1, 1908, following the assassination of his father, Dom Carlos I. Luis Filipe was himself mortally wounded in the attack, but survived his father by 20 minutes.

BEING A MONARCH CAN BE A JOB FOR LIFE—CHECK OUT THE RECORD REIGNS OF HISTORY'S MOST RESILIENT RULERS:

Longest ever reign:
94 years, by Phiops II, an Egyptian pharaoh whose reign began in 2281 B.C. when he was just six years old.

Longest reigning monarch—living:
64 years, by King Bhumibol Adulyadej of Thailand, who was crowned King on June 9, 1946.

Longest reign in Europe:
73 years 220 days, by Afonso I Henrique of Portugal, who ruled as count and then king from 1112 until 1185.

Native to Papua New Guinea, Bulmer's fruit bat (*Aproteles bulmerae*) is the **largest cave-dwelling bat**. Adult females have a wingspan of 3 ft. 3 in. (1 m).

ROYAL ROCKER Princess Stéphanie of Monaco is the only royal in the world to have had hit records in Europe. Her debut album, *Besoin*, has sold more than a million copies since its release in 1986.

○**YOUNGEST REIGNING MONARCH** King Oyo—aka Rukirabasaija Oyo Nyimba Kabamba Iguru Rukidi IV—is the 19-year-old ruler of Toro, a kingdom in Uganda. Born on April 16, 1992, he came to power at the age of three (pictured) and now rules over 3% of Uganda's 33-million-strong population. Despite his title, the King's influence is largely symbolic, as the country is governed by an elected president.

TALLEST CROWN PRINCE The heir to the Spanish throne, Príncipe de Asturias, Don Felipe de Borbón y Grecia, stands 6 ft. 5 in. (1.97 m) tall. The Crown Prince was a member of the Spanish Olympic sailing team that competed at the Barcelona Games in 1992.

A treat for a hungry fruit bat would be a juicy fig. In 2006, nine carbonized figs up to 11,400 years old were found in a Neolithic village in Israel. A variety that could only have been produced through human intervention, they are the **oldest examples of fruit cultivation**.

● **MOST LIVE STREAMS FOR A SINGLE EVENT** The YouTube broadcast of Prince William's marriage to Catherine Middleton (both UK) in London, UK, on April 29, 2011, achieved a record 72 million live views, as people from 188 countries around the world tuned in to watch the event on the company's official Royal Channel. Although this figure alone was enough to beat the 70 million streams achieved during the inauguration of U.S. President Barack Obama in 2009, the wedding's overall tally is likely to have been significantly higher when taking into account the millions watching via other live streaming services.

● **MOST PORTRAYED LIVING MONARCH** Queen Elizabeth II has been portrayed on stage and screen more than any other living monarch. Memorable portrayals include (clockwise from top left): Prunella Scales (UK) in the play *A Question of Attribution* (1988), Helen Mirren (UK) in the movie *The Queen* (2006), a cartoon cameo in *The Simpsons* (2003), and numerous stage, screen, and public appearances by Jeanette Charles (UK).

Oldest reigning monarch Born in 1924, King Abdullah bin Abdulaziz Al-Saud of Saudi Arabia became the world's oldest monarch, at the age of 82 years 253 days, after the death of the previous holder, Malietoa Tanumafili II of Samoa, on May 11, 2007. He was crowned in 2005.

Largest royal family The royal House of Saud of Saudi Arabia, currently presided over by King Abdullah bin Abdulaziz Al-Saud, has royal relatives numbering in the tens of thousands. The kingdom was established by King Abdul Aziz in 1932. With his 17 wives, he fathered a total of 44 sons, four of whom have gone on to rule the kingdom since his death in 1953.

78: The number of times you have to repeat the word "great" to describe the most recent ancestor that you and everyone else on the Earth (including the Queen) shares—the 78 great-grandparents of us all.

DURING HER LONG REIGN, HER MAJESTY, QUEEN ELIZABETH II HAS BROKEN NUMEROUS ROYAL RECORDS:

Longest reigning queen—living:
59 years 95 days from February 6, 1952, to May 12, 2011.

● **Oldest British monarch:**
85 years 21 days as of May 12, 2011.

○ **Wealthiest queen:**
$682 million, including fine art, jewelry, and property.

Most depicted person on international currencies:
35 countries feature Queen Elizabeth II on their national coinage.

MOST COUNTRIES RULED AS HEAD OF STATE SIMULTANEOUSLY The most powerful woman in the world, Queen Elizabeth II is the lawful head of state of 16 independent nations. While the Queen's role is nominal and ceremonial (exercising no political powers), 128 million people in 15 Commonwealth states, plus the UK, recognize her as monarch.

● **MOST PHOTOGRAPHED QUEEN** One of the most popular monarchs in history, Queen Elizabeth II (UK) is the most photographed queen, pictured here accepting a golden anniversary edition of *Guinness World Records* from Managing Director Alistair Richards.

○ **RICHEST MONARCH** According to Forbes.com, the richest monarch in the world is Thailand's King Bhumibol Adulyadej, King Rama IX of the Chakri Dynasty. In July 2010, the popular ruler's wealth was estimated to be around $30 billion.

○ **YOUNGEST REIGNING MONARCH OF A SOVEREIGN NATION** Born on February 21, 1980, Jigme Khesar Namgyel Wangchuck became the 5th King of Bhutan on December 14, 2006, and, at 31 years old, he is the youngest monarch of a sovereign nation. The Oxford-educated King presides over one of the world's most isolated countries, a tiny realm in the Himalaya Mountains where progress is measured in terms of "Gross Domestic Happiness."

CODES & CRYPTOGRAPHY

●**First use of an encryption technique** The Caesar Cipher was first used during the Gallic War *c.* 50 B.C. According to Roman historian Suetonius, Julius Caesar employed this cipher in his military campaigns, the earliest known use of an encryption technique. The cipher is fairly simple, and in this instance involved shifting each letter of the alphabet three places to the left to produce apparently meaningless groups of letters. The recipient of the cipher had merely to move each letter three places to the right to reveal the message from Caesar.

●**First use of a Cardan grille** Mathematician Gerolamo Cardano (Italy) first employed a "Cardan grille" to disguise a secret message in 1550. The technique is used to hide a message in an ordinary-looking document. The writer of the message places a piece of card with irregular slots cut into it—a Cardan grille—over a sheet of paper and writes the message in the slots, then removes the grille and fills in the gaps to create a seemingly ordinary message. The message can be read later by someone with a copy of the grille.

●MOST ENDURING ELECTRICAL CODING SYSTEM On May 24, 1844, Samuel Morse (U.S.A.) transmitted a line of code ("What hath God wrought?") by telegraph from Washington, DC, to a partner in Baltimore, Maryland (both U.S.A.)—the **first instant telecommunication**. It hailed the dawn of modern telecommunications. More than 160 years later, Morse code is still in use.

● **MOST DIFFICULT CODE TO CRACK** During World War II, the U.S. Marine Corps developed a code utilizing the Navajo language in tandem with encryptions and word substitutions to produce an unbreakable code. The code substituted Navajo words for common military terms (so "tank" became the Navajo word for turtle), and it also spelled out letters using Navajo words based on the first letter of the English translation of the word, e.g., "Wo-la-chee" means "ant" so represents the letter "A."

● **LONGEST TIME TO CRACK A CODE** The Vigenère Cipher, which uses a polyalphabetic system of encryption (left), was so effective that it was not broken for over 300 years. Invented by cryptographer Giovan Battista Bellaso (Italy) in 1553, it was finally cracked by mathematician and computer pioneer Charles Babbage (UK) in 1854.

Uri Gil (Israel, b. April 9, 1943), a brigadier general in the Israeli Air Force, flew from 1964 until his last flight in an F-16 on June 20, 2003, at the age of 60 years 72 days, making him the **oldest active fighter pilot**.

● **FIRST RECORDED USE OF STEGANOGRAPHY** Steganography (Greek: "concealed writing") is a way of sharing secret information in which only the sender and the intended recipient are aware that there is even a message. The first recorded use, according to the classical author Herodotus, was by the tyrant Histiaeus, who shaved the head of a servant before tattooing a message on the poor man's scalp. When the hair had grown back, the servant was sent to deliver his message—a warning of impending attack by the presumably slow-moving Persian army—which was revealed when the servant's head was once more shaved.

 By contrast, the East Asian country of Laos has the **youngest official soldiers**—the minimum age for military service in the country is 15 years. And it's compulsory!

●**SMALLEST CODE-BREAKING SUPERCOMPUTER Pico Computing (U.S.A.)** has created a desktop-sized mini supercomputer by adapting difficult-to-program silicon chips to make them more powerful than those found in larger supercomputers.

At $400, it is also the ●**cheapest code-breaking supercomputer.**

●**First use of postal codes** Sir Rowland Hill (UK) introduced a code for the postal system in London, UK, in 1857. The code divided the city into postal districts based on compass points. The present form of the postcode—a mix of letters and numbers that can be decoded by machine for faster sorting—was first used in Norwich, UK, in October 1959. The similar U.S. zip code arrived in July 1963.

●**First cryptic crossword** The earliest crossword comprising only cryptic clues appeared in 1925 in the *Saturday Westminster Gazette*. There had been cryptic elements within crosswords before, but Edward Powys Mathers (UK), who set crosswords for this newspaper under the name "Torquemada," and for *The Observer* from 1926, was the first compiler to use cryptic clues only.

First computer virus The earliest computer program that replicates itself surreptitiously was demonstrated by Fred Cohen (U.S.A.), a student at the University of Southern California, U.S.A., on November 11, 1983. Cohen described his creation as "a program that can 'infect' other programs by modifying them to include a . . . version of itself." Although computer viruses had been theorized previous to this, Cohen was the first to write and execute a working code. Today, more than a million such viruses exist, according to security firm Symantec.

Most attacks in a hacking competition A staggering 5.23 million attacks were made during eWeek's 17-day-long OpenHack III competition in January 2001, in which the latest security software, PitBull—by Argus Systems Group Inc.—was probed for weaknesses. Despite a $50,000 prize, no one could penetrate PitBull.

COLOR CODED By altering the numeric values a computer assigns to the green, red, or blue in a pixel, the spies hid binary code in photos. Details about Baltimore Airport (main photo) were hidden in this photo of the Washington Monument.

● **FIRST CONFIRMED USE OF SECRET CODES IN ONLINE PHOTOGRAPHY**
On June 28, 2010, the U.S. Justice Department announced charges against 11 people accused of working for the SVR—the Russian successor to the Soviet KGB. Among the charges was the accusation that they had slipped encoded messages into otherwise harmless-looking images on the internet (see above), the first confirmed use of this high-tech method of concealing data.

● **FIRST PRESIDENT WITH A SECRET CODE NAME**
Harry S Truman, who served as U.S. President from 1945 to 1953, was given the Secret Service code name "General." Advances in telecommunications technology, and the newly present danger that potentially threatening forces might be listening in, required that all presidents, senior staff, and their families be issued with code names from this point onward in an effort to confuse anyone who might be listening to them illicitly.

Longest prison sentence for computer hacking Brian Salcedo of Michigan, U.S.A., was sentenced to nine years in federal prison in Charlotte, North Carolina, U.S.A., on December 16, 2004 for computer hacking.

Salcedo was sentenced after pleading guilty to conspiracy and numerous hacking charges in August 2004 after he tried to steal credit card information from the computer systems of Lowe's hardware stores across the U.S.A.

●**Most popular cheat code** The Konami Code debuted in the NES version of the video game *Gradius*, released in 1986, and has since been included in 151 games—either in the form of the same button presses, or subtle variations of them. The effect of the code differs from game to game, but in most cases entering the code while the game is paused grants the player most of the game's available power-ups. For those players who have not encountered it, or have forgotten about it, the sequence is: Up, Up, Down, Down, Left, Right, Left, Right, B, A.

●**First hack into a network protected by quantum cryptography** In April 2007, a team from the Massachusetts Institute of Technology (MIT) carried out the first reported hack of a quantum network. Quantum networks were thought to be uncrackable until the team managed to set up what they describe as a quantum-mechanical "wire-tap" and extract data that previously had been considered beyond the reach of even the most determined code-breaker.

●**First synthetic genome to contain secret messages** In 2008, the J. Craig Venter Institute (U.S.A.) produced a man-made bacteria and placed five hidden "watermarks" within its genome (the complete list of its genetic material). This "secret" information was encoded in the form of single-letter amino acids (A, R, N, etc.), the names of which spelled out the Institute and people associated with the project: "CRAIGVENTER," "HAMSMITH," "CINDIANDCLYDE," "GLASSANDCLYDE," and "VENTERINSTITVTE" ("V" is used because there is no amino acid for the letter "U").

SCI-TECH &
ENGINEERING

CONTENTS

LARGEST MOTORIZED TRIKE Swiss carnival band Guggä-Rugger Buus built a trike 26 ft. 7 in. (8.1 m) in length and weighing 13,300 lb. (6,030 kg) as a mobile grandstand for all 30 members of the band. The machine has the 729-cu.-in. (12-liter) engine and chassis of a Saurer truck.

Band member Tom Brodbeck rides the trike, which was built in 2003 and is called Rösli.

COMPUTING FIRSTS

ENIAC Developed for the U.S.Army, the Electronic Numerical Integrator And Computer (ENIAC) was completed in 1946 and was the ●first general-purpose electronic computer.

THE STORY OF THE COMPUTER

The year 2012 has been designated "Alan Turing Year" in honor of the British code-breaker, mathematician, and computer pioneer, who was born on June 23, 1912. To mark the 100th anniversary of Turing's birth, and to acknowledge his contribution to computing, we look back over some key moments in the history of this now-ubiquitous invention.

BABY The Manchester Small-Scale Experimental Machine, known as "Baby," ran its first program at Manchester University, UK, in 1948 and was the ●first computer to store its program internally. Pictured is team leader Tom Kilburn (UK, 1921–2001) with a modern chip with the same capacity as Baby but a fraction of the size.

COLOSSUS Designed by a team of British engineers led by Tommy Flowers, the Colossus computers were used to decipher communications between German army commanders near the end of World War II and were the ●first digital programmable electronic computing devices. The first model began its work in February 1944.

ON YOUR MARKS . . . Ten Colossus computers were built in total—a Mark 1, followed by nine Mark 2 models. So rapid was their development that the first Mark 2 was five times faster than the Mark 1.

Tektites are pieces of rock formed when large meteorites and asteroids hit Earth. The **largest recorded tektite** weighs 7.04 lb. (3.2 kg). It was discovered in 1932 at Muong Nong, Laos.

1912 **ALAN TURING** Born on June 23, 1912, one year after IBM was founded. During World War II, he worked as a code-breaker at Bletchley Park, UK. Died on June 7, 1954.

1930 Vannevar Bush (U.S.A.) creates the Differential Analyzer, a prototype analog computer.

1938 Konrad Zuse (Germany) invents the Z1 Computer, a digital computer that uses punched tape.

1939 John Atanasoff and Clifford Berry (both U.S.A.) create the ●**first electronic digital computer**; William Hewlett and David Packard form Hewlett Packard.

1958 Work by Jack Kilby and Robert Noyce (both U.S.A.), working independently, results in the **first integrated circuit**, or silicon chip. Noyce goes on to cofound Intel, in 1968.

1964 The IBM 360 becomes the ●**first computer to use integrated circuits**.

1971 IBM produces the **first floppy disk**.

1976 Michael Shrayer (U.S.A.) develops the Electric Pencil, the ●**first word processor for microcomputers**.

1981 IBM PC introduced.

1989 Microsoft introduces Windows for IBM computers.

1990 Tim Berners-Lee (UK) and Robert Cailliau (Belgium) kick-start the world wide web by proposing a hypertext system; the internet goes public in 1991. Microsoft and IBM stop collaborating on operating systems.

2001 Approximately 1 billion PCs now sold. Apple sells its 5 millionth iMac.

2010 Launch of Apple's iPad tablet. Nearly 15 million devices are sold in a year.

The **largest known meteorite** is a block 9 ft. (2.7 m) long by 8 ft. (2.4 m) wide, estimated to weigh 65 tons (59 metric tons). It was found in 1920 at Hoba West, near Grootfontein in Namibia.

Computing Firsts

2,100: Data in gigabytes that you will store on CDs, DVDs, computer hard drives, digital cameras, mp3 players, cell phones, and websites.

THE MOUSE TALE
Douglas Engelbart (U.S.A.) created the first computer mouse in 1964. He was awarded a U.S. patent for it in 1970. It was called a mouse because of the wire's resemblance to a tail.

SUPER COMPUTERS In 1976, the first Cray-1 (far left) was installed at Los Alamos National Laboratory, U.S.A. It is the ●**first supercomputer.** The ○**fastest supercomputer,** China's Tianhe-1 (left), is capable of 2.5 quadrillion flops. (A "flop" is the number of mathematical operations involving decimal fractions that a computer can make in a second.)

ANTIKYTHERA MECHANISM
The 2,000-year-old Antikythera Mechanism was discovered c. 1900 in a shipwreck close to the Greek island of Antikythera. It is a collection of bronze gears (X-ray, inset) built with a mechanical complexity not evident in any other object prior to the 14th century, though it is now encrusted with sea accretions. It is regarded as the ●**oldest analog computer;** experts believe that it was used to predict eclipses.

COMPUTER ACE Turing designed the Automatic Computing Engine (ACE), an electronic computer with a stored program. (He likened it to "building a brain.") It first ran in 1950.

The ●**fastest speed attained skiing on sand dunes** is 57.24 mi./hr. (92.12 km/h) by Henrik May (Namibia) in Swakopmund, Namibia, on May 31, 2010.

PERSONAL COMPUTER Today, PCs are everywhere—in our homes, schools, and workplaces—and we take laptops and tablet models with us wherever we go. Here's a brief guide to the history of the personal computer:

1950: Simon, the ●**first personal computer (PC)** (top left), retails for $600. Memory is six 2-bit words—12 bits in total.

1972: HP 9830, the ●**first all-in-one desktop computer**, is launched. Intel releases the SIM4, the **first microcomputer**, which uses the Intel 4004 microprocessor, capable of 92,000 instructions per second.

1979: Regarded as the **first true laptop**, the GRiD Compass (middle left) is designed by William Moggridge (UK) for GRiD Systems Corporation (U.S.A.). It is introduced in 1982 with a RAM of 512K.

1983: The IBM PC/XT is the ●**first PC with a hard drive as standard.**

1984: The first Apple Macintosh (bottom left) is launched, with an 8-MHz processor and 128 KB of memory. It becomes the ●**first commercially successful PC with a graphical user interface (GUI)** rather than command line (text-only interface).

1998: IBM demonstrates a prototype processor capable of operating at 1 GHz.

4004 CHIP The first microprocessor was the 4004 chip, produced by Intel (U.S.A.) and dating from 1971. The size of a thumbnail, it was just as powerful as ENIAC (p. 297), the room-sized first electronic computer.

The ○**greatest distance traveled Nordic skiing in 24 hours** was 269.3 miles (433.4 km) and was achieved by Teemu Virtanen (Finland) at Kuortane, Finland, on November 16–17, 2010.

CUTTING-EDGE SCIENCE

●**Fastest movie** Conventional movies run through a projector at a rate of 24 frames per second, creating the appearance of fluid motion. In January 2011, researchers using the FLASH X-ray laser in Hamburg, Germany, revealed their technique for molecular movie-making using ultrafast X-ray pulses to create a superfast movie. They made a two-frame movie of the Brandenburg Gate, reducing the rate from 24 frames per second to 0.00000000000005 seconds, or 50 femtoseconds, between frames. (A femtosecond is one millionth of one billionth of a second.)

●**Largest seed vault** The Svalbard Global Seed Vault is an underground facility located on the Norwegian island of Spitsbergen. The facility is designed to store samples of the world's seeds as insurance against future threats to biodiversity. The heavily fortified vault opened on February 26, 2006, and has the capacity to store 4.5 million samples. On March 10, 2010, it received its 500,000th sample.

●**First antilaser** In February 2011, scientists from Yale University, U.S.A., unveiled their antilaser, the first device capable of absorbing and canceling out a laser beam. It uses an optical cavity made from silicon, which traps the laser energy and dissipates it as heat, and this prototype can absorb 99.4% of the laser light for a specific frequency. Researchers hope that the technology will have applications in the next generation of optical computing and in medical imaging.

●**First individual to win both a Nobel and an Ig Nobel Prize** Andre Geim (Russia) won an Ig Nobel Prize in 2000 for levitating a frog using magnets, and went on to win a Nobel Prize in Physics in 2010 for his research into graphene (see next entry), thereby becoming the first individual to win both prizes.

The Ig Nobels began in 1991 and are awarded for seemingly trivial advances in scientific research. They are organized by the *Annals of Improbable Research*, a U.S. publication that takes a humorous approach to science. The Nobel Prize, considered a more illustrious award by some, has been handed out since 1901 in recognition of significant cultural and scientific advances.

○**Largest sheet of graphene** Graphene—discovered by Nobel Prize winners Andre Geim and Konstantin Novoselov (both Russia)—is a sheet of carbon atoms arranged in a pattern just one atom thick, and is the **thinnest man-made material**. Strong, flexible, and an effective conductor of

⊕ The ○**fastest time to solve a Rubik's Cube using the feet** is 31.56 seconds and was achieved by Anssi Vanhala (Finland) at the Helsinki Open 2011, in Helsinki, Finland, on January 22–23, 2011.

electricity, graphene has great potential as an industrial material, but up to now it has proved impossible to produce in substantial amounts.

In June 2010, however, scientists at Sungkyunkwan University and Samsung (both South Korea) revealed they had devised a new method of increasing the amounts of graphene that can be made, and have produced continuous sheets with a width of 30 in. (76 cm).

●**LARGEST 3D EARTHQUAKE TABLE** E-Defense is a table used for research into the resilience of buildings and structures to earthquakes. Measuring 65 x 49 ft. (20 x 15 m), it can support structures weighing 1,320 tons (1,200 metric tons) and shake payloads with an acceleration of 1 *g* in two dimensions horizontally and an acceleration of 1.5 *g* vertically. 1 *g* = acceleration of gravity at sea level. E-Defense is located in Miki City, Japan.

●**FIRST ARSENIC-BASED LIFE-FORM** Life on Earth uses six basic "building block" elements to make up its molecular structure: carbon, nitrogen, hydrogen, oxygen, sulfur, and phosphorus. In December 2010, a team of NASA scientists led by Felisa Wolfe-Simon (U.S.A., pictured) announced its discovery of bacteria that shows the unique ability to incorporate arsenic into its DNA and proteins, as a substitute for phosphorus. It lives in the briny Mono Lake, California, U.S.A.

TOXIC TASTES The discovery that some bacteria can absorb arsenic is particularly surprising, as arsenic has long been used as a poison, notably in pesticides and insecticides.

The ●**fewest moves to complete a Rubik's Cube** in the usual way—with one's hands—is 22. Jimmy Coll (Belgium) set the record at the Barcelona Open 2009, in Terrassa, Spain, on April 24, 2009.

Highest man-made temperature In February 2010, scientists at Brookhaven National Laboratory's Relativistic Heavy Ion Collider on Long Island, New York, U.S.A., announced that they had smashed together gold ions at nearly the speed of light, briefly forming a state of matter known as a quark-gluon plasma, which has properties more similar to those of a liquid than a gas. During the experiment the plasma reached temperatures of approximately 7.2 trillion °F (4 trillion °C), some 250,000 times hotter than the center of the Sun.

This substance is believed to have filled the universe just microseconds after the Big Bang—the **greatest explosion ever**—and is also thought to be the **earliest form of matter**.

●**Smallest solar-powered sensor** In February 2010, scientists at the University of Michigan, U.S.A., unveiled a solar-powered sensor measuring 0.09 x 0.1 x 0.03 in. (2.5 x 3.5 x 1 mm). It consumes around one billionth of a watt of power and could operate indefinitely. This device could be used to monitor environmental conditions, or converted to run on body heat as a biomedical implant.

●**Highest-resolution optical microscope** On March 1, 2011, scientists at the University of Manchester, UK, announced that they had cre-

●**FIRST TRAPPING OF ANTIHYDROGEN** Antihydrogen—which consists of an antielectron (also known as a positron) and an antiproton—is the antimatter "opposite" of a hydrogen atom. In November 2010, researchers at CERN in Geneva, Switzerland, revealed that they had trapped and contained 38 atoms of this substance for around one-tenth of a second. Pictured is part of the "trap" where the positrons and antiprotons meet (right), and untrapped antihydrogen atoms annihilating on the inner surface of the trap (left).

●**LONGEST HI-FIDELITY SPACEFLIGHT SIMULATION** Mars500 is a collaboration between the European Space Agency, Russia, and China to simulate a 500-day manned mission to Mars. The crew of six entered their sealed facility (right), located in Moscow, Russia, in June 2010, to begin their 520 days of isolated simulation.

ated an optical microscope that can see objects just 50 nanometers across, such as the insides of living cells. The instrument uses tiny spherical particles known as microspheres to amplify its optical power.

●**First wedding conducted by robot** A humanoid robot named I-Fairy conducted the wedding ceremony of Tomohiro Shibata and Satoko Inoue in Tokyo, Japan, on May 16, 2010. The groom is a professor of robotics at the Nara Institute of Science and Technology, while his bride is an employee of Kokoro, the company that built I-Fairy.

●**First human killed by a robot** On January 25, 1979, Robert Williams (U.S.A.) was killed by a production-line robot in a Ford Motor Company casting plant in Michigan, U.S.A. The robot belonged to a parts-retrieval system that moved material around the factory. When the robot began running slowly, Williams climbed into the storage rack to retrieve parts manually and was struck on the head by the robotic arm.

NANOTECH

ENGINEERING THE INVISIBLE Join us on a journey down to the atomic level, where a single hair's width is considered colossal at 100 micrometers (μm)—millionths of a meter! Any smaller and we need to describe things in nanometers (nm)— billionths of a meter—or even picometers (pm), at a trillion to the meter! Here, scientists can manipulate individual atoms to create new objects and materials—pictured is a model of a toilet just 3 nm tall made by Takahashi Kaito (Japan). But there are also serious applications of this "nanotech," as our guide reveals. . . .

SMALLEST . . .

●**Robotic hand** In October 2006, scientists at the University of California, U.S.A., demonstrated a robotic hand only 0.039 in. (1 mm) wide. Using silicon "fingers" and molecular balloons for joints, the hand could be made to flex and grasp objects by inflating or deflating the balloon joints. Inventors Yen-Wen Lu and C. J. Kim developed the robotic hand to perform complex manipulations at the sub-millimeter scale for applications that could include microsurgery.

●**Jet engine** In September 2010, students at the Leibniz Institute for Solid State Physics and Materials Research in Dresden, Germany, produced a "nanorocket" measuring just 600 nm across and weighing 1 femtogram (10^{-15} g).

●**Book** Costing an enormous $15,000, the smallest book yet made comprises 30 micro-tablets carved on a pure crystalline silicon page, measuring just 70 x 100 μm. Etched using an ion beam at the Simon Fraser

○**SMALLEST TRANSISTOR**
Researchers at Australia's University of New South Wales have made a transistor of crystalline silicon, with seven of the silicon atoms replaced by phosphorus atoms. It is 4 nm wide; conventional transistors are about 40 nm wide.

○**SMALLEST NANOCALLIGRAPHY**
In March 2009, researchers at Stanford University (U.S.A., left) were able to compose letters from subatomic pixels no bigger than 0.3 nm. The team arranged individual carbon monoxide molecules on a copper surface, then used a constant flow of electrons to form the letters "S" and "U."

Seven contestants from Belgium's Big Brother TV show built the **largest flaming image using matches**. The image depicted the show's logo and measured 107 ft.² (10 m²) when the 329,700 matches were lit on November 19, 2000.

University, Canada, the book is called *Teeny Ted from Turnip Town*. It even has its own ISBN reference, ISBN-978-1-894897-17-4, though you will need a scanning electron microscope if you want to read a copy.

●**Working gears** Researchers at the Institute of Materials Research and Engineering in Singapore have developed working molecule-sized gears that can be fully controlled, rotating clockwise and counterclockwise. Based upon individual chains of molecules, they are arranged with arms issuing from each point on a hexagon.

●**Battery** Created in December 2010, the world's smallest battery was demonstrated at Sandia Laboratories, U.S.A. Just 0.118 in. (3 mm) long, the anode of the battery comprised a single nanowire of tin oxide only 100 nm in diameter by 10 μm long. Charged to 3.5 volts, the battery can sustain a current of only 1 picoampere (pA)—just a millionth of a microampere (mA). Work on miniaturization of batteries leads to better, smaller, and longer-lived rechargeable cells for cell phones and MP3 players.

●**Radio** Built using a single carbon nanotube, the world's smallest radio receiver measures only 10 μm in diameter by 100 μm in length. The car-

●**SMALLEST ROBOTIC MEDICAL DEVICE** In April 2009, scientists at Zurich's Federal Institute of Technology (Switzerland) announced they had created a micro-robot capable of swimming in human arteries. The corkscrew-shaped robot has a maximum length of 60 μm. It will be used to repair damaged blood vessels and remove arterial deposits.

The micro-robot swims in the same way as bacteria.

On December 10, 2009, a total of 118 employees of the drug company Sandoz created the **largest flaming image using candles** at the Hotel Serena in Faisalabad, Pakistan. It had an area of 9,800 ft.² (910.45 m²) and included 35,478 candles.

bon tube is electrically charged and can vibrate in harmony with incoming radio waves in the 40–400 Hz range. The precise tuning is achieved by changing the voltage applied to the tube to isolate individual radio frequencies.

●**Christmas card** Scientists at the University of Glasgow in Scotland, UK, saved on the cost of Christmas cards by making their own in 2010—but recipients would need a high-power microscope to read them! At 200 x 290 μm in size, 8,276 cards would fit on a postage stamp. The card features a Christmas tree etched onto a tiny piece of glass. The technology used to produce the card could be used to make Christmas presents such as TVs and cameras of exceptional quality and performance.

Automobile In 2005, scientists at Rice University in Texas, U.S.A., led by James Tour, revealed an "automobile"—made from a single molecule of mostly carbon atoms—measuring 3–4 nm wide. It includes four wheels made from "buckyballs" (carbon-60).

○**SMALLEST 3D MAP OF EARTH** Scientists at IBM (U.S.A.) have created an accurate 3D map of Earth so small that 1,000 of them could fit on a single grain of salt. Patterns of the Earth's continents were created using an incredibly sharp silicon knife to carve features as small as 15 nm on a polymer substrate measuring only 22 x 11 μm.

IT'S A SMALL WORLD The silicon cutting tip that created the 3D map is 100,000 times finer than a sharpened pencil tip, allowing scientists to recreate the Matterhorn (inset) at a scale of 1:50 million!

SMALLEST . . .

●PERIODIC TABLE: 89 μm wide. Scientists at the University of Nottingham, UK, etched a table of element symbols into a strand of hair plucked from the head of Prof. Martyn Poliakoff.

GUITAR 10 μm long. This blood-cell-size guitar, made by scientists at Cornell University in New York, U.S.A., has 50-nm-wide strings that can actually be strummed—using an ion beam!

●WEIGHING SCALES Groups from the University of Barcelona (Spain) and EPFL Microsystems Laboratory (Switzerland) have created scales to weigh vapor and gas, incorporating a balance beam just13 μm long.

●TEST-TUBE EXPERIMENT Less than 0.2 μm wide. Particle of gold melted inside a test tube 1,000th of the width of a human hair at the University of Texas (U.S.A.).

●KNIFE A cheese-wire-style knife, with a carbon nanotube edge that has a diameter of around 100 nm, made by the National Institute of Standards and Technology (NIST) and the University of Colorado (both U.S.A.).

CONSUMER TECH

●**Lightest Wi-Fi phone** The modu W weighs 2.2 oz (62.7 g). Made by modu (Israel), it was measured at The Standards Institution of Israel (SII) in Tel Aviv, Israel, on September 21, 2010.

○**Most expensive cell phone series** Although more expensive limited-edition cell phones exist, the priciest handset that is commercially available is the Ulysse Nardin Chairman. Models range from $13,000 to $50,000 for precious-metal versions. It has a 3.2-in. (81-mm) touch screen, 32 gigabytes of memory, and an 8-megapixel camera, and offers high-definition video playback. The phone includes a lacquered wooden docking station with built-in speakers.

This is also the ●**first cell phone with a self-winding rotor mechanism**, as in an automatic watch, which supplies backup kinetic energy to help keep the battery charged.

●**First dual-screen cell phone** Instead of one large and unwieldy 4.7-in. (11.9-cm) smartphone screen, the Kyocera Echo smartphone is equipped with twin 3.5-in. (8.9-cm) displays with a hinge in the middle. When it is closed, the phone is no larger than a regular touch slab-style-screen smartphone. Each screen can run a different application or display a different web page; alternatively, a single app can be run or a single web page can be displayed across both screens. One screen can display a QWERTY keyboard as well. The Echo runs Android 2.2 and is powered by a 1-GHz processor.

●**FIRST HANDHELD 3D GAME PLAYER** On March 27, 2011, Nintendo unveiled the 3DS, a portable 3D game player that does not require the user to wear 3D glasses. The 3DS has two screens; an upper 800 x 240 pixel, 3.53-in. (9-cm) widescreen 3D display and a lower 320 x 240 pixel, 3.02-in. (7.7-cm) screen. Players can increase or decrease the 3D depth perception via a slider, or can simply turn off the 3D capability to play in 2D. The device also features a dual lens 3D camera on the rear.

○**Largest screen on a cell phone** The Dell Streak 5 is a mobile 3G phone/tablet with a 5-in (12.7-cm) screen. It runs the Android 2.2 operating system, with a WVGA 800 x 480 thin-film transistor (TFT) LCD screen.

Highest-resolution cell phone camera In May 2009, Sony-Ericsson unveiled the Satio cell phone, equipped with a 12.1-megapixel camera. Shots can be framed in a 3.5-in. (8.9-cm) 16:9 color LCD, lit with a Xenon flash, and brought closer with a 12x digital zoom, also the world's highest on a cell phone.

○**Largest LCD television screen** Sharp's (Japan) LB-1085 is the world's largest LCD HDTV, with a screen measuring 108 in. (274 cm) diagonally. Introduced at CES 2007, the HDTV without the stand measures 101.26 x 62.64 x 8.03 in. (257.2 x 159.1 x 20.4 cm).

○**Largest LED screen** The largest high-definition video screen is an LED display that measures 820 x 98 ft. (250 x 30 m), giving a total surface area of 80,729 ft.² (7,500 m²). It is located at The Place, Beijing, China.

●**FASTEST-SELLING CONSUMER ELECTRONICS DEVICE** The concept of tablets—portable, lightweight, and thinner than conventional laptop computers—has existed for decades. The arrival of Apple's iPad, however—with its characteristic multitouch screen—proved a landmark release. Following its launch in April 2010, three million units were sold in the first 80 days, and thanks to the release of the iPad 2 on March 25, 2011, 4.69 million units were sold in the second quarter of the year—or 311,666 per day.

iBUY! The sales figure of 4.69 million iPads includes both iPad and iPad 2 sales—and even if only half of the sales were iPad 2, this is 156,333 units per day, meaning that iPad 2 has sold faster than any other consumer gadget ever!

○ THINNEST BLU-RAY PLAYER
Samsung's BD-D7500 Blu-ray player
is just 0.9 in. (22.86 mm) thick. Wall-
mountable, it plays 3D Blu-ray discs,
runs 200 Samsung HDTV apps, and
has built-in Wi-Fi to download these
apps and to access their online
content.

**● MOST ADJUSTABLE DIGITAL
CAMERA** The 3-in. (7.6-cm) touch-
screen LCD on the Casio Tryx digital
camera is swivel-mounted inside a
frame, on which the lens and flash
are affixed. The screen pops out
of the frame and can be swiveled
270° around and through the frame
in landscape mode, and swiveled
simultaneously 360° on its frame-
attached stem in portrait mode. The
Casio Tryx launched in the U.S.A.
and Japan in April 2011.

○ LARGEST PLASMA TV SCREEN Launched on July 1, 2010, Panasonic's
TH-152UX1 high-definition TV (HDTV) boasts a colossal 152-in. (386-cm)
plasma screen, which measures 5 ft. 10.9 in. (1.8 m) tall and 11 ft. 2.4 in.
(3.41 m) wide to give a screen area equivalent to nine 50-in. (127-cm)
HDTVs arrayed in a three-by-three grid. It is also the **● most expensive
commercially available TV**, with a retail price of around $500,000.

In 1953, the Kutiah Glacier in Pakistan advanced more than 7.4
miles (12 km) in three months, averaging some 367 ft. (112 m) per
day—the **fastest glacial surge.**

HANDS-FREE HEAVEN Using a gadget similar to a web camera, Kinect enables players to interact with Xbox 360 using physical movements and verbal commands rather than a conventional games console.

●**FASTEST-SELLING GAMING PERIPHERAL** Kinect for Xbox 360 sold an average of 133,333 units per day in its first 60 days on sale in November–December 2010, and by March 2011, the "controller-free" peripheral had surpassed sales of 10 million units. Until iPad sales figures were released in April 2011 (see p. 311), the Kinect also enjoyed the distinction of being the all-time fastest-selling piece of consumer tech.

○**Smallest digital voice recorder** The Edic-mini Tiny A31, by Telesystems (Russia), measures just 1.14 x 0.47 x 0.59 in. (29 x 12 x 15 mm) and weighs 0.21 oz. (6 g). It was introduced in May 2009.

○**Thinnest laptop** The Windows 7 Dell Adamo XPS ranges in size from 0.38 in. (9.7 mm) at its slimmest point to 0.41 in. (10.3 mm) at its thickest—an average of 0.39 in. (9.99 mm). For comparison, an iPhone 4 is just 0.37 in. (9.4 mm) thick. The Adamo stays skinny by repositioning key components and enclosing the keyboard fully inside the reinforced 13.4-in. (34-cm) display area when the unit is closed. It measures 13.39 x 10.78 x 0.39 in. (340 x 273.9 x 9.99 mm).

○**Highest-capacity digital music player** No other portable media player has ever had as much memory for music tracks, photos, or video as the Archos 5 Internet Tablet—a massive 500 GB, due to a built-in hard disk drive. The tablet runs the Android operating system, has a 4.8-in. (12.2-cm) 800 x 480-pixel LCD screen and can connect to the internet via Wi-Fi. Up to 32 GB of extra memory can be added via the microSD card slot.

A volcanic eruption under Europe's largest glacier, Vatnajokul in Iceland, in October 1996, topped Lake Grímsvötn with meltwater. This flowed from the lake at an estimated 1.6 million ft.^{3}/s (45,000 m^3/s), the **fastest-melting glacier**.

The Archos 5 is capable of storing up to 600 movies, 290,000 songs, or 5 million photos. It can record from any device with a standard video output (such as TVs, DVDs, and set-top cable boxes) via the optional digital video recording (DVR) station. It can receive FM radio, has built-in portable GPS navigation, an audio recording capability, and connects to an HDTV via a high-definition multimedia interface (HDMI) jack.

Deepest limit for a diving watch The 20,000-ft. model CX Swiss Military Watch is a mechanical divers' watch made by Montres Charmex SA (Switzerland) that can function at depths of 20,000 ft. (6,000 m). The wristwatch was tested at the Oceanographic Institute of the University of Southampton, UK, on January 5, 2009.

INTERNET

●**First computerized social network** The Community Memory project, established in Berkeley, California, U.S.A., in 1973, used a teletype terminal in a record store, connected to an SDS 940 computer in San Francisco. It allowed visitors to the store to enter and view messages left by others and was the first public computerized bulletin board system (BBS).

●**Most frequent social network users** According to market research company TNS, as of October 2010 social network users in Malaysia spend an average of nine hours a week on social network sites.

It therefore comes as no surprise to learn that Malaysia is the ●**country with the most digital friends**—in the same research study, TNS discovered that social network users in Malaysia have an average of 233 digital friends.

The ●**country with the fewest digital friends** is Japan, where social networkers have an average of just 29 friends.

●**LARGEST MILITARY INTERNET LEAK**
On October 22, 2010, the whistle-blowing website Wikileaks published online 319,882 field reports from the U.S. Army, documenting its operations in Iraq from 2004 to 2009. Known as the "Iraqi War Logs," they outline events previously unpublicized concerning the activities of U.S. and coalition troops in Iraq. UK-based Iraq Body Count, which attempts to monitor civilian casualties, claimed that the Iraqi War Logs reveal 15,000 extra civilian deaths that had not been included in public reports.

Wikileaks' editor-in-chief and spokesperson Julian Assange (Australia, pictured) was voted the 2010 Readers' Choice Person of the Year in *Time* magazine. At the time of going to press, he was living in the UK, appealing against extradition to Sweden, where he faces questioning about alleged assaults.

○ **MOST SEARCHED-FOR FEMALE ONLINE** Pop star Katy Perry (U.S.A., b. Katheryn Hudson) was the highest-ranking female on the "fastest-rising people" list for 2010, according to Google's end-of-year report. Interest in the singer peaked at various times, notably around the announcements of the MTV and Grammy awards.

● **MOST "LIKES" ON YOUTUBE** Judson Laipply's (U.S.A.) "Evolution of Dance" viral video—in which Judson performs a dance routine featuring moves from the history of dance—was uploaded to YouTube in 2006 and was viewed 70 million times in less than eight months. As of May 4, 2011, the video has been viewed 171,571,560 times and has earned a record 739,956 "likes."

"Evolution of Dance" features 32 songs in all.

DANCE, DANCE, DANCE! Judson's epic routine takes in landmark songs from the history of popular music, from Elvis Presley's 1956 hit "Hound Dog" to Jay-Z's "Dirt Off Your Shoulder" (2004).

By 2009, Facebook's revenue was estimated at $800 million.

○ **LARGEST ONLINE SOCIAL NETWORK** **As of January 2011, Facebook boasted over 600 million active users, according to the global investment bank Goldman Sachs, and an estimated market value of $50 billion.**

FACEBOOK

The world's most popular online social network (see main record text) has spawned a few more records for its fans, followers, and founder:

Record	Achievement	Details
Youngest billionaire (present day)	Mark Zuckerberg (U.S.A., b. May 14, 1984), CEO of Facebook	Estimated net worth of $1.5 billion when listed on Forbes.com on March 5, 2008
● Most fans on Facebook	34,757,671	*Texas Hold'em Poker* (Zynga). Achieved on January 31, 2011
● Most "likes" on a Facebook post in 24 hours	588,403, in response to a post made on February 15, 2011	Rapper Lil Wayne, aka Dwayne Carter, Jr. (U.S.A.)

According to the Nobel Foundation, as of 2002 Iceland had 3.36 Nobel Laureates for every 1 million head of population—the **most Nobel Prize Laureates per capita**.

200 BILLION: Neurons in your brain. Each neuron has 7,000 synapses, with each synapse making 1,000 connections. Your head contains more connections than all the computers, routers, and internet connections on Earth.

First Twitter tweet Twitter was invented by Jack Dorsey (U.S.A.) in 2006 as a microblogging and social networking tool. The very first tweet was posted by Dorsey at 9:50 p.m. (Pacific Standard Time) on March 21, 2006, and read: "just setting up my twittr."

●**Most friends on Twitter** U.S. President Barack Obama was following 703,744 friends as of February 14, 2011. But more important is the number of followers. . . .

○**Most followers on Twitter** Pop singer Lady Gaga (U.S.A., b. Stefani Germanotta) had 7,942,058 Twitter followers as of February 1, 2011.

●**Most responsive brand on Twitter** The most responsive corporate account on Twitter is Microsoft's @XboxSupport, aka the "Elite Tweet Fleet." From March 12 to 18, 2010, the Fleet responded to more than 5,000 questions—taking an average of 2 min. 42 sec. per question—to illustrate their commitment to customer service.

○**Largest video-sharing website** YouTube currently receives around 35 hours of content every minute, and in 2010, more than 13 million hours of video were uploaded to the site. Also in 2010, YouTube surpassed 700 billion playbacks.

●**MOST GOOGLE STREET VIEW APPEARANCES** The most verified appearances of an individual on Google Street View is 43, achieved by Wendy Southgate (UK), who was photographed repeatedly by the service's mobile camera while walking her dog in Elmswell, Suffolk, UK, in 2009.

In 1992, at the age of 33, Rigoberta Menchú Tum (Guatemala) became the **youngest-ever Nobel Peace Prize winner**; born in the Mayan village of Chimel, she was also the first indigenous person to receive the award.

○ **LARGEST INTERNET SEARCH ENGINE** Google no longer publishes its index size—owing, it says, to inaccurate data and duplicate sites. However, it remains the most popular search tool. In January 2011, Google enjoyed a 65.6% market share, with 11.1 billion searches that month in the U.S.A. alone.

Pictured is a pixelated "visualization" of the internet (left) created by nmap.org. It shows the logos of 328,427 websites, each scaled in proportion to the size of its web traffic. The largest icon, then, is Google's "g" (top right), with a total area of 11,936 pixels^2.

● **MOST COMMENTS ON A FACEBOOK POST** A post made on January 6, 2011, on the Facebook page for *CityVille* (Zynga, 2010) received 29,160 comments. The majority of the comments are requests for other players to link up, or "add," as friends on the game, which rewards community-based play. As such, the comment thread isn't so much a discussion of a topic but an open forum for players to attempt to attract people to add them as friends, thereby increasing their gameplay options.

● **Most common form of malware** Trojan-horse software performs unwanted tasks on a computer while masquerading as a useful application. It allows malicious software—aka malware or pestware—to be installed on a machine via a "back door." Data compiled by BitDefender in the first half of 2009 showed that Trojan horses accounted for some 83% of all malware on the internet.

NEED FOR SPEED

Fastest land-speed record The official land-speed record, measured over 1 mile (1.6 km), is 763.035 mi./hr. (1,227.985 km/h, or Mach 1.020). Andy Green (UK) became the most recent holder of this famous record on October 15, 1997, in the Black Rock Desert, Nevada, U.S.A., in *Thrust SSC*. When he set the land-speed record that day, Green also became the **first person on land to travel faster than the speed of sound** (usually around 768 mi./hr., or 1,236 km/h, in dry air at 68°F, or 20°C). The resultant sonic boom shook a school in the nearby town of Gerlach. He set the record 50 years and a day after the sound barrier was broken in the air by Chuck Yeager (U.S.A.).

RACING TOWARD A NEW RECORD? *Bloodhound SSC* has been built by the same team that created the record-breaking *Thrust SSC*. They hope to set a new land-speed record of around 1,000 mi./hr. (1,609 km/h)—significantly faster than the current record—in 2013. A site for the attempt has already been chosen at Hakskeen Pan, on the edge of South Africa's Kalahari Desert.

○**FASTEST SPEED IN A DIESEL-ENGINE AUTOMOBILE** Driving the *JCB DIESELMAX,* Andy Green (UK) reached 350.092 mi./hr. (563.418 km/h) at Bonneville Salt Flats, Utah, U.S.A., on August 23, 2006. In doing so, he broke his own record, which he had achieved the day before with a speed of 328.767 mi./hr. (526.027 km/h).

LAND-SPEED LANDMARKS

This table charts highlights from the history of the land-speed record, going back as far as the late 19th century. The speed is typically calculated over a two-way run measuring 1 km (0.6 miles).

Date	Vehicle	Driver	Location	Speed/Record
Dec. 18, 1898	*Jeantaud Duc* (electric)	Gaston de Chasseloup–Laubat (France)	Achères, Yvelines, France	39.24 mi./hr. **First recognized land-speed record**
Aug. 5, 1902	*Mors* (internal combustion [IC])	William Vanderbilt (U.S.A.)	Albis, near Chartres, France	76.080 mi./hr. **First internal combustion record**
Jul. 21, 1904	*Gobron-Brillié* (IC)	Louis Emile Rigolly (France)	Ostend, Belgium	103.561 mi./hr. **First to exceed 100 mi./hr.**
Jun. 24, 1914	*Benz #3* (IC)	L G "Cupid" Hornsted (UK)	Brooklands, Surrey, UK	124.095 mi./hr. **First two-way record attempt**
Mar. 29, 1927	*Sunbeam 1000* (IC)	Henry Segrave (U.S.A./UK)	Daytona, Florida, U.S.A.	203.792 mi./hr. **First to exceed 200 mi./hr.**
Sep. 3, 1935	*Railton Rolls-Royce Bluebird* (IC)	Sir Malcolm Campbell (UK)	Bonneville, Utah, U.S.A.	301.129 mi./hr. **First to exceed 300 mi./hr.**

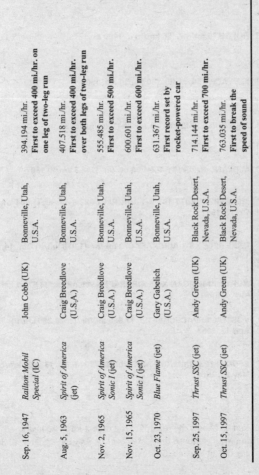

Date	Vehicle	Driver	Location	Speed / Achievement
Sep. 16, 1947	*Railton Mobil Special* (IC)	John Cobb (UK)	Bonneville, Utah, U.S.A.	394.194 mi./hr. **First to exceed 400 mi./hr. on one leg of two-leg run**
Aug. 5, 1963	*Spirit of America* (jet)	Craig Breedlove (U.S.A.)	Bonneville, Utah, U.S.A.	407.518 mi./hr. **First to exceed 400 mi./hr. over both legs of two-leg run**
Nov. 2, 1965	*Spirit of America Sonic I* (jet)	Craig Breedlove (U.S.A.)	Bonneville, Utah, U.S.A.	555.485 mi./hr. **First to exceed 500 mi./hr.**
Nov. 15, 1965	*Spirit of America Sonic I* (jet)	Craig Breedlove (U.S.A.)	Bonneville, Utah, U.S.A.	600.601 mi./hr. **First to exceed 600 mi./hr.**
Oct. 23, 1970	*Blue Flame* (jet)	Gary Gabelich (U.S.A.)	Bonneville, Utah, U.S.A.	631.367 mi./hr. **First record set by rocket-powered car**
Sep. 25, 1997	*Thrust SSC* (jet)	Andy Green (UK)	Black Rock Desert, Nevada, U.S.A.	714.144 mi./hr. **First to exceed 700 mi./hr.**
Oct. 15, 1997	*Thrust SSC* (jet)	Andy Green (UK)	Black Rock Desert, Nevada, U.S.A.	763.035 mi./hr. **First to break the speed of sound**

HISTORY'S FASTEST SPEEDS From speed on land to the all-time fastest methods of transport. Each entry on this chart was once the fastest way to travel, other than simply running. For more than 5,000 years, sledges were the fastest way to get around; and the air-speed record has not advanced since 1961. The *Apollo 10* mission represents the fastest speed at which humans have ever traveled.

Fastest speed by humans—6.88 mi./s 11.08 km/s

SLEDGE 25 mi./hr. (40 km/h) *c.* 6500 B.C.

HORSE 35 mi./hr. (56 km/h) *c.* 1400 B.C.

ICE YACHT 50 mi./hr. (80 km/h) A.D. 1600

DOWNHILL SKIER 87 mi./hr. (141 km/h) 1873

MIDLAND RAILWAY 4-2-4 90 mi./hr. (144.8 km/h) 1897

MESSERSCHMITT 163 V-1 AIRCRAFT 623.8 mi./hr. (1,004 km/h) Oct. 2, 1941

USAF BELL XS-1 AIRCRAFT 670 mi./hr. (1,078 km/h) Oct. 14, 1947

NORTH AMERICAN X-15 AIRCRAFT 2,905 mi./hr. (4,675.1 km/h) Mar. 7, 1961

VOSTOK 1 SPACECRAFT *c.* **17,560 mi./hr. (c. 28,260 km/h)** Apr. 12, 1961

APOLLO 10 **COMMAND MODULE 24,790 mi./hr. (39,897 km/h)** May 26, 1969

....

 Guatemala boasts the record for the **oldest known Mayan writing**, with evidence that dates back to 300–200 B.C. at a site in the city of San Bartolo, Guatemala.

....

> **LIGHT FANTASTIC** We are still lagging far behind the speed of light, at 983,571,056 ft./s (299,792,458 m/s) in a vacuum. At that speed, you could travel around the world seven times in a second!

○**FASTEST MOTORCYCLE LAND-SPEED RECORD** On September 25, 2010, Rocky Robinson (U.S.A.) achieved an average speed of 376.363 mi./hr. (605.697 km/h) in his *Top Oil-Ack Attack* streamliner over a measured kilometer (0.6 miles) at Bonneville Salt Flats, Utah, U.S.A.

Fastest land-speed record (female) The highest land-speed recorded by a woman is 512.710 mi./hr. (825.126 km/h), by Kitty Hambleton (U.S.A.) in the rocket-powered SM1 *Motivator* in the Alvord Desert, Oregon, U.S.A., on December 6, 1976. In these record attempts, average speeds are calculated from a number of different runs. The highest speed measured during Hambleton's runs was 524.016 mi./hr. (843.323 km/h), although it is probable that she touched 600 mi./hr. (965 km/h) momentarily.

Fastest wheel-driven vehicle The fastest speed ever reached by a vehicle powered through its wheels is 458.444 mi./hr. (737.794 km/h), by the turbine-powered *Turbinator* driven by Don Vesco (U.S.A.) at Bonneville Salt Flats, Utah, U.S.A., on October 18, 2001. It is also the ●**fastest turbine-engine automobile**.

 Going back even further, the Sumerians, who lived in what is now Iraq, created the **oldest surviving love poem** in the form of a clay tablet dating back to 3500 B.C.

Fastest automobile crash survived In September 1960, during trials to set a new land-speed record at Bonneville Salt Flats, Utah, U.S.A., Donald Campbell (UK) crashed his car *Bluebird* while traveling at 360 mi./hr. (579 km/h). The vehicle rolled over and Campbell fractured his skull, but against all the odds he survived.

In the 1950s and 1960s, he broke multiple world speed records. He was the son of Sir Malcolm Campbell (see table).

●**Fastest speed by a jet-powered motorcycle** On April 24, 2009, Kevin Martin (U.S.A.) achieved a speed of 202.55 mi./hr. (325.97 km/h) on his *Ballistic Eagle* jet-powered motorcycle at the Spring Nationals, Rockingham, North Carolina, U.S.A.

Fastest motorcycle wheelie Sweden's Patrick Fürstenhoff hit 191.3 mi./hr. (307.86 km/h) on the rear wheel of a Honda Super Blackbird 1100 cc Turbo at Bruntingthorpe Proving Ground, Leicestershire, UK, on April 18, 1999.

OIL

●**First oil wells** Humans first began drilling for oil in China as early as A.D. 347. Drilling was achieved to depths of 787 ft. (240 m) using rudimentary drill bits attached to "pipes" made from bamboo.

●**Oldest oil** In August 2000, Australian scientists announced their discovery of minute oil droplets within fluid inclusions (microscopic liquid or gas bubbles) trapped inside mineral grains in rocks dating back some 3.2 billion years.

●**HEAVIEST OFFSHORE OIL PLATFORM** With storage for 1.3 million barrels of oil, the 702,172-ton (637,000-metric-ton) Hibernia rig in the Atlantic can withstand iceberg impacts.

IN DEEP WATER The flames from the Deepwater Horizon fire were up to 300 ft. (91 m) high and could be seen 35 miles (56 km) away. The fire burned for 36 hours before the rig sank on April 22, 2010.

●LARGEST ACCIDENTAL MARINE OIL SPILL On April 20, 2010, an explosion on the *Deepwater Horizon* oil drilling rig in the Gulf of Mexico killed 11 workers and caused an environmental and economic disaster that is still unfolding. The oil spill from a gusher on the seafloor continued to flow until July 15, when the well was capped. In the meantime, 4.9 million barrels, or 171 million gal. (779 million liters), of crude had entered the ocean.

●**Oldest offshore platform** Neft Daslari is a town built in 1949 in the Caspian Sea 34.2 miles (55 km) off the coast of Azerbaijan. Oil production began there in 1951 and, at its peak, the town boasted hotels, a bakery, a power plant, and a total surface area of 17.3 acres (7 ha), consisting of separate "islands" connected by 124.3 miles (200 km) of bridges. Much of Neft Daslari has now been reclaimed by the sea, but its rigs still produce oil and its population remains around 5,000.

●**Deepest oil well** While operating in the Tiber oil field in the Gulf of Mexico in 2010, the *Deepwater Horizon* semi-submersible drilling rig achieved a drilling vertical depth of 33,011.8 ft. (10,062 m), working in water 4,130 ft. (1,259 m) deep.

●**Greatest drilling water depth** In November 2003, the drillship *Discoverer Deep Seas*, owned by Transocean Inc. (U.S.A.), drilled for oil and gas in 10,011 ft. (3,051 m) of water in the Gulf of Mexico.

To see the fastest "gas guzzlers" on the planet, turn to p. 472.

WHAT IS OIL? There are many types of oil, including those that we cook with, but the most useful—and sought after—is the dark, treacly "crude oil" that comes from deep within the Earth's crust. Crude is formed naturally from plants and animals that decayed under sand and mud millions of years ago, so it is known as a "fossil fuel." It is tricky to get to and has to be pumped to the surface by drilling rigs such as the Hibernia, then treated in an oil refinery to make it usable. The most common use for oil is as automobile fuel, but it is also found in plastics, clothes, fertilizers, foods, and almost everything else we use. Life without it would be very different.

A. 83–87% carbon
B. 10–14% hydrogen
C. 1–4% nitrogen, oxygen, sulfur, metals

●**LARGEST PROVEN OIL RESERVES** Residents of Saudi Arabia need not worry about the gas pumps running dry any day soon—the country has more proven oil reserves than any other, with 264.1 billion barrels, or almost 20% of the world's proven reserves, as of 2010.

BLACK GOLD Fortunes are made and lost in the oil business. One of the industry's biggest winners was U.S. tycoon John D. Rockefeller (1839–1937), the **first dollar billionaire**, who made $1.4 billion from "black gold."

The **first use of a graphite bomb** was during the Gulf War in 1991, when Allied forces used it to disable 85% of Iraq's power supplies. So-called G-bombs work by exploding thousands of ultrafine carbon-fiber wires over electrical installations, short-circuiting them.

Sci-tech & Engineering

61,331: Gallons of oil you will use in your lifetime. Maybe you're wearing some of it right now—artificial fibers are made from oil, and oil is made from things that died when dinosaurs walked the Earth, so you're actually wearing fossil clothes!

●**LARGEST OIL REFINERY COMPLEX** The Reliance Jamnagar complex in Gujarat, India, consists of two massive oil refineries adjacent to each other, completed in 1999 and 2008. Between them, the refineries have the capacity to process more than 1.2 million barrels (50 million gal.) of crude oil each day.

Longest crude oil pipeline The Interprovincial Pipe Line Inc. installation, which spans North America from Edmonton to Montreal (both Canada), covers a distance of 2,353 miles (3,787.2 km) and features 82 pumping stations, which maintain a flow of over 1.6 million barrels a day.

●**Largest oil tanker** The four T1 class ultra-large crude carriers—T1 Africa, T1 Asia, T1 Europe, and T1 Oceania—were constructed in 2002/03 by Daewoo Shipbuilding and Marine Engineering in South Korea. They are 1,243 ft. (379 m) long and 223 ft. (68 m) wide, and have a displacement of 570,621 tons (517,659 metric tons) fully loaded.

Largest tanker ship hijacked On November 15, 2008, off the coast of Somalia, pirates seized one of the world's largest tankers, the *Sirius Star* (UAE), along with its precious cargo of crude oil valued at $110 million. At 1,100 ft. (330 m) long and with a gross tonnage of 162,252, the tanker is the largest ever hijacked, and a ransom of $3 million had to be paid for its release.

●**MOST WELLS SABOTAGED** In 1991, retreating Iraqi forces in Kuwait burned 700 oil wells, with a loss of up to 1.5 billion barrels of oil. Unburned oil formed a layer of "tarcrete" over 5% of the land.

The O**most recent nuclear test** occurred underground in North Korea, on May 25, 2009. According to the U.S. Geological Survey, the explosion had a magnitude of 4.7 on the Richter scale.

●**Largest oil gusher** An oil gusher, or wildcat, is the uncontrolled release of oil from a well. On August 26, 1956, an enormous wildcat exploded to the surface near Qom, Iran, with some 120,000 barrels of crude oil per day spurting out in a fountain that reached 170.6 ft. (52 m) high. The Qom wildcat was extinguished after 90 days.

○**Largest oil consumption** A land full of road users, the U.S.A. is the world's most oil-thirsty nation, consuming an estimated 18.69 million barrels per day in 2009.

○**Lowest fuel price** Despite the soaring oil price, motorists in Venezuela were paying just 2.3 cents per liter of gas in November 2010—less than the market price of crude!

ALTERNATIVE ENERGIES

○**Greenest country** Based on the Environmental Sustainability Index—which measures a country's water use, biodiversity, and adoption of clean energies, among other things—Iceland is the greenest country, with a score of 93.5/100.

In terms of the **greenest city**, Masdar City in Abu Dhabi, UAE, is the first city envisaged to have no carbon emissions and no waste. Designed by Foster and Partners (UK), all of its power will be generated from renewable resources, and all waste material recycled. Automobiles will be banned in favor of electric, driverless, underground vehicles, so the city's projected 50,000 citizens should leave no carbon footprint. Phase 1 is due to be completed in 2015.

●LARGEST SOLAR FURNACE In Odeillo Font-Romeux, France, an array of heliostats direct the Sun's energy onto a 21,500-ft.² (2,000-m²) parabolic reflector, which then reflects the rays of the Sun to a focal point. The concentrated rays can create temperatures of up to 6,872°F at the focal point, where they are used to conduct research into materials science and solar engineering. The furnace was built in 1969.

70: Amount of energy, in joules, that your body uses every second. That's enough to power a 70-Watt light bulb. To keep it shining all the way through your life, you would have to eat 60,000,000 calories.

●**FIRST WAVE FARM** The Aguçadoura Wave Farm is located 3.1 miles (5 km) off the shore of Portugal. It uses three Pelamis wave energy conversion machines to generate up to 2.25 MW of electricity. These machines consist of connected sections that flex as waves pass and convert the flexing motion to electricity.

●**Largest CNG fuel station** The C-Nergy Compressed Natural Gas (CNG) station in Singapore has 46 filling hoses. It opened to the public on September 9, 2009.

○**Highest-capacity wind farm** Covering an area of almost 100,000 acres (400 km²), Roscoe Wind Farm in Texas, U.S.A., has 627 wind turbines and can generate up to 781.5 megawatts (MW).

Located in Emden in northwest Germany, the **largest wind generator** is the Enercon E-126, with a hub height of 443 ft. (135 m) and a rotor diameter of 416 ft. (127 m). Its capacity is rated at 7 MW—enough to fuel 5,000 households of four people in Europe!

VEHICLES

Longest journey by solar electric automobile The *Midnight Sun* solar automobile team from the University of Waterloo in Ontario, Canada, traveled 9,364 miles (15,070 km) through Canada and the U.S.A., leaving Waterloo on August 7, 2004, and finishing in Ottawa, Canada, on September 15, 2004.

On November 17, 2009, Tadashi Tateuchi (Japan) drove his electrically powered Mira EV for 345.23 miles (555.6 km), from Tokyo to Osaka, Japan, the ●**longest journey made by a non-solar-powered electric vehicle** without recharging the batteries.

○**FASTEST SOLAR-POWERED VEHICLE** *Sunswift IV* achieved a speed of 55.139 mi./hr. (88.738 km/h) at the naval base HMAS *Albatross* near Nowra, in NSW, Australia, on January 7, 2011. The car was built by the University of New South Wales Solar Racing Team and driven by Barton Mawer (Australia).

○**FASTEST SPEED ON A LAND YACHT** The highest speed officially recorded for a land yacht is 126.1 mi./hr. (202.9 km/h) by *Greenbird*, piloted by Richard Jenkins (UK), at Ivanpah Dry Lake, Prim, Nevada, U.S.A., on March 26, 2009.

●**LONGEST JOURNEY BY COFFEE-POWERED AUTOMOBILE** In March 2010, a 1988 Volkswagen Scirocco was driven 209 miles (337 km) from London to Manchester, UK, powered by coffee. The coffee granules are heated in a charcoal fire, where they then break down into carbon monoxide and hydrogen. The gas is then cooled and filtered before the hydrogen is combusted to drive the engine. Nicknamed the "Car-puccino," it can reach a speed of 60 mi./hr. (96.5 km/h) and achieve a rate of 1 mile per 56 espressos (1 km per 35). The process works because coffee granules contain a small amount of carbon, which is why the trip required enough coffee to make 11,760 espressos!

WOOD ALTERNATIVE In Europe, *c.* A.D. 1500, the overuse of wood for burning led to shortages owing to deforestation. People began burning coal instead of wood, and coal became the **oldest alternative fuel**.

●**LARGEST SOLAR-POWERED BOAT** *TÛRANOR PlanetSolar* measures 101 ft. (31 m) long—or 114 ft. (35 m) with flaps extended. It has a beam, or width, of 49 ft. (15 m)—75 ft. (23 m) with flaps—and a displacement of 93 tons (85 metric tons). The catamaran's upper surface is covered in 5,780 ft.^{2} (537 m^2) of solar panels, allowing the vessel to be powered by solar energy alone.

●**Longest journey by wind-powered automobile** Dirk Gion and Stefan Simmerer (both Germany) drove 3,106 miles (5,000 km) from Perth to Melbourne, Australia, in 18 days between January and February 2011. The *Wind Explorer* is powered by the wind; a wind turbine charges a lithium-ion battery pack to provide propulsion and, when the wind is strong enough, a kite resembling a parasail harnesses the power of the wind directly. Aside from about $10 worth of electricity when the wind was insufficient, the journey was entirely wind-powered.

WATER CRAFT Hydro power—techniques of harnessing the energy created by moving water—remains the ○**largest contributor to renewable energy**, reaching a capacity of 980 GW by the end of 2009.

●Fastest water-jet-powered automobile The greatest speed attained in a water-jet-powered automobile is 16.65 mi./hr. (26.8 km/h) and was achieved by Jason Bradbury (UK) on the set of *The Gadget Show* at Wattisham Airfield, Ipswich, UK, on March 15, 2010.

Fastest electric automobile The highest average speed achieved for an electric vehicle is 303.025 mi./hr. (487.672 km/h) by *Buckeye Bullet 2*. The vehicle was designed and built by engineering students at Ohio State University, U.S.A., at the university's Center for Automotive Research (CAR), and driven by Roger Schroer (U.S.A.) at the Bonneville Salt Flats, Utah, U.S.A., on September 25, 2009.

Fastest electric motorcycle The *KillaCycle* can accelerate from 0–60 mi./hr. (0–96 km/h) in less than a second and is powered by the same battery as a cordless drill. On October 23, 2008, it reached 167.99 mi./hr. (270.35 km/h), driven in a race by Scotty Pollacheck (U.S.A.) at Bandimere Speedway in Morrison, Colorado, U.S.A., and covered 0.25 miles (0.4 km) in 7.89 seconds.

○Best-selling hybrid vehichles Hybrid vehicles are powered by a combination of an internal combustion engine and an electric engine. They produce fewer harmful emissions than conventional cars and are highly energy-efficient. The best-selling hybrid vehicle is the Toyota Prius, launched in 1997. By September 2010, it had sold 2,011,800 units. The third-generation Prius was unveiled in 2009.

AUTOMOBILES

○FASTEST PRODUCTION AUTOMOBILE The super-quick Bugatti Veyron 16.4 Super Sport achieved a two-way timed speed of 267.86 mi./hr. (431.072 km/h) at the Volkswagen proving grounds in Ehra-Lessien near Wolfsburg, Germany, on June 26, 2010.

Although it had reached its full height of 1,082 ft. (330 m), the Ryugyong Hotel in Pyongyang, North Korea, was not finished when construction was halted in 1992. Twenty years later, it remains the **tallest unoccupied building**.

○**Best-selling automobile** As of February 2011, the Toyota Corolla is the best-selling automobile, with more than 35 million sold since 1966.

The Volkswagen Beetle is the ●**best-selling automobile of a single design**; the core structure and shape remained largely unchanged from 1938 to 2003. It was also the ●**first automobile to achieve 20 million sales**. The Beetle's tally when production ended in 2003 was 21,529,464.

The Ford Model T is the second best-selling car of a single design, and the ●**first car to achieve sales of 10 million**; it has now exceeded 15 million sales. More than 16.5 million were built between 1908 and 1927.

Mazda has produced at least 900,000 Miata sports cars, making it the ○**best-selling sports car**. Production of the open-top two-seater began in April 1989 in Hiroshima, Japan. The Miata is expected to eclipse 1 million sales by 2015.

○**Largest vehicle manufacturer** Japanese automobile manufacturer Toyota ended General Motors' 77-year reign as the best-selling vehicle

manufacturer in 2008, selling 8.97 million vehicles compared with GM's tally of 8.35 million vehicles in that calendar year. Toyota continued to be the world's top-selling vehicle manufacturer for three years in a row (2008, 2009, and 2010), although its lead over General Motors narrowed in 2010.

LARGEST AUTOMATED PARKING FACILITY The two 157-ft.-tall (48-m) "automobile towers" at Volkswagen's Autostadt in Wolfsburg, Germany, can each store 400 automobiles. Buyers can watch as their new vehicle is retrieved from one of the 20-story towers by an automated system that travels at speeds of up to 3 ft. 3 in./s. (2 m/s).

SPEEDY SERVICE Automobiles are transported to the two steel-and-glass towers at the Autostadt straight from the Volkswagen factory. The robotic "shuttles" can process a vehicle every 45 seconds.

By contrast, the Nisiyama Onsen Keiunkan hot-spring hotel in Yamanashi, Japan, has been finished and entertaining guests for a very long time. The world's ○**oldest hotel**, it dates back to A.D. 705.

OLDEST AUTOMOBILE IN PRODUCTION The Morgan 4/4 has been produced since 1935. Apart from a break during World War II (and from March 1951 to September 1955), it has been in production ever since. The engine, transmission, and brakes have been redesigned many times, but the body has remained largely unchanged and is still hand-built by the Morgan Motor Car Company of Malvern, UK.

○**Largest vehicle producer (country)** The country that produces the most automobiles is China, which in 2010 manufactured 18.265 million vehicles out of a world total of 77.610 million, the biggest year on record according to provisional data supplied by the International Organization of Motor Vehicle Manufacturers (OICA). Japan was second with 9.626 million and North America third with 7.761 million.

○**FASTEST AUTOMOBILE ON ICE** On March 6, 2011, Janne Laitinen (Finland) drove an Audi RS6 at an average top speed of 206.05 mi./hr. (331.61 km/h)—less than 0.6 mi./hr. (1 km/h) faster than the previous record—on an 8.6-mile (14-km) section of highway in the Gulf of Bothnia, Oulu, Finland.

RECORD-BREAKING AUTOS

Some people will spend a fortune to secure their dream auto. But as the table below shows, you don't have to be a millionaire to buy a record breaker!

Record	Price	Date
Most expensive automobile: Ferrari 250 GTO (above right)	$17,275,000	Sold May 14, 2010
Most expensive veteran automobile: 1904 Rolls-Royce	£3,521,500 ($7,242,916)	Sold Dec. 3, 2007
Most expensive production automobile: Mercedes-Benz CLK/LM	$1,547,620	Launched 1997
Least expensive present-day production automobile: Tata Nano (above left)	100,000 rupees ($2,500)	Launched Jan. 10, 2008
Least expensive production car ever: Red Bug	$122–$150 (approx. $1,600–$1,920 today)	Launched 1922

●**Largest vehicle sales (country)** In 2009, for the first time since automotive mass production began, China overtook North America as the world's biggest automobile market, with 13.6 million sales compared to North America's tally of 10.4 million. In 2010, China's tally exceeded 18.3 million sales.

> **NANO TECHNOLOGY** The groundbreaking Tata Nano was created to give poorer Indian families the chance to buy automobiles, rather than using motorcycles—often dangerously overladen—to get around.

●FIRST AUTOMOBILE WITH A CRASH-AVOIDANCE SYSTEM In 2008, Volvo (Sweden) released an automobile that constantly monitors the possibility of a nose-to-tail crash. A laser in the windscreen of the Volvo XC60 wagon monitors slow-moving traffic 19 ft. 8 in.–26 ft. (6–8 m) ahead of the front bumper. At speeds less than 18 mi./hr. (30 km/h), the City Safety system will bring the vehicle to an abrupt halt if the driver does not brake in time.

●Greatest fuel range The farthest distance driven on a single standard tank of fuel is 1,526.63 miles (2,456.88 km), by a Volkswagen Passat 1.6 TDI BlueMotion in an event organized by *The Sunday Times* (UK). It was driven by Gavin Conway (UK) between Maidstone, UK, and the A26 in France between August 3 and 5, 2010.

○Greatest vehicle mileage A 1966 Volvo P-1800S owned by Irvin Gordon (U.S.A.) had covered more than 2,850,000 miles (4,586,630 km) by December 2010. It is still driven on a daily basis and covers more than 100,000 miles (160,000 km) per year, thanks in part to being driven to numerous automobile shows in Europe and the U.S.A.

●First hydrogen-powered production automobile Honda introduced its FCX experimental vehicle on public roads in North America and Japan in October 2002, but Mercedes-Benz was first to lease an automobile (the A-class F-Cell) under special arrangements to a paying customer, Tokyo Gas, in December 2003. Hydrogen powers a "fuel cell" that creates electricity.

TRAINS & RAILROADS

First public electric railroad Unveiled on May 12, 1881, at Lichtervelde near Berlin, Germany, the earliest public electric railroad was 1.5 miles (2.5 km) long, ran on a 100-volt current, and carried 26 passengers at a speed of 30 mi./hr. (48 km/h).

Japan is home to PAC-Man, the **most successful coin-operated arcade game**. A total of 293,822 PAC-Man arcade machines were built and installed in arcade venues around the world between 1981 and 1987.

The Volk's Electric Railway, which runs along the seafront at Brighton, UK, is the world's ●**oldest electric railroad still in operation**. Designed by Magnus Volk (UK), the railroad first opened for business in August 1883.

○**FASTEST PASSENGER TRAIN** On December 3, 2010, a CRH380A-type unmodified passenger train reached 302 mi./hr. (486.1 km/h) on a stretch of track between Zaozhuang City in Shandong Province and Bengbu City in eastern Anhui Province, China. At the time of going to press, this is the fastest officially confirmed speed ever attained by an unmodified passenger train.

RUSH-RUSH HOUR! China is planning an ambitious high-speed route to link the major economic centers of Beijing and Shanghai. It will reduce journey time between the two cities from 14 hours to just five hours.

The Taiwanese gamer known only as "Little Gray" became the ●**first player to complete all the listed 986 quests and tasks in** *World of Warcraft*, on November 27, 2009.

○Longest rail tunnel On October 15, 2010, engineers working 6,560 ft. (2,000 m) beneath the Swiss Alps drilled through the last remaining rock blocking the creation of the world's longest rail tunnel. The 35-mile (57-km) Gotthard rail tunnel will take up to 300 trains a day when it officially opens in 2016. Until then, the Seikan rail tunnel in Japan remains the world's longest, at 33.46 miles (53.85 km).

Largest railroad station In terms of platform capacity, New York's Grand Central Terminal is the world's largest station. Currently covering 48 acres (19 ha), the station houses 44 platforms and 67 tracks over two below-ground levels. This is set to expand in 2016, when a new level will open beneath the existing ones, adding four new platforms and a further eight tracks. The station was constructed between 1903 and 1913.

●**FIRST ALL-FEMALE PASSENGER CAR** For a number of years, female-only passenger cars have been a feature of Japanese rail travel, but in July 2002 the West Japan Railway Company (JR West), based in Osaka, Japan, introduced the first female-only cars at rush hour. Other companies soon followed, and all-female cars are now available all day long on trains supplied by Hankyu Railway.

●**LARGEST TRAIN SET** The world's most extensive train set can be found in Hamburg, Germany. Its landscape is modeled on regions in Europe and the U.S.A. and it covers 12,378 ft.^{2} (1,150 m^2), but when completed in 2014, the 13 miles (20 km) of track will cover more than 24,756 ft.^{2} (2,300 m^2). The model comprises over 11,000 passenger cars and wagons, 900 signals, 3,500 buildings, and 200,000 figures.

 Taiwan is home to the **first fully bioluminescent pigs**. Three glowing pigs were born in 2005, created by Taiwan University's Department of Animal Science and Technology, who added DNA from bioluminescent jellyfish to pig embryos.

LONGEST RAIL NETWORKS

Placed end to end, the 10 longest rail networks would extend for 417,157 miles (671,350 km)—enough to stretch from the Earth to the Moon and three-quarters of the way back again.

Country	Length of network
U.S.A. *(pictured is an Amtrak—government-owned stock)*	140,695 miles (226,427 km)
Russia	54,156 miles (87,157 km)
China	48,363 miles (77,834 km)
India	39,777 miles (64,015 km)
Canada	29,010 miles (46,688 km)
Germany	26,032 miles (41,486 km)
Australia	23,522 miles (37,855 km)
Argentina	19,516 miles (31,409 km)
France	18,152 miles (29,213 km)
Brazil	17,930 miles (28,857 km)

SPEED

●**Fastest rail link** The line between the cities of Guangzhou and Wuhan in China carries trains averaging 217 mi./hr. (350 km/h), which cover the 664-mile (1,069-km) distance in just three hours. In France, the average speed for high-speed trains is 172 mi./hr. (277 km/h), while in Japan high-speed trains travel at a relatively sedate 150 mi./hr. (243 km/h).

Fastest speed between two scheduled rail stops Between Lorraine and Champagne-Ardennes, France, trains reach an average speed of 173.6 mi./hr. (279.4 km/h), according to an official *Railway Gazette International* World Speed Survey study.

This figure is almost half the **highest speed ever recorded by a train on a national rail system** (rather than a dedicated test track). A French SNCF modified version of the TGV, called V150, reached 357.1 mi./hr. (574.8 km/h) on April 3, 2007.

Located off the island of Vieques in Puerto Rico, Mosquito Bay is the **most bioluminescent bay** in the world, owing to the millions of tiny bioluminescent *Pyrodinium bahamense* microorganisms that live there.

●**LARGEST RAILROAD NETWORK UNDER A SINGLE MANAGEMENT** India may have only the fourth-largest rail network (see table p. 339), but it has the distinction of being the largest in the world under a single management. It is also the world's largest commercial employer, with more than 1.6 million employees.

Highest sustained train speed for 1,000 km The highest average speed by a train over a distance of 1,000 km (621 miles) is 190.37 mi./hr. (306.37 km/h), by a French SNCF TGV train between Calais and Marseille on May 26, 2001. The train, which was unmodified and therefore identical to regular-service Eurostar trains, covered the 663 miles (1,067 km) between the cities in 3 hr. 29 min. reaching a maximum speed of 227 mi./hr. (366 km/h). The feat was organized to mark the opening of a new stretch of high-speed line between Valence and Marseille.

○**Longest high-speed rail network** China had 4,679 miles (7,531 km) of high-speed track in service as of January 2011, according to the Chinese Ministry of Railroads. A further 10,560 miles (17,000 km) of track is being built, which by 2015 will extend China's high-speed network beyond 15,500 miles (25,000 km). (High-speed routes have an average speed of 124 mi./hr. [200 km/h] or higher.)

●**BUSIEST RAILROAD STATION** An average of 3.64 million passengers per day pass through Shinjuku Station in Tokyo, Japan. The station has more than 200 exits and serves the city's western suburbs via a range of intercity, commuter-rail, and metro services.

Fastest magnetic levitation train in regular service The Shanghai Transrapid "maglev" train links Pudong International Airport to the center of Shanghai (both China) and opened on January 1, 2004. It reaches a speed of 267 mi./hr. (431 km/h) in normal service. The **first maglev train in regular service** linked Birmingham International Airport and International rail station (both UK) between 1984 and 1995.

PETROL HEADS

FASTEST . . .

Amphibious vehicle With an engine based on the LS Corvette power train, the *WaterCar Python* is the fastest amphibious vehicle. It has a top speed of 60 mi./hr. (96 km/h; 52 knots) on water and can perform a 0–60 mi./hr. acceleration in 4.5 seconds on land. The *Python* is hand-built to order; prices start from $200,000.

●**Bed** Created and driven by Edd China (UK), the fastest mobile bed reached a speed of 69 mi./hr. (111 km/h) along a private road in London, UK, on November 7, 2008, as part of Guinness World Records Day 2008.

Caravan tow A Mercedes Benz S600 driven by Eugene Herbert (South Africa) reached 139.113 mi./hr. (223.881 km/h) towing a caravan at Hoedspruit Air Force Base, South Africa, on October 24, 2003.

○**Furniture** *Fast Food*, a motorized mock-up of a fully laid dining table, reached 113.8 mi./hr. (183.14 km/h) at the Santa Pod Raceway, Bedfordshire, UK, on September 5, 2010. It was driven by its creator, Perry Watkins (UK).

○**Hearse** Shane Hammond (Australia) covered 0.25 miles (0.4 km) in a hearse in 12.206 seconds on the TDRA Dragway in Tasmania, Australia, on February 20, 2010. (The time is an average from four runs.)

Hovercraft The highest recorded speed by a hovercraft is 85.38 mi./hr. (137.4 km/h), by Bob Windt (U.S.A.) at the 1995 World Hovercraft Championships on the Rio Douro River, Peso de Regua, Portugal. Windt was driving a streamlined 19-ft. (5.8-m) Universal UH19P hovercraft named *Jenny II*, with a 110-hp (82-kW) V6 automobile engine driving its two fans.

Race to p. 319 for more high-speed antics.

●**FASTEST MOBILITY SCOOTER** Colin Furze (UK) has supercharged a mobility scooter so that it can reach a top speed of 69 mi./hr. (111 km/h). It took Colin three months to convert the scooter, which features five gears, a 125cc motorbike engine, and twin exhausts.

FASTEST . . .

Office Edd China (UK) built a roadworthy desk that can reach a speed of 87 mi./hr. (140 km/h). Edd drove it across Westminster Bridge into the City of London, UK, on November 9, 2006, as part of GWR Day.

Powered street luge Joel King (UK) reached a speed of 112.7 mi./hr. (181.37 km/h) on his jet-engine-powered street luge at Bentwaters Airfield, UK, on August 28, 2007.

Snowmobile The speed record for the fastest snowmobile is 172.2 mi./hr. (277.13 km/h) and was set by Chris Hanson (U.S.A.) on Lake Nipissing in North Bay, Ontario, Canada, on March 13, 2004.

 The **largest dish radio telescope** is the partially steerable ionospheric assembly built over a natural bowl at Arecibo, Puerto Rico. The dish has a diameter of 1,000 ft. (305 m).

●**Towed Big Wheel** On November 18, 2008, Jim DeChamp (U.S.A.) rode a towed Big Wheel to a maximum speed of 59 mi./hr. (94.9 km/h) at Miller Motorsports Park in Tooele, Utah, U.S.A., for the MTV show *Nitro Circus*.

●**Towed toilet** Garrett Olson (U.S.A.) rode a towed toilet at a speed of 49.6 mi./hr. (79.83 km/h) at the Dunn Tire Raceway in Lancaster, New York, U.S.A., on September 2, 2009.

●**Waste container** The fastest waste container—built using a modified 0.43-gal (2-liter) turbo Subaru Impreza Type R rally car set within a 24-ft. (7.3-m) debris box—achieved a land-speed record of 93.92 mi./hr. (151.15 km/h) on the 0.25-mile (0.4-km) dragster track at the Santa Pod Raceway, Northants., UK, on November 3, 2007. The vehicle was driven by its owner, James Norvill (UK).

MOST CRASH TESTS ENDURED
By February 2003, traffic collision reconstructionist W. R. "Rusty" Haight (U.S.A.) had had 718 collisions in automobiles as a "human crash test dummy."

LONGEST MONSTER TRUCK RAMP JUMP On September 11, 1999, *Bigfoot 14*, driven by Dan Runte, jumped 202 ft. (61.57 m) over a Boeing 727 passenger jet at Smyrna Airport, Tennessee, U.S.A. During the runup, Dan also set the record for the **fastest speed for a monster truck**: 69.3 mi./hr. (111.5 km/h).

Bigfoot trucks were created by Bob Chandler (U.S.A.).

The **largest cosmic ray telescope** is the Pierre Auger Observatory, an array of some 1,600 particle detectors arranged across 1,158 miles^2 (3,000 km^2) of western Argentina.

$109,000: The cost of the 14 automobiles you will own in your lifetime. Almost all of the metal in old automobiles is recycled into new ones, so your 14th automobile may contain some of your first.

SMALLEST ROAD-WORTHY AUTOMOBILE
Created by Perry Watkins (UK), the world's smallest roadworthy automobile is *Wind Up*, which measures 41 in. (104.14 cm) high, 26 in. (66.04 cm) wide, and 52 in. (132.08 cm) long. It was measured in Wingrave, UK, on May 8, 2009.

○**FASTEST LAWNMOWER** Don Wales (UK), of Project Runningblade, rode a lawnmower at a world-beating speed of 87.83 mi./hr. (141.35 km/h) in Pendine, UK, on May 23, 2010.

●**FASTEST WEDDING CHAPEL** The *Best Man* achieved a speed of 62 mi./hr. (99 km/h) in Shelbyville, Illinois, U.S.A., on September 30, 2010.

FAST SERVICE The mobile chapel includes stained-glass windows, pews, a pulpit, a pipe organ, a 1,000-watt stereo system, and a three-tiered back porch with wrought-iron hand railings.

AIRCRAFT

●**Fastest plane (civil)** In August 2010, a Gulfstream G650 jet flown by Tom Horne and Gary Freeman reached Mach 0.995 (757 mi./hr.; 1,219 km/h) in a 16- to 18-degree dive in Savannah, Georgia, U.S.A. The U.S. plane can carry four crew and eight passengers nonstop from London, UK, to Buenos Aires, Argentina—a distance of 6,916 miles (11,130 km).

●**First commercially produced electric aircraft** The two-seater Yuneec e430 is an eco-friendly plane that carries no fuel and emits no fumes and little noise. It is a single-engined monoplane that can fly for up to 3 hours at a cruising speed of 52 knots (60 mi./hr.; 96 km/h).

●**First electric helicopter** Sikorsky unveiled the world's first all-electric helicopter on July 26, 2010. Called the *Firefly*, it is a modified Schweizer S-300C, weighing 2,125 lb. (963.9 kg). Powered by two lithium-ion battery packs producing about 370 volts, it is capable of flying for up to 15 minutes at a speed of 80 knots (92 mi./hr.; 148 km/h).

●**Most expensive helicopter** The cost for a proposed fleet of 28 Lockheed Martin (U.S.A.) VH71 Kestrel helicopters was estimated at a record $13.2 billion, making it the most expensive helicopter in the world at $471 million.

Q. WHICH AIRCRAFT MANUFACTURER HAS PRODUCED THE MOST AIRCRAFT TO DATE?

A. Not Boeing or Airbus, but in fact the Cessna Aircraft Company of Wichita, Kansas, U.S.A., which had built 192,967 aircraft up to 2010.

●**FIRST HUMAN-POWERED AIRCRAFT WITH FLAPPING WINGS** The *Snowbird*, which has a wingspan of 105 ft. (32 m)—comparable to a Boeing 737—is the first aircraft to be able to fly like a bird (once launched by a tow vehicle). On August 2, 2010, Canadian student Todd Reichert flew the carbon-fiber-and-balsa-wood craft for 19.3 seconds, averaging 16 mi./hr. (25.6 km/h) over a distance of 476 ft. (145 m) at the Great Lakes Gliding Club in Ontario, Canada.

●**FASTEST HELICOPTER (NON-FAI)** On September 15, 2010, the Sikorsky X2 set a new unofficial speed record for a helicopter, reaching 250 knots (288 mi./hr.; 463 km/h) at Sikorsky's Development Flight Center in Florida, U.S.A. The X2, which took its first flight in 2008, has coaxial rotors—two sets of blades that rotate in opposite directions.

●**Most expensive aircraft scrapped before becoming operational** In January 2011, nine new Nimrod MRA4 aircraft costing £450 million ($713 million) each were scrapped by the UK Ministry of Defence due to budget cuts.

○**Longest flight by a solar-powered UAV** At 6:41 a.m. on July 9, 2010, a Zephyr unmanned aerial vehicle (UAV) was launched from the U.S. Army's Yuma Proving Ground in Arizona, U.S.A., and flew for a record 336 hr. 22 min.—over two weeks—fueled only by solar power generated by paper-thin silicon arrays on the aircraft's wings. On the same flight, the battery-powered Zephyr also earned the record for the ●**highest altitude achieved by a solar-powered UAV**, soaring to an unprecedented height of 70,740 ft. (21,561 m).

○**LARGEST FIRE-FIGHTING AIRCRAFT** The Evergreen International Aviation Company (U.S.A.) has modified a Boeing 747-300 aircraft for fire-fighting duties. The Evergreen 747 Supertanker has a capacity of 17,070 gal (77,600 liters)— more than eight times that of the commonly used P-3A Orion aircraft—and was first used in July 2009 to fight huge fires in Cuenca, Spain.

Built in 2002 by Carlos Alberto Balbiani (Argentina), the world's **smallest pistol** is 2.1 in. (5.5 cm) long, 1.3 in (3.5 cm) in height, and weighs just 0.91 oz. (26 g). It fires 0.68 mm caliber bullets.

729: Balloons you will buy in a lifetime. If they were all filled with helium, they could together lift an average-sized newborn baby (7.5 lb.). To fly an average adult (168 lb.), you'd need more than 22 lifetimes' worth!

In 2004, "Rocket Man" Rossy became the first human to fly horizontally.

●**FIRST AERIAL LOOP USING A JET PACK** On November 5, 2010, former fighter pilot Yves Rossy (Switzerland) became the first man to complete an aerial loop using a jet-propelled carbon-fiber wing. After launching from a hot-air balloon at 7,874 ft. (2,400 m) over Lake Geneva, Switzerland, he performed two aerial loops before parachuting safely back to Earth.

●**First flight of a manned solar-powered aircraft** On April 7, 2010, German pilot Markus Scherdel flew the *Solar Impulse* on a 90-minute test flight at Payerne, Switzerland. The aircraft, the $93.8-million brainchild of Swiss adventurer Bertrand Piccard, is powered by 12,000 solar cells driving four electric motors and is destined for a future round-the-world record attempt.

●**First algae-powered aircraft** At the 2010 ILA Air Show in Berlin, Germany, the European defense company EADS showcased a twin-engine Diamond DA42 NG light aircraft powered by algae-derived biofuel.

○**Busiest airport (passengers, flights)** According to the Airports Council International, 88,032,086 people flew in or out of Hartsfield-Jackson Atlanta International Airport in Georgia, U.S.A., in 2009. Hartsfield-Jackson was also busiest by flight numbers, with 970,235 in and out.

BLADES OF GLORY: The **fastest helicopter** according to the Féderation Aéronautique Internationale (FAI) is a Westland Lynx that hit a speed of 216 knots (249 mi./hr.; 400 km/h) in 1986.

Much larger by comparison is the **most powerful cell phone gun**, a 0.22 in. caliber pistol disguised as a cell phone. Made in Croatia, the gun is triggered when the numbers 5, 6, 7, and 8 are pressed in quick succession.

●FIRST FLAPLESS AIRCRAFT WITHOUT CONVENTIONAL CONTROL SURFACES The UK aerospace company BAE Systems, in cooperation with 10 UK universities, has created an unmanned aerial vehicle (UAV) designed to fly without conventional control surfaces. The DEMON uses outputs from air jets to control airflow over the wing—based on a concept called "fluidic flight control"—manipulating lift and drag to control its flight path rather than using traditional mechanical elevators and ailerons. Its maiden flight took place in Cumbria, UK, on September 17, 2010.

●FIRST COMMERCIAL PASSENGER SPACE AIRCRAFT On March 23, 2010, the Virgin Space Ship *Enterprise* took its maiden test flight over California, U.S.A. The craft, attached to the mothership, *WhiteKnightTwo*, flew for 2 hr. 54 min. and reached 45,000 ft. (13,716 m). When passenger flights begin in 2012, the spaceship will rise to 50,000 ft. (15,240 m) and then, powered by a single rocket motor, detach from the mothership and carry its six "space tourists" to the edge of the Earth's atmosphere.

○Busiest airport (cargo) At Memphis International Airport in Tennessee, U.S.A., 4,075,304 tons (3,697,054 metric tons) of cargo were loaded and unloaded in 2009.

●Longest flight at hypersonic speed Launched from a B-52 bomber on May 26, 2010, a Boeing (U.S.A.) X-51A Waverider was propelled to nearly Mach 6—4,567 mi./hr. (7,350 km/h), or six times the speed of sound—by its air-breathing scramjet motor, which burned for more than 200 seconds. Scramjets are powered by hydrogen fuel, which is ignited by oxygen rushing in through the engine at supersonic speeds.

○Longest wingspan of an aircraft in production The colossal Airbus A380 airliner has a wingspan of 261 ft. 9.73 in. (79.8 m), which is nearly as long as a full-sized soccer field.

●First purpose-built commercial spaceport The construction of Spaceport America, by the Government of New Mexico, U.S.A., is due for completion toward the end of 2011 at a cost of around $200 million. It will comprise a space-age terminal and hangar and a 10,000-ft. (3,000-m) runway, and will be home to Virgin Galactic's (UK) space operations (see above).

WARSHIPS

●**Largest class of aircraft carrier** In terms of production numbers, the largest class of aircraft carrier is the Casablanca-class escort carrier. Between 1942 and 1945, a total of 50 were built for the U.S. Navy. They were 512 ft. (156.1 m) long with a displacement of 12,017 tons (10,902 metric tons) when fully loaded. Five Casablancas were lost during World War II and the rest have since been scrapped.

●**Largest aircraft to land on a carrier** In October 1963, a Lockheed KC-130F Hercules transport performed 21 unarrested landings and unassisted takeoffs on the USS *Forrestal* around 497 miles (800 km) off the U.S. coast in the North Atlantic. Despite weighing up to 121,000 lb. (54,844 kg), the aircraft managed to come to rest over a distance of just two wingspans without the aid of arresting gear to slow or stop it.

●**Oldest aircraft carrier in service** In 1959, the UK's Royal Navy commissioned the HMS *Hermes*, a Centaur-class carrier. Measuring 743 ft. (226.5 m) long, it displaces 31,636 tons (28,700 metric tons) and can reach 28 knots (32 mi./hr.; 52 km/h). After serving as the UK's flagship in the Falklands War with Argentina in 1982, it was sold to India in 1986 and now serves as India's flagship under the name INS *Viraat*.

●**Largest aircraft cruiser** Aircraft cruisers are capable of ship-to-ship combat as well as carrying aircraft. The largest of these is the Russian *Admiral Kuznetsov*, at 992 ft. (302.3 m) long and displacing 64,595 tons (58,600 metric tons). Armed with 12 Granit antiship missiles, 192 Kinzhal surface-to-air missiles, an antisubmarine rocket launcher, and antiaircraft guns, it can also carry 12 Su-33 and 5 Su-25 jets, along with 24 helicopters.

●**LAST BATTLESHIPS TO SEE COMBAT** The growing dominance of airpower and guided missiles in naval combat has rendered battleships effectively obsolete. The U.S. Navy's four Iowa-class battleships—*Missouri*, *Iowa*, *Wisconsin*, and *New Jersey*—were first commissioned in 1943 and, although they have spent much of their lives in mothballs, they have seen action in Korea (1950–53), Vietnam (1955–75), and the Persian Gulf (1990–91).

USS *TRUMAN* [CVN75]

The *Truman* is the eighth of 10 Nimitz-class nuclear-powered aircraft carriers—the world's largest warships.

Launch	September 7, 1996
Cost	$4.5 billion
Size	1,096 ft. (334 m) long; 251 ft. (76.5 m) wide
Displacement	116,342 tons (105,545 metric tons) full load
Speed	Over 30 knots (34 mi./hr.; 55 km/h)
Propulsion	Two A4W nuclear reactors, four screws
Crew	5,200 with embarked air wing, 3,000-plus without air wing
Aircraft	80 fixed-wing aircraft, 10 helicopters
Armaments	2 Sea Sparrow, 3 Phalanx CIWS, and 2 Rolling Airframe Missile (RAM) mounts

●**LARGEST FLEET OF AIRCRAFT CARRIERS** **Of the 22 aircraft carriers in service worldwide, the U.S. Navy accounts for exactly half of them, boasting one Enterprise-class carrier (the USS *Enterprise*, the first nuclear aircraft carrier) and 10 Nimitz-class carriers (the largest warships ever built), including the USS *Truman*, pictured. The remaining 11 belong to the UK, Russia, France, Brazil, India, Italy, Spain, and Thailand.**

The **largest truffle** was a white truffle (*Tuber magnatum pico*) found by Giancarlo Zigante (Croatia) near Buje, Croatia, on November 2, 1999. Weighing 2 lb. 8 oz. (1.31 kg), it was 7.6 in. (19.5 cm) long and estimated to be worth $5,080.

6,356 Cans of food you will eat in a lifetime. Canned food was invented in 1810 to feed armies on the march and navies at sea. These cans had to be chiseled open—the can-opener wouldn't be invented until 1855!

CLASH OF THE TITANS: In the Battle of the Coral Sea on May 4–8, 1942, Japanese and U.S.carriers fought the ●**first battle between aircraft carriers**. During the fray, neither ship caught sight of the other as the battle was fought by planes overhead.

●**Fastest speed by a battleship** The U.S. Iowa-class ships were powered by eight fuel-oil boilers and four propellers, delivering 212,000 shaft horsepower. In 1968, the USS *New Jersey* achieved a record speed of 35.2 knots (40.5 mi./hr.; 65.2 km/h) for a duration of six hours. Following this feat, the *New Jersey*'s captain ordered an emergency stop, and the ship took 2 miles (3.2 km) to come to rest.

●**First all-big-gun battleship** HMS *Dreadnought*, commissioned in 1906 by the UK's Royal Navy, revolutionized global battleship design. The vessel was the first to dispense with medium-caliber guns as main armaments, replacing them with more large-caliber main guns. In total, *Dreadnought* featured ten 12-inch guns mounted in five turrets.

●**Last monitor to see active service** Monitor-class warships are named after the first of their class, USS *Monitor*, which was commissioned in 1862. They are slow, heavy, and characterized by a low profile and single main turret. The Brazilian Navy's riverine Monitor *Parnaíba* (U-17) was commissioned in 1937 and is still in active service.

●**Largest cruiser fleet** Just three nations have cruisers in active service: the U.S.A., Russia, and Peru. The U.S. Navy has by far the largest fleet with 22 ships to Russia's five and Peru's one. The U.S. vessels are all Ticonderoga-class cruisers, built between 1980 and 1994. They are 568 ft. (173 m) long with a displacement of 10,919 tons (9,906 metric tons) and are armed with a vertical launch system for surface-to-air, cruise, antisubmarine, and antiship missiles. They also have two 5-inch guns, antimissile defenses, and torpedo tubes.

Tuber magnum pico is the **most expensive truffle species**, fetching up to $1,350 per pound. Limited to parts of Italy and Croatia, it grows as deep as 1 ft. (30 cm) underground and can only be located with the help of trained dogs.

●**Largest naval exercise** The Rim of the Pacific Exercise is an annual international maritime exercise that was first held in 1971. Its main participants are the U.S.A., Canada, and Australia, with the UK, Chile, Peru, Japan, and South Korea also taking part regularly. Although the scale of the exercise varies annually, the U.S.component can include up to 20,000 personnel and a full carrier battle group plus support ships.

●**Most ships scuttled** During World War II, on November 27, 1942, the French fleet in Toulon, France, was sunk to avoid capture by the Germans. Of some 73 ships lost, 57 were major vessels, including two battleships, two battle cruisers, four heavy cruisers, two light cruisers, an aircraft transport, 30 destroyers, and 16 submarines.

●**LARGEST SURFACE COMBAT SHIP IN ACTIVE SERVICE** Discounting carriers, amphibious assault ships, and subs, the largest combat ships are the Russian Kirov-class cruisers. At 827 ft. (252 m) long with a beam of 93 ft. 6 in. (28.5 m), they displace 30,865 tons (28,000 metric tons) fully loaded and have a top speed of 32 knots (37 mi./hr.; 59 km/h). Pictured is the 24,300-ton (22,044-metric-ton) *Admiral Lazarev* (laid down 1978).

MILITARY HARDWARE

●**Most effective body armor** In July 2010, BAE Systems (UK) demonstrated the effectiveness of kevlar body armor integrating "shear-thickening fluid" (STF). This substance, dubbed "bulletproof custard," thickens when impacted and absorbs the energy more than three times more effectively than untreated armor. STF also offers a reduction in uniform thickness by 45%.

●**LARGEST OPERATIONAL UAV** In February 2010, Israel Aerospace Industries unveiled the latest development of the Heron TP unmanned aerial vehicle (UAV), named the *Eitan*. The size of a Boeing 737, it has a maximum takeoff weight of 10,250 lb. (4,650 kg), a wingspan of 86 ft. (26.2 m), and a length of 46 ft. (14 m). Its 1,200-hp (895-kW) turbojet engine allows it to carry high-resolution cameras, electronic systems, and, possibly, weapons, while it can stay airborne for over 20 hours at 45,000 ft. (13,716 m).

CHINESE WHISPERS In early 2010, China tested its new Chengdu J-20 Powerful Dragon stealth fighter, destined to enter service in around 2017 to challenge the world's only fully stealthy aircraft, the U.S. F-22 Raptor.

●**LARGEST SPY SATELLITE** On November 21, 2010, a spy satellite, payload NROL-32, dubbed the world's largest by an official from the National Reconnaissance Office, was launched from Cape Canaveral, U.S.A., on a Delta 4-Heavy rocket—the most powerful rocket in the U.S. inventory. Although the satellite and its mission are top secret, the size of the rocket, which can launch payloads of up to 26.45 tons (24 metric tons), implies an extremely large satellite.

●**Most advanced electric uniforms** Intelligent Textiles Ltd (UK) have developed an "e-textile" with passive electronic circuits, allowing for electrical interconnectivity. In 2009, the e-textile was woven into an Osprey armor carrier vest, where it carried a current of 0.1–4 amperes. This technology helps lighten a soldier's load as it eradicates the need for heavy batteries and allows electrical equipment to be attached to power-points on their uniforms.

●**Most accurate electronic sniper detector** The Boomerang Warrior-X system, made by Raytheon (U.S.A.), is just 4 in.^{2} (10.2 cm^2) and detects enemy shooters by triangulating the sound of their gunfire up to 3,000 ft. (914 m) away. It displays the target's position on a screen and emits a warning signal.

●**Most ecofriendly spy plane** Powered by a highly efficient hydrogen propulsion system, the Phantom Eye is a prototype unmanned aircraft that was unveiled by Boeing (U.S.A.) on July 12, 2010. The reconnaissance plane can stay in the air for four days at 65,000 ft. (19,800 m), while its only by-product is water.

● **FIRST SUCCESSFUL KILL OF A BALLISTIC MISSILE BY AN AIRBORNE LASER SYSTEM** In February 2010, a U.S. prototype weapon system on board a modified Boeing 747-400F destroyed a ballistic missile in mid-flight off the coast of California, U.S.A. Low-energy lasers were first used to detect and track the missile before it was then engaged by a megawatt-class high-energy laser fired through a telescope in the nose of the plane.

● **FIRST PILOTLESS COMBAT HELICOPTER** The American, Connecticut-based helicopter manufacturer Sikorsky has embarked on a $1-billion program to produce the first pilotless combat helicopter, with a prototype set for 2011. Based on the same company's world-famous Black Hawk aircraft, the new helicopter is slated to enter service in 2015 at a cost of $17.25 million each.

RC AIRCRAFT The remote-control Black Hawk may be some way from service, but pilotless aircraft have been used in combat for years. The ● **first aerial battle involving a UAV** occurred when an Iraqi MiG downed a U.S. Predator drone over Iraq in December 2002.

On April 25, 2009, Italian Michele Pradelli performed the **longest standing jump on a motorcycle**, achieving a distance of 14 ft. (4.26 m) on the set of *Lo Show dei Record* in Milan, Italy.

$243: Your share of the $1.687 trillion the world spends on arms every year. If governments were persuaded to pay your share back to you each year, you'd save enough in a lifetime ($19,149) to buy a (used) armored vehicle.

● **MOST EFFECTIVE ANIMAL MINE-CLEARER** In Tanzania, the giant African pouched rat is trained by APOPO, a Belgian nongovernmental organization, to sniff out landmines. The work is not overly dangerous for rats as they are very light and therefore highly unlikely to trigger a mine. Training the rats to recognize the smell of TNT explosive takes about nine months, but, once up to speed, two rats can clear an area of 2,150 ft.^{2} (200 m^2) in two hours, whereas human mine-clearers would take a day to cover the same area.

● **FIRST REMOTE-CONTROL SEARCH DOGS** Researchers at the Canine Detection Research Institute at Auburn University in Alabama, U.S.A., have invented a harness that uses Global Positioning Systems (GPS) to remotely guide search dogs in dangerous situations. Carrying a GPS, a processor, spatial sensors, and a radio modem, the harness transmits vibrations to the dog on its left or right side so that it can be "steered" through extremely tight gaps in buildings such as airports or in other disaster scenarios.

● **Most ecofriendly bomb detectors** The University of Colorado (U.S.A.) has developed a computer program that can "train" plants to respond to explosives in the same way that they react to other threatening stimuli, by releasing chemicals called terpenoids, which change the color of their leaves.

● **Most ecofriendly ammunition** Although lethal to humans, the U.S. Army's new M855A1 Enhanced Performance Rounds are kinder to the environment as they are made of nonhazardous copper instead of lead. The bullets have been used by U.S. troops in Afghanistan since June 2010.

Of course, people do all kinds of things on bikes—motorcycle enthusiasts Peter Schmidl and Anna Turceková (both Slovakia) put on the **largest motorcycle wedding procession**, featuring 597 bikes, when they tied the knot in Bratislava, Slovakia, on May 6, 2000.

●**Most powerful electromagnetic railgun** Electromagnetic (EM) railguns use electricity to fire projectiles at speeds greater than Mach 7 and are capable of destroying targets 230 miles (370 km) away. On December 10, 2010, an EM railgun at the Naval Surface Warfare Center in Dahlgren, U.S.A., achieved a 33-megajoule shot—an amazing force, given that 1 megajoule can propel a 1.1-ton (1-metric-ton) vehicle at 100 mi./hr. (160 km/h).

●**Fastest landing vessel** In 2010, the UK agreed to test the Partial Air-Cushion Supported Catamaran, an aluminum landing craft capable of 30 knots (34.5 mi./hr.; 55.6 km/h).

●**Smallest guided missile** Weighing 5 lb. 4 oz. (2.4 kg), the U.S. Navy's Spike missile is perfectly suited to small unmanned aerial vehicles (UAVs). With its precise laser-guided targeting system, it can lock on to a target as small as a motorcycle.

●**Most advanced airborne surveillance system** In December 2010, the U.S. Air Force deployed its new Gorgon Stare surveillance system on an MQ-9 Reaper UAV in Afghanistan. The technology has nine cameras that can transmit 65 different live images at a time and can watch over an entire city.

BRIDGES

Oldest bridge Remnants of bridges dated *c.* 1600 B.C. exist over the River Havos in Mycenae, Greece. The oldest datable bridge still in use, though, is the slab-stone single-arch bridge over the River Meles in Izmir (formerly Smyrna), Turkey, which dates from 850 B.C.

●**LONGEST BRIDGE FOUNTAIN** The Banpo Grand Bridge over the Han River in Seoul, South Korea, measures 3,740 ft. (1,140 m) long. Running along its length are 380 nozzles that send 60 tons (54 metric tons) of water cascading 140 ft. (43 m) horizontally and 65 ft. (20 m) down into the river every minute. In the evening, LED lights illuminate the water spray, which "dances" in time to 100 different pieces of music.

440: Length in miles of a lifetime's-worth of hair if placed end to end. Spin it into a single strand and it would measure four times longer than the world's longest bridge.

Widest bridge The 1,650-ft.-long (503-m) Sydney Harbour Bridge in New South Wales, Australia, is 160 ft. (48.8 m) wide. It carries two electrical overhead railroad tracks, eight lanes of roadway, a cycle track, and footway. It opened on March 19, 1932.

Tallest bridge The Millau Viaduct, which crosses the Tarn Valley in France, is supported by seven concrete piers, the tallest of which measures 1,095 ft. 4 in. (333.88 m) from the ground to its highest point—more than twice the height of the Great Pyramid of Giza. (See pp. 364–368 for other Pyramid-related facts.)

○**LONGEST ROAD-AND-RAIL BRIDGE** The Wuhu Yangtze River Bridge in Anhui province, China, is a road-and-railroad bridge with a total length of 6.2 miles (10.02 km) and a main span of 1,023 ft. (312 m). The top deck carries four lanes of highway and a footpath, while the lower deck comprises a double-track grade-one railroad.

●**LONGEST BRIDGE OVER WATER** The six-lane Qingdao-Haiwan road bridge, which spans Jiaozhou Bay in China's Shangdong province, is 26.4 miles (42.5 km) long. The earthquake- and typhoon-proof bridge opened in 2011 and is designed to withstand the impact of a 300,000-metric-ton vessel. It is 2.53 miles (4.07 km) longer than the former record holder, the Lake Pontchartrain Causeway in Louisiana, U.S.A.
A. 496,040 tons of steel—enough to build 65 Eiffel Towers!
B. 81 million ft.^{3} of concrete—enough to fill 3,800 Olympic swimming pools!

For more epic engineering, turn to p. 360.

Most bridges walked across Donald H. Betty of Lancaster, Pennsylvania, U.S.A., has walked across 150 bridges (all suspension bridges), including 26 of the longest in the world. The longest bridge Betty has crossed is the Akashi-Kaikyo Road Bridge in Japan (see p. 360).

HIGHEST . . .

●**Railroad bridge** The Beipanjiang River Railway Bridge, near Liupanshui in Guizhou province, China, is an arch with a maximum deck height of 902 ft. (275 m).

○**Bridge (deck)** The deck of the suspension bridge over the Si Du River in Badong County, Hubei, China, is situated 1,549 ft. (472 m) above the valley—more than high enough to accommodate the Empire State Build-

ing beneath it. When the bridge was being constructed, the first suspension cable to be secured was fired across the 1,600-ft.-wide (500-m) valley, rather than flown across by helicopter, making it the ●**first suspension-bridge cable placed using a rocket**. The bridge was opened to traffic on November 15, 2009.

○**LONGEST BRIDGE** The Danyang-Kunshan Grand Bridge, on the Jinghu High-Speed Railway (aka Beijing–Shanghai High-Speed Railway), is 102 miles (164 km) long. This new line (open from June 2011) also crosses the 70.8-mile (114-km) Langfang–Qingxian viaduct, the second longest bridge in the world.

BUILDING BRIDGES The original Bay Bridge, built in 1936, cost $77 million—equivalent to $1.2 billion today. It needed more concrete than was used in the Empire State Building.

The record for the **largest collection of napkins** belongs to Antónia Kozáková (Slovakia), who had amassed 30,300 different ones as of April 27, 2007.

●**MOST EXPENSIVE BRIDGE** The five-lane San Francisco–Oakland Bay toll bridge opened in 1963, but was left crippled by the Loma Prieta earthquake in 1989. In 2002, restoration and replacement work began on the bridge at an estimated cost of $6.3 billion.

And those napkins would come in very handy at the Bawabet Dimashq (Damascus Gate) Restaurant in Damascus, Syria—with 6,014 seats, it is the **largest restaurant** in the world.

LONGEST . . .

●**Road bridge** The six-lane elevated Bang Na Expressway (aka the Bang Na-Bang Phil-Bang Pakong Expressway or the Burapha Withi Expressway) runs for 33.5 miles (54 km) through Bangkok, Thailand, and was constructed using 63.5 million ft.^{3} (1.8 million m^3) of concrete. It was opened on February 7, 2000, at a cost of $1 billion.

Transoceanic bridge The bridge spanning the greatest expanse of open ocean is the 22-mile (36-km) Hangzhou Bay Bridge, which links the cities of Cixi and Zhapu in Zhejiang province, China.

Suspension bridge The main span of the Akashi-Kaikyo Road Bridge linking Honshu and Shikoku, Japan, is 6,532 ft., or 1.24 miles (1,990.8 m) long. The overall suspended length with side spans totals 12,831 ft. 8 in., or 2.43 miles (3,911.1 m).

●**Footbridge** On October 3, 2009, the 6,767-ft., or 1.28-mile (2.06-km) Poughkeepsie Bridge (also known as the Walkway Over the Hudson State National Park) in New York, U.S.A., was reopened to the public as the world's longest pedestrian bridge. (Hornibrook Bridge across Bramble Bay in Queensland, Australia, is longer but is now closed to the public.)

○**Steel arch bridge** The Chongqing-Chaotianmen Bridge over the Yangtze River in China is a two-deck, steel truss-arch bridge with a main span of 1,811 ft. (552 m).

Tibetan bridge A 1,227-ft. (374-m) Tibetan bridge—a narrow walkway between two banks and supported loosely by cables or ropes—was strung across the Po River in Turin, Italy, in May 2004 by Experimenta (Italy).

EPIC ARCHITECTURE

○**Tallest tower** The Canton Tower, also known as the Guangzhou TV & Sightseeing Tower, rises 1,968 ft. 6 in. (600 m) to the top of its mast—twice as tall as Paris' Eiffel Tower. It is located in the Haizhu District, Guangzhou, China, and was designed by Mark Hemel and Barbara Kuit (both Netherlands) of the Dutch firm Information Based Architecture.

> Leans at an angle four times greater than that of the leaning Tower of Pisa.

FARTHEST-LEANING MAN-MADE BUILDING Capital Gate has an inclination of 18 degrees and is 524 ft. 11 in. (160 m) high. It was developed by the Abu Dhabi National Exhibitions Company and designed by RMJM. The external construction was completed in Abu Dhabi, UAE, in January 2010.

Epic Architecture

HIGHEST BUILDING TO HOUSE A HOTEL
The Park Hyatt Shanghai in Pudong, China, occupies floors 79 to 93 of the Shanghai World Financial Centre.

The hotel also incorporates the **highest observation deck** in the world, a glass construction known as the Skywalk. It is located on the building's 100th floor at a height of 1,554 ft. (473.9 m).

TALLEST BUILDING On January 4, 2010, the Burj Khalifa, developed by Emaar Properties in Dubai, UAE, topped out at 2,716 ft. 6 in. (828 m). The architects were Skidmore, Owings, & Merrill LLP. Construction began on September 21, 2004, with the exterior being completed on October 1, 2009. The Burj Khalifa is also the **tallest man-made structure on land**.

●**Tallest tensile structure** The Khan Shatyr Entertainment Centre, in Astana, Kazakhstan, soars 492 ft. (150 m) from its elliptical base. The tent-like structure covers an area of more than 1,076,390 ft.^{2} (100,000 m^2).

Largest hotel The First World Hotel, in the Genting Highlands Resort in Pahang Darul Makmur, Malaysia, has 6,118 rooms. The hotel was completed in 2005.

Tallest lighthouse The steel Marine Tower at Yamashita Park in Yokohama, Japan, is 348 ft. (106 m) tall, has a visibility range of 20 miles (32 km), and contains an observatory 328 ft. (100 m) above ground. It can project light with an intensity of 600,000 candelas.

Dating from A.D. 232, the **oldest surviving Christian church** is a house originally located in Qal'at es Salihiye (formerly Dura Europos) in eastern Syria.

● **MOST LANDMARKS ILLUMINATED IN 24 HOURS** On October 1, 2010, as part of Breast Cancer Awareness Month, The Estée Lauder Companies organized the lighting of 38 landmarks in 24 hours. A host of iconic structures were turned pink, including the Zappeion (above left) in Athens, Greece; the Freedom Tower (above right) in Miami, U.S.A.; Tokyo Tower in Japan; and the Burj Al Arab in Dubai, UAE. The event culminated in New York City, U.S.A., with the illumination of the Empire State Building.

○**Highest residential apartments** The Burj Khalifa in Dubai, United Arab Emirates, has the world's highest residential floor at 1,263 ft. (385 m). Floors 77 to 108 of the 163-floor building are given over to its 900 apartments.

Largest residential palace The palace (Istana Nurul Iman) of HM the Sultan of Brunei in the capital Bandar Seri Begawan was completed in January 1984 at a reported cost of $422 million. It features 1,788 rooms, 257 toilets, and 2,152,780 ft.^{2} (200,000m^2) of floor space—an area equivalent to 40 American football fields.

Tallest structure The Ursa tension-leg platform is a floating oil-production facility operated by Shell in the Gulf of Mexico. The top of its drilling rig is 4,285 ft. (1,306 m) above the seabed.

The **largest monolithic church** is in Lalibela, Ethiopia: Bet Medhane Alem is 110 ft. (33.5 m) long, 78 ft. (23.5 m) wide, and 36 ft. (11 m) high.

●TALLEST MAN-MADE LEANING TOWER
Completed in 1987, the Olympic Stadium Tower in Montreal, Canada, is 541 ft. 4 in. (165 m) high and curves at an angle of 45 degrees. The stadium was used as a venue at the 1976 Olympic Games, although the tower was unfinished at the time and the stadium did not have a retractable roof.

TALLEST RESIDENTIAL BUILDING Q1 in Gold Coast, Queensland, Australia, has a structural height of 1,060 ft. (323 m) and a roof height of 902 ft. (275 m), making it the tallest building in the world used purely for residential purposes. The building's 80 levels accommodate 527 apartments. It opened in October 2005 and is the tallest building in Australia.

Tallest hotel The Rose Rayhaan by Rotana hotel in Dubai, UAE, stands 1,092 ft. 6 in. (333 m) from ground level to the top of its mast. The hotel consists of 482 rooms spread over 72 floors and it opened on December 14, 2009.

PYRAMIDS

WHAT IS A PYRAMID?

Technically, a pyramid is described as a polyhedron (a three-dimensional straight-edged shape) with a polygonal (many-sided) base and triangular faces that meet at the apex (top). The most famous examples are the giant stone buildings on the Giza Plateau in Cairo, Egypt (above right), but pyramids come in all sorts of shapes and sizes, as this selection of records illustrates.

> **SUPER-SIZED** The **largest pyramid** is the Quetzalcóatl pyramid near Mexico City, Mexico. Its base covers nearly 45 acres (18.2 ha)—about the size of 34 American football fields!—and its volume is estimated at 167 million ft.³ (3.3 million m³).

TALLEST PYRAMID The Giza Plateau in Cairo, Egypt, is home to the pyramid of Khufu (pictured above right—the perspective of this shot makes it look smaller, and the middle pyramid is on higher ground). Also known as the Great Pyramid, it was 481 ft. 3 in. (146.7 m) high when completed around 4,500 years ago and was built as a mausoleum for the Pharaoh Khufu (aka Cheops), who reigned from 2589 to 2566 B.C.

A. QUEENS' PYRAMIDS
Three smaller tombs—a fifth of the size of the Great Pyramid—were used by the pharaohs' female relatives.

B. PYRAMID OF MENKAURE
The smallest of the Giza pyramids measures 339 ft. (103.4 m) at the base and 215 ft. (65.5 m) in height. It remains incomplete, helping archaeologists piece together how the pyramids were made.

C. PYRAMID OF KHAFRE
Second-tallest pyramid at 706 ft. (215.5 m) wide and rising to 448 ft. (136.4 m); looks taller than the Great Pyramid as it sits on bedrock 33 ft. (10 m) high.

D. PYRAMID OF KHUFU
The Great Pyramid, built *c*. 2560 B.C., is eroded now to 451 ft. (137.5 m) tall but is still the **tallest pyramid**. At its original height of 481 ft. 3 in. (146.7 m), it was the **tallest manmade construction** in the world until A.D. 1311 and the building of Lincoln Cathedral (UK).

E. Remnants of original, smooth limestone casing

ROCK LIKE AN EGYPTIAN The Great Pyramid has a volume of 88.2 million ft.^{3} (2.5 million m^3) and is built from 2.3 million stone blocks (see inset photo), some of which weigh up to 88 tons (80 metric tons).

● **LARGEST HUMAN WATERSKIING PYRAMID** Members of the Rock Aqua Jays Water Ski Team of Janesville, Wisconsin, U.S.A., formed a 44-person, triple four-tier pyramid at the National Water Ski Show Tournament held in Rockford, Illinois, U.S.A., in August 2003.

HIGHEST EIGHT-PERSON TIGHTROPE PYRAMID The Flying Wallendas (U.S.A.) performed an eight-person pyramid suspended at a height of 25 ft. (7.62 m) at Sarasota, U.S.A., on February 20, 2001.

HUMAN PYRAMIDS

On motorcycles The Dare Devils Team of the Indian Army Signal Corps traveled a distance of 424 ft. (129 m) while maintaining a pyramid formation of 201 men on 10 motorcycles at Gowri Shankar Parade Ground, Jabalpur, India, on July 5, 2001.

On skates A pyramid of 30 skaters from the NSA Roller Gymnastics Team (U.S.A.) traveled 155 ft. (47.2 m) in eight seconds in Philadelphia, U.S.A., in 1985.

MAN-MADE PYRAMIDS

Bottle caps On September 9, 2000, a group of 12 students from the Krasnystaw Cultural Centre in Krasnystaw, Poland, completed a pyramid of 308,945 bottle tops after nearly nine days of shift work.

....

Surprisingly, the **largest cowboy boot** was made not in the U.S.A. but in Ethiopia. The boot measured 8 ft. 2 in. (2.5 m) in height and 7 ft. 9 in. (2.38 m) in length and was made by Belachew Tola Buta (Ethiopia).

....

63: Tons of trash you'll throw away in your lifetime—enough to construct a scale model of the Great Pyramid of Giza 28 ft. high. A full-sized replica would require 49,163 lifetimes' worth of garbage.

Aluminum cans It was thirsty work for the students of INTI College Subang Jaya (Malaysia) as they built a pyramid of 9,455 drinks cans in just 24 minutes in Kuala Lumpur on September 23, 2000.

○**Bottle crates** A team of 200 volunteers spent two days erecting a bottle-crate pyramid 63,365 crates strong at an event organized by Foundation Limmen Ludiek in Limmen, the Netherlands, on June 11–12, 2005.

○**Paperboard boxes** From caps, cans, and crates to paperboard boxes—the largest pyramid consisted of 43,147 Calgon boxes, which were stacked into 46 layers measuring 21 ft. (6.44 m) tall. The towering structure was built by employees of the Reckitt Benckiser Cleaning Materials Industry and Trade Co. (Turkey) at CarrefourSA in Istanbul, Turkey, on October 30, 2010.

●**TALLEST COFFEE-CUP PYRAMID** A pyramid of 22,140 coffee cups was built by Melanie Lütkefent, Vanessa Höft, Miriam Plümer, Arman Schlieker, and Damian Krey (all Germany) in association with Aral AG at the Du Mont Carre, Cologne, Germany, on October 8, 2010.

TALLEST ICE-CREAM-SCOOP PYRAMID
Baskin-Robbins (U.S.A.) scooped the ice-cream pyramid title with 3,100 dollops of the company's own product in Hawaii, U.S.A., on May 8, 2000.

In terms of big boots, Latvian clown Coco (aka Nicolai Poliakoff) was clearly a step ahead. When he joined the Bertram Mills Circus (UK) in 1929, his 58½-U.S.-size shoes went down as the **largest clown boots** in history!

LARGEST CHAMPAGNE PYRAMID Luuk Broos (Netherlands) and his team created a 63-story champagne fountain using 43,680 glasses at the Wijnegem shopping mall, Belgium, on January 25, 2008.

●**Straw bales** The largest straw-bale pyramid stood 94 ft. 11 in. (28.95 m) high with a base of 82 ft. x 82 ft. (25 m x 25 m) and was constructed using 1,500 bales. It was made by members of Le Cercle des Jeunes Agriculteurs du Pays de Sarrebourg, in Voyer, Sarrebourg, France, on August 22, 2004.

Cookies The record for the tallest pyramid of cookies is 4 ft. 10 in. (1.49 m) and was achieved by Jan Vinzenz Krause and members of the diocese Essen (Germany) at the Centro shopping mall in Oberhausen, Germany, on September 16, 2006. The pyramid may not sound that tall, but it was made using 12,180 Leibniz butter cookies!

BACKYARD BEHEMOTHS

LARGEST . . .

○**Bead mosaic** A mosaic measuring 12 ft. 3 in. (3.74 m) wide by 8 ft. 10 in. (2.7 m) tall, with an area of 108.7 ft.² (10.1 m²) was made by the Fifth and Sixth grade of Scoil Naomh Iosaf Primary School (Ireland) in Baltinglass, Co. Wicklow, Ireland, on June 24, 2010.

○**Chandelier** Named "Reflective Flow," the largest chandelier weighs 39,680 lb. (18,000 kg) and consists of 165,000 LED units. The chandelier was measured in the Ali Bin Khalifa Al Hitmi & Co. building in Doha, Qatar, where it is installed, on June 23, 2010.

○**Soccer ball** KIA Motors and Emperors Palace Resort and Casino (both South Africa) created a soccer ball with a diameter of 51 ft. 4 in. (15.66 m). It was displayed in Johannesburg, South Africa, on July 5, 2010.

○**Inflatable beach ball** The world's largest inflatable beach ball is 48 ft. 2 in. (14.70 m) in diameter. Made by IDCL for MTN Nigeria (both

Think big: check out some garden giants on p. 251.

Nigeria), it was presented and measured in Lagos, Nigeria, on August 10, 2010.

●**Table tennis bat** Todd Thomas (U.S.A.) has constructed an outsize table tennis bat that is 8 ft. 9.9 in. (2.69 m) tall, with a diameter of 5 ft. 9.9 in. (1.77 m); its handle is 3 ft. 5.5 in. (1.05 m) tall. It was presented and measured at the DFW Table Tennis Club in Irving, Texas, U.S.A., on May 3, 2010.

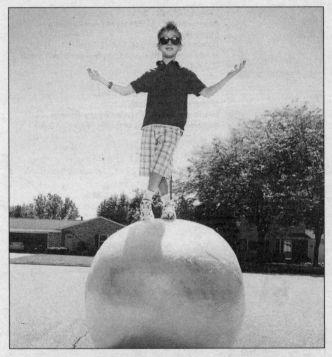

LARGEST BALL OF PLASTIC WRAP Jake Lonsway of Bay City, Michigan, U.S.A., created a ball of plastic wrap that had a circumference of 11.5 ft. (3.51 m) and weighed 281 lb. 8 oz. (127.7 kg) as of June 14, 2007.

CHEERS! The ○**largest pom-pom** was 4 ft. (1.21 m) high and 10 ft. 8 in. (3.25 m) in diameter. It was made by the children of the Sixth grade of the Salesian Primary School (all Ireland) on March 16, 2010.

LARGEST HAIR BALL
Weight: 167 lb. (75.7 kg)
Height: 4 ft. (1.2 m)
Collected by:
Henry Coffer (U.S.A.)

LARGEST PAINT BALL
Approximately 17,994 paint layers around a baseball!
Circumference: 9 ft. 1 in. (2.77 m)
Made by: Michael and Glenda Carmichael (both U.S.A.)

LARGEST PLASTIC-BAG BALL
Number of bags: 36,700
Made at: an event staged by the County of Los Angeles Department of Public Works (U.S.A.)

LARGEST TAPE BALL
Weight: 1,862 lb. (844.59 kg)
Circumference: 23 ft. 9 in. (7.23 m)
Made by: Tim and Ryan Funk (both Canada)

LARGEST RUBBER-BAND BALL
Weight: 9,032 lb. (4,097 kg)
Height: 6 ft. 7 in. (1.99 m)
Made by: Joel Waul (U.S.A.)

Eugene Gomberg (Latvia) bought the ●**most expensive picture postcard** in 2002. It cost $45,370.60 and dated from 1840.

6.5: Weight in tons of fruit you'll consume during your life—about the same weight as a bull elephant. Fruit is the only thing you eat that "wants" to be eaten—that's one of the ways it spreads its seeds.

●**Voodoo doll** The largest voodoo doll was 21 ft. 8 in. (6.6 m) high, and was created by Catherina Williams (U.S.A.) at the Sugar Mill in New Orleans, Louisiana, U.S.A., on November 17, 2010. The doll was blessed in the traditional manner of the voodoo religion, by a bona fide voodoo priestess.

○**Yo-yo** Jerry Havill's Team Problem Solving course (U.S.A.) devised a yo-yo weighing 1,625 lb. (738.64 kg) with an 11-ft. 6-in. (3.51-m) diameter at Bay de Noc Community College in Escanaba, Michigan, U.S.A., on July 6, 2010. Launched by a crane, it yo-yoed 30 times.

LARGEST SKATEBOARD
Designed by Rob Dyrdek and Joe Ciaglia (both U.S.A.), the largest skateboard is 36 ft. 7 in. (11.14 m) long, 8 ft. 8 in. (2.63 m) wide, and 3 ft. 7.5 in. (1.1 m) high. It was unveiled on MTV, on February 25, 2009.

●**LONGEST PICNIC TABLE** On October 30, 2009, Deirdre Sargent (U.S.A.) created one continuous picnic table, measuring 248 ft. 2 in. (75.65 m) long and made from solid pine wood, at the New Orleans City Park, New Orleans, U.S.A.

WHY "PICNIC"? The word "picnic" comes from the French word pique-nique. First used in the late 17th century, it described the practice of diners each bringing a dish, or perhaps a bottle of wine, to a communal meal.

There are two contenders for the title of **rarest stamp**: the Swedish 3-skilling-banco yellow color error stamp of 1855 and the British Guiana (now Guyana) 1-cent black on magenta stamp from 1856. Both are unique.

LONGEST . . .

●**Crochet chain** Anne Vanier-Drüssel (France) created a chain of crochet 80.78 miles (130 km) long—the distance from New York to Philadelphia, as the crow flies. It was presented and measured in Aniane, France, on October 14, 2009.

○**Pearl necklace** The world's longest single-strand pearl necklace was 728 ft. 4 in. (222 m) long. It was created by Shimashi Kanko Kyokai (Japan) at the 60th Pearl Festa in Kashikojima, Shima, Mie Prefecture, Japan, on October 22, 2010.

○**Tablecloth** Measuring 5,784 ft. 1 in. (1,763 m) long, the longest tablecloth was created by a group known as Gli Amici dell'Aia (Italy). On September 12, 2010, it was laid out along via Romana and via Della Noce between the towns of Albinea and Scandiano in Italy.

○**LARGEST ROCKING HORSE** On September 12, 2010, Ofer Mor (Israel) completed a rocking horse measuring an amazing 24 ft. 11 in. x 10 ft. 6 in. x 20 ft. (7.6 x 3.22 x 6.10 m) in Kadima, Israel.

20,000 screws, 2 tons of wood, 79 gallons of paint—worth: $50,000

●LARGEST BIRD-NEST BOX The Heighley Gate Garden Centre in Morpeth, UK, created a bird-nest box 4 ft. 1 in. (1.25 m) long and 3 ft. 11 in. (1.20 m) wide, with a height of 5 ft. 8 in. (1.75 m) at the front and 6 ft. 10 in. (2.10 m) at the back. It went on display on January 16, 2008.

BIG STUFF

LARGEST . . .

○**Backpack** Safta (Spain) has made a backpack 14 ft. 1 in. (4.31 m) tall, 10 ft. 6 in. (3.21 m) wide, and 4 ft. 9 in. (1.47 m) deep. It was measured at the Intergift IFEMA expo center in Madrid, Spain, on February 3, 2011.

Bed Mark Gerrick and Royal Sleep Products (both U.S.A.) created a bed 77 ft. (23.47 m) long and 46 ft. 6 in. (14.17 m) wide in Fort Worth, Texas, U.S.A., on September 11, 2008.

●**Belt buckle** On February 3, 2011, the world's largest belt buckle was unveiled at "*ESPN The Magazine*'s NEXT BIG Weekend" in Fort Worth, Texas, U.S.A. It is 6 ft. 6 in. (1.98 m) tall and 8 ft. 6 in. (2.59 m) wide and was created by ESPN with Kelly Graham (both U.S.A.).

●**Firework rocket** Weighing 29 lb. 8 oz. (13.4 kg), the largest firework rocket was produced and launched by Associaçao Nacional de Empresas de Produtos Explosivos (Portugal) at the 12th International Symposium on Fireworks in Oporto and Vila Nova de Gaia, Portugal, on October 13, 2010.

LARGEST MOTORIZED SHOPPING CART Edd China (UK) created a motorized shopping cart measuring 9 ft. 10 in. (3 m) long, 11 ft. 5 in. (3.5 m) tall, and 5 ft. 10 in. (1.8 m) wide. It was displayed at the Asda store, Watford, UK, on November 9, 2005.

525: Height in yards of all the toilet rolls you'll use in your lifetime—approximately 4,000—piled one on top of the other. That's about 328 ft. taller than the Empire State Building.

●**LARGEST VUVUZELA** At 114 ft. 9 in. (35 m) long and 18 ft. (5.5 m) in diameter at the front, the world's largest vuvuzela was created by Hyundai Automotive South Africa and was presented and measured in Cape Town, South Africa, on May 26, 2010.

LARGEST WATERING CAN A giant watering can built from galvanized steel was constructed for Utica Zoo, New York, U.S.A. The gigantic gardening tool arrived by truck on December 5, 2000. It weighs 2,000 lb. (907.1 kg) and measures 15 ft. 6 in. (4.7 m) high, with a diameter of 12 ft. (3.65 m).

LARGEST CHAINSAW A working chainsaw measuring 22 ft. 11 in. (6.98 m) long and 6 ft. (1.83 m) high was made by Moran Iron Works, Inc., of Onaway, Michigan, U.S.A., in 1996. Named "Big Gus," it was shown at Da Yoopers Tourist Trap at Ishpening, Michigan, U.S.A.

●**Flashlight** Moon Way General Trading LLC (UAE) produced a flashlight 7 ft. 5 in. (227 cm) long and 1 ft. 9 in. (55 cm) in diameter. It was presented and measured in Sharjah, UAE, on August 25, 2010.

●**Nativity village** *El Pesebre Mas Grande del Mundo*, the world's largest nativity village, was created by Fabian Rojas (Colombia) and opened on December 1, 2010, in Santiago de Cali, Colombia. It has an area of 185,440.6 ft.^{2} (17,228 m^2)—more than three times the size of an American football field—and features 339 figures.

The **most successful attorney** is Sir Lionel Luckhoo (Guyana), senior partner of Luckhoo and Luckhoo of Georgetown, Guyana, who succeeded in securing 245 successive homicide acquittals between 1940 and 1985.

MAKING IT BIG It took a month to plan how to create this huge beach towel, and eight days to actually make it. Hardly surprising when you consider that it's longer than a 747 jumbo jet.

○ **LARGEST BEACH TOWEL** Fateka SL manufactured a beach towel on behalf of the beverage group Compañía Cervecera de Canarias (both Spain) that measured 285 ft. 10 in. (87.14 m) long and 82 ft. 8 in. (25.20 m) wide. It was laid out at Playa de las Canteras in Las Palmas, Gran Canaria, Spain, on June 5, 2010.

● **Origami lei** "Network of Fukuoka Universities" (Japan) created a 6,594-ft.-long (2,010-m) origami lei (garland) at the Fukuoka City Hall, Fukuoka, Japan, on September 26, 2010.

ON THE BOARD While you're on the beach, you could try out the **longest surfboard**. Made by Nev Hyman (Australia) in 2005, it was 39 ft. 4 in. (12 m) long, 9 ft. 10 in. (3 m) wide, and 11.8 in. (30 cm) thick.

 By contrast, Pedro López (Colombia) was convicted of 57 counts of murder in Ecuador in 1980. Dubbed the "Monster of the Andes", he confessed to a total of 300 murders across Colombia, Peru, and Ecuador, making him the **most prolific serial killer** of all time.

Big and beautiful, or small but perfectly formed? You'll find people of every size and shape on p. 132.

○**Poster** On December 8, 2010, a poster for Michael Jackson's *Michael* album was unveiled at Rectory Farm in Hounslow, UK. Measuring 171 x 170 ft. (52.1 x 51.8 m), it was created by painter Kadir Nelson (U.S.A.) in 2009 as a commission from Sony Music UK.

●**Scratchcard** The Golden Casket Lottery (Australia) created a scratchcard 32 ft. 9 in. (10 m) tall and 16 ft. 4 in. (5 m) wide. It was unveiled and scratched in Brisbane, Queensland, Australia, on February 5, 2011.

○**Snowball** Wesley Fowlks and a team of nine other participants (all U.S.A.) rolled a snowball measuring 23 ft. 2.5 in. (7.07 m) in circumference at the University of Massachusetts' Dartmouth Campus, Massachusetts, U.S.A., on February 1, 2011.

●**Umbrella** Measuring 56 ft. (17.06 m) in diameter and 36 ft. (10.97 m) tall, the largest umbrella was made by Max New York Life Insurance (India) and unveiled at Ishanya Mall in Pune, India, on August 14, 2010.

○**Underpants** The largest underpants in the world measured 65 ft. 7 in. (20 m) across the waist and 39 ft. 4 in. (12 m) from waistband to crotch. They were presented by Pants to Poverty (UK) in London, UK, on September 16, 2010.

●**Wallet** Produced by the Big Skinny Corporation (U.S.A.), the largest wallet measures 10 ft. (3.14 m) long and 10 ft. 5 in. (3.06 m) high. It was presented and measured in Cambridge, Massachusetts, U.S.A., on November 26, 2010.

●**Worry beads** Also known as kombolói, worry beads are a set of beads threaded on to a string. They are designed as a tool to help people relax, by manipulating the beads. A colossal set of worry beads measuring 47 ft. 2 in. (14.4 m) long was made by the Kuwait Oil Company (Kuwait) in Al-Ahmadi, Kuwait, and completed on January 15, 2011.

POPULAR CULTURE

CONTENTS

COMIC-CON

STAR WARS: THE CLONE WARS The hit CGI TV series *Star Wars: The Clone Wars* pulled in an average viewership of 4 million at its launch on the Cartoon Network in 2008, making it the world's ●most watched sci-fi animation series. On hand to accept the GWR certificate were (left to right) producer Cary Silver, Turner Animation President and COO Stuart Snyder, and Supervising Director Dave Filoni.

○HIGHEST BOX-OFFICE GROSS FOR AN ANIMATED MOVIE ON OPENING DAY On its day of release in the U.S.A. on June 18, 2010, the hotly anticipated Disney/Pixar (both U.S.A.) movie *Toy Story 3* (U.S.A., 2010) took in $41 million at 4,028 locations across the country, beating the previous record of $38.4 million set by *Shrek the Third* (U.S.A., 2007) on May 18, 2007.

For more gargantuan gatherings, head straight to p. 174.

GUINNESS WORLD RECORDS VISITS THE WORLD'S LARGEST POPULAR CULTURE CONVENTION

More than 130,000 fans of comic books, movies, TV shows, and video games descended on San Diego in California, U.S.A., in July for Comic-Con 2010—the globe's ●largest pop-culture gathering . . . and GWR was there to present some record certificates.

ROCKY Actor/director Sylvester Stallone made a guest appearance to promote his new movie, *The Expendables*, but it was for his *Rocky* movies that he received a record certificate. Having grossed $556 million at the domestic box-office alone, the *Rocky* series is the ●most successful sports movie franchise. Pictured is GWR's Craig Glenday (▊▊▊) presenting to Stallone (▊▊▊) and *Rocky IV* co-star Dolph Lundgren.

Native to Ecuador (as well as Peru and Panama), the world's **largest winged cockroach** is *Megaloblatta longipennis*. A preserved female specimen in the collection of Akira Yokokura (Japan) measured 3.8 in. (97 mm) in length and 1.75 in. (45 mm) across.

GLEE Stars of the musical TV show *Glee* were excited to learn that they'd made it into the *Guinness World Records* book for the **most simultaneous tracks debuting in the UK chart**, with five in January 2010. So, too, were the "Gleeks" who turned up to mob the overwhelmed cast!

FUTURAMA With an average reviewer score of 80/100, the 6th season of the sci-fi comedy *Futurama* was the ●**most critically acclaimed animation on TV**. The show's creator—and multiple Guinness World Record holder—Matt Groening (top right) joined Executive Producer David X. Cohen on stage to receive their official certificates.

SAW With a total worldwide gross of $733 million over its first six installments, the *Saw* franchise is the world's ●**most successful horror movie series**. And who better to receive the award than the fearsome Jigsaw Killer himself—actor Tobin Bell.

The **largest aquatic insect** is the giant water bug (*Lethocerus maximus*), a carnivorous species that inhabits Venezuela (as well as Brazil). Although it can grow up to 4.53 in. (11.5 cm) long, it is not as heavy as some of the continent's burly beetles and stick insects.

23,973: Hours you will spend reading newspapers, books, and comic books. At an average rate of 300 words per minute, that's more than 448 million words in a lifetime. Or 3,400 copies of this book!

TODD KLEIN We were honored to meet record-breaking comic letterer Todd Klein, who won the **Most Eisner comic awards in one category** with 15. Here he is pictured with the 2011 GWR comic-books spread, for which Todd did the lettering.

STEAMPUNKS Comic-Con attracts fans of all kinds of pop culture, including Steampunks—the subculture inspired by an alternative history of steam-age technology and Victoriana. The 2010 Con brought together 185 like-minded people to set the first ever record for the ●**largest gathering of Steampunks.** Congratulations everyone!

The **highest mudslide death toll** occurred in December 1999 after torrential rains fell in Vargas State, Venezuela. An estimated 10,000 to 30,000 people died in the disaster.

VIDEO GAMING

○**Largest handheld game console party** On January 23, 2011, 849 children, parents, and friends played the game *Tokutenryoku Gakushu DS* (Benesse, 2008) on Nintendo DS for 10 minutes. The event, hosted by TV star Takahiro Azuma and actress Wakana Aoi, was organized by Odawara Gakuryoku Koji Iinkai in collaboration with Benesse in Odawara, Japan.

●**Fastest lap on *Crash Nitro Kart*** On May 31, 2010, gamer Alex Herrera (U.S.A.) of Lilburn, Georgia, U.S.A., achieved a lap time of just 37.77 seconds around the Jungle Boogie track on *Crash Nitro Kart* (Universal, 2003).

●**Longest marathon** In an epic session, Tony Desmet, Jesse Rebmann, and Jeffrey Gammon (all Belgium) played *Assassin's Creed Brotherhood* (Ubisoft, 2010) for 109 hours at the GUNKtv World Record Gaming Event in Antwerp, Belgium, on December 18–22, 2010.

○**Longest marathon (soccer game)** In the name of charity, soccer-mad Michael Puterflam (Australia) played *FIFA 11* (EA, 2010) for 30 hr. 1 min. at Westfield Bondi Junction, Sydney, Australia, on December 1–2, 2010. During the attempt, Michael faced more than 100 opponents, including celebrities, sports personalities, and the public.

●**Longest marathon (*Guitar Hero*)** In a performance streamed live over the internet, Zach Wong (Canada) played *Guitar Hero* (Harmonix, 2005) for a record 50 hr. 3 min. in Vancouver, Canada, on August 25–27, 2010.

●**MOST DOWNLOADED CELL PHONE VIDEO GAME** The ever-popular puzzle game *Tetris* (Alexey Pajitnov, 1985) is still going strong after 25 years, notching up its 100 millionth cell phone download by October 2010.

The ●**most people receiving a mud treatment** was achieved by 50 participants in an event organized by Bad Saarow Kur GmbH in Brandenburg, Germany, on March 28, 2009.

● MOST AUTOMOBILES IN A RACING VIDEO GAME Sony's *Gran Turismo 5* (2010) features 1,000 licensed vehicles from the world's top marques—and all are included on the game disk. Downloadable content is expected to increase this number even further.

● LONGEST GAMING SESSION IN INDOOR FREEFALL Suspended in a wind tunnel, the 6-ft. 5-in. (190-cm), 265-lb. (120-kg) Jesse Moerkerk (Netherlands) enjoyed an aerial Nintendo Wii gaming session lasting 18 min. 52 sec. at Indoor Skydive Roosendaal, the Netherlands, on January 11, 2011.

○ FASTEST-SELLING PC GAME Launched on December 7, 2010, *Cataclysm*, the third expansion for Blizzard Entertainment's *World of Warcraft*, sold 3.3 million copies in its first 24 hours, beating the previous record of 2.8 million set by its predecessor, *Wrath of the Lich King*, in 2008.

First maximum score on *PAC-Man* Billy Mitchell (U.S.A.) completed the first "perfect" game of *PAC-Man* (Namco, 1980) on July 3, 1999, notching up the maximum 3,333,360 points in just over six hours. The feat is considered one of the most difficult in video gaming, requiring the player to eat every dot, energizer, flashing ghost, and fruit in all 256 levels without losing a single life.

●Fastest completion of "Sniper-Fi" on *Call of Duty: Modern Warfare 2* In 2010, a U.S. gamer known as Janner, of online community weplayedcod.com, finished the special-ops mission "Sniper-Fi" on the PC version of *Call of Duty: Modern Warfare 2* (Infinity Ward, 2009) in a time of 1 min. 39.5 sec—16 seconds faster than the game's own developers!

Measuring 892 ft. 3 in. (271.97 m) in length, the world's **longest model train** was created by German model-maker Miniature Wunderland. Built in Hamburg, Germany, on July 25, 2008, the 1:87.1-scale train featured eight locomotives and 2,212 coaches!

34: Age of the average video game player. He (the average gamer is male) started playing 12 years ago and spends $126 a year on games. Curiously, the average video game buyer is 40 years old.

ARCADE ACTION: Guitars first came to arcades in 1999 when Konami released *GuitarFreaks*, a rhythm game for up to two players. The franchise is still going strong a decade later, with *GuitarFreaks* V8 released in 2011.

○ **HIGHEST SCORE ON *GUITAR HERO III* (FEMALE)** On September 30, 2010, at her home in California, U.S.A., Annie Leung (U.S.A.) proved she was a true guitar hero when she racked up a score of 789,349 playing the classic track "Through the Fire and Flames" on *Guitar Hero III: Legends of Rock* (Neversoft, 2007).

● **Most expensive virtual object** The greatest amount paid for a piece of virtual property is $6 million by SEE Virtual Worlds (U.S.A.) for Planet Calypso, a virtual planet within the online game *Entropia Universe* (MindArk, 2003). This "virtual real estate" was purchased on December 20, 2010.

 Speaking of models, the **largest collection of model automobiles** belongs to Nabil Karam (Lebanon), who had amassed 22,222 unique items by November 11, 2009.

FASTEST FINGERS: Ryota might want to try out the Venom Mini Dance Mat, which lets gamers play DDR with their fingers. Measuring just 4 in. (10 cm) by 4.5 in. (11.5 cm), it is the world's ●**first handheld dance mat**.

●**YOUNGEST GAMER TO ACHIEVE A PERFECT SCORE ON *DANCE DANCE REVOLUTION*** Aged just 9 years 288 days, Ryota Wada (Japan) achieved a perfect "AAA" rating on *Dance Dance Revolution* (Konami, 1998) when he mastered the song "Hyper Eurobeat" on the "Expert" difficulty setting at his home in Tokyo, Japan, on August 29, 2010.

Ryota made 237 perfect steps!

●**FIRST GAME TO HAVE AN OFFICIALLY RECOGNIZED DAY OF CELEBRATION** On its release, *Sid Meier's Civilization V* (2K Games, 2010) was honored by the Governor of Maryland, U.S.A., who stated that September 21, 2010, would henceforth be known as "Sid Meier's Civilization V Day."

COLLECTIBLE CARD GAMING

●**First trading card game** The world's oldest trading card game (TCG) appeared way back in 1904. The Base Ball Card Game, published by the Allegheny Card Co. (U.S.A.), contained 104 player cards and eight team "ball counter" cards. As the game proved unpopular in its day, these hand-cut card sets are today extremely rare, with a mint condition deck likely to fetch around $500.

●**First modern trading card game** Magic: The Gathering was unleashed on the world on August 5, 1993. Created by Richard Garfield (U.S.A.) and published by Wizards of the Coast, Inc., the game combines the excitement of competition with the thrill of trading and collecting. Players engage in combat to reduce their opponent's score from 20 to zero with a variety of attacks and defenses that unleash spells, artifacts, and mystical creatures. Still enormously popular, Magic is regarded as the origin of TCGs as we know them.

●**RAREST TRADING CARD Created for Magic: The Gathering (Wizards of the Coast, Inc., U.S.A.), the most elusive cards on the planet are the 1996 World Champion (left) and the Shichifukujin Dragon (right)—only one of each exists. The former was awarded to the winner of the 1996 World Championships, Tom Chanpheng (Australia), while the latter was created to celebrate the opening of the DCI Tournament Centre in Tokyo, Japan, in 1996.**

●**FIRST TRADING CARD GAME PATENT On September 2, 1997, Magic: The Gathering's inventor, Richard Garfield (U.S.A.), was granted U.S. patent 5,662,332 (A) for "the trading card game method of play"—the first-ever TCG patent.**

14,953: Sandwiches you will eat during your lifetime. Legend has it that the sandwich was invented as a convenient snack in 1760 by John Montague, the 4th Earl of Sandwich, so that he didn't have to leave the card table for meals.

COSTLY ERROR In 2009, a misprinted Yu-Gi-Oh! card went up for sale on eBay with an asking price of $100,000! This rare "Clock Tower Prison" card—incorrectly titled as "Miraculous Descent"—failed to raise the outrageous sum.

● **BEST-SELLING TRADING CARD GAME** The world's most popular trading card game is Yu-Gi-Oh!, created by Konami Digital Entertainment Co., Ltd. (Japan) and based on the comic books and animated TV series by artist Kazuki Takahashi (Japan). Fronted by lead character Yusei Fudo (left), the game sold a phenomenal 25,175,567,833 cards around the globe between 1999 and April 1, 2011, and has spawned spin-offs including video games and movies.

● **Most played trading card game** Since making its debut in 1993, the Magic: The Gathering trading card game has spread across the world while growing ever more popular. According to the publisher, Wizards of the Coast, Inc., the game, which has since been translated into nine languages, is now played in 52 countries by more than 6 million players.

Ashraf Makarem (Lebanon) and Khaled Othman (Kuwait) unveiled the world's O**largest flag**, a huge 710,148-ft.^{2} (65,975-m^2) Lebanese flag, in Rayak, Lebanon, on October 10, 2010.

Discover more collectibles on pp. 271–279.

●**LONGEST-RUNNING DIGITAL TRADING CARD GAME** Magic: The Gathering has been available in computer format since the release of the PC game *Magic: The Gathering* (Microprose) on March 27, 1997.

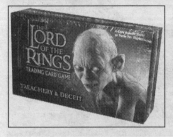

LONGEST TRADING CARD GAME MARATHON From December 27, 2002, to January 1, 2003, William Stone, Bryan Erwin, and Christopher Groetzinger (all U.S.A.) played 154 games of The Lord of the Rings Trading Card Game over 128 hours at The Courtyard, Colorado Springs, Colorado, U.S.A.

●**First online trading card game** When it went live on May 28, 1997, *Chron X*, developed by George Moromisato and published by Genetic Anomalies, became the first TCG to enter the virtual world. Free to play, *Chron X* is set on a dystopian Earth in the year 2096. The rights to the game were acquired by Darkened Sky Studios in 2007, who announced their plans for a sequel, *Chron X2*.

●**Largest trading card** Produced by Panini America (U.S.A.), the world's largest trading card was revealed on February 13, 2010. Carrying the image of the basketball player Kobe Bryant of the Los Angeles Lakers NBA team (both U.S.A.), the card was embossed with a 15-in.-by-15-in. (38-cm-by-38-cm) swatch of an official game jersey and measured a vast 7 ft. (2.13 m) tall by 4 ft. 11 in. (1.22 m) wide.

 A flag of that size would need quite a flagpole if it were to be flown, and a suitable candidate would be the ○**tallest unsupported flagpole**. It measures 531 ft. 5 in. (162 m) and was erected in Baku, Azerbaijan, on May 29, 2010.

HIGH STAKES TCG tournaments are big business—just ask pro Magic: The Gathering player Kai Budde. To date, the German has racked up career winnings of $352,620—the ●**highest earnings from TCG tournaments**.

●**LARGEST TRADING GAME TOURNAMENT** The Magic Grand Prix Madrid 2010, held over the weekend of February 27–28, 2010, in Madrid, Spain, saw 2,227 players battle it out over 19 rounds until just two remained: David Do Anh (Czech Republic) and Andreas Müller (Germany). In a close-fought final, Müller won through by a margin of 2–1, taking home $3,500.

●**First three-dimensional trading card game** Canadian games company Spin Master took TCGs to the next level when they unveiled the world's first 3D trading card game, Redakai, at the American International Toy Fair in New York, U.S.A., in February 2011. The game, which focuses on a group of teens searching for a mystical energy called Kairu, includes hologram cards that animate characters' attacks, as well as transparent cards that can be overlayed with others to create a variety of effects.

●**Largest cash prize for a TCG** The World of Warcraft TCG World Championship, held at the San Diego Convention Center (U.S.A.) between November 30 and December 2, 2007, saw Guillaume Matignon (France) beat over 400 of the world's best World of Warcraft warriors to claim a record payout of $100,000.

PUBLISHING

● **First crossword puzzle book** The earliest collection of crossword puzzles was published in the U.S.A. in 1924. *The Cross Word Puzzle Book* was the first publication by a new partnership formed by Dick Simon and Lincoln Schuster. A compilation of crossword puzzles from U.S. newspaper *New York World*, it was an instant success and helped to establish publishing giant Simon & Schuster, who still produce crossword books today.

○ **Most expensive published book sold at auction** On December 7, 2010, a rare, complete copy of John James Audubon's *Birds of America* sold for £7.3 million ($11.4 million) at Sotheby's in London, UK. It contains 1,000 life-size illustrations of 435 birds drawn and printed by Audubon between 1827 and 1838. The illustrations were originally sold a page at a time to collectors, and only 119 complete editions are known to exist.

● **Highest weekly newspaper circulation** Founded in 1978 in Moscow, Russia, *Argumenty i Fakty* ("Arguments and Facts") attained a circulation of 33,431,100 in May 1990, with an estimated readership of more than 100 million.

If you like life on a large scale, turn back to p. 373.

○ **LARGEST POP-UP BOOK** Measuring 13 ft. 1 in. x 9 ft. 10 in. (4 x 3 m) and featuring pop-ups 7 ft. 9 in. (2.35 m) tall, the largest pop-up book was made for a TV commercial advertising Pearle Opticiens (Belgium) in Ghent, Belgium, on September 6, 2010.

MY WORD! Entitled *My Word*, the book was a scaled-up version of a booklet available in the 160 Pearle Opticiens stores in Belgium. It took three months to complete the paper engineering and final build.

42: The meaning of life, the universe, and everything, according to writer Douglas Adams's memorable creation *The Hitchhiker's Guide to the Galaxy*. It's also how many years of your life are left over when you take off the time you'll spend sleeping and working.

○**Most books written and published in a year by an individual** Ryuho Okawa (Japan) wrote and published 52 books between November 23, 2009, and November 10, 2010.

Youngest person to have a book published The youngest commercially published author is Dorothy Straight (b. May 25, 1958), of Washington, DC, U.S.A., who wrote *How the World Began* in 1962, aged four. It was published in August 1964 by Pantheon Books.

○**Largest book (trimmed page size)** On March 21, 2010, Béla Varga, Béláné Varga (both Hungary), and 25 volunteers completed *Fragile Nature*—a book about the Aggtelek National Park in Hungary—which measured 13 ft. 8.5 in. x 12 ft. 4.3 in. (4.18 x 3.77 m) and weighed 3,130 lb. 9 oz. (1,420 kg). It runs to a length of 346 pages.

THE BOOKS WE LEAVE BEHIND

A 2010 survey of the thousands of books that guests most often leave behind at rooms in 452 Travelodge hotels in the UK gave the following Top Ten.

Book title	Author(s)
1. *Simon Cowell: The Unauthorized Biography*	Chas Newkey-Burden
2. *Ooh! What a Lovely Pair: Our Story*	Ant & Dec
3. *The Storm: The World Economic Crisis and What It Means*	Vince Cable
4. *The Lost Symbol*	Dan Brown
5. *The Girl with the Dragon Tattoo*	Stieg Larsson
6. *Breaking Dawn*	Stephenie Meyer
7. *The Girl Who Played with Fire*	Stieg Larsson
8. *Eclipse*	Stephenie Meyer
9. *The Girl Who Kicked the Hornets' Nest*	Stieg Larsson
10. *Eat, Pray, Love*	Elizabeth Gilbert

MAGIC AT THE MOVIES: Quite aside from her hugely popular books, J. K. Rowling also profits from the mega-successful Harry Potter movie series, which has earned $6.4 billion globally to date.

FIRST DOLLAR-BILLIONAIRE AUTHOR J. K. Rowling (UK) is one of only five self-made female billionaires, and the first billion-dollar author. Her seven Harry Potter books have sold 400 million copies worldwide. According to *Forbes*, Rowling has grossed more than $1 billion for her novels and from related earnings.

● **LONGEST-RUNNING CHILDREN'S MAGAZINE** *Murzilka* is a monthly literary and art publication for children aged six to 12, published by UAB "Editors Murzilka" (Russia). *Murzilka* launched on April 28, 1924, and has appeared monthly and without interruption for its 86 years of existence, except for 26 double issues in the years 1931 to 1933 and 1939 to 1946. Overall, 1,014 issues had been produced as of November 28, 2010.

● **First author to sell more than 1 million e-books** On July 6, 2010, the Hachette Book Group announced that James Patterson (U.S.A.), creator of the Alex Cross and Women's Murder Club series of novels, was the first author to exceed 1 million sales in electronic books, moving 1.14 million units of his books for devices such as Kindle and the iPad.

○ **Highest-earning adult fiction author** In terms of book sales and earnings, James Patterson (U.S.A.) is currently the best-selling author of adult fiction. In the year to June 1, 2010, he earned $70 million from his writing, and has sold more than 200 million books since 1992.

●**LARGEST GOVERNMENT PUBLISHING COMPANY** In 1813, the U.S. Congress decided that Americans should be kept informed about the workings of the government, leading to the creation of the U.S. Government Printing Office (GPO) and the "Keep America Informed" program. In 2010, the GPO employed 2,300 staff (and up to 332,000 private sector contract staff) supplying 1,220 libraries; more than 250,000 titles were available online, and 25 million documents were downloaded per month.

○**Highest initial print run (fiction)** *Harry Potter and the Deathly Hallows* had an initial print run of 12 million copies, the biggest initial print run in history. It was released at midnight on July 21, 2007. It is also the **fastest-selling fiction book in 24 hours**, shifting 8.3 million copies (or 345,833 books per hour) on the day of its release in the U.S.A., from 00:01 a.m. on July 21, 2007.

AT THE MOVIES

●**Most profitable cinema industry** The U.S. cinema industry made more than $11 billion in domestic box-office takings during 2010. Japan is in second place with $2.5 billion while India is in third place, with $2.2 billion.

○**Most expensive movie ever produced** *Pirates of the Caribbean: At World's End* (U.S.A., 2007) had an estimated budget of around $300 million. If the budgets of movies are adjusted for inflation to 2010 dollars, *Pirates of the Caribbean: At World's End* remains the most expensive production of all time, its $315-million budget narrowly beating *Cleopatra* (U.S.A., 1963), starring Elizabeth Taylor and Richard Burton (both UK), which cost $44 million in 1963, the equivalent of $310 million in 2010.

○**Most screen credits for a living actor** Brahmanandam Kanneganti (India), usually known just as Brahmanandam, played an astonishing 857 credited movie roles from 1987 to June 24, 2010.

○**Fastest $100-million box-office gross for an animation** *Toy Story 3* (U.S.A., 2010), the computer-animated movie from Walt Disney and Pixar Animation Studios, reached the $100-million mark at the U.S. box office in three days from its release on June 18, 2010, at 4,028 movie theaters, making it the fifth fastest-grossing movie ever.

The movie also holds the record for the ○**highest box-office gross for an animation**, having taken more than $1.05 billion at the global box office from June to October 2010.

○**HIGHEST-PAID ACTRESS** Star of the movies *The Proposal* and *The Blind Side* (both U.S.A., 2009), Sandra Bullock (U.S.A.) earned $56 million in the 12 months to June 2010.

○**HIGHEST-PAID ACTOR** *Pirates of the Caribbean* star Johnny Depp (U.S.A., seen here with costar Penélope Cruz) earned a treasure trove—$75 million—from June 2009 to June 2010.

○HIGHEST BOX-OFFICE GROSS FOR AN OPENING WEEKEND Sci-fi action movie *Inception* (U.S.A., 2010) racked up a record-breaking $62,785,337, across 3,792 theaters, on its opening weekend of July 16–18, 2010. Directed by Christopher Nolan and starring Leonardo DiCaprio, the movie was later nominated for eight Oscars, winning four.

THE OSCARS

Most wins (movie) Three movies share the record for the **most Oscars won**, with 11 wins each:
• *Ben-Hur* (U.S.A., 1959) won from 12 nominations in 1960.
• *Titanic* (U.S.A., 1997) won out of 14 nominations in 1998 (the **most nominations for a movie**, shared wth *All About Eve* [U.S.A., 1950] in 1951).
• *The Lord of the Rings: The Return of the King* (NZ/U.S.A., 2003) won all 11 of the categories in which it was nominated in 2004.

Azerbaijan and the area surrounding the Caspian Sea contain nearly 400 mud volcanoes. The **largest mud volcanoes** in Azerbaijan, and the world, are an average of 0.6 miles (1 km) across the base and hundreds of yards tall.

●**Most wins for best foreign language film** Federico Fellini (Italy) won four Oscars for Best Foreign Language Film as a director, with *La Strada* (1954), *Nights of Cabiria* (1957), *8½* (1963), and *Amarcord* (1973).

If Special Oscars are also considered (awarded before the category of Best Foreign Language Film was opened), Fellini shares his record with Vittorio De Sica (Italy). De Sica won Special Oscars for *Shoeshine* (1946) and *Bicycle Thieves* (1938), and Oscars for *Yesterday, Today, Tomorrow* (1963) and *Il Giardino dei Finzi Contini* (1970).

○**HIGHEST-GROSSING STUDIO Warner Bros. (U.S.A.)** claimed 18.2% of the movie market in 2010, its motion pictures grossing $1,923.9 million in all. The studio's impressive performance was helped by the fact that it distributes the highly profitable Harry Potter series, the penultimate installment of which appeared in November 2010 (see table p. 398).

MOVIE MAGIC: The seven Harry Potter movies have grossed $6.3 billion at the global box office to date, making them the ○**most successful movie franchise** of all time.

The **coldest erupting lava** is the natrocarbonatite lava of the volcano Oldoinyo Lengai, Tanzania, which erupts at temperatures of 930–1,110°F (500–600°C).

BOX-OFFICE HALL OF FAME

GWR proudly presents the movies that have grossed the most. The first list is purely in terms of today's money; the second accounts for the number of tickets sold, contemporary seat prices, and inflation, giving a truer picture of success.

	Movie	Non-adjusted gross (million)	Movie	Adjusted gross (million)
1	*Avatar* (2009)	$2,782.3	*Gone with the Wind* (1939)	$3,301.4
2	*Titanic* (1997)	$1,843.2	*Avatar* (2009)	$2,782.3
3	*The Lord of the Rings: The Return of the King* (2003)	$1,119.1	*Star Wars* (1977)	$2,710.8
4	*Pirates of the Caribbean: Dead Man's Chest* (2006)	$1,066.2	*Titanic* (1997)	$2,413.8
5	*Toy Story 3* (2010)	$1,063.2	*The Sound of Music* (1965)	$2,269.8
6	*Alice in Wonderland* (2010)	$1,024.3	*E.T.: The Extra-Terrestrial* (1982)	$2,216.8
7	*The Dark Knight* (2008)	$1,001.9	*The Ten Commandments* (1956)	$2,098.6
8	*Harry Potter and the Sorcerer's Stone* (2001)	$974.7	*Doctor Zhivago* (1965)	$1,988.6
9	*Pirates of the Caribbean: At World's End* (2007)	$961	*Jaws* (1975)	$1,945.1
10	*Harry Potter and the Deathly Hallows Part 1* (2010)	$952.2	*Snow White and the Seven Dwarfs* (1937)	$1,746.1

The record for the **fastest group of Maasai warriors to complete a marathon** is 5 hr. 24 min. 47 sec. and was achieved by six warriors from Tanzania at the Flora London Marathon, in London, UK, on April 13, 2008.

○**Most Oscar nominations without winning by an actor** Peter O'Toole (Ireland) has been nominated eight times for the Best Actor award, but has never won. O'Toole's nonwinning run has so far lasted 44 years, with *Lawrence of Arabia* (UK, 1962); *Beckett* (UK, 1964); *The Lion in Winter* (UK, 1968); *Goodbye Mr Chips* (UK, 1969); *The Ruling Class* (UK, 1972); *The Stunt Man* (U.S.A., 1980); *My Favorite Year* (U.S.A., 1982); and *Venus* (UK, 2006).

●**First remake to win best picture** The first—and only—remake to win Best Picture is *The Departed* (U.S.A., 2006), a remake of *Infernal Affairs* (Hong Kong, 2002). Many films share the same source material, but *The Departed* is the sole Best Picture winner to have been based on another film.

WORLD CINEMA

THE GLOBAL BOX OFFICE We've all heard about Hollywood and Bollywood. But what about the rest of the planet? GWR presents you with a guide to the biggest movie hits made (or, in some cases, co-produced) by some of the world's other film industries. All the figures listed are for the worldwide box-office gross of each film, unless otherwise stated.

BRAZIL
City of God (2003)
Dir.: Fernando Meirelles and Kátia Lund (both Brazil).
Box office: $30.6 million.

CHINA
Hero (2004)
Dir.: Yimou Zhang (China).
Box office: $177.4 million.

Jan Skorkovský (Czech Republic) juggled a soccer ball while running the 26.219-mile (42.195-km) Prague City Marathon in 7 hr. 18 min. 55 sec. on July 8, 1990, the **fastest marathon juggling a soccer ball**.

●FINLAND
The Man Without a Past **(2003)**
Dir.: Aki Kaurismäki (Finland).
Box office: $9.6 million.

●UK
Slumdog Millionaire **(2008)**
Dir.: Danny Boyle (UK) and Loveleen Tandan (India).
Box office: $378 million.

●ESTONIA
The Singing Revolution **(2006)**
Dir.: James and Maureen Castle Tusty (both U.S.A.).
Box office (U.S.): $335,700.

○FRANCE
Amélie **(2001)**
Dir.: Jean-Pierre Jeunet (France).
Box office: $174 million.

The Czech Republic is the **highest consumer of beer per capita**, with an estimated 35.3 gal (160.5 liters) quaffed annually by each citizen as of 2005.

GERMANY
Das Boot (1981)
Dir.: Wolfgang Petersen (Germany).
Box office: $84.915 million.

ITALY
Life Is Beautiful (1997)
Dir.: Roberto Benigni (Italy).
Box office: $229 million.

●JAPAN
Spirited Away (2002)
Dir.: Hayao Miyazaki (Japan).
Box office: $274.9 million.

●NEW ZEALAND
The Piano (1993)
Dir.: Jane Campion (NZ).
Box office (U.S.): $40 million.

 Muhamed Kahrimanovic (Bosnia and Herzegovina) holds the record for the ●**most cans crushed in one minute**, squeezing the life out of 65 full cans of beer with his bare hands in Vienna, Austria, on September 28, 2008.

300: Number of times a day you will be filmed on CCTV. At an average of three seconds at a time, you will rack up 7,186 hours on camera in a lifetime—or enough footage for 3,593 feature films starring you!

● **PORTUGAL**
The House of the Spirits (1993)
Dir.: Bille August (Denmark).
Box office (U.S.): $6.2 million.

○ **SWEDEN**
The Girl with the Dragon Tattoo (2010)
Dir.: Niels Arden Oplev (Denmark).
Box office: $104 million.

AUSTRALIA
Crocodile Dundee (1986)
Dir.: Peter Faiman (Australia).
Box office: $328 million.

● **RUSSIA**
Mongol (2008)
Dir.: Sergei Bodrov (USSR, now Russia).
Box office: $26.5 million.

MEXICO
Pan's Labyrinth (2006)
Dir.: Guillermo del Toro (Mexico).
Box office: $83.2 million.

BOLLYWOOD CINEMA Although often applied to all Indian movies, the term "Bollywood" actually refers to the Hindi-language film industry based in Mumbai. Typical Bollywood films are colorful and romantic, with songs, action, and comedy. India has the ○largest annual movie output, with 800 to 1,000 features produced each year by Mumbai's Bollywood studios—roughly double the number of Hollywood movies made each year. In 2009, 1,288 movies were made in India, in 24 different languages. By contrast, Hollywood made 606 feature films in 2008.

●**HIGHEST-EARNING BOLLYWOOD STAR** As the salaries of Bollywood stars are never officially revealed, financial success is usually ranked by the tax they pay each quarter. Shah Rukh Khan, star of *Devdas* (2002) and *My Name Is Khan* (2010), paid Rs 5 crore ($1.06 million) in tax for the second quarter of financial year 2011. (The term "crore" stands for 10 million.)

●**HIGHEST-EARNING BOLLYWOOD ACTRESS** Bollywood budgets remain much lower than those of Hollywood blockbusters, but top Indian stars can command a high percentage of a movie's production budget—reportedly up to 40%. Katrina Kaif, star of *Singh Is Kinng* (2008) and *De Dana Dan* (2010), paid Rs 1.3 crore ($289,000) in tax in the second quarter of 2011.

○**HIGHEST BOX-OFFICE GROSS FOR A BOLLYWOOD MOVIE** Starring R. Madhavan, Sharman Joshi, and Aamir Khan (all India), *3 Idiots* (2009) has grossed Rs 202,57,00,000, or Rs 2.0257 billion ($44.9 million), at the box office to date, seeing off competition from the 2010 movies *Dabangg, Golmaal 3,* and *Raajneeti* by a considerable margin.

MUSIC

○**Most consecutive no. 1 singles** KinKi Kids (Japan)—Tsuyoshi Domoto and Koichi Domoto (both Japan)—saw 30 singles in a row go straight to No.1 on the Japanese chart between July 28, 1997, and November 14, 2010. The duo's 30th hit was "Family—hitotsu ni narukoto."

Best-selling single of all time Yuletide favorite "White Christmas," written by Irving Berlin (Israel) and first recorded by Bing Crosby (U.S.A.) on May 29, 1942, is estimated to have sold in the region of 100 million copies across all formats, including 78s, 45s, and albums. The popular single has been reissued every Christmas since 1942.

●**Most R&B no. 1 singles** Since accurate sales figures were introduced in the U.S.A. in 1991, no artist has amassed more R&B No. 1 hits than the multitalented Usher (U.S.A.). The singer, songwriter, producer, actor, model, and designer has a total of 11 No.1s to his name, from 1997's "You Make Me Wanna . . ." to "There Goes My Baby," released on August 14, 2010.

●**Longest chart run in the UK by a group (one single)** On March 26, 2011, Snow Patrol's (UK) "Chasing Cars" spent a world record 100th nonconsecutive week in the UK Top 75.

●**MOST NO.1 SINGLES PRODUCED BY AN INDIVIDUAL** Johnny Kitagawa (Japan) has achieved the No. 1 position more often than any other music producer, with a record 232 chart-toppers for over 40 of Japan's best-selling groups between 1974 and 2010. He also holds the record for the ●**most concerts produced by an individual**, having put on an amazing 8,419 shows between 2000 and 2010.

Where there's music, there's dance—on p. 163.

On May 7, 2010, Bosnia and Herzegovina played host to the ○**largest waltz**, with 1,510 couples dancing up a storm at an event organized by Radio Kameleon in Tuzla's Freedom Square.

○**MOST CONSECUTIVE WEEKS AT NO. 1 ON THE UK ALBUMS CHART (FEMALE)** On April 9, 2011, Adele's (UK) second album, *21*, achieved its 10th consecutive week at No.1 on the UK albums chart, beating the 21-year-old record of nine weeks set by Madonna's (U.S.A.) *The Immaculate Collection* in 1990. Adele's album went on to spend 11 consecutive weeks at the top before dropping to No. 2 on April 23, 2011. However, it returned to No. 1 the following week, and at the time of going to press had spent a total of 16 weeks there—the ●**most non-consecutive weeks at No. 1 on the UK albums chart (female)**.

 The **longest single line of dancers** consisted of 2,354 participants performing the "Toe Dance" in an event organized by the Rääma Young People Union "Youth" in Audru, Estonia, on June 14, 2008.

Rihanna is the "only girl in the world" to have achieved 10 no. 1 hits on the U.S. hot digital songs chart.

●MOST U.S. NO. 1 SINGLES IN A YEAR (FEMALE) In 2010, Barbados-born singer Rihanna became the only female artist to have four U.S. Hot 100 No. 1 singles in a calendar year: "Rude Boy," "Love the Way You Lie" (featuring Eminem), "What's My Name?" (featuring Drake), and "Only Girl (In the World)." She is also the ●first female artist to have UK No. 1 singles in five consecutive years (2007–11).

1,023: Hit singles that will make it to No. 1 in your lifetime. The average hit is four minutes long, so it would take 4.25 days to listen to them all back to back, discounting the time you are asleep.

COUNTRY QUEEN Although tied with Carrie for country No. 1s, Reba McEntire is in a class of her own as the world's ⚪**best-selling female country artist**, with 23 gold, 19 platinum, and 9 multiplatinum albums as of February 2011.

⚫MOST COUNTRY NO. 1 HITS IN THE U.S.A. BY A FEMALE ARTIST Since the introduction of accurate sales records in the U.S.A. in 1991, U.S. stars Reba McEntire (left) and Carrie Underwood (right), winner of talent show *American Idol* in 2005) have each amassed a record 10 U.S. Hot Country Songs chart-toppers.

⚫**Most simultaneous U.S. hot 100 hits by a female artist** On November 13, 2010, Taylor Swift (U.S.A.) had 11 singles on the U.S. Hot 100, with 10 of those tracks making their chart debuts—another record for a female artist.

DOUBLE TOP Adele (UK) is the ⚫**first female to reach the UK Top 5 with two singles and two albums simultaneously**, achieving the feat on February 26, 2011 with singles "Someone Like You" and "Rolling in the Deep" and albums *19* and *21*.

●**Longest run on the U.S. hot country songs chart** By September 25, 2010, Lee Brice's (U.S.A.) "Love Like Crazy" had spent an incredible 56 weeks—more than a year—on the U.S. Hot Country Songs chart.

●**Most U.S. hot 100 entries** By April 2, 2011, cast members of the TV show *Glee* (U.S.A.) had notched up 131 Hot 100 entries—beating Elvis Presley's (U.S.A.) 108, which remains the ●**most U.S. Hot 100 entries (solo)** since the chart began in 1958. In 2010, Glee also claimed the ○**most hit singles in a year (UK)**, with 45 making the Top 75.

●**Oldest group to enter the UK album chart** On November 20, 2010, The Chelsea Pensioners (UK) entered the UK album chart at No. 14 with *Men in Scarlet*. The all-male group, British war veterans from the Royal Hospital Chelsea (UK), had an average age of 78.

●**Biggest hit act (UK)** Rock Choir (UK), a gospel, pop, and Motown ensemble, entered the UK album Top 20 at No. 5 on July 17, 2010, with *Rock Choir Vol. 1*. The group has around 4,500 members, 1,000 of whom contributed vocals to the debut album.

Best-selling group The Beatles (UK) have sold more music than any other band in history. All-time global sales have been estimated at more than 1 billion disks and tapes, with around 177 million sales in the U.S.A. alone. Elvis Presley (U.S.A.) is the **best-selling solo artist**, with 1 billion sales worldwide (129.5 million in the U.S.A.).

○**Best-selling contemporary jazz musician** American saxophone player Kenny G is the world's most popular jazz artist, with 15 gold, 11 platinum, and eight multiplatinum albums to his name, as well as total record sales of over 75 million.

●**MOST U.S. HOT 100 HITS BY A RAP ARTIST** Between December 4, 1999, and October 16, 2010, U.S. rapper Lil Wayne (b. Wayne Carter) appeared in the Hot 100 chart on an incredible 64 different tracks, which roughly equates to a successful single release every two months for nearly a decade.

SOUNDS OF SILENCE If you think today's music is just a lot of noise, you might enjoy "4'33"" (1952) by John Cage or the aptly titled "Two Minute Silence" (2010) by the Royal British Legion—not a note is played or sung on either.

●Highest-earning deceased artist According to *Forbes*' 2010 list of Top-Earning Dead Celebrities, the late Michael Jackson (U.S.A.) made more than the rest of the Top 10 combined, with $275 million for the year. In the 12 months following his death on June 25, 2009, his estate is reported to have earned $1.017 billion in revenue, with album sales of more than 33 million worldwide.

○Highest-grossing music tour By April 10, 2011, Irish rock band U2 had raked in over $558 million on their 360° world tour, making it the most lucrative on record. In total, over 7 million tickets have been sold for the tour's 110 shows between July 2009 and July 2011.

●Most successful album series by a solo artist All five albums released by Rod Stewart (UK) in his Great American Songbook series (2002–10) have reached the U.S. Top 5 and the UK Top 10, with *Stardust: The Great American Songbook, Volume III* topping the U.S. chart in 2004.

●Most album sales in the 21st century (UK) As a solo artist, Robbie Williams (UK) has notched up an astonishing 13,339,555 album sales up to October 2010, achieving eight UK No. 1 albums in the process.

●FIRST BRITISH FEMALE ARTIST TO TOP THE U.S. AND UK ALBUM CHARTS WITH TWO RELEASES In 2010, Susan Boyle (UK) achieved her second transatlantic No. 1 album with *The Gift*, matching the success of 2009's *I Dreamed a Dream*. On November 20, 2010, the 49-year-old Boyle also became the **●oldest female to top the UK album chart with a newly recorded album**, while *The Gift* was also the **●first Christmas album to top the UK chart**.

○HIGHEST CONCERT Singer James Blunt (UK) played a concert at 42,080 ft. (12,825 m) to a ticketed audience of over 100 people on June 29, 2010. The gig—which lasted 21 min. 15 sec.—took place on a Boeing 767-300 ER operated by Titan Airways that left Stansted Airport in London, UK, and flew in circles between Norwich and Cambridge until it reached maximum altitude.

Bieber was the most searched for celebrity on the internet in July 2010!

● **MOST VIEWED MUSIC VIDEO ONLINE** The video for the hit single "Baby," performed by Justin Bieber (Canada) and directed by Ray Kay (Norway), had been viewed 463,820,304 times by February 16, 2011, making it the most watched music video online and also the ●**most popular video of any kind online.** Alongside Bieber, the video also features R&B singer/actress Jasmine Villegas (U.S.A.) and U.S. rapper Ludacris.

● **Most successive U.S. no. 1 albums by a solo artist** Eminem, aka Marshall Mathers III (U.S.A.), has hit the top spot in the U.S. album chart six times in a row, with his latest success, *Recovery*, debuting at No. 1 on July 10, 2010. He also holds the record for **most album sales in the 21st century (U.S.A.),** with 32,241,000 sales by the end of 2009.

● **Youngest U.S. top 3 album act** On December 4, 2010, the album *O Holy Night* entered the U.S. chart at No. 2, making *America's Got Talent* runner-up Jackie Evancho (U.S.A.), at 10 years and 7 months, the youngest person ever to have a Top 3 album in the U.S.A. Only *Britain's Got Talent* winner Susan Boyle prevented her reaching the No. 1 spot.

● **Oldest chart duo** At the ripe old ages of 68 and 62, respectively, American singers Carole King (b. February 9, 1942) and James Taylor (b. March 12, 1948) hit No. 4 in the U.S. Billboard 200 chart with their album *Live at the Troubadour* on May 22, 2010.

Intan Pragi (Estonia) spun a roulette wheel more than 1,650 times in a 48-hour period during the **longest croupier marathon** at the Olympic Casino in Tallinn, Estonia, on February 18–20, 2005.

●MOST SUCCESSFUL COMPILATION SERIES It was announced in May 2010 that the *Now That's What I Call Music!* series had passed the 200-million sales mark around the world. The series was launched by Virgin Records (UK) in the UK in 1983 and has since become a global phenomenon.

●**Oldest artist to achieve a U.S. no. 1 dance hit** Ono, aka Yoko Ono (Japan), widow of the late Beatle John Lennon, made chart history on March 12, 2011, when "Move On Fast" became the 78-year-old's eighth chart-topper and sixth successive No. 1 on the U.S. Hot Dance Club Songs chart.

○FASTEST-SELLING DOWNLOAD ALBUM (UK) Take That's (UK) album *Progress*, which saw the return of ex-member Robbie Williams, sold a record 79,807 digital copies on November 15, 2010, its first day of release. Across all formats, the album's first-week sales hit 518,601—more than any other album this century.

Take That sold a record 1.3 million tickets in a day for their 2011 tour.

On the subject of gambling, the **longest time spent dealing blackjack** is 51 hr. 33 min., achieved by Stephen De Raffaele (Malta) at the Oracle Casino, Qawra, Malta, from August 24 to 27, 2001.

Most popular music download site On February 25, 2010, "Guess Things Happen That Way" by Johnny Cash (U.S.A.) became the 10 billionth track to be downloaded from the iTunes music store since its launch in April 2003.

●**Best-selling digital album (UK)** *The Fame* (2008), the debut album of American singer and fashionista Lady Gaga, passed the 300,000 mark in digital sales on March 1, 2011.

FASHION MIS-STEAK? Trend-setter Lady Gaga pulled off another fashion first at the 2010 MTV Video Music Awards when she turned up to receive her eight awards wearing a dress and hat (below) made of raw meat!

●**MOST WEEKS ON THE U.S. HOT DIGITAL SONGS CHART** Lady Gaga's (U.S.A.) track "Poker Face" spent a record 83 weeks on the U.S. Hot Digital Songs chart in the course of 2009 and 2010.

●**YOUNGEST TRANSATLANTIC TOP 20 ARTIST** Willow Smith (b. October 31, 2000), daughter of U.S. actor and rap star Will Smith, is the youngest artist to have had a single in the U.S. and UK Top 20s. At the age of 10 years 48 days, her single "Whip My Hair" entered the UK chart at No. 2 on December 18, 2010, following a U.S. debut at No. 11 on November 13, 2010.

YOUNG AT HEART: Before Willow was born, Jimmy Osmond (U.S.A.) took "Long-Haired Lover from Liverpool" to the top of the UK chart on December 23, 1972, making him the ●**youngest UK No. 1 artist** at 9 years 250 days old.

●FIRST SOLO ARTIST TO ACHIEVE FOUR UK NO. 1 ALBUMS IN FOUR SUCCESSIVE DECADES Australian vocalist Kylie Minogue first topped the UK chart with *Kylie!—The Album* in 1988, and she has revisited the No. 1 slot four times, with *Enjoy Yourself* (1989), *Greatest Hits* (1992), *Fever* (2001), and *Aphrodite* (2010).

●**Fastest-selling digital album by a female artist (U.S.A.)** Taylor Swift's (U.S.A.) album *Speak Now* shifted 278,000 digital copies in the week ending November 13, 2010.

●**First single to reach 1 million downloads (UK)** A year after its release in June 2009, The Black Eyed Peas' (U.S.A.) "I Gotta Feeling" became the first song to be downloaded more than a million times in the UK, reaching the landmark in June 2010. Gwen Stefani's (U.S.A.) "Hollaback Girl" (2005) was the **first digital million-seller worldwide**.

●**Most U.S. no. 1 music videos** With the release of *Sticky & Sweet Tour* (2010), Madonna (U.S.A.) enjoyed her ninth No. 1 on the U.S. Music Video chart on April 24, 2010.

MUSICAL MAYHEM

●**Fastest fiddle player** Fiddler Frankie Gavin (Ireland) played "The Foxhunter's Reel" at 150 bpm. The live performance took place at the Aula Maxima at the National University of Ireland (Galway), in Co. Galway, Ireland, on September 20, 2010.

The ●**fastest violinist** is Guo Siyan (China), who sped through "Flight of the Bumblebee" in a mere 54.922 seconds in Beijing, China, on December 21, 2010.

●OLDEST DJ Ruth Flowers (UK) played more than 38 sets at clubs and festivals worldwide in 2010, as Mamy Rock. GWR has established Ruth's date of birth, and precise age, but at her request we have decided to print only her "stage age": 69.

○LARGEST VIOLIN The Vogtland masters of violin- and bow-making (Germany) created a violin 14 ft. (4.27 m) long and 4 ft. 6 in. (1.4 m) at its widest. It was completed on June 14, 2010.

With 785 anglers, the ○**largest sea angling contest** took place at Malta's 2010 Blue Sea—Puttinu Fishing Festival.

> **LONG BOW:** This fantastic fiddle—plus its 17-ft.-long (5.2-m) bow—is seven times larger than the real thing. It takes three people to play a tune on it—one to press the strings and two to move the bow.

LARGEST ENSEMBLES

Instrument	No.	Organized/Led by	Date
●Barrel organ	82	On Leiden Barrel Organ Day (Netherlands)	May 3, 2008
●Can drum	770	Pringles Xtreme and Jake Sasseville (U.S.A.)	October 10, 2010
○Car horn	185	Funda Vanroy (Germany)	October 8, 2010
○Dhol drum	632	King Gucharan Mall (UK)	May 2, 2009
○Flute	2,320	Aomori Nebuta Festival and the Aomori Nebuta Executive Committee (both Japan)	August 1, 2010
○Guitar	6,346	Thanks Jimi Festival (Poland)	May 1, 2009
●Horn	264	Suffolk County Music Educators Association (U.S.A.)	January 15, 2010
●Orchestra on recycled materials	617	Allegro gra Eko (Poland)	August 1, 2010
○Saxophone	918	Taizhong City Government Cultural Department (Taiwan)	October 18, 2008
○Spoons	888	Conducted by Tang-Chi Chung (China)	July 6, 2009
○Ukulele	851	DeQuincy Prescott (UK)	June 20, 2009

○**Most concerts in 12 hours** Weltrekorder (Germany) played 35 live concerts at venues across Cologne, Germany, between August 21 and 22, 2010.

The ○**most concerts performed in 24 hours** is 55, by Kesiraju Srinivas (India) at venues in and around Narasapur, Bhimavaram, and Palakol, India, from September 23 to 24, 2010.

Staying on the fishing front, the **heaviest Guinean barracuda caught** weighed 101 lb. 3 oz. (45.9 kg) and was landed by Dr. Cyril Fabre (France) off the coast of Gabon on December 27, 2002.

3: Sets of hearing aids you'll need in later life. Better to be below average here! Most deafness is a result of damage caused by too much noise in daily life, so take care of your ears!

The Matterhorn

●**LARGEST ALPHORN ENSEMBLE** A group of 366 musicians played six songs on alphorns on the Gornegrat mountain near Zermatt, Switzerland, on August 20, 2009. The alphorn is a traditional Swiss instrument that was once used to enable people to communicate with each other over distance.

○**Most people whistling at once** On June 6, 2010, a group of 329 whistlers performed at Grandberry Mall, Tokyo, Japan, in an event staged by the TMD Corporation (Japan). They whistled the tune "Sapo," from the film *My Neighbour Totoro*, for over five minutes.

●**Most people singing live on a radio broadcast** In an event organized by the Children's Aid Society of Ottawa (Canada), 622 people sang "Lean on Me." The performance was broadcast by HOT 89.9 live from the Place D'Orleans Shopping Mall in Ottawa, Canada, on October 2, 2010.

○**Longest concert by a group** From April 14 to 16, 2009, Bodhi Foundation & Maharashtra Youth Development Organization & Group (India) played a concert 64 hr. 5 min. 7 sec. long at the Veterinary Hall, Seminary Hills, Nagpur, India.

Richard Deschamps (France) performed the ○**longest solo concert**, for 40 hr. 40 min. 40 sec., on guitar and piano in Caen, France, on December 4–5, 2010.

Q. WHAT'S THE DIFFERENCE BETWEEN A FIDDLE AND A VIOLIN?

A. There is no real difference, but classical musicians are more likely to refer to their instruments as violins, while folk musicians tend to call theirs fiddles. This is why GWR recognizes records for both.

●**Longest drumroll by an individual** Mickey Grimm (U.S.A.) played a drumroll lasting 5 hr. 20 min. at the Coffee House, New Harmony, Indiana, U.S.A., on October 24, 2009.

○**Longest solo singing marathon** On October 14–17, 2010, Swaradhika Dhari Pancham'Da (India) sang for 82 hr. 15 min. at Aarshiwad Complex in Vasna, Ahmedabad, India.

○**Longest singing marathon by multiple singers** A group of 389 artists sang 1,488 songs in 103 hr. 9 min. 26 sec. at an event staged by nonprofit organization Titanus (Italy) at the Teatro Cinema Astra in Pesaro, Italy, between the dates of September 21 and 25, 2010.

○**Longest marathon playing guitar** Guillermo Terraza (Argentina) played guitar for a finger- numbing 100 hours at La Fabrica in Comodoro Rivadavia, Chubut, Argentina, from May 12 to 17, 2010. Terraza has previously held this record four times, in 2000, 2003, 2005, and 2008.

●**Largest piano** Daniel Czapiewski (Poland) has built a piano 8 ft. 2 in. (2.49 m) wide, 19 ft. 10 in. (6.07 m) long, and 6 ft. 3 in. (1.92 m) high. It featured in a concert at Szymbark, Poland, on December 30, 2010.

●**Largest conductor's baton** Harmonie Amicitia Roggel (Netherlands) made a 13-ft.-11-in.-long (4.25-m) baton. It was first used by Bas Clabbers (Netherlands) for a concert in Heythuysen, the Netherlands, on October 30, 2010.

WHAT'S ON TV

○**Most hours of TV watched (nation)** Americans watched more television than ever in 2010, according to media research company Nielsen. Viewing of broadcast networks and basic cable channels rose about 1% for the year, to an average of 34 hours per person per week.

○**HIGHEST-RATED NEW SHOW (U.S.)** Crime drama *Hawaii Five-0* (CBS) drew an audience of 19.34 million for its highest-rated episode on January 23, 2011. The new series is a "reimagining" of the 1968 original.

●BIGGEST-SELLING TV DVD As of the end of 2010, the chart-topper on both sides of the Atlantic—and in some territories beyond—was the box-set of the 10-part mini-series *The Pacific* (HBO), a sister project to the hugely successful *Band of Brothers*. In 2010, U.S. sales alone reached 1,488,763 units, generating a revenue of more than $65 million.

○MOST EXPENSIVE TV EPISODE
The opening episode of *Boardwalk Empire* (HBO), directed by Martin Scorsese (U.S.A.), is reputed to have cost $50 million. The Prohibition-Era drama, which aired on HBO on September 19, 2010, stars Steve Buscemi (U.S.A., pictured left) as underworld kingpin Enoch "Nucky" Thompson.

The Okla natural fossil reactors, found underground in Gabon in 1972, are evidence of the **oldest nuclear chain reaction**. The fission happened 2 billion years ago, powered by natural uranium ore.

861: Number of batteries you'll get through in a lifetime. You only need one if it's rechargeable, as it can be used 1,000 times. But if you want to use your TV's remote control, which takes two batteries, you'll need help from a friend!

HOUSEHOLD NAME: Medical drama *House* is currently the world's **most-watched TV show**, broadcast in 66 countries and watched by an amazing 81.8 million viewers.

●HIGHEST-PAID ACTOR IN A TV DRAMA Hugh Laurie (UK) reportedly earns $400,000 per episode as the titular star of the U.S. medical drama *House* (Fox). The success of the show (see box above), now in its seventh series, currently makes Laurie ○TV's most- watched leading man.

●**First show based on a Twitter feed** *$h*! My Dad Says* premiered on September 23, 2010, on CBS (U.S.A.) and is based on the hugely popular Twitter feed by Justin Halpern (U.S.A.).

The sitcom documents the life of a struggling author (played by Jonathan Sadowski) who finally finds work writing about his father's politically incorrect rants. Starring in the role of Dad is veteran TV actor William Shatner.

A new Japanese series, *Hard to Say I Love You*, aired in April 2010 and was inspired by Twitter but was not an actual feed.

○**Longest-running sitcom (years)** The UK's *Last of the Summer Wine* (BBC) finished in 2010 after a record-breaking 37 years and 31 series. Every single episode was written by Roy Clarke (UK), the world's ●**most prolific writer of sitcoms**.

More than 1.7 million people were exposed to radiation—and 31 died—in the 1986 Chernobyl accident in the Ukraine, the **worst nuclear reactor disaster**.

○ **HIGHEST-PAID ACTOR ON TV**
Before Charlie Sheen left *Two and a Half Men* amid a storm of controversy and media attention, he was the highest paid TV star, earning $1.25 million per episode.

○ **HIGHEST-PAID TV CHILD STAR** Angus T. Jones (U.S.A., b. October 8, 1993), who stars as Jacob David "Jake" Harper (pictured above right) in the CBS hit comedy *Two and a Half Men*, is reported to earn $250,000 per episode. At the time of going to press, the 17-year-old's stellar paychecks make Jones—aka the "Half"—the highest-paid under-18-year-old on TV, although other juvenile performers may earn more annually through endorsements, royalties, and appearance fees.

○ **HIGHEST-PAID ACTRESS ON TV** As of 2010, Mariska Hargitay (U.S.A., left)—star of *Law & Order: Special Victims Unit* (NBC)—has regained her title as the world's highest-paid actress per episode, taking home a tidy $395,000 for every show.

The ●**highest-paid teen actress on TV** is Miranda Cosgrove (U.S.A., b. May 14, 1993), who earns the sum of $180,000 per episode of Nickelodeon's sitcom *iCarly*.

○ **MOST POPULAR TV SHOW (2010)** The first series of the ITV drama *Downton Abbey* scored 92 out of 100 on Metacritic, making it the highest-scoring reviewer-rated show of the year. The series, conceived and written by the actor Julian Fellowes (UK), follows the lives and loves of those living upstairs and downstairs in the estate of Robert, Earl of Grantham from 1912 to 1914.

○**LONGEST-RUNNING TV SOAP OPERA** With the ending of CBS's *As the World Turns* in 2010, the UK's *Coronation Street* (ITV) is now the all-time longest-running drama serial on TV. *"The Street"* first aired on December 9, 1960, and introduced us to the character of Ken Barlow—a role still played by William Roache (UK), the ○**longest-serving actor in a TV show**.

○**Longest-running sitcom (episodes)** It was announced in November 2010 that *The Simpsons* had been renewed for a 23rd season, which means that the series will rack up over 500 episodes. The show has featured the **most celebrity guests**, with at least 555 as of series 21.

○**Longest-running animation** The longest-running animated series by years is *Sazae-san* (Fuji Television), which first aired in October 1969 and continues to the present day.

●**First 3D Drama** Debuting in January 2011, Fuji TV's (Japan) *Tokyo Control* is a ten-part all-3D drama series about Tokyo's Air-Traffic Control Centre, airing on SKYPerfecTV's dedicated 3D channel. The technology behind the show was produced by Sony.

●**Longest gap between original TV show and sequel** When costume drama *Upstairs Downstairs* (ITV) returned to UK screens in 2010, it was 35 years after the original series ended. Actress Jean Marsh returned as the same character (Rose Buck), verifying this as a direct sequel (i.e., one that features one or more members of the original cast).

●**Longest gap between TV appearances** When Philip Lowrie (UK) rejoined the cast of *Coronation Street* in 2011, he reprised the role of Dennis Tanner, a part he first essayed in 1960. The last time he played this role was 43 years ago in 1968.

TV ACTION HEROES

●**First TV spy series** TV's first spy series was the U.S.A.'s *Shadow of the Cloak* (DuMont, 1951–52), which featured Helmut Dantine as Peter House, an agent working for International Security Intelligence. Another spy series, *Dangerous Assignment* (U.S.A., syndicated), starring Brian Donleavy as U.S. Government Agent Steve Mitchell, was produced at the same time but didn't air until some months later.

9: Years of your life you'll spend watching TV. Five activities will take up 70% of your life: 27 years of sleep, 10 years of work, nine years of TV, 5.7 years lounging about at home, and 4.7 years of eating.

●**HIGHEST-RATED TV SPY SHOW** Season 1 of *Archer*, an animated series based on the exploits of spy Sterling Archer, scored a rating of 78 (out of 100) on Metacritic.com. The website assembles an average rating from reviews by a range of entertainment critics.

●**FIRST 3D SPY** On February 2, 2009, NBC presented *Chuck vs the Third Dimension*, an all-3D episode of the hit comedy spy series *Chuck*. Viewers accessed the 3D using glasses that had been made available from various retailers. Many viewers would have worn the glasses the day before, to enjoy an all-3D commercial break in the 2009 Super Bowl presentation.

The Kiev dam across the Dnieper River, Ukraine, was completed in 1964. It has a crest length of 25.6 miles (41.2 km), making it the **longest dam wall** in the world.

●Longest-running spy series U.S. series *The FBI* (ABC) was broadcast from 1965 to 1974, running to 240 episodes. The series featured adaptations of many real-life FBI cases and was partly inspired by the 1959 movie *The FBI Story*.

●First private-eye TV series Running from 1949 to 1954, the U.S. series *Martin Kane, Private Eye* (NBC) was the first authentic private-eye show, though the character of a private investigator had featured in short dramatized segments as part of various guess-the-ending panel shows. In its five-year run, four different actors played Martin Kane: William Gargan, Lloyd Nolan, Lee Tracy, and Mark Stevens.

●DETECTIVE MOST OFTEN PORTRAYED ON TV From early small-screen appearances on NBC experimental programming in 1937 to the present day, more than 30 actors have essayed the role of Sherlock Holmes. In the latest incarnation, *Sherlock* (BBC, 2010), Benedict Cumberbatch (left) plays the cerebral hero alongside Martin Freeman as Dr. Watson (right, both UK).

SUPER SLEUTH: Created by Sir Arthur Conan Doyle (UK), Sherlock Holmes is also the **most portrayed literary character at the movies**, with at least 81 actors appearing in more than 220 movies.

 The world's **highest dam** is the Nurek dam on the Vakhsh River in Tajikistan. It is 984 ft. (300 m) high and was completed in 1980.

First TV superhero Superman—created by Jerry Siegel and Joe Shuster and sold to Detective Comics in 1938—was the first comic-strip superhero to appear in his own TV series. *The Adventures of Superman* (syndicated, 1952) starred George Reeves as the Man of Steel and was sponsored by Kellogg's. Initially filmed in monochrome, the show was shot in color from 1955 onward.

Most valuable costume from a TV series The Superman suit from the 1955 series of *The Adventures of Superman* (U.S.A.)—starring George Reeves (U.S.A.)—was sold for $129,800 at the Profiles in History auction in Los Angeles, U.S.A., on July 31, 2003. Until 1955, the show was filmed in black and white, and a brown and white outfit was used to create extra definition.

Most portrayed superhero on TV The character of Superman has featured in four live-action television series and been played by five different American actors:
• **George Reeves** (*The Adventures of Superman*, syndicated, 1951–57)
• **John Haymes Newton** and **Gerard Christopher** (*Superboy*, syndicated, 1988–91)
• **Dean Cain** (*Lois & Clark: The New Adventures of Superman*, ABC, 1993–97)
• **Tom Welling** (*Smallville*, Warner Bros., later CW, 2001–11).
   A sixth actor, Johnny Rockwell (U.S.A.), played the character in *The Adventures of Superboy* (1961), an untransmitted pilot for an unrealized series.

FIRST WESTERN ACTRESS TO PERFORM KUNG FU ON TV In 1965, the combat choreographers Ray Austin (UK) and Chee So (UK/China) incorporated kung-fu moves into several action scenes performed by Diana Rigg (UK, later Dame Diana Rigg) in *The Avengers*.

MAN APPEAL: Diana Rigg (above) played the role of Emma Peel (a play on the words M-Appeal or Man Appeal) in *The Avengers* in the 1960s, a role for which the U.S. TV *Guide* named her the "Sexiest TV Star of All-Time."

●**FIRST FEMALE JUNGLE HERO** In the syndicated series *Sheena Queen of the Jungle* (U.S.A., 1955–56), actress Irish McCalla played the lead. The character of Sheena had first appeared in comic strips in the 1930s, and was the ●**first female character to star in her own comic book**.

FEMALE TV FIRSTS

●**Action hero** Cowgirl Annie Oakley became the first female action-hero character to have a show built around her in the Western series *Annie Oakley* (U.S.A., 1954–57), a syndicated show starring Gail Davis as the sharpshooter from the Buffalo Bill traveling show.

●**Detective** The earliest female detective (i.e., paid investigator, not amateur sleuth) character to front a television show was Stacey Smith (played by Hattie Jaques) in the UK series *Miss Adventure* (ABC, 1964).

The ●**first U.S. female detective** to headline her own show was Honey West (played by Anne Francis, U.S.A.) in *Honey West* (ABC, 1965–66). The character of West had first appeared in books during the 1950s.

● **FIRST FEMALE TV SPY** British series *The Avengers* (ABC, 1961–69) pioneered the concept of the action spy heroine, but it was American agent April Dancer (played by U.S. actress Stefanie Powers) who was TV's first female spy with her own show: *The Girl from UNCLE* (NBC, 1966–67).

● **Sleuth** The earliest female sleuth to front her own show was Mme Lui-Tsong in the U.S. series *The Gallery of Mme Lui-Tsong* (DuMont, 1951). Lui-Tsong—played by Chinese-American actress Anna May Wong—was a globe-trotting art gallery owner who doubled as a sleuth and became involved in various international intrigues.

TV's ● **most prolific female amateur sleuth** was Jessica Fletcher (played by British actress Angela Lansbury), the hero of *Murder, She Wrote* (CBS, 1984–96), who investigated crimes over the course of 265 episodes and four feature-length movies. Agatha Christie's Miss Marple has had fewer small-screen cases, but in various incarnations has been on and off air since 1956. On that first occasion, she was played by Gracie Fields for the U.S. one-off *A Murder is Announced* (NBC).

The Pamir gardens near Khorog, Tajikistan, are the **highest botanical gardens** in the world, located at an elevation of 6,889–11,483 ft. (2,100–3,500 m) above sea level. The 30-acre (12-ha) site features more than 2,000 species of flora.

TV DOCUMENTARIES

1. FIRST EMMY AWARD FOR SPECIAL EFFECTS The 13-part series *Cosmos* (1980), produced and hosted by astrophysicist Carl Sagan (U.S.A.), won an Emmy for its impressive set, which was built to look like the inside of a space station.

**THE CAMERA ROLLED ON AND ON FOR THESE
TV DOCUMENTARY RECORD HOLDERS . . .**

● **Longest-running nonterrestrial TV documentary series:**

Explorer (National Geographic) has been running on cable in the U.S.A. since its Nickelodeon debut on April 7, 1985.

Longest video documentary

The Definitive Elvis Collection (Passport International Productions, U.S.A.)—released on July 16, 2002—ran for 13 hr. 52 min. and featured over 200 interviews with Elvis Presley's friends, family, and fans.

● **Longest-running medical TV show**

Hosted by Dr. Jayalath Jayawardena (Sri Lanka), *Vaidaya Hamuwa* has been regularly broadcast for 14 years 7 months as of April 2011.

One plant found at altitude that would suit the Pamir gardens is the giant bromeliad P*uya raimondii*, discovered at a height of 12,992 ft. (3,960 m) in Bolivia. The flower cluster emerges after 80–150 years of the plant's life, making it the **slowest-flowering plant**.

$7,381: How much you will spend on buying six televisions in a lifetime. This means that your nine years of small-screen viewing will cost you about $820 per year or 9¢ per hour—so spend it wisely!

2. ●LONGEST-RUNNING SCIENCE DOCUMENTARY SERIES Canada's award-winning *Nature of Things* (CBC), hosted by geneticist David Suzuki since 1979, has been on TV screens since its debut on November 6, 1960.

3. LONGEST-SERVING TV HOST Amateur astronomer Sir Patrick Moore (UK) is the most durable host in the history of television, having hosted his monthly astronomy show, *The Sky at Night*, since April 24, 1957.

4. ●LONGEST-RUNNING TV DOCUMENTARY SERIES NBC's news interview series *Meet the Press* (U.S.A.) has been airing since November 6, 1947. The weekly show, which focuses on political interviews, has had 11 hosts in its history.

LONG HAUL The 11-part series *Planet Earth* (BBC), screened in the UK in 2006, holds the record for the **most days filming on location for a natural world TV show**, with 40 crew shooting for 2,000 days in 200 locations on every continent.

5. ◯LONGEST CAREER AS A TV NATURALIST Sir David Attenborough's (UK) career as a writer and host of TV nature programs dates back to 1954's *Zoo Quest* and continues today with *Frozen Planet*, scheduled for 2011.

6. ◯HIGHEST-RATED TV DOCUMENTARY According to review site Metacritic, *Beyond Scared Straight: Season 1* achieved an average rating of 84/100. The U.S. show followed students visiting prisons to find out more about life behind bars.

7. ◯LONGEST-RUNNING TV DOCUMENTARY SERIES— SINGLE SUBJECT First aired in May 1964, *UP* is a UK series that has followed 14 people since they were seven years old; it returns every seven years to see how their lives have developed.

8. ●FIRST VIDEO GAME TO INSPIRE A HISTORICAL DOCUMENTARY Telling the story of the U.S. 101st Airborne Division in World War II, the History Channel's *Brothers in Arms* (2005) was inspired by a 2005 video game of the same name.

9. MOST EXPENSIVE TV DOCUMENTARY SERIES PER MINUTE Depicting how dinosaurs lived, reproduced, and became extinct, the BBC's *Walking with Dinosaurs* (1999) cost over £37,654 ($61,112) per minute to produce.

10. LARGEST AUDIENCE FOR A TV DOCUMENTARY CBS's *9/11*, broadcast in the U.S.A. on March 10, 2002, achieved the highest viewing figures for a documentary, with 39 million people tuning in to the documentary about the 2001 terrorist attacks.

The **highest restaurant** on the planet is found at the Chacaltaya ski resort, Bolivia, 17,520 ft. (5,340 m) above sea level. Lake Titicaca, the world's **highest commercially navigable lake**, can be glimpsed through the restaurant's windows.

ART & SCULPTURE

1. HIGHEST INSURANCE VALUATION The world's most famous painting, Leonardo da Vinci's (Italy) *Mona Lisa* was valued at $100 million ahead of its move from the Louvre in Paris, France, for a special U.S. exhibition in 1962–63. In the end, the insurance was not taken up because the cost of security for the artwork was less expensive than the price of insuring it.

2. ●MOST HANDMADE ELEMENTS IN AN ARTWORK *Sunflower Seeds*, by Chinese artist Ai Weiwei, comprises 100 million replica sunflower seeds, with each "seed" crafted in porcelain and hand-painted by a team of 1,600 skilled artisans. The work, laid out in a 10,764-ft.² (1,000-m²) rectangle, was displayed in the Turbine Hall at Tate Modern, London, UK, between October 12, 2010, and May 2, 2011.

On December 14, 2009, food manufacturer Kraft Foods Philippines scooped the record for the ○**most different dishes on display**, serving up 5,845 plates of food—all containing Kraft Eden cheese—at Araneta Coliseum in Quezon City, the Philippines.

3. LARGEST GUM MOSAIC A
209-ft.² (19.4-m²) mosaic of Nelson Mandela made with 100,000 Cadbury Chappies was created by TBWA Digerati and ID Productions in Johannesburg, South Africa, on August 17, 2004.

4. ○LONGEST PAINTING
On May 28, 2010, a group of 3,000 school students created a painting on paper 19,690 ft. (6,001.5 m) long in San Luis Potosí, Mexico.

5. ●HIGHEST ART GALLERY
Owned by artist-mountaineer Miguel Doura (Argentina), the Nautilus art gallery is located in a tent on Mount Aconcagua, Argentina, 14,108 ft. (4,300 m) above sea level.

6. ⭕ **HIGHEST TOTAL AUCTION SALES** Long after his death in 1973, Pablo Picasso (Spain) continues to be a hit in the auction room, with sales of $2 billion to date. A significant contributor to this total was *Nude, Green Leaves,* and *Bust* (1932), which sold for $106.5 million in 2010 to become the world's ⭕ **most expensive painting at auction.**

7. LEAST VALUABLE ART The collection of the Museum of Bad Art (MOBA) in Boston, U.S.A., has the lowest value of any public art collection. Its 573 works are worth a total of just $1,197.35!

ART OR GRAFFITI? In 1998, a vast "drawing" of an Aboriginal man appeared on the landscape at Finniss Springs, near Maree in South Australia. At 2.6 miles (4.2 km) long, it is the largest **human image ever**, but its artist remains a mystery.

5.25: Area in square feet you could cover if you collected all the flakes of earwax you produce in a lifetime. That's enough for two 12.4-in.-high hollow replicas of the Statue of Liberty—one for each ear!

TALLEST SCULPTURE MADE OF COAT HANGERS Standing at an imposing height of 9 ft. 11 in. (3.02 m), *Silver Streak* is a male gorilla made out of 6,000 metal coat hangers and weighing 661 lb. (300 kg). Created by British sculpture and installation artist David Mach, it was unveiled at the Royal Academy, London, UK, in June 2010.

WALKING TALL Although smaller than *Silver Streak*, Alberto Giacometti's (Switzerland) *Walking Man I* (1961) is the world's ○**most expensive sculpture**, selling for £65 million ($104.3 million) at Sotheby's, UK, on February 3, 2010.

SPORTS

CONTENTS

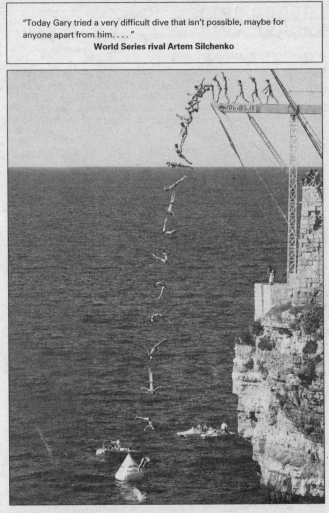

●**FIRST CLIFF-DIVING RUNNING TAKEOFF** On August 8, 2010, UK diver Gary Hunt executed the first running takeoff ever performed in cliff-diving competition, launching into four front-piked somersaults with 2.5 twists (captured here using time-lapse photography). Hunt's death-defying aerial feat, from a height of 88 ft. (26.8 m) at Polignano a Mare (Italy), helped him clinch first place in the first Red Bull Cliff-Diving World Series.

LONDON 2012

ALL EYES ON LONDON

Following in the footsteps of the phenomenally successful Beijing Olympics of 2008, London 2012 certainly has much to live up to—but so far it is shaping up to be one of the most spectacular Games ever. As the world's elite athletes, the global media, and millions of excited fans converge on the Olympic city in July and August, records are certain to be shattered—both in and out of the shiny new stadia.

ONES TO WATCH With the Olympics only coming around once every four years, the world's elite athletes will be going all out to make their mark in 2012. World and Olympic 100 m and 200 m record holder Usain Bolt (Jamaica, bottom left) has set his sights on smashing his own times of 9.58 sec. and 19.19 sec., respectively, while fellow runner Haile Gebrselassie (Ethiopia, top left) is aiming to better the marathon record of 2:03.59 he set in Germany in 2008. In the water, former record breaker Ian "Thorpedo" Thorpe (Australia, above right) is set to return from retirement to renew his rivalry with the current king of the pool, Michael Phelps (U.S.A.).

For more sporting feats, turn to p.501.

OLYMPIC ICONS Launched in June 2007, the 2012 logo (above left), designed by Wolff Olins (UK), is the ●**most expensive Olympic logo** ever, costing £400,000 ($645,645) to design. The Olympic mascots, Wenlock and Mandeville (above right), are named after the British towns Much Wenlock, where modern Olympics founder Baron de Coubertin got his inspiration for the Games, and Stoke Mandeville, home of the hospital that was central to the birth of the Paralympics.

SECURITY! Despite the huge security operation at Beijing 2008 (left), London 2012 is set to go one step further, with the ●**largest security budget for an Olympics**—$1.3 billion (£838 million) as of December 2010.

OLYMPIC HERITAGE London is no stranger to the Olympics—the city hosted only the fourth Games of the modern era in 1908, stepping in for Rome at the last minute when the Italian capital pulled out after the eruption of Mt. Vesuvius. The Games returned to London in 1948, with a record 59 nations taking part as the world sought to put the trauma of World War II behind it. In winning the right to host the Games for a third time in 2012, London saw off the challenges of New York, Madrid, Paris, and Moscow to take the record for the ●**most Summer Olympics hosted**.

160: Days spent on sport and outdoor activities in a lifetime. This is 27 days less than the first London Olympics, which lasted for 187 days from April 27 to Halloween (October 31) 1908.

ECO-FRIENDLY GAMES Located in the heart of East London, the brand-new Olympic Stadium is the focal point of London 2012 and the place where, for the athletes, dreams will be made or dashed in the blink of an eye. However, the stadium is also central to London's aim to be the greenest Games on record, and as well as 80,000 seats for spectators, the stadium boasts 525 bird boxes, 150 bat boxes, and numerous otter holts. Elsewhere in the park, there will be 4,000 trees and 300,000 wetland plants planted, creating habitats for numerous bird and mammal species.

TOP VELO-CITY London's 6,000-seat velodrome was the first 2012 venue to open, in January 2011, and the £100-million ($161-million) track has already been hailed as the world's fastest by cyclists who have tried it.

On May 22, 1998, the Central Bank of Manila (Philippines) issued the world's **largest legal banknote**, a special 100,000-peso note measuring 8 x 11 in. (22 x 33 cm).

TAKE YOUR SEAT With around 500,000 visitors expected to descend on London's Olympic venues every day during the 2012 Games, there will be plenty of competition for the 8.8 million tickets up for grabs. The organizing committee, led by former athlete Seb Coe (UK, left), hopes to raise £441 million ($710.5 million) from ticket sales, and a fair proportion of that will come from the opening ceremony on July 27. With a price tag of £2,012 ($3,250), the top seats are the ●most expensive Olympic tickets ever!

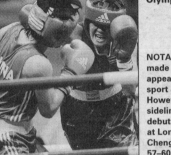

NOTABLE FIRSTS Women's boxing made its first and only Olympic appearance as a demonstration sport at the 1904 Paris Games. However, after a century on the sidelines, the sport will make its debut as an official Olympic sport at London 2012, with China's Dong Cheng (left) tipped for success in the 57–60 kg category.

OLYMPIC MILESTONES

THE OLYMPIC STORY BEGINS The ancient Olympics, so called as they were held on the plains of Olympia in Greece, date back at least as far as 776 B.C. They attracted famous names such as Socrates and Aristotle, who competed in events including running, discus, javelin, and wrestling. However, in A.D. 393, after 1,000 years of competition, the Games were terminated by order of Emperor Theodosius I, who considered them a "pagan cult."

The honor for the **largest denomination banknote** goes to Zimbabwe, which issued a $100-billion bill on July 22, 2008—it was enough to buy two loaves of bread.

FIRST MODERN OLYMPIC GAMES Conceived by the French academic and sports enthusiast Pierre de Fredi, Baron de Coubertin (1863–1937), the modern Olympic Games are inaugurated in Athens, Greece, the birthplace of Olympic sport, on April 6, 1896. The first ever modern Games were a modest affair by today's standards, with just 241 participants representing 14 different countries and competing in 43 events.

776 B.C.–A.D. 393 Olympia

1896 Athens

1900 Paris

   ●**First female Olympic athletes**
Paris 1900 sees 22 women compete in tennis, golf, and croquet. Tennis player Charlotte Cooper (UK) becomes the ●**first female Olympic champion**.

   ●**Lowest attendance at an Olympic event**
The women's croquet event is attended by just one paying spectator.

1904 St. Louis

   ●**First gold medals**
Until St. Louis 1904, just two medals were awarded to competitors: a silver for first place and a bronze for second.

 The people with the **fewest toes** are members of the Wadomo tribe of the Zambezi Valley, Zimbabwe, who, along with the Kalanga tribe of the eastern Kalahari Desert, Botswana, have just two very large digits due to a hereditary genetic condition.

151,891: Kilowatt-hours of electricity you will use in a lifetime—that's enough to power the 532 floodlights of the London 2012 Olympic Stadium 24 hours a day for six days.

1908 London

1912 Stockholm
●**Last solid-gold medals**
After Stockholm, gold medals are cast in silver and coated in 0.21 oz. (6 g) of gold.

1920 Antwerp

1924 Paris
●**First Olympic village**
To keep all the athletes in one place and avoid the expense of hotels, a "village" of cabins is erected close to the Olympic Stadium.
●**First Olympics to be broadcast live on radio**
The 1924 Games are heard on the airwaves across the home nation of France.

●**FIRST WINTER OLYMPIC GAMES**
The Winter Olympics, originally established to support snow- and ice-based sports not suited to the summer, are held for the first time in Chamonix, France, between January 25 and February 5, 1924.

1928 Amsterdam

1932 Los Angeles
●**First three-tiered victory podium**
Los Angeles 1932 are the most lavish Games to date, with the first victory podium, the ●**first raising of the gold medalist's flag,** and the ●**first playing of national anthems.**

The Padaung and Kareni tribes of Burma engage in active body modification. The females are known to have the world's **longest necks**, measuring up to 15.75 in. (40 cm), which they "grow" by adding successive copper rings over a number of years (see page 125).

1936 Berlin

● **First Olympic torch relay**
The torch is carried 1,980 miles (3,187 km) from Olympia to Berlin by 3,331 runners.

● **FIRST TELEVISED OLYMPIC GAMES**
The 1936 Berlin Games are beamed out live in black and white to athletes in the Olympic village and to special viewing rooms in Berlin and Potsdam. Color pictures arrive on screens much later, in 1968, when Mexico City becomes the ● **first Olympics to be televised in color.**

1948 London

● **First Olympic use of starting blocks**
Previously, athletes had been forced to dig holes in the track to gain a foothold.

1952 Helsinki

1956 Melbourne

● **FIRST SOUTHERN HEMISPHERE GAMES** The Olympics travel south of the Equator for the first time when hosted by Melbourne, Australia, in 1956. It would be another 44 years before they will again visit such southerly climes, with Sydney putting on the event in 2000.

1960 Rome

1964 Tokyo

● **First billion-dollar Games**
One of the best ever Games, Tokyo comes with an eye-watering price tag of $1.9 billion!

● **FIRST OLYMPIC TEAM SPORT FOR WOMEN** Volleyball is introduced at the 1964 Tokyo Games, becoming the first Olympic team sport for female athletes. The event is won easily by the hosts, who lose just a single set in the tournament.

1968 Mexico City

● **First use of gender testing at summer Olympics**
Testing introduced to stop male athletes competing as women.

● **FIRST "FOSBURY FLOP"** Dick Fosbury (U.S.A.) wins gold in the 1968 high jump with a revolutionary new technique, leaping over the bar back first (rather than head on) and changing the sport forever.

1972 Munich
1976 Montreal
1980 Moscow
1984 Los Angeles
1988 Seoul
1992 Barcelona
1996 Atlanta

○ **LARGEST ATTENDANCE AT AN OLYMPICS** A total of 8.3 million tickets are sold for the 1996 Games held in Atlanta, Georgia, U.S.A.—often referred to as the "Centennial Olympics." This equates to more than half a million spectators watching on each day of the two-week event, which is dominated by Michael Johnson's (U.S.A., pictured) gold-medal-winning runs in the 200 m and 400 m. By comparison, "only" 6.8 million tickets are sold for the 2008 Games in Beijing.

2000 Sydney
2004 Athens
2008 Beijing

○ **Most participants at an Olympics**
Beijing attracts a record 10,942 athletes from 204 countries.

2012 *London*
2016 *Rio De Janeiro*

AS SEEN ON TV The Beijing Games also attracted the ○**largest TV audience for an Olympic Games**. Over the two-week period, 4.7 billion people tuned in—that's two out of every three people on the planet!

○**MOST EXPENSIVE OLYMPIC GAMES** The 2008 Games in Beijing, China, cost 295 billion yuan ($43 billion). Accounting for a small part of the cost are the 958 medals awarded to the athletes, comprising 302 golds, 303 silvers, and 353 bronzes—the ○**most medals awarded at an Olympics.**

○**MOST EVENTS AT A SUMMER OLYMPICS** The XXIX Olympiad held in 2008 in Beijing, China, featured a record 302 events, nine of which are new to the Games, including the discipline of BMX racing.

The world's ●**heaviest bell ever** was the Tsar Kolokol, cast on November 25, 1735, in Moscow, Russia. The 222.6-ton (202-tonne) bell was never rung—it was cracked in a fire in 1737 while still in the casting pit.

OLYMPIC LEGENDS

Longest time as an Olympic athlete Four men have competed in the Olympics over a period of 40 years: Ivan Joseph Martin Osiier (Denmark) in fencing, in 1908–32 and 1948; Magnus Andreas Thulstrup Clasen Konow (Norway) in sailing, in 1908–20, 1928, and 1936–48; Paul Elvstrom (Denmark) in sailing, in 1948–60, 1968–72, and 1984–88; and Durward Randolph Knowles (UK, then Bahamas) in sailing, in 1948–72 and 1988.

Oldest summer Olympics champion Aged 64 years 258 days, Oscar Swahn helped the Swedish team win the Running Deer shooting event at the 1912 Games in Stockholm, Sweden. At the 1920 Antwerp Games in Belgium, he became the oldest silver medalist in the event at 72 years 280 days old.

Youngest summer Olympics champion At the 1936 Berlin Games in Germany, Marjorie Gestring (U.S.A.) became the youngest gold medalist when she won the springboard diving at the age of just 13 years 268 days.

MOST CONSECUTIVE OLYMPIC GOLD MEDALS IN AN ENDURANCE EVENT Britain's most decorated Olympian, Steve Redgrave won five consecutive gold medals between 1984 and 2000, competing in the coxed four (1984), coxless pair (1988–96), and coxless four (2000). Redgrave also won a bronze in the coxed pair in 1988.

●**MOST OLYMPIC DISCUS GOLD MEDALS** During a glittering Olympic career, Al Oerter (U.S.A.) won four discus gold medals in a row, in 1956 in Melbourne, Australia, 1960 in Rome, Italy, 1964 in Tokyo, Japan, and 1968 in Mexico City, Mexico. This feat also makes Oerter a joint holder of the record for the **most consecutive Olympic gold medals won in an individual event** (see also Carl Lewis on p. 449).

The **heaviest bell still in use** is the 101.4-ton (92-tonne) Mingun bell in Mandalay, Burma.

MOST OLYMPIC GOLD MEDALS U.S. swimmer Michael Phelps has won a record 14 individual and team gold medals in the pool—six at the 2004 Games in Athens, Greece, and eight at the 2008 Games in Beijing, China. His 2008 tally was also the most gold medals won at a single Olympic Games, comprising titles in the 100 m butterfly; 200 m freestyle, butterfly, and medley; 400 m medley; 4 x 100 m freestyle and medley relays; and the 200 m freestyle relay.

NO. 1 FAN Since attending the 1932 Olympics in Los Angeles, U.S.A., sports-mad Harry Nelson (U.S.A.) has gone on to attend every Games to date (except Berlin 1936), making the 89-year-old something of an Olympic legend in his own right.

●MOST OLYMPIC LONG JUMP GOLD MEDALS Carl Lewis (U.S.A.) won the Olympic long jump four times in a row, in 1984 in Los Angeles, U.S.A., 1988 in Seoul, South Korea, 1992 in Barcelona, Spain, and 1996 in Atlanta, U.S.A. Alongside Paul Elvstrom (Denmark) and Al Oerter (U.S.A.)—see p. 447—Lewis holds the record for the **most consecutive Olympic gold medals won in an individual event.**

○MOST OLYMPIC ATHLETICS MEDALS (FEMALE) Jamaican sprinter Merlene Ottey won nine Olympic 100 m and 200 m medals—three silver and six bronze—between the 1980 Games in Moscow, Russia, and the 2000 Games in Sydney, Australia. The bronze won in the individual 100 m in Sydney was awarded in 2009, after the gold medalist, Marion Jones (U.S.A.), was stripped of her title due to a drugs offense.

Most consecutive Olympic gold medals Fencer Aladár Gerevich (Hungary) won gold in saber events at every Games he competed in: a total of six, in 1932–36 and 1948–60.

Most Olympic medals With 18 gymnastics medals (nine gold, five silver, and four bronze) won in 1956–64, Larisa Semyonovna Latynina (USSR) is the most successful Olympian ever. Her nine golds are also the **most Olympic gold medals by a female**, while her 14 medals in solo events rank as the ●**most individual Olympic medals**.

●**Most medals won at one Olympics (female)** The record medal haul by a female competitor at one Olympics is gymnast Maria Gorokhovskaya's (USSR) two golds and five bronzes at Helsinki, Finland, in 1952.

See more aerial antics on p. 207.

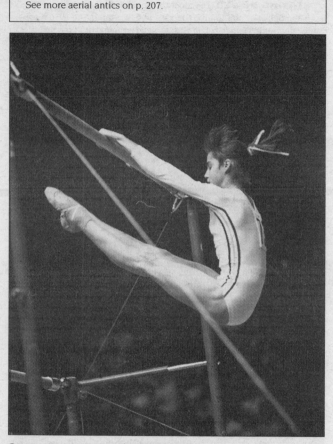

● **FIRST PERFECT 10 IN OLYMPIC GYMNASTICS** Nadia Comaneci (Romania) was the first athlete to earn a perfect score of 10/10 at an Olympic gymnastics event, for her uneven bars routine in the team competition in Montreal, Canada, on July 18, 1976.

 Lake Baikal in eastern Siberia, Russia, is the **deepest lake** in the world. It is 385 miles (620 km) long and 20–46 miles (32–74 km) wide. In 1974, the lake's Olkhon Crevice was measured to be 5,371 ft. (1,637 m) deep, of which 3,875 ft.(1,181 m) is below sea level.

MOST MEDALS WON AT THE SUMMER OLYMPICS (1896–2008)

1.	U.S.A.	2,298 overall (931 gold, 729 silver, 638 bronze)
2.	USSR*	1,010 overall (395 gold, 319 silver, 296 bronze)
3.	Germany**	852 overall (247 gold, 284 silver, 321 bronze)

MOST MEDALS WON AT A SINGLE SUMMER OLYMPICS

1.	U.S.A.	239 overall (78 gold, 82 silver, 79 bronze) at St. Louis 1904 (U.S.A.)
2.	USSR*	195 overall (80 gold, 69 silver, 46 bronze) at Moscow 1980 (USSR)
3.	Great Britain	145 overall (56 gold, 51 silver, 38 bronze) at London 1908 (UK)

MOST GOLD MEDALS WON AT A SINGLE SUMMER OLYMPICS

1.	U.S.A.	83 at Los Angeles 1984 (U.S.A.)
2.	USSR*	80 at Moscow 1980 (USSR)
3.	U.S.A.	78 at St. Louis 1904 (U.S.A.)

* Includes USSR only (1952–80 and 1988); does not include Russia, Unified Team, or Russian Federation

** Includes Germany (1896–1912, 1928–36, 1952, 1992–2008), United Team (1956–64), and FRD (1968–1976, 1984–88)

●**Most medals won at one Olympics (male)** Just two men in Olympic history have walked away from a single Games with eight medals: gymnast Aleksandr Nikolayevich Dityatin (USSR), who won three golds, four silvers, and one bronze at the 1980 Games in Moscow, Russia, and U.S. swimmer Michael Phelps (U.S.A.), who has achieved the feat twice. Phelps won six golds and two bronzes at Athens 2004 in Greece, and a remarkable eight golds at Beijing 2008 in China. Phelps's overall tally of 16 medals is the ○**most Olympic medals by a male**.

●**Most Olympic track and field gold medals** Distance runner Paavo Nurmi (Finland), nicknamed "The Flying Finn," claimed a total of nine Olympic golds in track and field between 1920 and 1928. The only man to

The **deadliest lake** is Lake Nyos in Cameroon, where toxic gases have claimed nearly 2,000 lives in recent decades. One night in August 1986, up to 1,800 people and many animals were killed by a large release of carbon dioxide.

match this feat is Carl Lewis (U.S.A.), who took gold in the 100 m, 200 m, 4 x 100 m relay, and long jump from 1984 to 1996.

●**Most Olympic boxing gold medals** Boasting a trio of gold medals each, the most successful pugilists in Olympic history are Laszlo Papp (Hungary), Teofilo Stevenson (Cuba), and Felix Savon (Cuba), who all won titles in three consecutive Games, in 1948–56, 1972–80, and 1992–2000, respectively.

●**Most Olympic canoe/kayak medals** Birgit Fischer (Germany) paddled her way to 12 medals in canoeing and kayaking events between 1980 and 2004, securing an impressive eight golds and four silvers.

●**First athlete to set three sprinting world records at one Olympic Games** At the 2008 Beijing Games in China, Usain Bolt (Jamaica) smashed the world records in three sprint events—the 100 m, 200 m, and 4 x 100 m relay—the first Olympian to do so in history. Bolt won the 100 m in 9.69 seconds, the 200 m in 19.30 seconds, and the relay in 37.10 seconds, alongside his Jamaican team-mates Asafa Powell, Nesta Carter, and Michael Frater.

PARALYMPICS

●**Most medals won at the summer Paralympics** Since the first Paralympics, in Rome, Italy, in 1960, the U.S.A. has been by far the most successful nation, with its athletes picking up a record 1,870 medals over the years.

●**MOST GOLD MEDALS WON AT THE SUMMER PARALYMPICS BY AN INDIVIDUAL** Trischa Zorn (U.S.A.) is the most successful Paralympian in history, racing to a record 32 individual golds and nine team golds in the pool between 1980 and 2004. The visually impaired athlete—who was born blind but later received two iris implants to boost her vision—has been almost unstoppable, winning 55 medals overall: 41 golds, nine silvers, and five bronzes.

The **most consecutive matches played in the Africa Cup of Nations soccer tournament** is 34, by defender Rigobert Song (Cameroon) between 1996 and 2010.

BOCCIA Similar to bowls, boccia is played in over 50 countries and made its Paralympic debut in 1984. Athletes with cerebral palsy and similar conditions throw balls as near as possible to a white target ball (the "jack") to win.

● **MOST FEMALE WHEELCHAIR BASKETBALL COMPETITORS** The 2008 Paralympic Games held in Beijing, China, saw the largest turnout of female wheelchair basketball players in the event's history, with 120 athletes from 10 nations competing for glory on the court. The tournament favorites, the U.S.A. (pictured in white), eventually won through, defeating Germany 50–38 in the final.

WHEELCHAIR RUGBY Dubbed "murderball" due to its intense physicality, wheelchair rugby is played on a basketball court by teams of four, who must carry the ball across the opposing goal line to score. A cross between basketball and ice hockey, it is a hugely popular sport.

 The record for the **fastest soccer goal by a substitute at the World Cup Finals** is 18 seconds, scored by Uruguay's Richard Morales against Senegal in Suwon, South Korea, on June 11, 2002.

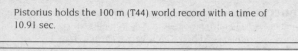

Pistorius holds the 100 m (T44) world record with a time of 10.91 sec.

●**FASTEST MEN'S 400 M (T44)** Dubbed the "Blade Runner," Oscar Pistorius (South Africa) set the track alight at the 2008 Paralympics in Beijing, China, winning the 100 m, 200 m, and 400 m titles and setting a 400 m record of 47.49 seconds on September 16, 2008. Born without his fibulae, Oscar had his legs amputated below the knees and today runs on carbon-fiber blades in the T44 class. He is bidding to become the first amputee sprinter to compete at the Olympics, in 2012.

1.23: Gallons of blood your heart pumps during each one of the 41,393,520 minutes of your life. Plumbed into an Olympic-sized swimming pool, you would fill it to within 6.3 in. of the regulation depth over the course of your life.

● **Most gold medals won at a single summer Paralympics** The host nations dominated proceedings at the 1984 Games in New York (U.S.A.) and Stoke Mandeville (UK), with the U.S.A. winning 136 golds and Great Britain picking up 107. The U.S.A. has also won the ● **most Paralympic gold medals** overall—665 to date.

● **MOST COUNTRIES REPRESENTED AT A SUMMER PARALYMPICS** The best-represented Paralympics on record was the 2008 Games hosted by Beijing, China, which was attended by 146 nations from around the globe. Beijing also claimed the record for ○ **most participants at a summer Paralympics**, with a total of 3,951 athletes turning up to compete for the 1,431 medals on offer.

● **FIRST PARALYMPIAN TO COMPETE IN THE OLYMPIC GAMES** After representing her nation in archery at the 1980 Paralympics in Arnhem, the Netherlands, Neroli Fairhall (New Zealand) became the first Paralympian to take on able-bodied athletes at the Olympic Games, competing with her bow at the 1984 Summer Olympics in Los Angeles, U.S.A. Neroli, who won gold at the Paralympics, eventually finished 35th at the Olympics.

PARALYMPIC COMPETITION

First held in 1960, the Paralympic Games is an international multisport event that runs every four years in parallel with the Olympics. Featuring many Olympic sports and several unique events (see boxes on p. 453 and below), the Paralympics sees athletes of all levels of disability compete for glory on the world stage.

CLASSIFICATION

Athletes are classified according to the nature and extent of their disabilities, to ensure that they compete on equal terms. The main categories listed below are further subdivided according to severity.

Amputee	Athletes with partial or complete loss of one or more limbs; must be missing a major joint
Cerebral palsy	Athletes with motor conditions that cause impaired movement, balance, or muscle control
Visual impairment	Athletes with any condition that impacts on vision; includes total blindness
Spinal cord injuries	Athletes who must compete in wheelchairs due to some loss of functioning in lower limbs
Intellectual disability	Athletes with impaired mental functioning, including communication or social disorders
Les autres	French for "the others"; applies to athletes with disabilities not covered above

●**First televised summer Paralympics** The 1976 Games in Toronto, Canada, represented the first time that the Paralympics had been televised in its entirety. Events were broadcast daily to more than half a million viewers across Ontario, Canada.

●**First amputee and visually impaired athletes at the Paralympics** Blind, partially sighted, and amputee athletes competed in the Paralympics for the first time at the 1976 Games hosted by Toronto, Canada. Wheelchair racing over distances of 200 m, 400 m, 800 m, and 1,500 m was added to the lineup along with goalball, a sport aimed at visually impaired athletes (see below). The standout athlete was Arnie Boldt (Canada), an 18-year-old leg amputee, who won gold in the long jump and the high jump.

GOALBALL Invented as a rehab aid for blinded World War II veterans, goalball is similar to soccer. It is played indoors by teams of three players wearing blackout masks, who score by throwing the ball into the opposition net. Bells in the ball help players keep track of where it is.

●**First Paralympic racing wheelchairs** Wheelchair racing debuted at the 1964 Paralympic Games in Tokyo, Japan, but athletes had no option but to race in standard chairs, which were heavy and awkward to control. By Toronto 1976, however, things had changed, and the development of special racing chairs, which were lighter, faster, and far more maneuverable, led to a glut of new speed records.

●**Fastest wheelchair marathon (T52)** At the 2008 Games in Beijing, China, Austrian wheelchair athlete Thomas Geierspichler won gold in the men's T52-class marathon (no lower limb function), setting a world-record time of 1 hr. 40 min. 7 sec. on September 17, 2008.

The ●**first wheelchair marathon** took place at the 1984 Games co-hosted by New York (U.S.A.) and Stoke Mandeville (UK).

Most Paralympic wheelchair basketball titles The kings of the court in men's basketball are the Americans, with five titles won to date, in 1960, 1964, 1972, 1976, and 1988. More recently, the balance of power has shifted to Canada and Australia, with each country winning gold twice and silver once in the course of the last four Games. In the female category, Canada's women have replicated the success of its men by winning in 1992, 1996, and 2000.

●**Fastest Paralympic men's 5,000 m (T13)** At Beijing 2008, Kenyan track star Henry Kiprono Kirwa claimed gold in the men's 5,000 m in a record time of 14 min. 24.02 sec., competing in the T13 category—the minimum level of visual impairment.

●**Fastest Paralympic men's 5,000 m (T46)** Abraham Cheruiyot Tarbei (Kenya) ran the quickest 5,000 m in the men's T46 class at the 2008 Games in Beijing, China, taking gold in 14 min. 20.88 sec. on September 13, 2008. The T46 class covers track athletes with impaired arm or trunk functioning or an amputation above or below the elbow.

●**Fastest Paralympic 50 m freestyle swim (S12)** At the 2008 Games in Beijing, China, champion swimmer Maksym Veraska (Ukraine) set a new Paralympic record of 23.45 seconds in the S12 class of the 50 m freestyle. On the same day, September 14, 2008, Oxana Savchenko (Russia) won the women's category in a record 23.43 seconds. The S12 class is for those with an intermediate degree of sight loss.

●**Most medals won at the summer Paralympics by a male athlete** Sweden's Jonas Jacobsson has won more medals than any other male athlete at the Paralympics. Having competed at every Games since Arnhem 1980 in the Netherlands, Jonas has amassed a record 27 shooting medals, including 16 golds. At Beijing 2008, he won three titles, in the Air Rifle Standing, the Free Rifle 3x40, and the Mixed Free Rifle Prone.

HIGHEST EARNERS

THE INCREDIBLE INCOMES OF SPORT'S TOP TALENT

Meet the super-talented athletes whose hard work and natural ability have been rewarded with skyscraping salaries and lucrative sponsorship deals. This top ten, based on *Forbes* magazine's "Sports Money 50-50" list of the most powerful people in sports, is ranked according to total earnings between June 2009 and June 2010.

$38.3M
TERRELL RAYMONN SUGGS
U.S.A., B. 10/11/82, LINEBACKER,
BALTIMORE RAVENS A $63-million contract in 2009, and bonus of $33 million, made Suggs the best-paid National Football League (NFL) linebacker in history.

$39.9M
ELI MANNING U.S.A., B. 1/3/81,
QUARTERBACK, NEW YORK
GIANTS Manning is now officially the highest-earning NFL player, following a $97.5-million, six-year contract signed with the New York Giants in August 2010.

3 BILLION: Number of people (almost half of the world's population) living on less than $2.50 a day. Of these, more than half live without electricity.

$42M
MANNY PACQUIAO PHILIPPINES, B. 12/17/78, WBO WELTERWEIGHT WORLD CHAMPION Fights against Miguel Cotto and Joshua Clottey netted "Pac-Man" a cool $35 million alone. In 2010, he became a member of Congress in the Philippines.

$42.8M
LEBRON RAYMONE JAMES U.S.A., B. 12/30/84, SMALL FORWARD/ GUARD, MIAMI HEAT James enjoys lucrative deals with Nike and McDonald's, among others. In 2010, *Forbes* rated him the second most influential athlete, after U.S. cyclist Lance Armstrong.

$43M
ROGER FEDERER SWITZERLAND, B. 8/8/81, 16-TIME GRAND SLAM WINNER As of August 2010, Federer had won $56.9 million in prize money. His Nike deal is the most lucrative in tennis, worth over $10 million a year.

STRIKING IT RICH IN THE WORLD OF SPORT

$52M	Oscar de la Hoya's (U.S.A.) purse for his WBC Light Middleweight fight against Floyd Mayweather Jr. on May 5, 2007
$30M	The spoils pocketed by the Spanish national soccer association when its team lifted the 2010 FIFA World Cup
$13M	The prize pot scooped by the Stanford Superstars on their victory in the 2008 Stanford Series of Twenty20 cricket
$12M	The record jackpot earned by Jamie Gold (U.S.A.) for winning the World Series of Poker Main Event in 2006
$10M	The huge haul for claiming the FedEx Cup, a points-based golf competition that spans several tournaments
$6M	The riches paid out by the most lucrative horse race in the world—the prestigious Dubai World Cup
$1.7M	The top purse in tennis, awarded to the men's and women's singles champions at the U.S. Open
$1.5M	The glittering prize up for grabs in the biggest race of the NASCAR season—the Daytona 500
$1M	The windfall paid by the now-defunct IAAF Golden League to any athlete who won all of their events in a season
$400K	The cash on the table for the winner of the snooker World Championship, played at the Crucible, Sheffield, UK

$43.7M
DAVID R. J. BECKHAM UK, B. 5/2/75, MIDFIELDER, LOS ANGELES GALAXY
The English soccer hero and celebrity is still a financial top draw. Of the $40 million he earned in 2009, almost $33 million came via sponsorship.

Emilio Arenas (Uruguay) has the ○**largest collection of pencils**. His collection, which he started in 1956, includes a total of 11,856 different pencils from 55 countries.

$46M
**PHIL ALFRED MICKELSON U.S.A.,
B. 6/16/70, 2010 MASTERS GOLF
CHAMPION** Mickelson is the world
golfing number two, but his prize
money is dwarfed by his lucrative
endorsements from companies such
as ExxonMobil, Rolex, and Barclays.

$48M
**KOBE BEAN BRYANT U.S.A., B.
8/23/78, SHOOTING GUARD, LOS
ANGELES LAKERS** With 25,970
points as of April 2010, Bryant is
the Los Angeles Lakers' all-time
top scorer. He is set to earn $30.5
million in the 2013–14 season just
from playing.

The **largest collection of pencil sharpeners**, meanwhile, is
held by Demetra Koutsouridou (Greece), who has amassed 8,514
different pencil sharpeners since 1997.

Highest Earners

$65M
FLOYD JOY MAYWEATHER JR.
U.S.A., B. 2/24/77, UNBEATEN
BOXER IN FIVE CLASSES
Undefeated in his professional
career (his 41 wins include 25
knockouts), this boxing sensation
can boast nine world titles in five
different weight classes.

$105M
ELDRICK TONT "TIGER" WOODS
U.S.A., B. 12/30/75, 14-TIME PRO
GOLF CHAMPION The golfing
legend's income includes an annual
$30-million payment from sponsor
Nike. He has won the Masters four
times, most recently in 2005.

TOP MARKSMEN

● **Most three-point field goals in an NBA finals game** Ray Allen (U.S.A.) scored eight three-pointers for the Boston Celtics in game two of the 2010 NBA Finals in Los Angeles, U.S.A., on June 6, 2010. He also scored the **most three-point field goals in an NBA playoff game**: nine.

○ **Most three-point field goals (WNBA)** Between 1999 and the end of the 2010 season, Katie Smith (U.S.A.) scored 785 three-pointers for the Minnesota Lynx, Detroit Shock, and Washington Mystics (all U.S.A.).

Muralitharan's 800th wicket came with the final ball of his last over in Test cricket.

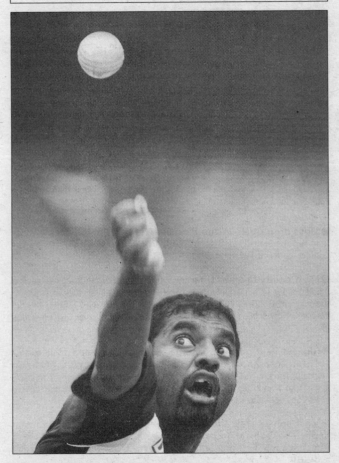

◯ **MOST WICKETS IN TEST MATCH CRICKET** Muttiah Muralitharan (Sri Lanka, above) took 800 wickets in 133 Tests from August 28, 1992, to July 22, 2010. He also has the ◯ **most international wickets:** 1,347, from 1992 to the World Cup final on April 2, 2011. Muttiah's compatriot, Chaminda Vaas, has the **most wickets in a one-day international match**, with 8–19 against Zimbabwe at Colombo, Sri Lanka, on December 8, 2001.

Top Marksmen

1,735: Weight in pounds of a lifetime's supply of chocolate. You're going to eat 10 times your own body weight of chocolate. Alternatively, you could make it all into an edible, life-size model of a basketball team.

●**MOST POINTS IN A TRI-NATIONS MATCH** Morne Steyn (South Africa) scored 31 points against New Zealand at ABSA Stadium, Durban, South Africa, on August 1, 2009.

●**MOST ACES SERVED IN A PROFESSIONAL TENNIS MATCH** John Isner (U.S.A.) served 113 aces in his epic match—from June 22 to 24—against Nicolas Mahut (France) at the 2010 Wimbledon Championships in London, UK. The feat also gives Isner the records for the ●**most aces in a Wimbledon match** and the ○**most aces in a Grand Slam tournament match.**

●**Most drop goals in the Five/Six Nations Championship** England rugby union fly-half Jonny Wilkinson scored 11 drop goals for his country between 1998 and 2011.

○**Most points in an NFL career** Morten Andersen (Denmark) scored 2,544 points in his National Football League (NFL) career as a place-kicker from 1982 to 2007. He played for the New Orleans Saints, Atlanta Falcons, New York Giants, Kansas City Chiefs, and Minnesota Vikings (all U.S.A.).

●**Highest field goal percentage in an NFL career** By the end of 2010–11, Nate Kaeding (U.S.A.) had converted 173 of 200 field goal attempts for the San Diego Chargers (U.S.A.), posting an 86.5% average. Mike Vanderjagt (Canada) lies in second place, averaging 86.47% (230/266) between 1998 and 2006.

●**Most consecutive Champions League matches scored in** Marouane Chamakh (Morocco) scored in six UEFA Champions League games in a row for Bordeaux (France) and Arsenal (UK) between 2009 and 2010.

Sophia Vaharis of Athens, Greece, has gathered the ○**most labels from champagne and wine bottles**: 15,255 different items, representing 50 different countries.

●HIGHEST FIELD GOAL PERCENTAGE IN AN NBA CAREER As of April 12, 2011, Boston Celtics center Shaquille O'Neal (U.S.A.) boasted a career field goal percentage of .5823, making him the most accurate points-scorer in the history of the National Basketball Association (NBA).

●MOST COMPETITIVE 147 BREAKS IN SNOOKER Ronnie O'Sullivan and Stephen Hendry (both UK) have both achieved a record 10 maximum 147 breaks in competitive snooker. The most recent was Hendry's (pictured) clearance in the opening frame against Stephen Maguire in their Welsh Open match on February 17, 2011.

Most Darts World Championships Phil Taylor (UK) has won 15 World Championship titles: the World Darts Organization (WDO) in 1990 and 1992, and the Professional Darts Corporation (PDC) in 1995–2002, 2004–06, and 2009–10.

●Most 180s scored in a Darts PDC Championship The most maximum scores by an individual darter in a Professional Darts Corporation (PDC) World Championship is 60 by Adrian Lewis (UK) at Alexandra Palace, London, UK, in January 2011.

○Most goals in an NHL debut On October 9, 2010, Derek Stepan (U.S.A.) became only the fourth player in National Hockey League (NHL) history to score a hattrick on his debut, for the New York Rangers in a 6–3 victory over the Buffalo Sabres (both U.S.A.). He shares the record with Fabian Brunnstrom (Sweden) of the Dallas Stars (U.S.A.), Alex Smart of the Montreal Canadiens, and Real Cloutier of the Quebec Nordiques (all Canada).

Commandaria, the sweet dessert wine from Cyprus, is the world's **oldest manufactured wine**. Its origins can be traced as far back as 2000 B.C.

Check out the crazier side of sport on p. 512.

○**Most Test cricket runs scored** Sachin Tendulkar (India) scored 14,692 runs in his Test match career between November 15, 1989 and January 6, 2011. He also holds the record for the ○**most runs scored in one day in an international career**: 18,111 runs, at an average of 45.16, between December 18, 1989, and the 2011 World Cup final on April 2, 2011.

●**MOST GRAND SLAM HOME RUNS IN A GAME** The Major League Baseball (MLB) record for the greatest number of grand slam home runs in one game is two and has been accomplished by 13 players. The most recent batter to achieve this feat was Josh Willingham (U.S.A., left) for the Washington Nationals against the Milwaukee Brewers (both U.S.A.) on July 27, 2009.

MOST POINTS SCORED IN AN NHL CAREER Wayne Gretzky (Canada) scored 2,857 points during his National Hockey League (NHL) career, playing for the Edmonton Oilers (Canada), Los Angeles Kings, St. Louis Blues, and New York Rangers (all U.S.A.) from 1979 to 1999. This total comprises 894 goals and 1,963 assists, achieved in 1,487 games.

MOST GOALS IN A SOCCER CAREER Edson Arantes do Nascimento (Brazil), known as Pelé, scored 1,279 goals in 1,363 games from September 7, 1956 to October 1, 1977. His best year was 1959, with 126 goals.

SPORTING LANDMARKS

Record	Tally	Holder
Most goals in a single FIFA World Cup	13	Just Fontaine (France)
Most Test cricket centuries	51	Sachin Tendulkar (India)
Most UEFA Champions League goals	71	Raúl González Blanco (Spain)
Most NFL touchdowns	208	Jerry Rice (U.S.A.)
Most English Premier League goals	260	Alan Shearer (UK)
Most NFL field goals	565	Morten Andersen (Denmark)
Most MLB home runs	762	Barry Bonds (U.S.A.)
Most Rugby Union international points	1,195	Jonny Wilkinson (UK)
Most WNBA points	6,413	Tina Thompson (U.S.A.)
Most NBA field goals	15,837	Kareem Abdul-Jabbar (U.S.A.)

WORLD'S FASTEST . . .

FASTEST . . .

English Premier League goal by a substitute Playing for Arsenal, super-sub Nicklas Bendtner (Denmark) scored just six seconds after coming on against Tottenham Hotspur in a Premier League soccer match at the Emirates Stadium, London, UK, on December 22, 2007.

UEFA Champions League goal Marginally slower than Bendtner, striker Roy Makaay (Netherlands) scored the opening goal for Bayern Munich against Real Madrid in just 10 seconds in Munich, Germany, on March 7, 2007.

> **CRAZY GOLF** On June 19, 2005, Ben Crosby, Andrew Crawford, John Lyon, and Russell Hayhoe (all UK) played the
> ● **fastest round of golf (fourball)** at Ponteland Golf Course, Northumberland, UK, finishing in 1 hr. 4 min. 25 sec.

FIFA World Cup goal Hakan Şükür's 11-second strike for Turkey against Korea Republic at Daegu, Korea, on June 29, 2002, is the fastest ever scored in a soccer World Cup finals match.

● **NFL touchdown** Playing for the Dallas Cowboys against the Philadelphia Eagles on October 12, 2003, receiver Randal Williams (U.S.A.) ran in the NFL's fastest ever touchdown. On the opening play of the game, the Eagles tried an onside kick, but Williams caught the ball and returned it 37 yards for a TD. The play, which set up a 23–21 Cowboys win, took just three seconds off the clock.

FASTEST MEN AND WOMEN Crossing land, air, ice, and water at breakneck speeds, these athletes are the fastest in their class. In the ultimate sporting showdown, we pitch rowers and runners against skiers, skaters, swimmers, and skydivers to discover the fastest sport on the planet!

50 M FREESTYLE, LONG COURSE (FEMALE) Britta Steffen (Germany) is the fastest woman in the pool over 50 m, finishing in 23.73 seconds at the World Championships in Rome, Italy, on August 2, 2009.
AVERAGE SPEED: 4.71 mi./hr. (7.59 km/h)

2,000 M ROW, SINGLE SCULLS At the 2009 World Championships in Poznan, Poland, Mahé Drysdale (NZ) won the 2 km sprint in style, beating his own world record in a time of 6 min. 33.35 sec.
AVERAGE SPEED: 10.46 mi./hr. (16.83 km/h)

- -

The ○ **largest skewer of kebab meat** weighed 8,866 lb. 15 oz. (4,022 kg) and was prepared by Zith Catering Equipment Ltd and the Municipality of Pafos (both Cyprus) in Pafos, Cyprus, on December 31, 2008.

- -

0.9 TRILLION: Distance in miles you'll travel in space. Our galaxy spins through the universe at 360 mi/s, so don't ever let anyone accuse you of sitting still—right now you're going at 1,296,000 mi./hr.!

MARATHON (FEMALE) Over 26.2 miles, Paula Radcliffe (UK) is the queen of the road, with a record time of 2:15.25 achieved in the London Marathon (UK) on April 13, 2003.
AVERAGE SPEED: 11.61 mi./hr. (18.68 km/h)

1 MILE RUN Fastest over 1,500 m and 2,000 m, Moroccan running machine Hicham El Guerrouj also holds the mile record, setting a time of 3:43.13 in Rome, Italy, on July 7, 1999.
AVERAGE SPEED: 16.13 mi./hr. (25.96 km/h)

110 M HURDLES Dayron Robles (Cuba) leaped into the record books with his 12.87-second finish over the sprint hurdles at the Golden Spike event in Ostrava, Czech Republic, on June 12, 2008.
AVERAGE SPEED: 19.12 mi./hr. (30.77km/h)

The **most meat consumed at an outdoor event** was 57,639 lb. (26,145 kg), cooked up by La Pastoral Social Arquidiocesana de Asunción y amigos, at La Asociacion Rural de Paraguay, Mariano Roque Alonso, Paraguay, on October 26, 2008.

100 M SPRINT Dubbed "the fastest man in the world," Usain Bolt (Jamaica) cruised to the 100 m record in 9.58 seconds in Berlin, Germany, on August 16, 2009.
AVERAGE SPEED: 23.35 mi./hr. (37.58 km/h)

1,000 M SPEED SKATE In between winning two Olympic golds (2006, 2010), Shani Davis (U.S.A.) set a new record for the 1,000 m event, posting a time of 1:06.42 in Salt Lake City, Utah, U.S.A., on March 7, 2009.
AVERAGE SPEED: 33.69 mi./hr. (54.21 km/h)

SPEED SKIING (FEMALE) Sanna Tidstrand (Sweden), the world champion speed skier since 2006, reached a death-defying 150.73 mi./hr. (242.59 km/h) on the slopes of Les Arcs, France, on April 20, 2006.
AVERAGE SPEED: 150.73 mi./hr. (242.59 km/h)

NHL hat-trick Nobody has broken Bill Mosienko's (Canada) phenomenal record of smashing three goals in just 21 seconds playing for the Chicago Blackhawks against the New York Rangers (both U.S.A.) on March 23, 1952.

●Rugby Union Super Rugby try The Super Rugby competition, contested by teams from Australia, New Zealand, and South Africa, saw its quickest ever try on May 12, 2001, when the Highlanders' (NZ) lock Vula Maimuri (Fiji) crossed the line just 12 seconds into a match against the Crusaders (NZ) at Christchurch, NZ.

BIGGEST HITTERS

From pacey pitches to speedy shuttlecocks, check out some of the fastest throws, tosses, whacks, and smashes from around the world of sport!

Category	Speed	Holder	Date
Cricket bowl	100.2 mi./hr. (161.3 km/h)	Shoaib Akhtar (Pakistan)	Feb. 22, 2003
Baseball pitch	100.9 mi./hr. (162.3 km/h)	Lynn Nolan Ryan (U.S.A.)	Aug. 20, 1974
● Ice hockey shot	110.3 mi./hr. (177.5 km/h)	Denis Kulyash (Russia)	Feb. 5, 2011
● Lacrosse shot	111.0 mi./hr. (178.6 km/h)	Paul Rabil (U.S.A.)	Jul. 8, 2010
Soccer shot (UK)	114.0 mi./hr. (183.0 km/h)	David Hirst (UK)	Sep. 16, 1996
○ Tennis serve	156.0 mi./hr. (251.0 km/h)	Ivo Karlovic (Croatia)	Mar. 5, 2011
Jai alai throw	188.0 mi./hr. (302.0 km/h)	José Ramón Areitio (Spain)	Aug. 3, 1979
● Golf drive	204.0 mi./hr. (328.3 km/h)	Jason Zuback (Canada)	Dec. 1, 2007
● Badminton smash	206.0 mi./hr. (332.0 km/h)	Fu Haifeng (China)	May 15, 2005

○**Cricket World Cup century** During the 2011 World Cup, Irish all-rounder Kevin O'Brien hit 100 runs off just 50 balls—an average of 12 per over, or two per ball! O'Brien went on to score 113 in a three-wicket win over England at Bangalore's M Chinnaswamy Stadium, India, on March 2, 2011.

○**SPEED SKYDIVE** Thanks to gravity—and a 12,139-ft. (3,700-m) plunge from a plane—speed skydiving is the world's fastest sport. On June 5, 2010, at the Speed World Series in Utti, Finland, Christian Labhart (Switzerland) hit a freefall speed of 327.41 mi./hr. (526.93 km/h)—fast enough to outpace a Bugatti Veyron supercar at full pelt (267.86 mi./hr.; 431.07 km/h).

Cricket World Cup final century Australian wicket-keeper Adam Gilchrist chalked up the quickest ton in a cricket World Cup final, hitting 100 runs off 72 balls against Sri Lanka at Kensington Oval, Bridgetown, Barbados, on April 28, 2007.

Snooker maximum break (147 points) True to his name, Ronnie "The Rocket" O'Sullivan holds the record for the fastest 147 break, recording a time of 5 min. 20 sec. in his first-round match against Mick Price at the World Championships in Sheffield, UK, on April 21, 1997. Sinking 15 reds, each followed by a black, then all seven colors, he averaged a pot every 8.65 seconds!

FASTEST ON WHEELS

FASTEST . . .

●**Average speed in an F1 Grand Prix** Michael Schumacher (Germany) averaged a record 153.842 mi./hr. (247.585 km/h) in his Ferrari on his way to winning the Italian Grand Prix at Monza on September 14, 2003. Despite advances in race technology, the German's speed remains unbeaten.

●**FASTEST INDY 500 OPENING LAP** The fastest start to an Indianapolis 500 was set by Brazilian driver Tony Kanaan, who fired his Honda round the opening lap of the 2007 race in a record 41.335 seconds, at an average speed of 217.728 mi./hr. (350.39 km/h). Pictured above left setting the pace for the Andretti Green team, Kanaan eventually fell back to finish eighth.

3.5: Number of speeding tickets you'll get in a lifetime. You'll also make nine claims on your motor insurance. Perhaps unsurprisingly, the average driver rates their driving ability as being above average.

●**FASTEST OUTRIGHT SPEED IN AN F1 RACE** Driving a McLaren-Mercedes, Juan Pablo Montoya (Colombia) accelerated to 231.5 mi./hr. (372.6 km/h) at Monza in the Italian Grand Prix on September 4, 2005. Montoya started and finished the race in first place.

●**FASTEST FIRS INLINE SPEED SKATING ROAD 200 M (MALE)** On July 6, 2006, inline speed skater Gregory Duggento (Italy) set a new record of 16.209 seconds in the men's 200 m time trial at the 2006 World Road Championships held in Anyang, South Korea.

Completion of the Indy 500 Dutchman Arie Luyendyk is the fastest driver ever to grace the 500-mile (804.5-km) race at the Indianapolis Motor Speedway in Indiana, U.S.A. On May 27, 1990, his Lola-Chevrolet cruised home in 2 hr. 41 min. 18.404 sec., averaging 185.981 mi./hr. (299.307 km/h).

Lap in the Le Mans 24-hour race On June 10, 1989, Alain Ferté (France) drove the fastest lap in the history of the 24 Hours of Le Mans, recording a time of 3 min. 21.27 sec. in his Jaguar XJR-9LM at the Circuit de la Sarthe, Le Mans, France, with his brother Michel also on board.

Average speed in the Tour de France Lance Armstrong (U.S.A.) won the 2005 Tour de France in 86 hr. 15 min. 2 sec., averaging 25.882 mi./hr. (41.654 km/h) on the 2,241-mile (3,607-km) course. After his record-breaking 7th Tour victory in a row, Armstrong announced his retirement, only to return in 2010 to finish in 23rd place. One of the world's greatest athletes, he gave up pro sports for good in February 2011.

○**3 km cycle, standing start (female team)** On May 12, 2010, Dotsie Bausch, Sarah Hammer and Lauren Tamayo (U.S.A.) won the 3 km team pursuit in Aguascalientes, Mexico, in 3 min. 19.569 sec.

MARATHON MAN Fearnley's big-race credentials were tested to the max at the 2004 Paralympics in Athens, Greece. With 3 miles (5 km) to go, Fearnley suffered a flat tire, but still pushed on to take gold.

●**FASTEST NEW YORK WHEELCHAIR MARATHON** On November 5, 2006, Australian Kurt Fearnley powered to victory in the wheelchair marathon in New York City, U.S.A., in a blistering 1 hr. 29 min. 22 sec. A talented athlete, Fearnley also holds the record across the Atlantic, achieving the **fastest London Wheelchair Marathon** in 1 hr. 28 min. 57 sec. in 2009. His most recent success was gold in the 1,500 m at the 2010 Commonwealth Games.

The **most recent tribal first contact** was with a subgroup of the Ayoreo-Totobiegosode peoples of Paraguay, who were forced from the forest in March 2004 when their land and waterholes were taken over by cattle ranchers.

○FASTEST OUTRIGHT SPEED IN NHRA DRAG RACING, PRO STOCK MOTORBIKE The highest speed for a gas-driven, piston-engined motorcycle (Pro Stock) is 197.65 mi./hr. (318.08 km/h), by Michael Phillips (U.S.A.) at Baton Rouge, Louisiana, U.S.A., on July 18, 2010.

Completion of the London Wheelchair Marathon (female)

Just months prior to winning a Paralympic bronze in the marathon at the 2008 Beijing Games, Swiss wheelchair athlete Sandra Graf saw off her rivals Amanda McGrory and Shelly Woods to win the London Wheelchair Marathon in a record time of 1 hr. 48 min. 4 sec. on April 13, 2008.

○Outright speed in NHRA drag racing, pro stock car On March 27, 2010, drag racer Greg Anderson (U.S.A.) tore up the tarmac to record a speed of 212.46 mi./hr. (341.92 km/h) in a gas-driven, piston-engined car (Pro Stock) at Concord, North Carolina, U.S.A.

Lap at the Isle of Man TT (female) With a super-quick time of 19 min. 22.6 sec. and an average speed of 116.83 mi./hr. (188.02 km/h), Jenny Tinmouth (UK) is the fastest female rider ever to lap the daunting 37.73-mile (60.75-km) Isle of Man TT course. She claimed the record on June 12, 2009, and has since gone on to become the ●**first woman to race in the British Superbike Championship**, appearing for the Split-lath Motorsport team in the 2011 season.

Isle of Man TT At the 2009 Isle of Man TT (UK), British Superbike rider John McGuinness won the Superbike category in a record time of 1 hr. 46 min. 7.16 sec. on June 8, 2009.

McGuinness also achieved the double feat of **overall fastest lap** and ●**overall fastest average speed**, completing the arduous circuit in 17 min. 12.3 sec. and averaging 131.578 mi./hr. (211.754 km/h) on his Honda CBR1000RR.

For more thrills on wheels, turn to p. 332.

The **shortest known tribe** are the Mbutsi people of the Democratic Republic of the Congo, whose average height is just 4 ft. 6 in. (1.37 m) for men and 4 ft. 5 in. (1.35 m) for women.

FASTEST 500 M CYCLE, UNPACED FLYING START (MALE) On May 13, 2007, Chris Hoy (UK) raced round the Alto Orpavi velodrome in La Paz, Bolivia, to shatter the "flying 500 m" record in a time of 24.758 seconds—more than a second quicker than Arnaud Duble's (France) 2001 record.

●**Speed by a newcomer at the Isle of Man TT** The 2009 British Supersport Champion Steve Plater (UK) made his Isle of Man TT debut in 2007 and, despite his inexperience on the course, steered his 1,000-cc Yamaha into the record books with a top speed of 125.808 mi./hr. (202.468 km/h).

●**FIRS inline speed skating track 10,000 m (male)** At the 2009 Fédération Internationale de Roller Sports (FIRS) World Roller Speed Skating Championships in Haining, China, Bart Swings (Belgium) won the track 10,000 m event in a record time of 14 min. 41.425 sec. He achieved this incredible feat at the age of 18 on September 18, 2009.

●**FIRS inline speed skating track 300 m (female)** On the same day of the same 2009 championships, South Korea's So Yeong Shin achieved a record of her own in the junior women's track 300 m. Finishing in a blistering 26.426 seconds, she even outpaced the winner of the senior race, and her time is the overall world record.

○**4 km cycle, unpaced standing start (male)** On February 2, 2011, Australia's Jack Bobridge broke Chris Boardman's (UK) 15-year-old 4 km record in the Cycling Australia Track National Championships in Sydney, Australia. Crossing the line in 4 min. 10.534 sec., he was just half a second quicker than Boardman's 1996 record—a barrier once thought unbeatable.

YOUNGEST & OLDEST

Oldest no. 1–ranked tennis player (male) The oldest male tennis player to be ranked No. 1 by the Association of Tennis Professionals (ATP) is Andre Agassi (U.S.A., b. April 29, 1970), who became the highest seeded men's player on May 11, 2003, aged 33 years 13 days. During his career, Agassi was ranked No. 1 for a total of 101 weeks.

●YOUNGEST JUDO CHAMPION (MALE)
The youngest male Judoka to win a World Championship is Teddy Riner (France, b. April 7, 1989), who was 18 years 192 days old when he took gold in the Heavyweight category at the 2007 World Championships in Rio de Janeiro, Brazil.

●OLDEST PLAYER TO SCORE A GOAL IN THE UEFA CHAMPIONS LEAGUE
On April 26, 2011, Ryan Giggs (UK, b. November 29, 1973) made Champions League history by scoring the opener in Manchester United's (England) 2–0 semi-final win over German side Schalke 04 at the age of 37 years 148 days.

Oldest Wimbledon tennis champion Martina Navratilova (U.S.A., b. October 18, 1956) was 46 years 261 days old when she won the mixed doubles with Leander Paes (India) on July 6, 2003.

Oldest winner of the French Open tennis tournament Elizabeth Ryan (U.S.A., b. February 8, 1892) won the 1934 women's doubles with Simone Mathieu (France) at 42 years 88 days old.

Oldest Davis Cup tennis player The oldest player ever to take to the court in the Davis Cup team tennis competition is Yaka-Garonfin Koptigan (Togo), who played for his country against Mauritius aged 59 years 147 days on May 27, 2001.

●Youngest player to win a career tennis Grand Slam (male) Tennis ace Rafael Nadal (Spain) was 24 years 101 days old when he achieved a career Grand Slam—winning all four major tournaments: the French Open, the Australian Open, Wimbledon, and the U.S. Open. He completed the feat by winning the U.S. Open on September 14, 2010.

●Oldest player to score in the NFL Super Bowl On February 7, 2010, Indianapolis Colts (U.S.A.) placekicker Matt Stover (U.S.A.) became the oldest American football player ever to score in the NFL's season finale, when, aged 42 years 11 days, he struck a 38-yard field goal against the New Orleans Saints (U.S.A.) in Super Bowl XLIV. In taking the field, he had also earned the record for the **oldest player to appear in the Super Bowl**.

●**YOUNGEST RIDER TO WIN A GRAND PRIX** Scott Redding (UK, b. January 4, 1993) won his first Grand Prix motorcycle race aged 15 years 170 days when he took the checkered flag in the British 125 cc Grand Prix at Donington Park, UK, on June 22, 2008.

●**Youngest NBA scoring champion** At 21 years 197 days old, basketball player Kevin Durant (U.S.A., b. September 29, 1988) of the Oklahoma City Thunder (U.S.A.) became the youngest single-season scoring champion in NBA history, averaging 30.1 points per game in 2009–10.

●**Youngest player to hit 600 home runs in an MLB career** New York Yankees (U.S.A.) third baseman Alex Rodriguez (U.S.A., b. July 27, 1975) hit his 600th home run aged 35 years 8 days against the Toronto Blue Jays (Canada) on August 4, 2010. In doing so, "A-Rod" broke the record set by baseball legend "Babe" Ruth (U.S.A., 1895–1948) with a year to spare.

Oldest rower to win the University Boat Race Mike Wherley (U.S.A., b. March 15, 1972) was 36 years 14 days old when he helped Oxford beat Cambridge (both UK) in the 2008 river race in London, UK.

●**Youngest rower to win the University Boat Race** On March 25, 2000, Oxford's Matt Smith (UK, b. July 14, 1981) became the boat race's youngest victor, aged just 18 years 255 days.

Youngest figure-skating champion Tara Lipinski (U.S.A., b. June 10, 1982) won the individual world title on March 22, 1997, aged 14 years 286 days.

Redding won rookie of the year for his landmark win.

$495: The amount you will spend on antiperspirant and deodorant in your lifetime. You'll spend most of it between the ages of 16 and 24, when you're at your most sporty—and your most self-conscious!

●**OLDEST OLYMPIC SWIMMING MEDALIST** On August 9, 2008, 41-year-old Dara Torres (U.S.A.) defied the years to earn a silver medal for the Americans in the pool at the Beijing Olympics, swimming the anchor leg in the 4 x 100 m freestyle relay.

●**YOUNGEST GOLFER TO MAKE THE CUT AT THE U.S. MASTERS** Matteo Manassero (Italy, b. April 19, 1993) was just 16 years 355 days old when he made it through the first two rounds of the U.S. Masters tournament held at Augusta National Golf Club, Georgia, U.S.A., on April 9, 2010.

○**Youngest driver to win an F1 championship point** Three years before he was crowned World Champion, Sebastian Vettel became the youngest driver to claim a point in the Championship, finishing eighth in the U.S. Grand Prix on June 17, 2007, aged 19 years 349 days.

Youngest driver to finish an F1 world championship race For the new drivers on the grid, the first aim is to get around the track without crashing out. On July 26, 2009, Jaime Alguersuari (Spain, b. March 23, 1990) became the youngest driver to pass this test, racing home in 15th place in the Hungarian Grand Prix, aged 19 years 125 days.

QUICK SILVER When Dara Torres (U.S.A., top) won silver at Beijing 2008 to become the **oldest Olympic swimming medalist**, she broke a record that had stood for a century, since 38-year-old William Robinson (UK) won silver at the 1908 Olympic Games.

WHEN IT COMES TO SINKING PUTTS AND POTS, THESE YOUTHS ARE IN A LEAGUE OF THEIR OWN. . . .

Youngest hole-in-one golfer (male):
Christian Carpenter (U.S.A.), 4 years 195 days on December 18, 1999.

Youngest hole-in-one golfer (female):
Soona Lee-Tolley (U.S.A.), 5 years 103 days on July 1, 2007.

Youngest century-break snooker player:
Michael White (UK), 9 years 268 days on March 24, 2001.

Youngest 147-break snooker player:
Ronnie O'Sullivan (UK), 15 years 98 days on March 13, 1991.

○**YOUNGEST F1 CHAMPION** Sebastian Vettel (Germany, b. July 3, 1987) clinched his first Formula One title aged 23 years 134 days when he won the Abu Dhabi Grand Prix, UAE, on November 14, 2010, the last day of the season. Before the race, he was trailing Championship leader Fernando Alonso (Spain) by 15 points, but his last-gasp victory saw him just edge past his rival in the standings.

●**Youngest winner of the Le Mans 24-hour race** Before switching to F1, Alexander Wurz (Austria, b. February 15, 1974) cut his teeth in the world's oldest and most prestigious endurance race: the Le Mans 24 Hours. On June 15–16, 1996, driving for Joest Racing (Germany), he became the French event's youngest-ever winner, aged just 22 years 123 days.

○**Youngest driver to win a NASCAR race** On June 28, 2009, Joey Logano (U.S.A., b. May 24, 1990) became the youngest driver to win a NASCAR event, speeding to victory in the Lenox Industrial Tools 301 at New Hampshire Motor Speedway, U.S.A., aged 19 years 35 days.

●**Oldest player to make a FIFA World Cup finals debut** David James (UK) made his first FIFA World Cup finals appearance at the ripe old age of 39 years 322 days, playing in goal for England against Algeria in Cape Town, South Africa, on June 18, 2010. The game ended 0–0, giving James a clean sheet on his debut.

The crater of the shield volcano Mount Nyiragongo in the Democratic Republic of the Congo holds the world's **largest lava lake**, measuring 820 ft. (250 m) across.

●Youngest goalkeeper to appear in a UEFA Champions League final Iker Casillas (Spain) appeared for Real Madrid against Valencia (both Spain) at the age of 19 years 4 days at the Stade de France in Paris, France, on May 24, 2000. Casillas kept a clean sheet in Real's 3–0 victory.

Oldest goal scorer in a UEFA Champions League final AC Milan (Italy) captain Paolo Maldini (Italy, b. June 26, 1968) was 36 years 333 days old when he scored the opener in the Champions League final against Liverpool (England) on May 25, 2005. This was the **fastest Champions League goal ever**, coming in the first minute; despite leading 3–0 at halftime, Milan went on to lose on penalties.

Oldest player in a FIFA World Cup Roger Milla (Cameroon, b. May 20, 1952) played against Russia at U.S.A. '94 on June 28, 1994, aged 42 years 39 days. During the game, he also scored, becoming the **oldest scorer in the FIFA World Cup finals**.

●Youngest golfer to win the U.S. Masters One of the greatest golfers of all time, Tiger Woods (U.S.A., b. December 30, 1975) was just 21 years 104 days old when he won the 1997 U.S. Masters at Augusta National Golf Club, Georgia, U.S.A., on April 13, 1997. Woods now has 14 major championships to his name, including three further U.S. Masters: 2001, 2002, and 2005.

DISTANCE & DURATION

Longest running race The 1929 transcontinental foot race from New York City to Los Angeles, U.S.A., covered a lung-busting 3,635 miles (5,850 km). Finnish-born Johnny Salo won in 79 days, with a time of 525 hr. 57 min. 20 sec., placing him just 2 min. 47 sec. ahead of Pietro "Peter" Gavuzzi (UK).

●Longest individual Test cricket innings During a Test match against the West Indies played in Barbados on January 17–23, 1958, Pakistan opener Hanif Mohammad made up for a poor first-innings score of 17 by hitting 337 runs in a heroic knock that saw him remain at the crease for 16 hr. 10 min.

 On December 18, 2009, U.S. scientists revealed that they had filmed the **deepest volcanic eruption** on record, more than 3,900 ft. (1,200 m) down in the Pacific Ocean, near Samoa. The footage, of the West Mata volcano, was captured by a robotic submersible.

449,061: Distance in miles you will travel in the 18,193 hours of your life spent in an automobile—enough to drive to the Moon and then travel around it 31 times at an average speed of 24.7 mi./hr.

● **MOST SKI JUMPS OVER 200 M** One of the greatest ski jumpers in the history of the sport, four-time World Champion Adam Małysz (Poland) passed the 200-m (656-ft.) mark a record 106 times in competition between 1994 and 2011. His longest jump ever was 225 m (738 ft.) in 2003, which places him joint 10th in the all-time list.

Adam is the only ski jumper to win the World Cup three times in a row (2001–03).

● **SHORTEST F1 CIRCUIT** By lap distance, the prestigious Circuit de Monaco in Monte Carlo, Monaco, is the shortest on the Formula One race calendar. The course, which has staged races since 1929, has varied in length over the years, with its shortest incarnation between 1929 and 1979, when it measured just 1.9 miles (3.1 km) in length.

GOING THE DISTANCE Before the Queensberry Rules brought in round limits in 1867, Jack Jones defeated Patsy Tunney (both UK) in a fight lasting 276 rounds in Cheshire, UK, in 1825—the **most rounds in a boxing match**.

●**LONGEST NFL KICK RETURN BY AN OFFENSIVE LINEMAN** Although better known for his strength than his speed, 313-lb. (142-kg) New England Patriots lineman Dan Connolly (U.S.A.) returned a kick 71 yards against the Green Bay Packers in Foxboro, Massachusetts, U.S.A., on December 19, 2010. He made it to the 4-yard line, only just missing out on a touchdown.

●**LONGEST FEMALE GRAND SLAM TENNIS MATCH** At the 2011 Australian Open, Francesca Schiavone (Italy) beat Svetlana Kuznetsova (Russia) in an epic last-16 match on January 23, 2011. Level after two sets, the pair took 30 games to settle the third, with the Italian finally winning through 4–6, 6–1, 16–14 after 4 hr. 44 min.

Longest golf putt in a major tournament Two players have managed to hole out from 110 ft.(33.5 m) in a major: Jack Nicklaus (U.S.A.) in the 1964 Tournament of Champions and Nick Price (Zimbabwe) in the 1992 U.S. PGA.

Longest drop goal in Rugby Union Gerald Hamilton Brand scored from 255 ft.(77.7 m) for South Africa against England at Twickenham, UK, in 1932.

●**Longest nine-innings baseball game** On August 18, 2006, the second game of a double-header between fierce rivals the New York Yankees and the Boston Red Sox (both U.S.A.) lasted 4 hr. 45 min. at Fenway Park, Boston, U.S.A., with the Yankees finally emerging victorious by a score of 14–11.

●**Most consecutive 30-win seasons to start an NHL goaltender career** Since joining the National Hockey League with the New York Rangers (U.S.A.), Henrik Lundqvist (Sweden) has become the only goaltender to record five straight seasons with 30-plus wins, achieving the run from 2005/06 to 2009/10.

●**Longest soccer tournament** With the first ball kicked on January 2 and the trophy lifted on November 14, the 2010 Copa Telmex in Mexico was equivalent in duration to more than 11 back-to-back FIFA World Cups! The competition also qualified as the ○**largest football tournament**, with 201,287 players and 11,777 teams competing for glory.

○FARTHEST HAMMER THROW On July 6, 2010, Anita Wlodarczyk (Poland) gave the performance of her career to achieve a throw of 256 ft. 10 in. (78.3 m) at the Enea Cup in Bydgoszcz, Poland, thus breaking her own 2009 world record of 255 ft. 9 in. (77.96 m).

●LONGEST-SERVING PREMIER LEAGUE SOCCER MANAGER Sir Alex Ferguson (UK) has managed Manchester United (England) for all 19 seasons since the birth of the Premier League in 1992.

●LONGEST PRO TENNIS MATCH On June 22–24, 2010, in the first round of the 2010 Wimbledon Championships (UK), John Isner (U.S.A.) and Nicolas Mahut (France) played out the longest match in tennis history, both in terms of time and number of games. After 11 hr. 5 min. on the court, and 183 games, Isner finally broke Mahut's spirited resistance, winning 6–4, 3–6, 6–7, 7–6, 70–68!

Longest FA Cup tie When Alvechurch met Oxford City (both UK) in the fourth qualifying round of the FA Cup in November 1971, the tie went to a record five replays, with Alvechurch breaking the deadlock after 11 hours of play by winning the sixth game 1–0.

....

The **smallest spider** is the Patu marplesi (family *Symphytognathidae*) of Western Samoa. A male found at around 2,000 ft.(600 m) in Madolelei on the island of Upolu in January 1965 had a leg-span of just 0.017 in. (0.43 mm)—about the size of a period on this page.

....

○**Longest soccer penalty shootout** In a nail-biting finish, the final of the 2005 Namibian Cup had to be settled by a record-breaking 48 penalty kicks, with KK Palace holding their nerve to defeat the Civics 17–16, following a 2–2 draw in regular time.

●**Longest unbeaten run at home by a soccer manager** Wherever he has managed, José Mourinho's (Portugal) home ground has been a fortress. Incredibly, he did not taste defeat on home soil for over nine years, between February 22, 2002, and March 12, 2011, during which time he managed Porto (Portugal), Chelsea (England), Inter Milan (Italy), and Real Madrid (Spain). The record run finally came to an end on April 2, 2011, when Real Madrid lost 1–0 to Sporting Gijón (Spain).

SPORTING FIRSTS

●**First official 147 break in snooker** On January 22, 1955, Joe Davis (UK) achieved an officially ratified maximum break against Willie Smith (UK) in London. The 147 break requires a player to pot all the balls in one turn and in a specified order—15 reds (15 points), each followed by the black (105 points), and then all six colors (27 points). The **first televised 147** was achieved by Steve Davis (UK) at the Lada Classic on January 11, 1982.

First basketball game on television Basketball hit U.S. TV screens on February 28, 1940, when Fordham's match against the University of Pittsburgh (both U.S.A.) was aired by broadcaster NBC. Pittsburgh won 57–37.

●**FIRST PERSON TO RUN A MILE IN LESS THAN FOUR MINUTES** On May 6, 1954, Roger Bannister (UK) became the first athlete to run a sub-four-minute mile. In front of a 3,000-strong crowd at Oxford University's Iffley Road track, the 25-year-old recorded a time of 3 min. 59.4 sec., achieving what was then believed by many to be an impossible feat.

Far larger than a period, the **heaviest spider** was a captive female goliath bird-eating spider (*Theraphosa blondi*) named Rosi, who weighed 6.17 oz. (175 g) on July 27, 2007 and belonged to Walter Baumgartner of Andorf, Austria.

FIRST WILDCARD ENTRANT TO WIN A TENNIS GRAND SLAM In 2001, Goran Ivanisevic (Croatia) won the men's singles at the Wimbledon Championships (UK). Ranked 125th in the world, Ivanisevic entered the competition as a wildcard and beat Pat Rafter (Australia) 6–3, 3–6, 6–3, 2–6, 9–7 in a nail-biting final.

●**First broadcast use of Hawk-Eye** Hawk-Eye, which tracks and predicts the path of a ball in flight using cameras placed around the playing field, has revolutionized sport. Developed in 1999, Hawk-Eye made its TV debut in 2001 in an England–Pakistan Test match at Lord's cricket ground in London, UK.

●**First quadruple jump in ice-skating** On March 25, 1988, Canadian Kurt Browning landed a toe loop jump with four aerial rotations at the World Championships in Hungary.

First opening kickoff return for a touchdown in the Super Bowl In Super Bowl XLI, played on February 4, 2007, Chicago Bears receiver Devin Hester (U.S.A.) returned the opening kickoff the length of the field for a touchdown. Despite the best start in the history of the Super Bowl, the Bears went on to lose the game to the Indianapolis Colts 29–17.

Ivanisevic hit 213 aces at Wimbledon 2001, the most ever at a Grand Slam.

4 MILLION: Tennis balls used at the Wimbledon Championships in your lifetime. An amazing 52,000 were supplied by Slazenger in 2010 alone—but what happened to them all afterwards? Each year, the All-England Tennis Club sells the used balls to raise money for charity.

Q. WHO MADE THE ●FIRST DOUBLE CENTURY IN A ONE-DAY INTERNATIONAL?

A. No, not Richards, Lara, or Botham. In fact, it was only in 2010 that a player finally hit a double ton, with India's Sachin Tendulkar making 200 off 147 balls vs. South Africa.

FIRST DRIVER TO WIN THE INDIANAPOLIS 500, DAYTONA 500, AND FORMULA 1 WORLD TITLE Mario Andretti (U.S.A.) is the only driver to win the Indy 500 (1969), Daytona 500 (1967), and Formula One world championship (1978)—three of motorsport's most prestigious titles.

FIRST ENGLISH PREMIER LEAGUE SOCCER TEAM TO GO UNBEATEN IN A SEASON In the 2003/04 season, Arsenal FC emerged unbeaten from all 38 league games, winning 26 and drawing 12. In total, they netted 73 goals and conceded just 26, finishing the season with 90 points following a 2–1 win over Leicester City on May 15, 2004.

FIRST NFL TEAM TO GO UNBEATEN IN A REGULAR SEASON The New England Patriots (U.S.A.) achieved a 16–0 record in 2007, becoming the first team to finish the regular season undefeated since the NFL switched to a 16-game schedule in 1978. The Patriots eventually reached the Super Bowl, but lost 17–14 to the New York Giants.

DECADE AT THE TOP Joe Louis (U.S.A.) was the **first boxing champion to reign for a decade**, holding the heavyweight title for 11 years 252 days (1937–49). Supermiddleweight Joe Calzaghe (UK) achieved the feat in 1997–2007.

FIRST CHAMPION BOXER TO GO UNDEFEATED IN A CAREER Rocky Marciano (U.S.A., right), is the only champion of any division to have won every fight of his professional career, from March 17, 1947, to September 21, 1955. Of his 49 fights, 43 were by either knock-out or stoppage.

Tony Hawk won 16 medals in his X Games career.

FIRST 900 ON A SKATEBOARD On June 27, 1999, skateboard legend Tony Hawk (U.S.A.) became the first person to achieve a 900 in competition at the ESPN X Games in San Francisco, U.S.A. The trick— two-and-a-half 360° aerial spins—is one of the most difficult in vert skateboarding.

OLLIE WHO? Tony Hawk may be the biggest name in skateboarding, but the first ever board trick came long before his time, when in 1976 Alan Gelfand (U.S.A.) pioneered the famous "Ollie," one of the most popular jumps in the sport.

● **FIRST PERSON TO RUN 100 M IN LESS THAN 10 SECONDS** At the 1968 Olympics, Jim Hines (U.S.A.) earned the title of "fastest man on the planet" when he broke through the 10-second barrier in the 100 m event. With a time of 9.95 seconds, Hines stormed to Olympic gold and set a new record that remained unbroken for 15 years.

● **First golden goal at a FIFA World Cup** On June 28, 1998, French defender Laurent Blanc scored the first golden goal in World Cup history in a match against Paraguay in Lens, France. Blanc scored in the 113th minute, in the second period of extra time, to give France a 1–0 win and send them into a quarter-final match against European rivals Italy. France went on to win the competition, defeating the favorites, Brazil, 3–0 in the final.

● **First ice hockey team to win world and Olympic titles in the same year** Having already taken gold at the 2006 Turin Olympics, Sweden's ice hockey team went on to win the world championship with a 4–0 shutout of the Czechs in Riga, Latvia, on May 21, 2006.

MARATHONS

Fastest marathon The official IAAF marathon world record is held by Haile Gebrselassie (Ethiopia), who raced home in 2 hr. 3 min. 59 sec. in Berlin, Germany, on September 28, 2008. *(See also box on p. 490 and p. 438.)*

Fastest London Marathon The fastest man over the London course is Samuel Wanjiru (Kenya), who won the event in 2 hr. 5 min. 10 sec. on April 26, 2009.

Set on April 13, 2003, Paula Radcliffe's (UK) time of 2 hr. 15 min. 25 sec. remains not only the fastest London Marathon (UK) by a female runner but also the fastest marathon by a woman outright (see also p. 469).

○ **MOST MONEY RAISED BY A MARATHON RUNNER** Marathon man Steve Chalke (UK) raised over £2,000,000 ($3,264,480) in sponsorship money for the charity Oasis UK by completing the Virgin London Marathon in London, UK, on April 17, 2011. In raising the huge sum, Steve beat his own previous record of £1,841,138 ($3,669,325), which he set at the same event, for the same charity, four years earlier on April 22, 2007.

●**Fastest Tokyo Marathon** Viktor Rothlin (Switzerland) completed the Tokyo Marathon in Tokyo, Japan, in a record 2 hr. 7 min. 23 sec. on February 17, 2008.

Japan's own Mizuho Nasukawa became the fastest female over the distance the following year, recording a time of 2 hr. 25 min. 38 sec. on March 22, 2009.

Fastest New York Marathon On November 4, 2001, Tesfaye Jifar (Ethiopia) won the New York Marathon in 2 hr. 7 min. 43 sec., setting a record time that remains unbeaten over a decade later.

Kenyan runner Margaret Okayo set the women's record on November 2, 2003, finishing in 2 hr. 22 min. 31 sec.

●**Fastest Chicago Marathon** Samuel Wanjiru (Kenya, see below) ran the Chicago Marathon in a time of 2 hr. 5 min. 41 sec. on October 11, 2009, thus breaking Khalid Khannouchi's (U.S.A.) 10-year-old course record of 2 hr. 5 min. 42 sec. by just one second.

Paula Radcliffe (UK, see p. 469 and p. 489) holds the female record, winning in 2 hr. 17 min. 18 sec. on October 13, 2002.

○**MOST WINS OF THE WORLD MARATHON MAJORS (MALE)** The World Marathon Majors comprises annual races in London (UK), Berlin (Germany), Boston, Chicago and New York (all U.S.A.), with athletes scoring points for top-five finishes over two calendar years. Kenya's Samuel Kamau Wanjiru (1986–2011) is the only man to have won the series twice, in 2008–09 and 2009–10.

FAST FINISH On April 18, 2011, Kenya's Geoffrey Mutai won the Boston Marathon (U.S.A.) in 2 hr. 3 min. 2 sec., beating Gebrselassie's world record time. However, his effort was not ratified, as the IAAF does not recognize times set in Boston due to the steep drops in elevation.

The **largest hand-forged horseshoe** is 1 ft. 10 in. (56 cm) tall and 2 ft. (61.5 cm) wide and was created by six clients and two employees of Caritas Tagesstätte Krumbach (all Austria) on June 21, 2008.

○ **MOST LINKED RUNNERS TO COMPLETE A MARATHON** Paris Centipede (UK)—a team of 53 runners tied together—completed the 2011 Paris Marathon in Paris, France, on April 10, 2011, raising $49,000 for charity.

● **FASTEST MARATHON BY A MARCHING BAND** The 20 musicians of the Huddersfield University Marching Band (UK) completed the 2011 Virgin London Marathon in 7 hr. 55 min. in London, UK, on April 17, 2011.

Oldest person to complete a marathon on each continent Margaret Hagerty (U.S.A.), who ran a marathon on all seven continents between 1995 and 2004, began her quest aged 72 years 225 days and finished aged 81 years 101 days. The ● **fastest marathon on each continent and at the North Pole (female)** was 324 days by Ginny Turner (U.S.A.), starting with the North Pole race on April 8, 2006, and finishing on King George Island, Antarctica, on February 26, 2007.

● **Fastest completion of 10 marathons in 10 days (male)** Adam Holland (UK) ran 10 marathons in just 32 hr. 47 min. 3 sec. to win the 2009 Brathay Challenge, held at Brathay Hall, Ambleside, UK, between May 8 and 17, 2009. Adam averaged 3 hr. 16 min. 42 sec. per marathon, and beat the previous record holder, Steve Edwards (who came second in 2009), by over two-and-a-half hours.

● **Fastest marathon barefoot** Running without shoes, Abebe Bikila of Ethiopia covered the marathon distance in a (blistering) 2 hr. 15 min. 16.2 sec. at the 1960 Olympic Games in Rome, Italy, on September 10, 1960.

○ **MOST WINS OF THE WORLD MARATHON MAJORS (FEMALE)** Irina Mikitenko (Germany) is the most successful female runner in World Marathon Majors history, topping the leaderboard in both 2007–08 and 2008–09.

Huaso ex-Faithful, the thoroughbred that made the **highest jump by a horse**, was wearing regular horseshoes. On February 5, 1949, the former Chilean racehorse leapt to a height of 8 ft. 1.25 in. (2.47 m)!

2011 VIRGIN LONDON MARATHON: NEW WORLD RECORDS

While marathon running is a serious business for elite athletes, for others it is a great excuse to have some fun on the run—and where better to have it than at the world's premier marathon event: the London Marathon? Since the first London Marathon in 1981, athletes of all ages, shapes, and sizes have donned their running shoes (and many an outrageous costume) to raise some cash for charity. Here, we take a look at some of the key characters from the class of 2011 . . .

A	●	**Fastest in a bomb disposal suit**	John Bedford (UK)	9 hr. 40 min. 1 sec.
B	○	**Fastest on crutches**	John Sandford Hart (UK)	6 hr. 24 min. 48 sec.
C	●	**Fastest by a parent and child (mixed sex, aggregate)**	Libby and Richard Collinson (both UK)	6 hr. 22 min. 5 sec.
D	●	**Fastest by a married couple (aggregate)**	Jez and Lucy Mancer (both UK)	5 hr. 46 min. 53 sec.
E	○	**Fastest carrying a 60-lb. pack**	Carl Andrew Creasey (UK)	4 hr. 50 min. 56 sec.
F	●	**Most Rubik's Cubes solved (100)**	Uli Kilian (Germany)	4 hr. 45 min. 43 sec.
G	●	**Fastest as Mr. Potato Head**	Peter Barlow (UK)	4 hr. 17 min. 38 sec.
H	●	**Fastest in a wedding dress**	Eleanor Franks (UK)	4 hr. 11 min. 1 sec.
I	●	**Fastest as a vegetable**	Julie Tapley (UK)	4 hr. 6 min. 17 sec.
J	●	**Fastest as a Roman soldier**	Les Slinn (UK)	4 hr. 5 min. 34 sec.
K	○	**Fastest carrying a 40-lb. pack**	Lee Riley (UK)	4 hr. 1 min. 17 sec.
L	●	**Fastest as a nun**	Ben Bradley (UK)	4 hr. 0 min. 28 sec.
M	●	**Fastest as an astronaut**	Darren Cox (UK)	3 hr. 55 min. 21 sec.
N	●	**Fastest in a gas mask**	Andy McMahon (UK)	3 hr. 54 min. 55 sec.
O	●	**Fastest as a bottle (male)**	Gavin Rees (UK)	3 hr. 53 min. 26 sec.
P	●	**Fastest as a gingerbread man**	David Smith (UK)	3 hr. 42 min. 20 sec.
Q	●	**Fastest as an animal (female, peacock)**	Barbara Stcherbatcheff (U.S.A.)	3 hr. 42 min. 11 sec.
R	●	**Fastest as a sailor**	Subhashis Basu (UK)	3 hr. 24 min. 12 sec.
S	○	**Fastest as a TV character (male, Captain James T. Kirk)**	Simon Bryant (UK)	3 hr. 21 min. 20 sec.
T	●	**Fastest as a fairy (female)**	Emily Foran (UK)	3 hr. 20 min. 52 sec.
U	●	**Fastest as a Viking**	Ben Afforselles (UK)	3 hr. 12 min. 11 sec.
V	○	**Fastest as a jester**	Alexander Scherz (Switzerland)	3 hr. 11 min. 57 sec.
W	●	**Fastest as a fairy (male)**	David Hellard (UK)	3 hr. 10 min. 56 sec.
X	●	**Fastest in a police uniform**	Paul Swan (UK)	3 hr. 9 min. 52 sec.
Y	○	**Fastest as an animal (male, ostrich)**	Martin Indge (UK)	3 hr. 4 min. 0 sec.
Z	○	**Fastest as Dennis the Menace**	David Ross (UK)	3 hr. 2 min. 30 sec.
AA	○	**Fastest as a nurse (male)**	Kevin Harvey (UK)	2 hr. 52 min. 26 sec.
BB	○	**Fastest as a superhero (male, Superman)**	David Stone (UK)	2 hr. 42 min. 46 sec.

Marathons

STRENGTH & ENDURANCE

○**Most boxing titles in different divisions** Manny Pacquiao (Philippines) has won world titles in eight weight divisions: WBC Super Welterweight, Flyweight, Super Featherweight and Lightweight; The Ring Featherweight; IBF Super Bantamweight; IBO and The Ring Light Welterweight; and WBO Welterweight.

●**Fastest win of the Tour du Léman** The annual Tour du Léman à l'Aviron is the **longest rowing race** in the world, covering 99 miles (160 km) around the circumference of Lake Léman in Switzerland—equivalent to crossing the sea between England and France five times without a break. The fastest race time on record is 11 hr. 55 min. 19 sec., achieved by Matthias Auer, Olaf Behrend, Jochen Domscheit, Christian Klandt, and Markus Neuman (all Germany), who won the men's coxed fours category in the 2007 race.

●**Farthest breath-hold swim under ice (fins and wetsuit)** Nikolay Linder (Germany) swam 354 ft. (108 m) under ice 1 ft. (31 cm) thick at Lake Weissensee, Austria, on January 15, 2011, staying under the freezing water for 1 min 16 sec.

●**MOST RUNNERS IN AN ULTRA-MARATHON** On May 30, 2010, a record 14,343 runners hit the road for the 85th Comrades Marathon, a grueling 56-mile (89.28-km) race from Pietermaritzburg to Durban, South Africa. The men's race was won by Stephen Muzhingi (Zimbabwe), while Elena Nurgalieva (Russia) was the leading female.

○**MOST UFC MIDDLEWEIGHT CHAMPIONSHIPS** As of February 5, 2011, mixed martial artist Anderson Silva (Brazil, far left) has won a record nine Middleweight title bouts in the Ultimate Fighting Championship. Known as "The Spider," he is a black belt in Judo, Tae Kwon Do, and Brazilian Jiu-Jitsu.

The **largest bunch of grapes** on record weighed a hefty 20 lb. 11.5 oz. (9.4 kg) and was grown by Bozzolo Y. Perut Ltda of Santiago, Chile, in 1984.

336: Hours you will spend kissing in a lifetime. That's two weeks—equivalent to a kiss that begins with the opening serve of the Wimbledon tennis championships (UK) and doesn't end until the winning shot!

BOXING CLEVER Another boxer with a killer punch is Tyrone Brunson (U.S.A.), who began his career with 19 first-round KOs in a row! His record run ended with a draw against Antonio Soriano (Mexico) on August 15, 2008.

●**MOST FLASH KNOCKOUTS** A flash knockout is when a boxer KOs his opponent less than a minute into a fight. Mike Tyson (U.S.A.) did this nine times in his pro career (1985–2006), against Trent Singleton (U.S.A.) in 52 sec., Ricardo Spain (U.S.A.) in 39 sec., Michael Johnson (U.S.A.) in 39 sec., Robert Colay (U.S.A.) in 37 sec., Sterling Benjamin (Trinidad & Tobago) in 54 sec., Mark Young (U.S.A.) in 50 sec., Marvis Frazier (U.S.A.) in 30 sec., Lou Savarese (U.S.A.) in 38 sec., and Clifford Etienne (U.S.A., left) in 49 sec.!

●**Farthest breath-hold swim under water (female)** In Mexico on January 7, 2011, Ai Futaki (Japan) swam under water with and without fins for distances of 328 ft. (100 m) and 295 ft. (90 m), respectively.

●**Most wins of the Yukon Quest** The Yukon Quest sled dog race, which runs 1,000 miles (1,600 km) between Fairbanks, Alaska, U.S.A., and Whitehorse, Yukon, Canada, has been won four times each by Hans Gatt (Canada), in 2002–04 and 2010, and Lance Mackey (U.S.A.), in 2005–08.

●**Most wins of the Skyrunner World Series (female)** Three athletes have won the women's Skyrunner World Series twice: Angela Mudge (UK) in 2006 and 2007; Corinne Favre (France) in 2005 and 2008; and Emanuela Brizio (Italy) in 2009 and 2010.

Bozzolo's grapes would have provided ample ammunition for champion grape-spitter Anders Rasmussen (Norway), who achieved the world's **longest grape spit**—an astonishing 28 ft. 7.25 in. (8.72 m)—at Myra, Arendal, Norway, on September 4, 2004.

Strength & Endurance

Aneta was the first Polish woman to lift 500 kg (1,102 lb.)!

● **MOST WINS OF THE STRONGWOMAN WORLD CHAMPIONSHIPS** Aneta Florczyk (Poland) began powerlifting in 1998 at just 16 years old, but by 2003 she had already earned her first Strongwoman world title. Since then, she has achieved three further wins in the competition, in 2005, 2006, and 2008, to become its most successful athlete.

FROM POWERFUL WOMEN TO MUSCLE-BOUND MEN, CHECK OUT THE WORLD'S STRONGEST, YOUNGEST, OLDEST, AND HEAVIEST!

○ **Most wins of the Strongman World Championships:**
Mariusz Pudzianowski (Poland)—five, in 2002, 2003, 2005, 2007, and 2008.

Youngest entrant in the Strongman World Championships:
Kevin Nee (U.S.A.)—20 years 37 days old at the 2005 competition held in China.

● **Oldest bodybuilder:**
Ray Moon (Australia)—81 years old at the 2010 NABBA championships held in Australia.

Heaviest living athlete:
Sumo wrestler Emmanuel "Manny" Yarborough (U.S.A.)—708 lb. (321 kg).

The **longest knitted scarf** is 11,364 ft. (3,463.73 m) in length and was completed after 23 years of knitting by Helge Johansen (Norway) in Oslo, Norway, on November 10, 2006.

Discover more tough guys on p. 178.

MOST KING OF THE MOUNTAINS TITLES IN THE TOUR DE FRANCE Richard Virenque (France) has been crowned King of the Mountains seven times, claiming the famous red-and-white polka-dot jersey in 1994–97, 1999, and 2003–04.

●**MOST WINS OF THE SKYRUNNER WORLD SERIES (MALE)** The annual Skyrunner series of high-altitude endurance races has been won three times each by the Catalan athletes Kilian Jornet Burgada (pictured), in 2007–09, and Agustí Roc Amador, in 2002–04.

Fastest crossing of the U.S.A. by bicycle In the 1992 Race Across America (RAAM), cyclist Rob Kish (U.S.A.) pedaled 2,911 miles (4,685 km) from Irvine, California, to Savannah, Georgia, in 8 days 3 hr. 11 min.—a record that still stands today. The race is one of the most arduous of all cycling ultra-marathons, requiring competitors to cover up to 22 hours per day with little rest or sleep.

●**Most weight lifted by arm curls in one hour** Multiple record holder Eamonn Keane (Ireland) curled a total of 51,314 lb. 12 oz. (23,276 kg) in an hour in Dublin, Ireland, on October 5, 2007. He performed 1,058 reps of a 48-lb. 8-oz. (22-kg) weight.

WINNING WAYS

●**Most match wins in the Rugby Union Six Nations Championship** Since the Five Nations became Six, with the addition of Italy in 2000, France has claimed 44 wins up to the end of the 2011 tournament. Despite England's victory that year, France still holds the ○**most Six Nations titles**, with five, in 2002, 2004, 2006–07; and 2010.

In 1995, Belarusian artist Alexander Kishchenko completed the **largest piece of needlework**—a hand-woven tapestry with a total area measuring 2,863 ft.^{2} (266 m^2).

○**MOST CONSECUTIVE WINS OF A FINA DIVING WORLD CHAMPIONSHIP** Jingjing Guo (China) topped the podium in both the individual and the synchronized 3 m platform in 2001, 2003, 2005, 2007, and 2009. Between her last two victories, the talented diver also won gold in both categories at the 2008 Olympics in Beijing, China.

○**Most Rugby Union Tri-Nations titles** New Zealand has won the annual three-way contest with Australia and South Africa a record 10 times, in 1996–97, 1999, 2002–03, 2005–08, and 2010.

○**Most Davis Cup tennis titles** The U.S. Davis Cup team has dominated the Davis Cup over the years, recording 32 wins between 1900 and 2007.

○**Most cricket World Cup titles** Since the cricket World Cup began in 1975, the standout team has been Australia, with a total of four wins from nine tournaments: the first in 1987 and the other three, in a row, in 1999, 2003, and 2007.

○**Most Indian Premier League titles** Cricket's glitziest tournament, the Indian Premier League, started in 2008 and has been won by three separate teams, the Rajasthan Royals (2008), the Deccan Chargers (2009), and the Chennai Super Kings (2010).

●**LATEST GOAL TO WIN A FIFA WORLD CUP** In the FIFA World Cup final on July 11, 2010, Spain midfielder Andrés Iniesta (far left) made history by netting the winner in the 116th minute to claim the Cup for Spain. The 1–0 victory, over the Netherlands in South Africa, was Spain's first ever World Cup title and the first by a European team on another continent.

MOST MOTO GP WORLD TITLES Valentino Rossi (Italy) has won motorcycle racing's most prestigious prize a record six times, in 2002–05, and 2008–09. He has also won the 125 cc, 250 cc, and 500 cc titles, giving him a total of nine different world championships in a glittering career that began in karting as a five-year-old.

○**Most Solheim Cup golf wins** The female version of golf's Ryder Cup is contested every two years between Europe and the U.S.A.'s top players, with the U.S.A. coming out on top eight times, in 1990, 1994, 1996, 1998, 2002, 2005, 2007, and 2009.

●**Most kiteboard freestyle World Championships** The most Kiteboard Pro World Tour Freestyle World Championships won by a male rider is two, by Sebastien Garat (France), in 2006–07. The competition's most successful female is Gisela Pulido (Spain) with three wins, in 2004–06.

●**Most consecutive wins of the FIS Speed Ski World Cup** North America's fastest speed skier, Tracie Sachs (U.S.A.) won Alpine skiing's greatest prize a record five times in a row, between 2003 and 2007.

Most ESPN Summer X Games medals BMX biker and rally driver Dave Mirra (U.S.A.) has won more Summer X Games medals than any other athlete, with 24 as of March 2010.

○**MOST CAREER STEEPLECHASE WINS** By the end of the 2011 racing season, the 15-times champion jump jockey Tony McCoy (UK) had ridden a record 3,368 winners in the course of his career. McCoy brought up an unprecedented 3,000th win on the back of Restless D'Artaix at Plumpton (UK) on February 9, 2009.

McCoy has been the British jump racing champion every year since 1996.

NEW START Proving that everyone can be a winner, the Caltech Beavers (U.S.A.) college basketball team broke a 310-game losing streak on February 22, 2011, with a 46–45 win over Occidental College (U.S.A.). None of the players were alive when the team last won—in 1985.

○**MOST NBA CHAMPIONSHIPS** The Boston Celtics (U.S.A.) are the most successful team in basketball history, winning the NBA title 17 times, in 1956–57, 1958–66, 1967–69, 1973–74, 1975–76, 1980–81, 1983–84, 1985–86, and 2007–08. They have also finished runner-up on four occasions, in 1957–58, 1984–85, 1986–87, and 2009–10, when the Los Angeles Lakers (U.S.A.) beat them 4–3 in the NBA Finals, the seven-game season finale.

●**Most wins in a WNBA season** In 2010, the Seattle Storm (U.S.A.) won 28 of 34 games on their way to winning the women's National Basketball Association championship.

○**Most career wins, NHRA drag racing** John Force (U.S.A.) has finished first in 132 races as of the end of the 2010 season.

○**Most hockey Asia Cup titles (male)** Two nations have won the Asia Cup a record three times: Pakistan and South Korea. Pakistan led the way in the early years, blitzing their way to three successive titles, in 1982, 1985, and 1989, each time defeating India in the final. South Korea enjoyed wins of their own in 1993 (again against India), 1999, and, more

On November 15, 1995, Aleksandr Bendikov (Belarus) built the world's **largest coin pyramid**, consisting of 880 coins stacked on the edge of a coin free-standing vertically on a table.

○**MOST DAKAR RALLY WINS BY A MANUFACTURER** Between 1985 and 2007, a Mitsubishi Pajero (Japan) won the Dakar Rally on 12 occasions—an exceptional record in what is considered to be the world's most punishing off-road endurance race, covering 3,107 miles (5,000 km) through the deserts, canyons, and mountains of South America. (The rally was formerly held between Paris, France, and Dakar, Senegal, but was relocated in 2009 for security reasons.)

recently, in 2009. Incredibly, India has been in seven out of the tournament's eight finals, winning in 2003 and 2007.

●**Most D1 Grand Prix titles** The only driver to win the Japanese Professional Drift Grand Series twice is Youichi Imamura (Japan), in 2003 and 2009.

○**Most Africa Cup of Nations titles** Egypt has proved itself to be the best soccer team in Africa seven times, winning the Africa Cup of Nations in 1957, 1959, 1986, 1998, 2006, 2008, and 2010.

○**Most match wins in the UEFA Champions League** Between September 15, 1993, and May 4, 2011, Manchester United (England) notched up 93 European wins.

●**Most UEFA Champions League titles (country)** As of April 2011, the Champions League (formerly the European Cup) has been won 12 times each by teams from Spain and Italy. Spain's first triumph came through Real Madrid in 1956, while its most recent was in 2009, with Barcelona. Italy won for the first time with AC Milan in 1963, and is home to the 2010 champions, Inter Milan.

GREAT ACHIEVEMENTS

○**Most appearances in international hockey matches** Two-times Olympic hockey champion Teun de Nooijer (Netherlands) made 431 appearances for the Netherlands between 1994 and January 25, 2011.

Tahar Douis (Morocco) supported 12 members of the Hassani Troupe on his shoulders to form the **largest-ever human pyramid**, weighing 1,700 lb. (771 kg), at BBC TV studios in Birmingham, UK, on December 17, 1979.

●**Most consecutive tennis Grand Slam semifinals (male)** Between 2004 and 2010, Roger Federer (Switzerland) made a record 23 Grand Slam semifinal appearances in a row. His extraordinary run came to an end when he was beaten by Robin Soderling (Sweden) in the French Open quarterfinals on June 1, 2010.

●**GREATEST COMEBACK IN THE ENGLISH PREMIER LEAGUE On** February 5, 2011, Newcastle United earned a 4–4 draw with Arsenal at St. James' Park in Newcastle, UK, after coming back from 4–0 down with four goals in the last 22 minutes.

●**MOST CONSECUTIVE BWF SUPER SERIES MASTERS FINALS TITLES (SINGLES)** Badminton world No. 1 Lee Chong Wei (Malaysia) has won the Badminton World Federation Super Series Masters Finals in every year that it has been held, three times from 2008 to 2010.

●**MOST CONSECUTIVE WINS IN SPAIN'S TOP SOCCER DIVISION** Between October 16, 2010, and February 5, 2011, La Liga champions Barcelona achieved 16 league wins in a row. Spearheaded by Argentina striker Lionel Messi (pictured center), they outscored their opponents by a goal margin of 60–6.

Turn to p. 221 for more icy achievements.

With 10 victories to his name (1997, 1999–2007), Lahcen Ahansai (Morocco) holds the record for ●**most wins of the Marathon des Sables**, a six-day ultradistance running race that covers 156 miles (254 km) across the Sahara Desert in Morocco.

DANCING ON ICE From the grace of figure skating to the power of NHL ice hockey, Alex Ovechkin (Russia) of the Washington Capitals (U.S.A.) is the ●**fastest player to reach 2,000 career shots on goal**, achieving the feat in 2011 after just 4.5 seasons.

●**MOST FIGURE-SKATING TRIPLE AXELS EXECUTED IN ONE COMPETITION (FEMALE)** During the 2010 Winter Olympic Games in Vancouver, Canada, champion figure skater Mao Asada (Japan) performed the notoriously difficult triple axel—three aerial spins, shown in time-lapse photography above right—a record three times: once in her short program on February 23 and twice in her long program on February 25.

●**Most consecutive wins in Twenty20 internationals** The England cricket team won eight 20-over matches in a row between May 6, 2010, and January 12, 2011, beating Pakistan three times, Australia twice, and South Africa, New Zealand, and Sri Lanka once.

●**Most Canadian football pass receptions** The Canadian Football League (CFL) record for most career pass receptions is 1,017, by Ben Cahoon (U.S.A.) playing for the Montreal Alouettes (Canada) from 1998 to 2010.

○**Most consecutive MLB seasons with 200-plus hits** Ichiro Suzuki (Japan) has recorded at least 200 hits in a Major League Baseball season for a record 10 consecutive years while playing for the Seattle Mariners (U.S.A.) from 2001 to 2010. Ichiro also holds the record for **most hits in an MLB season**, with an impressive 262 in 2004.

●**Most Scottish Premier League goals** Scottish striker Kris Boyd scored a record 164 goals for Kilmarnock and Rangers between 2001 and 2010.

A less punishing but equally impressive feat, the ●**most wins of the IAAF Half Marathon World Championships (male)** is four, by Zersenay Tadese (Eritrea) in 2006–09.

● **MOST GAMES PLAYED IN A WNBA CAREER** Since she began her career in 1998, Tangela Smith (U.S.A.) has competed in 415 Women's National Basketball Association (WNBA) games, playing forward/center for the Sacramento Monarchs, Charlotte Sting, Phoenix Mercury, and, from February 2011, the Indiana Fever (all U.S.A.).

○ **Most goals scored by a goalkeeper** Better known for scoring goals than saving them, São Paulo FC's Rogério Ceni (both Brazil) netted his 100th career goal on March 27, 2011. His long-range free kick secured a 2–1 win over rivals Corinthians.

● **Most Rugby Union Heineken Cup points** Ronan O'Gara (Ireland) is the most prolific points-scorer in Heineken Cup history, notching up 1,196 points for his province, Munster (Ireland), from 1997 to 2009.

● **Most pass completions in an NFL season** In the 2010–11 season, Indianapolis Colts quarterback Peyton Manning (U.S.A.) set the National Football League record for most pass completions in a season, throwing 450 successful passes.

● **Most kick returns for a touchdown in an NFL career** The most successful kick returner in American football history is the Chicago Bears' receiver/return specialist Devin Hester (both U.S.A.), who had run back a record 14 kicks for touchdowns by the end of the 2010 regular season. Hester's impressive haul came from 10 punts and four kickoffs.

○ **MOST SUMO BOUTS WON IN A CALENDAR YEAR** Hakuhō Shō (Mongolia) grappled his way to a record 86 wins in his 90 regulation bouts in 2009. Promoted to yokozuna, sumo wrestling's top rank, in 2007, Hakuhō has won 18 championship tournaments in his career.

CAPTAIN MARVELS

○**Most successful Test match captain** On December 19, 2010, Ricky Ponting won his 48th Test in charge of Australia in the third Test of the Ashes series against England in Perth, Australia. He is also the ●**most successful cricket World Cup captain**—with Clive Lloyd of the West Indies—having guided his team to glory in 2003 and 2007.

Longest-serving Test match captain Prolific batsman Allan Border led out the Australia Test cricket team 93 times in a row from 1978 to 1994.

Oldest captain to win the UEFA Champions League When Paolo Maldini lifted the Champions League trophy for the second time, in 2007, he became the oldest captain ever to do so. Playing for AC Milan (Italy) at the age of 38 years 331 days, he presided over a 2–1 victory against Liverpool (UK) in Athens, Greece, on May 23. The next season, he broke his own record for the ○**oldest player to captain a UEFA Champions League team**, when, aged 39 years 239 days, his side drew 0–0 with Arsenal (UK) in London, UK, on February 20, 2008.

○**Youngest Test match cricket captain** On May 6, 2004, Tatenda Taibu (Zimbabwe) was promoted to captain of the Zimbabwe cricket team at the age of 21 years 2 days, taking the helm for a match against Sri Lanka in Harare, Zimbabwe.

Most runs in a Test match by a captain In the first of three Tests against India in 1990, England skipper Graham Gooch smashed 456 runs—333 in the first innings, 123 in the second—in a 247-run victory at Lord's, UK, on July 26–31.

●**MOST SUCCESSFUL UEFA CHAMPIONS LEAGUE CAPTAIN** Carles Puyol (Spain) is one of just two soccer captains to have lifted the UEFA Champions League trophy twice, with Spanish giants FC Barcelona in 2006 and 2009. The only captain to have matched him is the now-retired Paolo Maldini (Italy), who led AC Milan to the title in 2003 and 2007. As of going to press, however, Puyol was in the running for an historic third title, with his side set to face Manchester United (England) in the 2011 final.

For more great leaders, turn to p. 284.

MOST CONSECUTIVE AFL MATCHES AS CAPTAIN Stephen Kernahan (Australia) led the Australian Football League side Carlton 226 times between 1986 and 1997, becoming the club's all-time record goal scorer in the process, with 738 strikes.

LONGEST-SERVING INTERNATIONAL RUGBY UNION CAPTAIN Springboks legend John Smit skippered the South Africa rugby union team in a record 67 international matches between 2003 and 2009.

First man to win the FIFA World Cup as player and manager Regarded as Germany's greatest ever soccer player, Franz Beckenbauer, aka *Der Kaiser* ("The Emperor"), is the only man to have won the game's premier event both as captain and manager, in 1974 and 1990, respectively. The 1974 triumph was particularly special as it was capped by a 2–1 win over the "Total Football" of the Dutch.

Most matches as captain in the FIFA World Cup finals The diminutive genius Diego Maradona led Argentina in 16 World Cup finals matches between 1982 and 1994. In this time, he experienced numerous highs and lows, including lifting the Cup in 1986, losing the final to Beckenbauer's West Germany in 1990, and being sent home for a failed drugs test in 1994.

According to the World Health Organization's first report on global road safety, Eritrea, in Africa, is the **deadliest place to travel by road** in terms of deaths per capita, with 48 deaths per 100,000 people in 2007.

LONGEST-SERVING ICE HOCKEY CAPTAIN Steve Yzerman (Canada) served as captain of the Detroit Red Wings (U.S.A.) for 20 years, from 1986 to 2006, leading his team to three Stanley Cup championships (1997–98 and 2002). In recognition, his jersey number, 19, was retired in a ceremony at the team's Joe Louis Arena on January 2, 2007.

●**MOST CONSECUTIVE TEST WINS BY A CAPTAIN** Between December 26, 2005, and January 2, 2008, the Australia cricket captain Ricky Ponting (pictured holding the trophy) led his team on a record-equaling run of 16 consecutive Test match victories, matching the win streak achieved by his predecessor, Steve Waugh, between October 14, 1999, and February 27, 2001. Ponting skippered his side on the field in all 16 matches, whereas Waugh did so in only 15, having missed the 13th Test match because of a muscle injury.

●**Most successful Rugby Union World Cup captain (female)** On beating England 25–17 in the 2006 IRB World Cup final, New Zealand's Farah Palmer took her title tally to three, having also guided the Black Ferns to victory in 1998 and 2002. Under her decade-long stewardship, from 1996 to 2006, New Zealand lost once—to England in 2001.

●**Most Rugby Union Tri-Nations won by a captain** Following on from Palmer's success in the women's game, Richie McCaw has demonstrated his own leadership qualities in the men's, steering the New Zealand All Blacks to four wins in the annual Tri-Nations tournament, against Australia and South Africa, in 2006–08 and 2010.

●**Most British and Irish Lions Rugby Union tours as captain** Only one player has led the Lions on two separate tours: Martin Johnson (UK) in 1997 and 2001. In 1997, the team triumphed in South Africa, while in 2001 they lost a tight series 2–1 in Australia.

Avoiding the perils of the road, the world's **most expensive franked letter** traveled by sea from Mauritius in the Indian Ocean to Bordeaux, France, in 1847. It sold at auction in 1993 for CHF5.75 million ($3.9 million) due to its rare Mauritian stamps.

JACK OF ALL TRADES Alaa El-din Gabr (Egypt) has captained his country in no fewer than three different sports: swimming (1970–78), modern pentathlon (1980), and tenpin bowling (1997–98).

●**MOST ODI CRICKET MATCHES AS CAPTAIN** Australian Belinda Clark captained her country in 101 One-Day International matches between 1994 and 2005. Talented with a bat, she also holds the record for the highest score at a World Cup, racking up 229 against India in 1997.

●**First captain to win the NFL MVP award unanimously** On February 6, 2011, the New England Patriots' captain and quarterback Tom Brady (U.S.A.) was voted Most Valuable Player of 2010, winning every one of the 50 available votes for the first time in the award's 53-year history.

●**Most successful Stanley Cup ice hockey captain** The only player to captain two teams to the Stanley Cup—the trophy awarded to the annual champion of the National Hockey League—is Mark Messier (Canada), playing center for the Edmonton Oilers (Canada) in 1990 and the New York Rangers (U.S.A.) in 1994.

Youngest captain to win the Stanley Cup At the age of 21 years 309 days, Sidney Crosby (Canada, b. August 7, 1987) became the youngest captain to win ice hockey's Stanley Cup, when the Pittsburgh Penguins (U.S.A.) defeated the Detroit Red Wings (U.S.A.) 4–3 in the final game of the 2009 playoffs on June 12. By this time, Crosby already held the record for the **youngest captain of an NHL team**, having been appointed to the position on May 31, 2007, at the age of 19 years 297 days.

Most successful Ryder Cup golf captain In his time as U.S. captain, Walter Hagen (U.S.A.) orchestrated a record four wins in golf's prestigious Ryder Cup contest between the U.S.A. and Europe, outwitting his opponents in 1927, 1931, 1935, and 1937.

●**Most successful AFL Premiership captain** Three captains have won the Australian Football League Premiership title on four occasions: Syd Coventry (Australia) for Collingwood in 1927–30, Dick Reynolds (Australia) for Essendon in 1942, 1946, 1949, and 1950, and Michael Tuck (Australia) for Hawthorn in 1986, 1988–89, and 1991.

BIG AIR

●**Largest parachuting canopy formation (female)** An international team of 250 female parachutists took part in a canopy formation over Perris Valley, California, U.S.A., on October 17, 1997.

The **largest women's free-flying head-down parachuting formation** consisted of 41 parachutists and was formed by an international team on November 26, 2010.

Eugene Andreev (Russia, then USSR) holds the official World Air Sports Federation (FAI) record for the **longest free-fall parachute jump**. On November 1, 1962, he fell 80,380 ft. (24,500 m)—almost as far as the height of the highest mountain in the Solar System, Olympus Mons on the planet Mars—from an altitude of 83,523 ft. (25,458 m) near the city of Saratov, Russia.

●**Most paragliding World Championships (female)** Louise Crandal (Denmark) won three paragliding World Championships, in 1999, 2001, and 2005.

The ●**most paragliding World Championships won by a national team** is two, by two teams: Switzerland in 1991 and 1993, and the Czech Republic in 2007 and 2009.

●**MOST PILOTS IN A RED BULL AIR RACE WORLD CHAMPIONSHIP** Fifteen pilots took part in the six races of the 2009 installment of this competition—the seventh championship in the series to date. Paul Bonhomme (UK) won the title that year for the first time.

LONGEST JOURNEY BY POWERED PARAGLIDER From May 15 to August 24, 2009, Benjamin Jordan (Canada) flew west to east across Canada from Tofino (British Columbia) to Bay St. Lawrence (Nova Scotia) by powered paraglider, a distance of 4,976 miles (8,008 km).

●**FASTEST TIME TO COMPLETE A SKYDIVE ON SIX CONTINENTS** Martin Downs (UK) took 8 days 7 hr. 30 min. to perform a skydive on six continents: Africa, Europe, South America, North America, Oceania, and finally Asia. Martin completed his last skydive in Nha-Trang, Vietnam, on March 6, 2008.

●**Most World Glider Aerobatic Championships (team)** The greatest number of wins at the World Glider Aerobatic Championships by a national team is eight, by Poland in 1985, 1987, 1989, 1991, 1993, 1999, 2001, and 2003.

The **most wins of the World Glider Aerobatic Championships by an individual** is six, by Jerzy Makula (Poland) in 1985, 1987, 1989, 1991, 1993, and 1999.

●**Most BASE Race victories** The BASE Race is an annual BASE-jumping wingsuit flying contest that has been held three times. Launching themselves into midair from a high point, competitors race over a 2,460-ft. (750-m) course; the fastest person to complete the course wins the race. Three Norwegian competitors share the record for most victories, with one win each: Ronny Risvik in 2008, Frode Johannessen in 2009, and Espen Fadnes in 2010.

●**Highest flat spin on inline skates** Sven Boekhorst (Netherlands) cleared a bar set at 15 ft. (4.6 m) with a flat spin on inline skates on the set of *L'Été de Tous les Records* in Biscarrosse, France, on July 1, 2004.

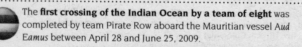

The **first crossing of the Indian Ocean by a team of eight** was completed by team Pirate Row aboard the Mauritian vessel *Aud Eamus* between April 28 and June 25, 2009.

●FASTEST SPEED KITE SURFING (FEMALE) Charlotte Consorti (France) registered a speed of 50.43 knots (58 mi./hr.; 93 km/h) while kite surfing at the 2010 Luderitz Speed Challenge in Luderitz, Namibia, on October 28, 2010.

The **●highest 900-degree McTwist performed on inline skates off a half-pipe ramp** is 3 ft. 9 in. (1.15 m), by Kevin Marron (Belgium) on the set of *L'Été de Tous les Records* in La Tranche-sur-Mer, France, on July 28, 2005.

The **●highest McTwist on inline skates** is 7 ft. 8 in. (2.35 m) and was set by Taïg Khris (France) on the set of *L'Été de Tous les Records* in Benodet, France, on August 2, 2004.

Taïg also registered an inline-skate jump of 10 ft. 2 in. (3.1 m) from a halfpipe on the set of *L'Émission des Records*, Paris, France, on December 6, 2000, the **highest indoor vertical air**.

○**Longest ramp jump on a snowmobile** On March 26, 2009, Paul Thacker (U.S.A.) carried out a huge 301-ft. (91.7-m) jump on a snowmobile—greater than the length of a 747 jumbo jet—in Brainerd, Minnesota, U.S.A.

●**Longest backflip** Lukas Steiner (Germany) executed a 13-ft. 6-in. (4.11-m) backflip on the set of *Zheng Da Zong Yi—Guinness World Records Special* in Beijing, China, on May 25, 2010.

○**Longest journey kite surfing** Phillip McCoy Midler (U.S.A.) kite-surfed from South Padre Island to Matagorda (both Texas, U.S.A.) between May 10 and 11, 2010, covering 199.63 nautical miles (229.73 miles; 369.71 km).

The **●fastest speed kite surfing** was 55.65 knots (64 mi./hr.; 103 km/h), achieved by Rob Douglas (U.S.A.) at the 2010 Luderitz Speed Challenge in Luderitz, Namibia, on October 28, 2010.

Highest-scored high dive In 2000, during the Cliff-Diving World Championships in Kaunolu, Hawaii, U.S.A., Orlando Duque (Colombia) performed a double-back somersault with four twists from 80 ft. (24.4 m). For this dive he earned a perfect 10 from all seven judges and scored 159.00 points.

 Elsewhere in the Indian Ocean: Huvadhu Atoll in the Maldives covers an area of around 1,120 miles^2 (2,900 km^2) and contains some 255 islands within its boundary, the **most islands within an atoll**.

Highest high dive from a board The world record high dive from a
diving board is 176 ft. 10 in. (53.9 m)—higher than the Statue of Liberty—by Olivier Favre (Switzerland) at Villers-le-Lac, France, on August
30, 1987.

Highest high jump Javier Sotomayor (Cuba) performed an 8-ft. 0.45-in.
(2.45-m) high jump in Salamanca, Spain, on July 27, 1993.

The **highest indoor high jump** measured 7 ft. 11.66 in. (2.43 m) and was
also achieved by Javier, in Budapest, Hungary, on March 4, 1989.

Stefka Kostadinova (Bulgaria) recorded the **highest high jump by a
woman**, which measured 6 ft. 10.28 in. (2.09 m). She achieved the feat in
Rome, Italy, on August 30, 1987.

The **highest indoor high jump by a woman** was 6 ft. 9.8 in. (2.08 m)
and was performed by Kajsa Bergqvist (Sweden) in Arnstadt, Germany, on
February 4, 2006.

Highest pole vault On July 31, 1994, legendary Ukrainian athlete Sergei Bubka launched himself into history's highest pole vault: 20 ft. 1.73 in.
(6.14 m). The feat took place in Sestriere, Italy. The previous year, on February 21, 1993, he had recorded the all-time **highest indoor pole vault**,
in Donetsk, Ukraine, reaching 20 ft. 2.12 in. (6.15 m). The remarkable
Bubka broke the world pole-vaulting record 35 times in a 20-year period.

The **highest pole vault by a woman** measured 16 ft. 7 in. (5.06 m) and
was executed by Yelena Isinbayeva (Russia) in Zürich, Switzerland, on
August 28, 2009. She also holds the world record for the **highest indoor
pole vault by a woman**, clearing 16 ft. 4 in. (5 m) on February 15, 2009,
in Donetsk, Ukraine.

SPORTING MADNESS

**MOST PEOPLE EXTREME IRONING
UNDERWATER** A group of 86
adventurous folk from the National
Diving and Activity Centre near
Chepstow, Gloucestershire, UK, donned
their wetsuits and scuba gear for a
10-minute session of extreme ironing
underwater on January 10, 2009.

BOG STANDARD The World Bog Snorkeling Triathlon, held in Llanwrtyd Wells, UK, consists of a 7.5-mile (12-km) run, a two-way snorkel through a 135-ft. (41-m) peat bog, and finally a grueling 19-mile (31-km) cycle race!

○ **FASTEST BOG SNORKELING TRIATHLON—MALE AND FEMALE** Daniel and Natalie Bent (both UK) are the world's top brother–sister bog snorkeling duo, with Daniel setting the men's triathlon record of 2 hr. 21 min. 5 sec. in July 2009 and Natalie setting the women's record of 2 hr. 45 min. 40 sec. in July 2010.

○ **Most competitors at the World Bog Snorkeling Championship** On August 31, 2009, a record 200 bog snorkelers took part in the World Championship at Waen Rhydd peat bog, Llanwrtyd Wells, Wales, UK.

● **Fastest World Bog Snorkeling Championship wins** New men's and women's records were set at the 2010 World Championship, with Dan Morgan (UK) snorkeling to victory in 1 min. 30.66 sec. and Dineka Maguire (Ireland) finishing in 1 min. 31.90 sec.

● **Longest-running man vs. horse race** The Man vs. Horse Marathon has been held annually since 1980 in Llanwrtyd Wells. The race, between runners and riders on horseback, covers 22 miles (35.4 km) of rugged Welsh terrain.

OTHER FAST FINISHES FROM THE WACKY WORLD OF SPORT:

Fastest 100 m on a space hopper: 30.2 sec. (Ashrita Furman, U.S.A.)

Fastest 100 m while throwing and catching a yo-yo: 13.9 sec. (Taro Yamashita, U.S.A.)

Fastest 50 m on can-and-string stilts: 9.7 sec. (Steven Bell, U.S.A.)

Fastest ferret over 10 m: 12.59 sec. ("Warhol" the albino ferret, owned by Jacqui Adams, UK)

Fastest marathon with an egg and spoon: 3 hr. 47 min. (Dale Lyons, UK)

LONGEST-RUNNING FINGER WRESTLING CONTEST *Fingerhakeln* (finger-wrestling contests) are known to have been staged in Bavaria, Germany, since the 14th century, when rivals competed for women's favors. The contests continue to this day, and the aim remains the same: to pull your rival (seated opposite) across a table using a finger lash wrapped around your fingers.

●**Most wins by a runner in the Man vs. Horse Marathon** Just two runners have ever beaten the riders in the Man vs. Horse Marathon: Huw Lobb (UK) in 2004 and Florian Holzinger (Germany) in 2007. Lobb's victory earned him a prize of £25,000 ($45,777).

○**Most competitors in a high-heel race** On September 11, 2010, 967 runners raced in high heels at Headwaters Park in Fort Wayne, Indiana, U.S.A. The event, staged by Women's Bureau, Inc. (U.S.A.), smashed the previous record of 763.

Most "ringers" in a horseshoe-pitching world championship (female) In the target sport of horseshoe pitching, the aim is to throw horseshoes over stakes in the ground. In 2008, Sylvianne Moisan (Canada) scored a record 126 "ringers"—the horseshoe-pitching equivalent of a bullseye.

○**MOST GURNING WORLD CHAMPIONSHIP WINS (MALE)** The only male gurner to win the world title an amazing 12 times is Tommy Mattinson (UK), whose flexible face took the top prize at the annual Gurning World Championship at Egremont Crab Fair, Cumbria, UK, in 1986–87 and then 10 times between 1999 and 2010.

WHY THE LONG FACE? Another face-pulling high-achiever is Anne Woods (UK), who has cringed and contorted her way to 27 Championship wins since 1977, the ●**most gurning world titles** ever won.

The **longest milk tooth** is from Ahmed Afrah Ismail (Maldives): 0.91 in. (2.3 cm) long, comprising a 0.39-in. (1-cm) crown and a 0.51-in. (1.3-cm) root.

0.3: Number of skateboards you'll buy in a lifetime—although the average person doesn't own or ride a skateboard. The average skater, however, will buy eight decks and 10 sets of wheels.

FASTEST 1,000 MARTIAL ARTS SWORD CUTS Samurai Isao Machii (Japan) sliced through 1,000 rolled straw mats in 36 min. 4 sec. on the set of *The Best House 123* in Tokyo, Japan, on September 19, 2007.

●**Longest-running Kubb Championship** Held in Gotland, Sweden, the Kubb World Championship has been running annually since 1995. Kubb is a target sport in which competitors have to knock down wooden blocks by throwing sticks.

Most Men's Pea Shooting World Championships Deadeye Mike Fordham (UK) has blown his way to a record seven Men's Pea Shooting World Championships, in 1977–78, 1981, 1983–85, and 1992.

Farthest winkle spit The farthest distance anyone has ever spat a periwinkle is 34 ft. 1.4 in. (10.4 m). The record is held by Alain Jourden (France), who retained his Winkle Spitting World Championship crown in Moguériec, France, on July 16, 2006, with a spit of 30 ft. 9.2 in. (9.38 m).

●**Highest bobbage jump** In Association Bobbage, competitors wearing flippers must jump into a swimming pool without letting their heads go under the water. The highest ever successful jump is 7 ft. 10 in. (2.4 m), achieved by Laszlo Fazekas (Hungary) in 2002.

For more conventional sporting successes, have a look at the great achievements on page 501.

The **most people brushing their teeth simultaneously in a single venue** is 13,380, at an event staged by Colgate Palmolive (Central America) Inc. at the Cuscatlaiun Stadium, City of San Salvador, El Salvador, on November 5, 2005.

First Chess Boxing World Champion

The first Chess Boxing World Championship was held in Amsterdam, the Netherlands, in 2003 and was won by Lepe Rubingh (Netherlands). Chess boxing is a hybrid of chess and boxing, alternating between each discipline for a total of 11 brain- and body-bruising rounds. Only boxers who have at least a Class-A chess rating can take part.

●**Most wins of the Mashed Potato Wrestling championships** Steve O'Gratin, aka Steve Barone (U.S.A.), has won the Mashed Potato Wrestling title a record four times since 2006. The championship, which takes place in Barnesville, Minnesota, U.S.A., is contested in a ring filled to the brim with piles of mashed potato. Barone, a musician, filmmaker, and comedian, is also the founder of the Mashed Potato Wrestling Federation, which sanctions the event.

SPORTING EXTREMES

●**Highest base jump from a building** On January 5, 2010, Nasser Al Neyadi and Omar Alhegelan (both UAE) performed the highest BASE jump from a building, plummeting 2,205 ft. (672 m) from the 160th floor of the Burj Khalifa tower in Dubai, UAE. The duo hit 137 mi./hr. (220 km/h) before their parachutes opened.

●**HIGHEST SKI-JUMPING HILL** The most forbidding purpose-built ski-jumping slope to regularly host international competition is Vikersundbakken in Vikersund, Norway. Officially ratified at a height of 738 ft. (225 m), it is the equivalent of nearly five Statues of Liberty stood one on top of another.

1.7: Weight in tons of cookies you'll eat in a lifetime. Cookies are not traditionally a key element of any athlete's training regime. In a lifetime, you will eat the weight of 10 sumo wrestlers in cookies.

Highest base jump To perform the highest BASE jump on record, Australians Glenn Singleman and Heather Swan turned to the mountains of India. On May 23, 2006, they climbed Mount Meru and then, wearing wingsuits and parachutes, leapt from a cliff edge 21,666 ft. (6,604 m) to the ground below.

○**Highest bungee jump (commercial)** The world's highest bungee jump available to paying customers is the 764-ft. (233-m) AJ Hackett Macau Tower Bungy Jump, located on the Macau Tower in Macau, China, and opened on December 17, 2006.

Highest bungee jump Curtis Rivers (UK) performed a bungee jump from a hot-air balloon at 15,200 ft. (4,632 m) over Puertollano, Spain, on May 5, 2002.

●**LARGEST ICE CANOEING RACE** Each year, the icy St. Lawrence River in Quebec City, Canada, hosts the world's largest canoe race, with the 2011 event attracting 49 five-man teams.

MOST SOUTHERLY MARATHON The Antarctica Marathon and Half Marathon are the only sporting events that take place on the world's most southerly continent. Held every February on King George Island, the route runs from the Uruguayan Antarctic base through bases belonging to Russia, Chile, and China. Despite the extreme conditions, the intrepid runners must compete in ordinary running shoes.

● **MOST DANGEROUS MOTORSPORTS CIRCUIT**
Home to the Isle of Man TT and Manx Grand Prix motorcycle races, the Isle of Man's Snaefell Mountain Course is the most dangerous circuit in the world. Since racing began there in 1911, the treacherous, winding course has claimed 229 lives.

● **Most ultra-trail du Mont Blanc wins** The 166-mile (267-km) race through the Alps has been won twice by Marco Olmo (Italy), in 2006–07, and Kilian Jornet (Spain), in 2008–09.

● **Most consecutive days running an ultramarathon** Extreme athlete Enzo Caporaso (Italy) ran seven ultramarathons in seven consecutive days between June 13 and 19, 2010. All the races covered 62.14 miles (100 km) in Ruffini Park, Turin, Italy, and were sanctioned by the Italian Athletics Federation. Caporaso ran the first in 11 hr. 28 min. 43 sec., but slowed to 19 hr. 23 min. 11 sec. by his last.

Highest marathon The Everest Marathon in Nepal takes place every two years, setting out from Gorak Shep, at 17,100 ft. (5,212 m), and finishing at Namche Bazar, at 11,300 ft. (3,444 m). Hari Roka (Nepal) is the event's fastest man, with a time of 3 hr. 50 min. 23 sec. in 2000, while Anna Frost (NZ) is the fastest woman, finishing in 4 hr. 35 min. 4 sec. in 2009.

The **largest pupusa**, an El Salvadorian tortilla with cheese and meat, measured 10 ft. 2 in. (3.09 m) in circumference and was made by the Chamber of Commerce El Salvador-California and Liborio Markets, Inc. (both U.S.A.) in Los Angeles, U.S.A., on June 3, 2007.

DEEPEST MAN ON EARTH Herbert Nitsch is truly the king of the deep, with 31 freediving world records. It is a phenomenal feat, given the risks—up to 40 people die each year diving without oxygen.

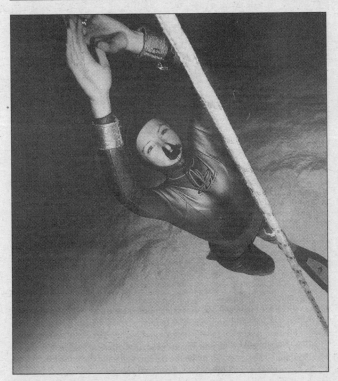

DEEPEST FREEDIVE, NO LIMITS (FEMALE) Tanya Streeter (UK) only took up freediving at the age of 25, but soon found she had a natural talent for it. On August 17, 2002, she plunged 525 ft. (160 m) into waters off the Turks and Caicos Islands, briefly wresting from the men the overall no-limits record.

Another sizeable tortilla dish, the world's **largest flour taco** weighed 1,654 lb. (750 kg) and was made by the city of Mexicali and Cocinex SA de CV, in Mexicali, Baja California, Mexico, on March 8, 2003.

○LARGEST WAVE SURFED On January 5, 2008, surfer Mike Parsons
(U.S.A.) rode a huge wave estimated to be 77 ft. (23.4 m) tall at Cortes Bank,
an underwater mountain range 100 miles (160 km) off the coast of south
California, U.S.A. The fearsome wave was generated by a powerful storm in
the area on January 4–6 that resulted in giant swells and buoy readings of
80–100 ft. (25–30 m).

Mike "Snip" Parsons was inducted into the Surfers' Hall of Fame
in 2008.

Most northerly marathon The North Pole Marathon has been held annually since 2002, and the course at the geographic North Pole has been
certified by the Association of International Marathons and Road Races.

The fastest runner to date is Thomas Maguire (Ireland), who finished in
3 hr. 36 min. 10 sec. in 2007, while the fastest woman is Cathrine Due (Denmark), who achieved a time of 5 hr. 7 min. 40 sec. in 2008.

Fastest road race The Silver State Classic, run on Route 318 in Nevada,
U.S.A., is the world's fastest road race, with drivers averaging speeds of
over 190 mi./hr. (305 km/h) over the 90-mile (145-km) course. The 2010
winners in the unlimited speed category were Pal-Arvid Blytt and Vegard
Robberstad (both Norway), who averaged 183.10 mi./hr. (294.67 km/h) in
a 1986 Pontiac TransAM.

Deepest freedive, no limits (male) Although Tanya Streeter briefly
held the overall no-limits apnea record, it was soon regained by the men,

first by Loïc Leferme (France) in 2002 and then by the "Deepest Man on Earth," Herbert Nitsch (Austria), who descended to 702 ft. (214 m) near Spetses, Greece, on June 14, 2007.

●**Longest breath-hold swim under water (open water)** In a single breath, freediver Carlos Coste (Venezuela) managed to cover a record 492 ft. 1 in. (150 m) submerged in the Dos Ojos cave system in Quintana Roo, Mexico, on November 3, 2010. During the attempt, Coste stayed under for 2 min. 32 sec.

Highest-altitude scuba-diving Scuba-dives have been made on several occasions at an altitude of 19,357 ft. (5,900 m), in a lagoon in the crater of Licancabur, a volcano on the border between Chile and Bolivia.

Highest-latitude windsurfing On July 14, 1985, Gerard-Jan Goekoop (Netherlands) windsurfed alongside the pack ice of the Arctic Ocean at a latitude of 80°40.3'N, 13°43'E, north of the Spitsbergen archipelago.

Highest-altitude golf course Located at 13,025 ft. (3,970 m) above sea level, the Yak golf course in Kupup, East Sikkim, India, opened to the public on October 10, 2006.

●**Longest sled-dog race** The Iditarod Trail sled-dog race covers 1,049 miles (1,688 km) across the icy wastes of Alaska, U.S.A. Racers experience extreme weather conditions and temperatures as low as -100°F (-73°C). The ●**fastest time to complete the Iditarod Trail** is 8 days 18 hr. 46 min. 39 sec., by John Baker (U.S.A.) in 2011.

SPORTS REFERENCE

★ ATHLETICS—OUTDOOR TRACK EVENTS ★

MEN	TIME	NAME & NATIONALITY
100 m	9.58	Usain Bolt (Jamaica)
200 m	19.19	Usain Bolt (Jamaica)
400 m	43.18	Michael Johnson (U.S.A.)
○ 800 m	1:41.01	David Lekuta Rudisha (Kenya)
1,000 m	2:11.96	Noah Ngeny (Kenya)
1,500 m	3:26.00	Hicham El Guerrouj (Morocco)
1 mile	3:43.13	Hicham El Guerrouj (Morocco)
2,000 m	4:44.79	Hicham El Guerrouj (Morocco)
3,000 m	7:20.67	Daniel Komen (Kenya)
5,000 m	12:37.35	Kenenisa Bekele (Ethiopia)
10,000 m	26:17.53	Kenenisa Bekele (Ethiopia)
20,000 m	56:26.00	Haile Gebrselassie (Ethiopia)
1 hour	21,285 meters	Haile Gebrselassie (Ethiopia)
25,000 m	1:13:55.80	Toshihiko Seko (Japan)
30,000 m	1:29:18.80	Toshihiko Seko (Japan)
3,000 m steeplechase	7:53.63	Saif Saaeed Shaheen (Qatar)
110 m hurdles	12.87	Dayron Robles (Cuba)
400 m hurdles	46.78	Kevin Young (U.S.A.)
4 x 100 m relay	37.10	Jamaica (Asafa Powell, Nesta Carter, Michael Frater, Usain Bolt)
4 x 200 m relay	1;18.68	Santa Monica Track Club, U.S.A. (Michael Marsh, Leroy Burrell, Floyd Heard, Carl Lewis)
4 x 400 m relay	2:54.29	U.S.A. (Andrew Valmon, Quincy Watts, Harry Reynolds, Michael Johnson)
4 x 800 m relay	7:02.43	Kenya (Joseph Mutua, William Yiampoy, Ismael Kombich, Wilfred Bungei)
4 x 1,500 m relay	14:36.23	Kenya (Geoffrey Rono, Augustine Choge, William Tanui, Gideon Gathimba)

WOMEN	TIME	NAME & NATIONALITY
100 m	10.49	Florence Griffith-Joyner (U.S.A.)
200 m	21.34	Florence Griffith-Joyner (U.S.A.)
400 m	47.60	Marita Koch (GDR)
800 m	1:53.28	Jarmila Kratochvílová (Czechoslovakia)
1,000 m	2:28.98	Svetlana Masterkova (Russia)
1,500 m	3:50.46	Qu Yunxia (China)
1 mile	4:12.56	Svetlana Masterkova (Russia)
2,000 m	5:25.36	Sonia O'Sullivan (Ireland)
3,000 m	8:06.11	Wang Junxia (China)
5,000 m	14:11.15	Tirunesh Dibaba (Ethiopia)
10,000 m	29:31.78	Wang Junxia (China)
20,000 m	1:05:26.60	Tegla Loroupe (Kenya)
1 hour	18,517 meters	Dire Tune (Ethiopia)
25,000 m	1:27:05.90	Tegla Loroupe (Kenya)

LOCATION	DATE
Berlin, Germany	Aug. 16, 2009
Berlin, Germany	Aug. 20, 2009
Seville, Spain	Aug. 26, 1999
Rieti, Italy	Aug. 29, 2010
Rieti, Italy	Sep. 5, 1999
Rome, Italy	Jul. 14, 1998
Rome, Italy	Jul. 7, 1999
Berlin, Germany	Sep. 7, 1999
Rieti, Italy	Sep. 1, 1996
Hengelo, the Netherlands	May 31, 2004
Brussels, Belgium	Aug. 26, 2005
Ostrava, Czech Republic	Jun. 26, 2007
Ostrava, Czech Republic	Jun. 27, 2007
Christchurch, New Zealand	Mar. 22, 1981
Christchurch, New Zealand	Mar. 22, 1981
Brussels, Belgium	Sep. 3, 2004
Ostrava, Czech Republic	Jun. 12, 2008
Barcelona, Spain	Aug. 6, 1992
Beijing, China	Aug. 22, 2008
Walnut, U.S.A.	Apr. 17, 1994
Stuttgart, Germany	Aug. 22, 1993
Brussels, Belgium	Aug. 25, 2006
Brussels, Belgium	Sep. 4, 2009

MEN'S OUTDOOR 800 M On August 29, 2010, David Lekuta Rudisha (Kenya) ran the men's 800 m in 1 min. 41.01 sec. at the IAAF World Challenge in Rieti, Italy, beating the record he had set in Germany a week earlier by eight seconds.

LOCATION	DATE
Indianapolis, U.S.A.	Jul. 16, 1988
Seoul, South Korea	Sep. 29, 1988
Canberra, Australia	Oct. 6, 1985
Munich, Germany	Jul. 26, 1983
Brussels, Belgium	Aug. 23, 1996
Beijing, China	Sep. 11, 1993
Zurich, Switzerland	Aug. 14, 1996
Edinburgh, UK	Jul. 8, 1994
Beijing, China	Sep. 13, 1993
Oslo, Norway	Jun. 6, 2008
Beijing, China	Sep. 8, 1993
Borgholzhausen, Germany	Sep. 3, 2000
Ostrava, Czech Republic	Jun. 12, 2008
Mengerskirchen, Germany	Sep. 21, 2002

★ ATHLETICS—OUTDOOR TRACK EVENTS ★

WOMEN	TIME	NAME & NATIONALITY
30,000 m	1:45:50.00	Tegla Loroupe (Kenya)
3,000 m steeplechase	8:58.81	Gulnara Samitova-Galkina (Russia)
100 m hurdles	12.21	Yordanka Donkova (Bulgaria)
400 m hurdles	52.34	Yuliya Pechonkina (Russia)
4 x 100 m relay	41.37	GDR (Silke Gladisch, Sabine Rieger, Ingrid Auerswald, Marlies Göhr)
4 x 200 m relay	1:27.46	United States "Blue" (LaTasha Jenkins, LaTasha Colander-Richardson, Nanceen Perry, Marion Jones)
4 x 400 m relay	3:15.17	USSR (Tatyana Ledovskaya, Olga Nazarova, Maria Pinigina, Olga Bryzgina)
4 x 800 m relay	7:50.17	USSR (Nadezhda Olizarenko, Lyubov Gurina, Lyudmila Borisova, Irina Podyalovskaya)

★ TRACK AND FIELD—INDOOR TRACK EVENTS ★

MEN	TIME	NAME & NATIONALITY
50 m	5.56	Donovan Bailey (Canada)
60 m	6.39	Maurice Greene (U.S.A.)
	6.39	Maurice Greene (U.S.A.)
200 m	19.92	Frank Fredericks (Namibia)
400 m	44.57	Kerron Clement (U.S.A.)
800 m	1:42.67	Wilson Kipketer (Denmark)
1,000 m	2:14.96	Wilson Kipketer (Denmark)
1,500 m	3:31.18	Hicham El Guerrouj (Morocco)
1 mile	3:48.45	Hicham El Guerrouj (Morocco)
3,000 m	7:24.90	Daniel Komen (Kenya)
5,000 m	12:49.60	Kenenisa Bekele (Ethiopia)
50 m hurdles	6.25	Mark McKoy (Canada)
60 m hurdles	7.30	Colin Jackson (GB)
4 x 200 m relay	1:22.11	Great Britain & Northern Ireland (Linford Christie, Darren Braithwaite, Ade Mafe, John Regis)
4 x 400 m relay	3:02.83	U.S.A. (Andre Morris, Dameon Johnson, Deon Minor, Milton Campbell)
4 x 800 m relay	7:13.94	Global Athletics & Marketing, U.S.A. (Joey Woody, Karl Paranya, Rich Kenah, David Krummenacker)
5,000 m walk	18:07.08	Mikhail Shchennikov (Russia)

··

In 1997, Mexican Sergio Rodriguez Villarreal crafted the **largest ornamental Christmas candle**, measuring 12 ft. 9 in. (3.9 m) tall and 10 ft. 2 in. (3.1 m) wide. It featured 1,789 pieces of mirrored glass and 1,164 bottles.

··

LOCATION	DATE
Warstein, Germany	Jun. 6, 2003
Beijing, China	Aug. 17, 2008
Stara Zagora, Bulgaria	Aug. 20, 1988
Tula, Russia	Aug. 8, 2003
Canberra, Australia	Oct. 6, 1985
Philadelphia, U.S.A.	Apr. 29, 2000
Seoul, South Korea	Oct. 1, 1988
Moscow, Russia	Aug. 5, 1984

LOCATION	DATE
Reno, U.S.A.	Feb. 9, 1996
Madrid, Spain	Feb. 3, 1998
Atlanta, U.S.A.	Mar. 3, 2001
Liévin, France	Feb. 18, 1996
Fayetteville, U.S.A.	Mar. 12, 2005
Paris, France	Mar. 9, 1997
Birmingham, UK	Feb. 20, 2000
Stuttgart, Germany	Feb. 2, 1997
Ghent, Belgium	Feb. 12, 1997
Budapest, Hungary	Feb. 6, 1998
Birmingham, UK	Feb. 20, 2004
Kobe, Japan	Mar. 5, 1986
Sindelfingen, Germany	Mar. 6, 1994
Glasgow, UK	Mar. 3, 1991
Maebashi, Japan	Mar. 7, 1999
Boston, U.S.A.	Feb. 6, 2000
Moscow, Russia	Feb. 14, 1995

OFFICIAL WEBSITES

ULTRARUNNING
www.iau-ultramarathon.org

TRACK & FIELD
www.iaaf.org

Energisa Sergipe (Brazil) organized the creation of the ○**largest Christmas tree structure**, a 419-ft.-10-in.-tall (127.99-m) decorated tree that was exhibited in Aracaju, Sergipe, Brazil, in December 2009.

★ TRACK AND FIELD—INDOOR TRACK EVENTS ★

WOMEN	TIME	NAME & NATIONALITY
50 m	5.96	Irina Privalova (Russia)
60 m	6.92	Irina Privalova (Russia)
	6.92	Irina Privalova (Russia)
200 m	21.87	Merlene Ottey (Jamaica)
400 m	49.59	Jarmila Kratochvílová (Czechoslovakia)
800 m	1:55.82	Jolanda Ceplak (Slovenia)
1,000 m	2:30.94	Maria de Lurdes Mutola (Mozambique)
1,500 m	3:58.28	Yelena Soboleva (Russia)
1 mile	4:17.14	Doina Melinte (Romania)
3,000 m	8:23.72	Meseret Defar (Ethiopia)
5,000 m	14:24.37	Meseret Defar (Ethiopia)
50 m hurdles	6.58	Cornelia Oschkenat (GDR)
60 m hurdles	7.68	Susanna Kallur (Sweden)
4 x 200 m relay	1:32.41	Russia (Yekaterina Kondratyeva, Irina Khabarova, Yuliya Pechonkina, Yulia Gushchina)
4 x 400 m relay	3:23.37	Russia (Yulia Gushchina, Olga Kotlyarova, Olga Zaytseva, Olesya Krasnomovets)
O 4 x 800 m relay	•8:06.24	Moscow (Aleksandra Bulanova, Yekaterina Martynova, Elena Kofanova, Anna Balakshina)
3,000 m walk	11:40.33	Claudia Stef (Romania)

•Still awaiting ratification at the time of going to press

★ TRACK AND FIELD—ULTRA LONG DISTANCE [TRACK] ★

MEN	TIME/DISTANCE	NAME & NATIONALITY
50 km	2:48:06	Jeff Norman (GB)
100 km	6:10:20	Donald Ritchie (GB)
100 miles	11:28:03	Oleg Kharitonov (Russia)
1,000 km	5 days 16:17:00	Yiannis Kouros (Greece)
1,000 miles	11 days 13:54:58	Peter Silkinas (Lithuania)
6 hours	60.4 miles (97.2 km)	Donald Ritchie (GB)
12 hours	100.91 miles (162.4 km)	Yiannis Kouros (Greece)
24 hours	188.59 miles (303.506 km)	Yiannis Kouros (Greece)
48 hours	294.21 miles (473.495 km)	Yiannis Kouros (Greece)
6 days	645.51 miles (1,038.851 km)	Yiannis Kouros (Greece)

WOMEN	TIME/DISTANCE	NAME & NATIONALITY
50 km	3:18:52	Carolyn Hunter-Rowe (GB)
100 km	7:14:06	Norimi Sakurai (Japan)
100 miles	14:25:45	Edit Bérces (Hungary)
1,000 km	7 days 1:28:29	Eleanor Robinson (GB)
1,000 miles	13 days 1:54:02	Eleanor Robinson (GB)
6 hours	57.7 miles (83.2 km)	Norimi Sakurai (Japan)
12 hours	91.71 miles (147.6 km)	Ann Trason (U.S.A.)

LOCATION	DATE
Madrid, Spain	Feb. 9, 1995
Madrid, Spain	Feb. 11, 1993
Madrid, Spain	Feb. 9, 1995
Liévin, France	Feb. 13, 1993
Milan, Italy	Mar. 7, 1982
Vienna, Austria	Mar. 3, 2002
Stockholm, Sweden	Feb. 25, 1999
Moscow, Russia	Feb. 18, 2006
East Rutherford, U.S.A.	Feb. 9, 1990
Stuttgart, Germany	Feb. 3, 2007
Stockholm, Sweden	Feb. 18, 2009
Berlin, Germany	Feb. 20, 1988
Karlsruhe, Germany	Feb. 10, 2008
Glasgow, UK	Jan. 29, 2005
Glasgow, UK	Jan. 28, 2006
Moscow, Russia	Feb. 18, 2011
Bucharest, Romania	Jan. 30, 1999

○**WOMEN'S INDOOR 4 X 800 M** The Russian team of Yekaterina Martynova, Aleksandra Bulanova, Anna Balakshina, and Elena Kofanova (pictured left to right) recorded a time of 8 min. 6.24 sec. in the 4 x 800 m at the Russian Indoor Championships in Moscow on February 18, 2011. In doing so, the quartet shaved more than six seconds off the previous record, set by another Russian team in 2010.

LOCATION	DATE
Timperley, UK	Jun. 7, 1980
London, UK	Oct. 28, 1978
London, UK	Oct. 20, 2002
Colac, Australia	Nov. 26–Dec. 1, 1984
Nanango, Australia	Mar. 11–23, 1998
London, UK	Oct. 28, 1978
Montauban, France	Mar. 15–16, 1985
Adelaide, Australia	Oct. 4–5, 1997
Surgères, France	May 3–5, 1996
Colac, Australia	Nov. 20–26, 2005

LOCATION	DATE
Barry, UK	Mar. 3, 1996
Verona, Italy	Sep. 27, 2003
Verona, Italy	Sep. 21–22, 2002
Nanango, Australia	Mar. 11–18, 1998
Nanango, Australia	Mar. 11–23, 1998
Verona, Italy	Sep. 27, 2003
Hayward, U.S.A.	Aug. 3–4, 1991

○**WOMEN'S 48 HOURS (TRACK)** On May 21–23, 2010, Inagiki Sumie (Japan) broke the 48-hour track record at Surgères, France, with a distance of 246.75 miles (397.103 km). Above, she is seen completing a 24-hour race in Finland in January 2010.

★ TRACK AND FIELD—ULTRA LONG DISTANCE [TRACK] ★

WOMEN	TIME/DISTANCE	NAME & NATIONALITY
○ 24 hours	158.09 miles (254.425 km)	Kudo Mami (Japan)
○ 48 hours	246.75 miles (397.103 km)	Inagiki Sumie (Japan)
6 days	549.06 miles (883.631 km)	Sandra Barwick (New Zealand)

★ TRACK AND FIELD—ROAD RACE ★

MEN	TIME	NAME & NATIONALITY
○ 10 km	26:44	Leonard Patrick Komon (Kenya)
○ 15 km	41:13	Leonard Patrick Komon (Kenya)
20 km	55:21	Zersenay Tadese (Eritrea)
Half marathon	58:23	Zersenay Tadese (Eritrea)
25 km	1:11:50	Samuel Kiplimo Kosgei (Kenya)
30 km	1:27:49	Haile Gebrselassie (Ethiopia)
Marathon	2:03:59	Haile Gebrselassie (Ethiopia)
100 km	6:13:33	Takahiro Sunada (Japan)
Road relay	1:57:06	Kenya (Josephat Ndambiri, Martin Mathathi, Daniel Mwangi, Mekubo Mogusu, Onesmus Nyerere, John Kariuki)

WOMEN	TIME	NAME & NATIONALITY
10 km	30:21	Paula Radcliffe (GB)
15 km	46:28	Tirunesh Dibaba (Ethiopia)
○ 20 km	•1:02:36	Mary Jepkosgei Keitany (Kenya)
○ Half marathon	•1:05:50	Mary Jepkosgei Keitany (Kenya)
○ 25 km	•1:19:53	Mary Jepkosgei Keitany (Kenya)
30 km	1:38:49	Mizuki Noguchi (Japan)
Marathon	2:15:25	Paula Radcliffe (GB)
100 km	6:33:11	Tomoe Abe (Japan)
Road relay	2:11:41	China (Jiang Bo, Dong Yanmei, Zhao Fengting, Ma Zaijie, Lan Lixin, Li Na)

•Still awaiting ratification at the time of going to press

The **largest published book** is a 128-page edition of Antoine de Saint-Exupéry's *The Little Prince* measuring 6 ft. 7 in. (2.01 m) high and 10 ft. 1 in. (3.08 m) wide when open. It was published by Ediouro Publicações SA (Brazil) in 2007.

LOCATION	DATE
Taipei, Taiwan	Dec. 12–13, 2009
Surgères, France	May 21–23, 2010
Campbelltown, Australia	Nov. 18–24, 1990

LOCATION	DATE
Utrecht, the Netherlands	Sep. 26, 2010
Nijmegen, the Netherlands	Nov. 21, 2010
Lisbon, Portugal	Mar. 21, 2010
Lisbon, Portugal	Mar. 21, 2010
Berlin, Germany	May 9, 2010
Berlin, Germany	Sep. 20, 2009
Berlin, Germany	Sep. 28, 2008
Tokoro, Japan	Jun. 21, 1998
Chiba, Japan	Nov. 23, 2005

LOCATION	DATE
San Juan, Puerto Rico	Feb. 23, 2003
Nijmegen, the Netherlands	Nov. 15, 2009
Ras Al Khaimah, UAE	Feb. 18, 2011
Ras Al Khaimah, UAE	Feb. 18, 2011
Berlin, Germany	May 9, 2010
Berlin, Germany	Sep. 25, 2005
London, UK	Apr. 13, 2003
Tokoro, Japan	Jun. 25, 2000
Beijing, China	Feb. 28, 1998

○ **15 KM ROAD RACE**
Leonard Patrick Komon (Kenya) won the 15 km road race in a record time of 41 min. 13 sec. in Nijmegen, the Netherlands, on November 21, 2010, adding to the 10 km record he achieved two months earlier.

The **largest coloring book** is a super-sized version of a popular coloring book aimed at teaching young people to brush their teeth. It measures 5 ft. 10 in. (1.8 m) high and 4 ft. 11 in. (1.5 m) long and was created by Salma Al-Jeddi (Kuwait) in 2008.

29.5: Length, in feet, of your intestines. If you were to stretch them all out in a straight line, they would extend slightly farther than the current men's long jump world record of 8.95 m.

★ TRACK AND FIELD—RACE WALKING ★

MEN	TIME	NAME & NATIONALITY
20,000 m	1:17:25.6	Bernardo Segura (Mexico)
20 km (road)	1:17:16	Vladimir Kanaykin (Russia)
30,000 m	2:01:44.1	Maurizio Damilano (Italy)
○ 50,000 m	•3:35:27.2	Yohann Diniz (France)
50 km (road)	3:34:14	Denis Nizhegorodov (Russia)

WOMEN	TIME	NAME & NATIONALITY
10,000 m	41:56.23	Nadezhda Ryashkina (USSR)
20,000 m	1:26:52.3	Olimpiada Ivanova (Russia)

•Still awaiting ratification at the time of going to press

★ TRACK AND FIELD—INDOOR FIELD EVENTS ★

MEN	RECORD	NAME & NATIONALITY
High jump	7 ft. 11.66 in. (2.43 m)	Javier Sotomayor (Cuba)
Pole vault	20 ft. 2.12 in. (6.15 m)	Sergei Bubka (Ukraine)
Long jump	28 ft. 10.06 in. (8.79 m)	Carl Lewis (U.S.A.)
○ Triple jump	•58 ft. 9.51 in. (17.92 m)	Teddy Tamgho (France)
Shot	74 ft. 4.12 in. (22.66 m)	Randy Barnes (U.S.A.)
○ Heptathlon*	•6,568 points	Ashton Eaton (U.S.A.)

WOMEN	RECORD	NAME & NATIONALITY
High jump	6 ft. 9.8 in. (2.08 m)	Kajsa Bergqvist (Sweden)
Pole vault	16 ft. 4 in. (5.00 m)	Yelena Isinbayeva (Russia)
Long jump	24 ft. 2.15 in. (7.37 m)	Heike Drechsler (GDR)
Triple jump	50 ft. 4.72 in. (15.36 m)	Tatyana Lebedeva (Russia)
Shot	73 ft. 9.82 in. (22.50 m)	Helena Fibingerová (Czechoslovakia)
Pentathlon†	4,991 points	Irina Belova (EUN)

*60 m, 6.66 seconds; long jump, 7.77 m; shot, 14.45 m; high jump, 2.01 m; 60 m hurdles, 7.60 seconds; pole vault, 5.20 m; 1,000 m, 2 min. 34.74 sec.

†60 m hurdles, 8.22 seconds; high jump, 1.93 m; shot, 13.25 m; long jump, 6.67 m; 800 m, 2 min. 10.26 sec.

•Still awaiting ratification at the time of going to press

LOCATION	DATE
Bergen, Norway	May 7, 1994
Saransk, Russia	Sep. 29, 2007
Cuneo, Italy	Oct. 3, 1992
Reims, France	Mar. 12, 2011
Cheboksary, Russia	May 11, 2008

LOCATION	DATE
Seattle, U.S.A.	Jul. 24, 1990
Brisbane, Australia	Sep. 6, 2001

50,000 M RACE WALK
Yohann Diniz (France)
completed the 50,000 m
race walk in a world
record 3 hr. 35 min.
27.2 sec. in Reims, France,
on March 12, 2011.

LOCATION	DATE
Budapest, Hungary	Mar. 4, 1989
Donetsk, Ukraine	Feb. 21, 1993
New York City, U.S.A.	Jan. 27, 1984
Paris, France	Mar. 6, 2011
Los Angeles, U.S.A.	Jan. 20, 1989
Tallinn, Estonia	Feb. 6, 2011

LOCATION	DATE
Arnstadt, Germany	Feb. 4, 2006
Donetsk, Ukraine	Feb. 15, 2009
Vienna, Austria	Feb. 13, 1988
Budapest, Hungary	Mar. 6, 2004
Jablonec, Czechoslovakia	Feb. 19, 1977
Berlin, Germany	Feb. 15, 1992

OFFICIAL WEBSITES

ATHLETICS &
RACE WALKING
www.iaaf.org

CYCLING
www.uci.ch

★ TRACK AND FIELD—OUTDOOR FIELD EVENTS ★

MEN	RECORD	NAME & NATIONALITY
High jump	2.45 m (8 ft. 0.45 in.)	Javier Sotomayor (Cuba)
Pole vault	6.14 m (20 ft. 1.73 in.)	Sergei Bubka (Ukraine)
Long jump	8.95 m (29 ft. 4.36 in.)	Mike Powell (U.S.A.)
Triple jump	18.29 m (60 ft. 0.78 in.)	Jonathan Edwards (GB)
Shot	23.12 m (75 ft. 10.23 in.)	Randy Barnes (U.S.A.)
Discus	74.08 m (243 ft. 0.53 in.)	Jürgen Schult (USSR)
Hammer	86.74 m (284 ft. 7 in.)	Yuriy Sedykh (USSR)
Javelin	98.48 m (323 ft. 1.16 in.)	Jan. Železný (Czech Republic)
Decathlon*	9,026 points	Roman Šebrle (Czech Republic)

WOMEN	RECORD	NAME & NATIONALITY
High jump	2.09 m (6 ft. 10.28 in.)	Stefka Kostadinova (Bulgaria)
Pole vault	5.06 m (16 ft. 7.21 in.)	Yelena Isinbayeva (Russia)
Long jump	7.52 m (24 ft. 8.06 in.)	Galina Chistyakova (USSR)
Triple jump	15.50 m (50 ft. 10.23 in.)	Inessa Kravets (Ukraine)
Shot	22.63 m (74 ft. 2.94 in.)	Natalya Lisovskaya (USSR)
Discus	76.80 m (252 ft.)	Gabriele Reinsch (GDR)
○ Hammer	78.30 m (256 ft. 10.67 in.)	Anita Wlodarczyk (Poland)
Javelin	72.28 m (253 ft. 6 in.)	Barbora Špotáková (Czech Republic)
Heptathlon†	7,291 points	Jacqueline Joyner-Kersee (U.S.A.)
Decathlon**	8,358 points	Austra Skujyte (Lithuania)

*100 m, 10.64 seconds; long jump, 8.11 m; shot, 15.33 m; high jump, 2.12 m; 400 m,
47.79 seconds; 110 m hurdles, 13.92 seconds; discus, 47.92 m; pole vault, 4.80 m; javelin,
70.16 m; 1,500 m, 4 min. 21.98 sec.
†100 m hurdles, 12.69 seconds; high jump, 1.86 m; shot, 15.80 m; 200 m, 22.56 seconds; long
jump, 7.27 m; javelin, 45.66 m; 800 m, 2 min. 8.51 sec.
**100 m, 12.49 seconds; long jump, 6.12 m; shot, 16.42 m; high jump, 1.78 m; 400 m,
57.19 seconds; 100 m hurdles, 14.22 seconds; discus, 46.19 m; pole vault, 3.10 m; javelin,
48.78 m; 1,500 m, 5 min. 15.86 sec.

★ CYCLING—ABSOLUTE TRACK ★

MEN	TIME/DISTANCE	NAME & NATIONALITY
200 m (flying start)	9.572	Kevin Sireau (France)
500 m (flying start)	24.758	Chris Hoy (GB)
Team 750 m (standing start)	42.950	Great Britain (Chris Hoy, Jason Kenny, Jamie Staff)
1 km (standing start)	58.875	Arnaud Tournant (France)
○ 4 km (standing start)	4:10.534	Jack Bobridge (Australia)
Team 4 km (standing start)	3:53.314	Great Britain (Ed Clancy, Paul Manning, Geraint Thomas, Bradley Wiggins)
1 hour	*49.7 km	Ondrej Sosenka (Czech Republic)

*Some athletes achieved better distances within an hour with bicycles that are no longer allowed
by the Union Cycliste Internationale (UCI). The 1-hour records given here are in accordance
with the new UCI rules.

LOCATION	DATE
Salamanca, Spain	Jul. 27, 1993
Sestriere, Italy	Jul. 31, 1994
Tokyo, Japan	Aug. 30, 1991
Gothenburg, Sweden	Aug. 7, 1995
Los Angeles, U.S.A.	May 20, 1990
Neubrandenburg, Germany	Jun. 6, 1986
Stuttgart, Germany	Aug. 30, 1986
Jena, Germany	May 25, 1996
Götzis, Austria	May 27, 2001

LOCATION	DATE
Rome, Italy	Aug. 30, 1987
Zurich, Switzerland	Aug. 28, 2009
St Petersburg, Russia	Jun. 11, 1988
Gothenburg, Sweden	Aug. 10, 1995
Moscow, Russia	Jun. 7, 1987
Neubrandenburg, Germany	Jul. 9, 1988
Bydgoszcz, Poland	Jun. 6, 2010
Stuttgart, Germany	Sep. 13, 2008
Seoul, South Korea	Sep. 24, 1988
Columbia, U.S.A.	Apr. 15, 2005

WOMEN'S JAVELIN
Barbora Špotáková (Czech Republic) achieved a distance of 253 ft. 6 in. (72.28 m) in the first round of the 2008 IAAF World Athletics Final in Stuttgart, Germany, on September 13, 2008.

LOCATION	DATE
Moscow, Russia	May 30, 2009
La Paz, Bolivia	May 13, 2007
Beijing, China	Aug. 15, 2008
La Paz, Bolivia	Oct. 10, 2001
Sydney, Australia	Feb. 2, 2011
Beijing, China	Aug. 18, 2008
Moscow, Russia	Jul. 19, 2005

★ CYCLING—ABSOLUTE TRACK ★

WOMEN	TIME/DISTANCE	NAME & NATIONALITY
○ 200 m (flying start)	10.793	Simona Krupeckaite (Lithuania)
500 m (flying start)	29.655	Erika Salumäe (USSR)
500 m (standing start)	33.296	Simona Krupeckaite (Lithuania)
○ Team 500 m (standing start)	32.923	Australia (Kaarle McCulloch, Anna Meares)
○ 3 km (standing start)	3:22.269	Sarah Hammer (U.S.A.)
○ Team 3 km (standing start)	3:19.569	U.S.A. (Sarah Hammer, Lauren Tamayo, Dotsie Bausch)
1 hour	*46.065 km	Leontien Zijlaard-Van Moorsel (Netherlands)

*Some athletes achieved better distances within an hour with bicycles that are no longer allowed by the Union Cycliste Internationale (UCI). The 1-hour records given here are in accordance with the new UCI rules.

★ FREEDIVING ★

MEN'S DEPTH DISCIPLINES	DEPTH/TIME	NAME & NATIONALITY
Constant weight with fins	124 m (406 ft. 9 in.)	Herbert Nitsch (Austria)
○ Constant weight without fins	101 m (331 ft. 4 in.)	William Trubridge (New Zealand)
Variable weight	142 m (465 ft. 10 in.)	Herbert Nitsch (Austria)
No limit	214 m (702 ft.)	Herbert Nitsch (Austria)
○ Free immersion	• 121 m (393 ft. 8 in.)	William Trubridge (New Zealand)

MEN'S DYNAMIC APNEA	DEPTH/TIME	NAME & NATIONALITY
○ With fins	265 m (869 ft. 5 in.)	Dave Mullins (New Zealand)
○ Without fins	218 m (715 ft. 2 in.)	Dave Mullins (New Zealand)

MEN'S STATIC APNEA	DEPTH/TIME	NAME & NATIONALITY
Duration	11 min. 35 sec.	Stephane Mifsud (France)

WOMEN'S DEPTH DISCIPLINES	DEPTH/TIME	NAME & NATIONALITY
○ Constant weight with fins	• 100 m (328 ft. 1 in.)	Natalia Molchanova (Russia)
Constant weight without fins	62 m (203 ft. 5 in.)	Natalia Molchanova (Russia)
○ Variable weight	126 m (413 ft. 4 in.)	Annelie Pompe (Sweden)
No limit	160 m (524 ft. 11 in.)	Tanya Streeter (U.S.A.)
Free immersion	85 m (278 ft. 10 in.)	Natalia Molchanova (Russia)

LOCATION	DATE
Moscow, Russia	May 29, 2010
Moscow, Russia	Aug. 6, 1987
Pruszków, Poland	Mar. 25, 2009
Copenhagen, Denmark	Mar. 25, 2010
Aguascalientes, Mexico	May 11, 2010
Aguascalientes, Mexico	May 12, 2010
Mexico City, Mexico	Oct. 1, 2003

○ **TEAM 500 M STANDING START** On March 25, 2010, Kaarle McCulloch (left) and Anna Meares (both Australia) achieved the fastest-ever team sprint by a female pair, winning the event in 32.923 seconds and breaking their own world record for a second time on the same day.

LOCATION	DATE
The Bahamas	Apr. 22, 2010
The Bahamas	Dec. 16, 2010
The Bahamas	Dec. 7, 2009
Spetses, Greece	Jun. 14, 2007
The Bahamas	Apr. 10, 2011

LOCATION	DATE
Porirua, New Zealand	Sep. 2, 2010
Porirua, New Zealand	Sep. 27, 2010

LOCATION	DATE
Hyères, France	Jun. 8, 2009

LOCATION	DATE
The Bahamas	Apr. 16, 2011
The Bahamas	Dec. 3, 2009
Sharm el Sheik, Egypt	Oct. 5, 2010
Turks and Caicos Islands	Aug. 17, 2002
Crete, Greece	Jul. 27, 2008

○ **WOMEN'S FREEDIVING, VARIABLE WEIGHT** On October 5, 2010, Annelie Pompe (Sweden) achieved a record depth of 413 ft. 4 in. (126 m) in the variable weight discipline in Sharm el Sheik, Egypt.

★ FREEDIVING ★

WOMEN'S DYNAMIC APNEA

	DEPTH/TIME	NAME & NATIONALITY
With fins	225 m (738 ft. 2 in.)	Natalia Molchanova (Russia)
Without fins	60 m (524 ft. 11 in.)	Natalia Molchanova (Russia)

WOMEN'S STATIC APNEA

	DEPTH/TIME	NAME & NATIONALITY
Duration	8 min. 23 sec.	Natalia Molchanova (Russia)

•Still awaiting ratification at the time of going to press

★ ROWING ★

MEN	TIME	NAME & NATIONALITY
Single sculls	6:33.35	Mahe Drysdale (New Zealand)
Double sculls	6:03.25	Jean-Baptiste Macquet, Adrien Hardy (France)
Quadruple sculls	5:36.20	Christopher Morgan, James McRae, Brendan Long, Daniel Noonan (Australia)
Coxless pairs	6:14.27	Matthew Pinsent, James Cracknell (GB)
Coxless fours	5:41.35	Sebastian Thormann, Paul Dienstbach, Philipp Stüer, Bernd Heidicker (Germany)
Coxed pairs*	6:42.16	Igor Boraska, Tihomir Frankovic, Milan Razov (Croatia)
Coxed fours*	5:58.96	Matthias Ungemach, Armin Eichholz, Armin Weyrauch, Bahne Rabe, Jörg Dederding (Germany)
Eights	5:19.85	Deakin, Beery, Hoopman, Volpenhein, Cipollone, Read, Allen, Ahrens, Hansen (U.S.A.)

LIGHTWEIGHT	TIME	NAME & NATIONALITY
Single sculls*	6:47.82	Zac Purchase (GB)
Double sculls	6:10.02	Mads Rasmussen, Rasmus Quist (Denmark)
Quadruple sculls*	5:45.18	Francesco Esposito, Massimo Lana, Michelangelo Crispi, Massimo Guglielmi (Italy)
Coxless pairs*	6:26.61	Tony O'Connor, Neville Maxwell (Ireland)
Coxless fours	5:45.60	Thomas Poulsen, Thomas Ebert, Eskild Ebbesen, Victor Feddersen (Denmark)
Eights*	5:30.24	Altena, Dahlke, Kobor, Stomporowski, Melges, März, Buchheit, Von Warburg, Kaska (Germany)

*Denotes non-Olympic boat classes

....

The ●largest gathering of people dressed as nurses was achieved by 116 participants at an event organized by the Kuwait Medical Students' Association at Dar Al Shifa Hospital in Kuwait on October 11, 2008.

....

LOCATION	DATE
Moscow, Russia	Apr. 25, 2010
Aarhus, Denmark	Aug. 20, 2009

LOCATION	DATE
Aarhus, Denmark	Aug. 21, 2009

LOCATION	DATE
Poznan, Poland	Aug. 29, 2009
Poznan, Poland	Jun. 17, 2006
Beijing, China	Aug. 10, 2008
Seville, Spain	Sep. 21, 2002
Seville, Spain	Sep. 21, 2002
Indianapolis, U.S.A.	Sep. 18, 1994
Vienna, Austria	Aug. 24, 1991
Athens, Greece	Aug. 15, 2004

LOCATION	DATE
Eton, UK	Aug. 26, 2006
Amsterdam, the Netherlands	Jun. 23, 2007
Montreal, Canada	Aug. 1992
Paris, France	1994
Lucerne, Switzerland	Jul. 9, 1999
Montreal, Canada	Aug. 1992

OFFICIAL WEBSITES

FREEDIVING
www.aida-international.org

ROWING
www.worldrowing.org

SPEED SKATING
www.isu.org

Laurence Wicks (UK) completed the ○**fastest marathon dressed as a doctor (male)** in 4 hr. 16 min. 9 sec. at the Leicester Marathon in Leicester, UK, on August 10, 2010.

1,491: Length, in miles, of the airways in your lungs—more than seven times as long as the New York City subway. Flattened out, your lungs would cover about 807 ft.^{2}—an area the size of half a tennis court inside your chest.

★ ROWING ★

WOMEN	TIME	NAME & NATIONALITY
Single sculls	7:07.71	Rumyana Neykova (Bulgaria)
Double sculls	6:38.78	Georgina and Caroline Evers-Swindell (New Zealand)
Quadruple sculls	6:10.80	Kathrin Boron, Katrin Rutschow-Stomporowski, Jana Sorgers, Kerstin Köppen (Germany)
Coxless pairs	6:53.80	Georgeta Andrunache, Viorica Susanu (Romania)
Coxless fours*	6:25.35	Robyn Selby Smith, Jo Lutz, Amber Bradley, Kate Hornsey (Australia)
Eights	5:55.50	Mickelson, Whipple, Lind, Goodale, Sickler, Cooke, Shoop, Francia, Davies (U.S.A.)

LIGHTWEIGHT	TIME	NAME & NATIONALITY
Single sculls*	7:28.15	Constanta Pipota (Romania)
Double sculls	6:49.77	Dongxiang Xu, Shimin Yan (China)
Quadruple sculls*	6:23.96	Hua Yu, Haixia Chen, Xuefei Fan, Jing Liu (China)
Coxless pairs*	7:18.32	Eliza Blair, Justine Joyce (Australia)

*Denotes non-Olympic boat classes

★ SPEED SKATING—LONG TRACK ★

MEN	TIME/ POINTS	NAME & NATIONALITY
500 m	34.03	Jeremy Wotherspoon (Canada)
2 x 500 m	68.31	Jeremy Wotherspoon (Canada)
1,000 m	1:06.42	Shani Davis (U.S.A.)
1,500 m	1:41.04	Shani Davis (U.S.A.)
3,000 m	3:37.28	Eskil Ervik (Norway)
5,000 m	6:03.32	Sven Kramer (Netherlands)
10,000 m	12:41.69	Sven Kramer (Netherlands)
500/1,000/500/1,000 m	137.230 points	Jeremy Wotherspoon (Canada)
500/3,000/1,500/5,000 m	146.365 points	Erben Wennemars (Netherlands)
500/5,000/1,500/10,000 m	145.742 points	Shani Davis (U.S.A.)
Team pursuit (eight laps)	3:37.80	Netherlands (Sven Kramer, Carl Verheijen, Erben Wennemars)

LOCATION	DATE
Seville, Spain	Sep. 21, 2002
Seville, Spain	Sep. 21, 2002
Duisburg, Germany	May 19, 1996
Seville, Spain	Sep. 21, 2002
Eton, UK	Aug. 26, 2006
Eton, UK	Aug. 27, 2006

LOCATION	DATE
Paris, France	Jun. 19, 1994
Poznan, Poland	Jun. 17, 2006
Eton, UK	Aug. 27, 2006
Aiguebelette-le-Lac, France	Sep. 7, 1997

LOCATION	DATE
Salt Lake City, U.S.A.	Nov. 9, 2007
Calgary, Canada	Mar. 15, 2008
Salt Lake City, U.S.A.	Mar. 7, 2009
Salt Lake City, U.S.A.	Dec. 11, 2009
Calgary, Canada	Nov. 5, 2005
Calgary, Canada	Nov. 17, 2007
Salt Lake City, U.S.A.	Mar. 10, 2007
Calgary, Canada	Jan. 18–19, 2003
Calgary, Canada	Aug. 12–13, 2005
Calgary, Canada	Mar. 18–19, 2006
Salt Lake City, U.S.A.	Mar. 11, 2007

★ SPEED SKATING—LONG TRACK ★

WOMEN	TIME/ POINTS	NAME & NATIONALITY
500 m	37.00	Jenny Wolf (Germany)
2 x 500 m	74.42	Jenny Wolf (Germany)
1,000 m	1:13.11	Cindy Klassen (Canada)
1,500 m	1:51.79	Cindy Klassen (Canada)
3,000 m	3:53.34	Cindy Klassen (Canada)
○ 5,000 m	•6:42.66	Martina Sáblíková (Czech Republic)
500/1,000/500/1,000 m	149.305 points	Monique Garbrecht-Enfeldt (Germany)
	149.305 points	Cindy Klassen (Canada)
500/1,500/1,000/3,000 m	155.576 points	Cindy Klassen (Canada)
500/3,000/1,500/5,000 m	154.580 points	Cindy Klassen (Canada)
Team pursuit (six laps)	2:55.79	Canada (Kristina Groves, Christine Nesbitt, Brittany Schussler)

•Still awaiting ratification at the time of going to press

★ SPEED SKATING—SHORT TRACK ★

MEN	TIME/ POINTS	NAME & NATIONALITY
500 m	40.651	Sung Si-Bak (South Korea)
1,000 m	1:23.454	Charles Hamelin (Canada)
1,500 m	2:10.639	Ahn Hyun-Soo (South Korea)
3,000 m	4:32.646	Ahn Hyun-Soo (South Korea)
5,000 m relay	6:38.486	South Korea (Kwak Yoon-Gy, Lee Ho-Suk, Lee Jung-Su, Sung Si-Bak)

WOMEN	TIME/ POINTS	NAME & NATIONALITY
500 m	42.609	Wang Meng (China)
1,000 m	1:29.049	Zhou Yang (China)
1,500 m	2:16.729	Zhou Yang (China)
3,000 m	4:46.983	Jung Eun-Ju (South Korea)
3,000 m relay	4:06.610	China (Sun Linlin, Wang Meng, Zhang Hui, Zhou Yang)

LOCATION	DATE
Salt Lake City, U.S.A.	Dec. 11, 2009
Salt Lake City, U.S.A.	Mar. 10, 2007
Calgary, Canada	Mar. 25, 2006
Salt Lake City, U.S.A.	Nov. 20, 2005
Calgary, Canada	Mar. 18, 2006
Salt Lake City, U.S.A.	Feb. 18, 2011
Salt Lake City, U.S.A.	Jan. 11–12, 2003
Calgary, Canada	Mar. 24–25, 2006
Calgary, Canada	Mar. 15–17, 2001
Calgary, Canada	Mar. 18–19, 2006
Calgary, Canada	Dec. 6, 2009

WOMEN'S 500 M LONG TRACK Jenny Wolf (Germany) sped to a new world record of 37 seconds in the 500 m event at the ISU World Cup Speed Skating Championships in Salt Lake City, U.S.A., on December 11, 2009.

LOCATION	DATE
Marquette, U.S.A.	Nov. 14, 2009
Montreal, Canada	Jan. 18, 2009
Marquette, U.S.A.	Oct. 24, 2003
Beijing, China	Dec. 7, 2003
Salt Lake City, U.S.A.	Oct. 19, 2008

LOCATION	DATE
Beijing, China	Nov. 29, 2008
Vancouver, Canada	Feb. 26, 2010
Salt Lake City, U.S.A.	Feb. 9, 2008
Harbin, China	Mar. 15, 2008
Vancouver, Canada	Feb. 24, 2010

WOMEN'S 1,000 M SHORT TRACK On February 26, 2010, China's Zhou Yang broke the 1,000 m short track world speed skating record by almost half a second, achieving a time of 1 min. 29.049 sec. at the 2010 Vancouver Winter Olympics in Vancouver, Canada.

★ SWIMMING—LONG COURSE [50 M POOL] ★

MEN	TIME	NAME & NATIONALITY
50 m freestyle	20.91	Cesar Cielo Filho (Brazil)
100 m freestyle	46.91	Cesar Cielo Filho (Brazil)
200 m freestyle	1:42.00	Paul Biedermann (Germany)
400 m freestyle	3:40.07	Paul Biedermann (Germany)
800 m freestyle	7:32.12	Zhang Lin (China)
1,500 m freestyle	14:34.56	Grant Hackett (Australia)
4 x 100 m freestyle relay	3:08.24	U.S.A. (Michael Phelps, Garrett Weber-Gale, Cullen Jones, Jason Lezak)
4 x 200 m freestyle relay	6:58.55	U.S.A. (Michael Phelps, Ricky Berens, David Walters, Ryan Lochte)
50 m butterfly	22.43	Rafael Muñoz (Spain)
100 m butterfly	49.82	Michael Phelps (U.S.A.)
200 m butterfly	1:51.51	Michael Phelps (U.S.A.)
50 m backstroke	24.04	Liam Tancock (UK)
100 m backstroke	51.94	Aaron Peirsol (U.S.A.)
200 m backstroke	1:51.92	Aaron Peirsol (U.S.A.)
50 m breaststroke	26.67	Cameron van der Burgh (South Africa)
100 m breaststroke	58.58	Brenton Rickard (Australia)
200 m breaststroke	2:07.31	Christian Sprenger (Australia)
200 m medley	1:54.10	Ryan Lochte (U.S.A.)
400 m medley	4:03.84	Michael Phelps (U.S.A.)
4 x 100 m medley relay	3:27.28	U.S.A. (Aaron Peirsol, Eric Shanteau, Michael Phelps, David Walters)

WOMEN	TIME	NAME & NATIONALITY
50 m freestyle	23.73	Britta Steffen (Germany)
100 m freestyle	52.07	Britta Steffen (Germany)
200 m freestyle	1:52.98	Federica Pellegrini (Italy)
400 m freestyle	3:59.15	Federica Pellegrini (Italy)
800 m freestyle	8:14.10	Rebecca Adlington (UK)
1,500 m freestyle	15:42.54	Kate Ziegler (U.S.A.)
4 x 100 m freestyle relay	3:31.72	Netherlands (Inge Dekker, Ranomi Kromowidjojo, Femke Heemskerk, Marleen Veldhuis)
4 x 200 m freestyle relay	7:42.08	China (Yang Yu, Zhu Qian Wei, Liu Jing, Pang Jiaying)
50 m butterfly	25.07	Therese Alshammar (Sweden)
100 m butterfly	56.06	Sarah Sjöström (Sweden)
200 m butterfly	2:01.81	Liu Zige (China)
50 m backstroke	27.06	Zhao Jing (China)
100 m backstroke	58.12	Gemma Spofforth (UK)
200 m backstroke	2:04.81	Kirsty Coventry (Zimbabwe)
50 m breaststroke	29.80	Jessica Hardy (U.S.A.)
100 m breaststroke	1:04.45	Jessica Hardy (U.S.A.)
200 m breaststroke	2:20.12	Annamay Pierse (Canada)
200 m medley	2:06.15	Ariana Kukors (U.S.A.)
400 m medley	4:29.45	Stephanie Rice (Australia)
4 x 100 m medley relay	3:52.19	China (Zhao Jing, Chen Huijia, Jiao Liuyang, Li Zhesi)

LOCATION	DATE
Sao Paulo, Brazil	Dec. 18, 2009
Rome, Italy	Jul. 30, 2009
Rome, Italy	Jul. 28, 2009
Rome, Italy	Jul. 26, 2009
Rome, Italy	Jul. 29, 2009
Fukuoka, Japan	Jul. 29, 2001
Beijing, China	Aug. 11, 2008
Rome, Italy	Jul. 31, 2009
Malaga, Spain	Apr. 5, 2009
Rome, Italy	Aug. 1, 2009
Rome, Italy	Jul. 29, 2009
Rome, Italy	Aug. 2, 2009
Indianapolis, U.S.A.	Jul. 8, 2009
Rome, Italy	Jul. 31, 2009
Rome, Italy	Jul. 29, 2009
Rome, Italy	Jul. 27, 2009
Rome, Italy	Jul. 30, 2009
Rome, Italy	Jul. 30, 2009
Beijing, China	Aug. 10, 2008
Rome, Italy	Aug. 2, 2009

MEN'S 100 M FREESTYLE
On July 30, 2009, Cesar Cielo Filho (Brazil) broke the men's 100 m long-course freestyle world record by just 0.03 seconds, finishing in a time of 46.91 seconds in the event's final at the 13th FINA World Championships in Rome, Italy.

LOCATION	DATE
Rome, Italy	Aug. 2, 2009
Rome, Italy	Jul. 31, 2009
Rome, Italy	Jul. 29, 2009
Rome, Italy	Jul. 26, 2009
Beijing, China	Aug. 16, 2008
Mission Viejo, U.S.A.	Jun. 17, 2007
Rome, Italy	Jul. 26, 2009
Rome, Italy	Jul. 30, 2009
Rome, Italy	Jul. 31, 2009
Rome, Italy	Jul. 27, 2009
Jinan, China	Oct. 21, 2009
Rome, Italy	Jul. 30, 2009
Rome, Italy	Jul. 28, 2009
Rome, Italy	Aug. 1, 2009
Federal Way, U.S.A.	Aug. 7, 2009
Federal Way, U.S.A.	Aug. 7, 2009
Rome, Italy	Jul. 30, 2009
Rome, Italy	Jul. 27, 2009
Beijing, China	Aug. 10, 2008
Rome, Italy	Aug. 1, 2009

WOMEN'S 200 M BUTTERFLY
China's Liu Zige—pictured while competing in the 2009 FINA World Championships in Rome, Italy—claimed the world record in the 200 m long-course butterfly on October 21 of the same year, covering the distance in a time of just 2 min. 1.81 sec. in Jinan, China.

8,150: Portions of French fries you will eat in a lifetime—a total weight of 1.8 tons, or the equivalent of the 12 players and four officials on the ice at any one time during an ice hockey game.

★ SWIMMING—SHORT COURSE [25 M POOL] ★

MEN	TIME	NAME & NATIONALITY
50 m freestyle	20.30	Roland Schoeman (South Africa)
100 m freestyle	44.94	Amaury Leveaux (France)
200 m freestyle	1:39.37	Paul Biedermann (Germany)
400 m freestyle	3:32.77	Paul Biedermann (Germany)
800 m freestyle	7:23.42	Grant Hackett (Australia)
1,500 freestyle	14:10.10	Grant Hackett (Australia)
4 x 100 m freestyle relay	3:03.30	U.S.A. (Nathan Adrian, Matt Grevers, Garrett Weber-Gale, Michael Phelps)
4 x 200 m freestyle relay	6:49.04	Russia (Nikita Lobintsev, Danila Izotov, Evgeny Lagunov, Alexander Sukhorukov)
50 m butterfly	21.80	Steffen Deibler (Germany)
100 m butterfly	48.48	Evgeny Korotyshkin (Russia)
200 m butterfly	1:49.11	Kaio Almeida (Brazil)
50 m backstroke	22.61	Peter Marshall (U.S.A.)
100 m backstroke	48.94	Nick Thoman (U.S.A.)
200 m backstroke	1:46.11	Arkady Vyatchanin (Russia)
50 m breaststroke	25.25	Cameron van der Burgh (South Africa)
100 m breaststroke	55.61	Cameron van der Burgh (South Africa)
200 m breaststroke	2:00.67	Daniel Gyurta (Hungary)
100 m medley	50.76	Peter Mankoc (Slovenia)
○ 200 m medley	1:50.08	Ryan Lochte (U.S.A.)
○ 400 m medley	3:55.50	Ryan Lochte (U.S.A.)
4 x 100 m medley relay	3:19.16	Russia (Stanislav Donets, Sergey Geybel, Evgeny Korotyshkin, Danila Izotov)

WOMEN	TIME	NAME & NATIONALITY
50 m freestyle	23.25	Marleen Veldhuis (Netherlands)
100 m freestyle	51.01	Lisbeth Trickett (Australia)
200 m freestyle	1:51.17	Federica Pellegrini (Italy)
400 m freestyle	3:54.92	Joanne Jackson (UK)
800 m freestyle	8:04.53	Alessia Filippi (Italy)
1,500 freestyle	15:28.65	Lotte Friis (Denmark)
4 x 100 m freestyle relay	3:28.22	Netherlands (Hinkelien Schreuder, Inge Dekker, Ranomi Kromowidjojo, Marleen Veldhuis)

UK cricketer David Gower batted for 119 Test match innings in a row without being dismissed for a duck (zero runs) between 1982 and 1990, the **most consecutive Test match innings without a duck**.

LOCATION	DATE
Pietermaritzburg, South Africa	Aug. 8, 2009
Rijeka, Croatia	Dec. 13, 2008
Berlin, Germany	Nov. 15, 2009
Berlin, Germany	Nov. 14, 2009
Melbourne, Australia	Jul. 20, 2008
Perth, Australia	Aug. 7, 2001
Manchester, UK	Dec. 19, 2009
Dubai, UAE	Dec. 16, 2010
Berlin, Germany	Nov. 14, 2009
Berlin, Germany	Nov. 15, 2009
Stockholm, Sweden	Nov. 10, 2009
Singapore	Nov. 22, 2009
Manchester, UK	Dec. 18, 2009
Berlin, Germany	Nov. 15, 2009
Berlin, Germany	Nov. 14, 2009
Berlin, Germany	Nov. 15, 2009
Istanbul, Turkey	Dec. 13, 2009
Istanbul, Turkey	Dec. 12, 2009
Dubai, UAE	Dec. 17, 2010
Dubai, UAE	Dec. 16, 2010
St Petersburg, Russia	Dec. 20, 2009

○ **MEN'S 4 X 200 M FREESTYLE RELAY** Nikita Lobintsev, Danila Izotov, Evgeny Lagunov, and Alexander Sukhorukov (all Russia) swam the men's 4 x 200 m freestyle relay in 6 min. 49.04 sec. at the 10th FINA World Swimming Championships (25 m) in Dubai, UAE, on December 16, 2010.

LOCATION	DATE
Manchester, UK	Apr. 13, 2008
Hobart, Australia	Aug. 10, 2009
Istanbul, Turkey	Dec. 13, 2009
Leeds, UK	Aug. 8, 2009
Rijeka, Croatia	Dec. 12, 2008
Birkerod, Denmark	Nov. 28, 2009
Amsterdam, the Netherlands	Dec. 19, 2008

OFFICIAL WEBSITES

SWIMMING
Federation Internationale
de Natation
www.fina.org

Sri Lankan Muttiah Muralitharan has recorded the **most man of the series awards in Test cricket by an individual player**, with 11 titles between 1992 and 2009.

★ SWIMMING—SHORT COURSE [25 M POOL] ★

WOMEN	TIME	NAME & NATIONALITY
○ 4 x 200 m freestyle relay	7:35.94	China (Chen Qian, Tang Yi, Kiu Jing, Zhu Qianwei)
50 m butterfly	24.38	Therese Alshammar (Sweden)
100 m butterfly	55.05	Diane Bui-Duyet (France)
200 m butterfly	2:00.78	Liu Zige (China)
50 m backstroke	25.70	Sanja Jovanovic (Croatia)
100 m backstroke	55.23	Sakai Shiho (Japan)
200 m backstroke	2:00.18	Sakai Shiho (Japan)
50 m breaststroke	28.80	Jessica Hardy (U.S.A.)
100 m breaststroke	1:02.70	Rebecca Soni (U.S.A.)
200 m breaststroke	2:14.57	Rebecca Soni (U.S.A.)
100 m medley	57.74	Hinkelien Schreuder (Netherlands)
200 m medley	2:04.60	Julia Smit (U.S.A.)
400 m medley	4:21.04	Julia Smit (U.S.A.)
4 x 100 m medley relay	3:47.97	U.S.A. (Margaret Hoelzer, Jessica Hardy, Dana Vollmer, Amanda Weir)

★ WEIGHTLIFTING ★

MEN	CATEGORY	WEIGHT	NAME & NATIONALITY
56 kg	Snatch	138 kg	Halil Mutlu (Turkey)
	Clean & jerk	168 kg	Halil Mutlu (Turkey)
	Total	305 kg	Halil Mutlu (Turkey)
62 kg	Snatch	153 kg	Shi Zhiyong (China)
	Clean & jerk	182 kg	Le Maosheng (China)
	Total	326 kg	Zhang Jie (China)
69 kg	Snatch	165 kg	Georgi Markov (Bulgaria)
	○ Clean & jerk	198 kg	Liao Hui (China)
	○ Total	358 kg	Liao Hui (China)
77 kg	Snatch	174 kg	Lu Xiaojun (China)
	Clean & jerk	210 kg	Oleg Perepetchenov (Russia)
	Total	378 kg	Lu Xiaojun (China)
85 kg	Snatch	187 kg	Andrei Rybakou (Belarus)
	Clean & jerk	218 kg	Zhang Yong (China)
	Total	394 kg	Andrei Rybakou (Belarus)
94 kg	Snatch	188 kg	Akakios Kakhiasvilis (Greece)
	Clean & jerk	232 kg	Szymon Kolecki (Poland)
	Total	412 kg	Akakios Kakhiasvilis (Greece)
105 kg	Snatch	200 kg	Andrei Aramnau (Belarus)
	Clean & jerk	237 kg	Alan Tsagaev (Bulgaria)
	Total	436 kg	Andrei Aramnau (Belarus)
105+ kg	Snatch	213 kg	Hossein Rezazadeh (Iran)
	Clean & jerk	263 kg	Hossein Rezazadeh (Iran)
	Total	472 kg	Hossein Rezazadeh (Iran)

LOCATION	DATE
Dubai, UAE	Dec. 15, 2010
Singapore	Nov. 22, 2009
Istanbul, Turkey	Dec. 12, 2009
Berlin, Germany	Nov. 15, 2009
Istanbul, Turkey	Dec. 12, 2009
Berlin, Germany	Nov. 15, 2009
Berlin, Germany	Nov. 14, 2009
Berlin, Germany	Nov. 15, 2009
Manchester, UK	Dec. 19, 2009
Manchester, UK	Dec. 18, 2009
Berlin, Germany	Nov. 15, 2009
Manchester, UK	Dec. 19, 2009
Manchester, UK	Dec. 18, 2009
Manchester, UK	Dec. 18, 2009

WOMEN'S 200 M BREASTSTROKE
On December 18, 2009, during the Duel in the Pool in Manchester, UK, Rebecca Soni (U.S.A.) swam the women's 200 m short-course breaststroke in a record time of 2 min. 14.57 sec.

LOCATION	DATE
Antalya, Turkey	Nov. 4, 2001
Trencín, Slovakia	Apr. 24, 2001
Sydney, Australia	Sep. 16, 2000
Izmir, Turkey	Jun. 28, 2002
Busan, South Korea	Oct. 2, 2002
Kanazawa, Japan	Apr. 28, 2008
Sydney, Australia	Sep. 20, 2000
Antalya, Turkey	Sep. 21, 2010
Antalya, Turkey	Sep. 21, 2010
Goyang, South Korea	Nov. 24, 2009
Trencín, Slovakia	Apr. 27, 2001
Goyang, South Korea	Nov. 24, 2009
Chiang Mai, Thailand	Sep. 22, 2007
Ramat Gan, Israel	Apr. 25, 1998
Beijing, China	Aug. 15, 2008
Athens, Greece	Nov. 27, 1999
Sofia, Bulgaria	Apr. 29, 2000
Athens, Greece	Nov. 27, 1999
Beijing, China	Aug. 18, 2008
Kiev, Ukraine	Apr. 25, 2004
Beijing, China	Aug. 18, 2008
Qinhuangdao, China	Sep. 14, 2003
Athens, Greece	Aug. 25, 2004
Sydney, Australia	Sep. 26, 2000

○**MEN'S 69 KG: CLEAN & JERK, TOTAL** Liao Hui (China) achieved records of 198 kg in the clean & jerk category and 358 kg in the total category at the World Championships in Antalya, Turkey, on September 21, 2010. These feats earned him a second 69 kg World Championships gold medal to add to the one he picked up a year earlier competing in Goyang, South Korea (pictured).

16: The average age of the average body. Apart from your eyes, heart, and brain, your cells live less than 16 years before being replaced. At the age of 17, your first memory is already one of the oldest "parts" of you.

★ WEIGHTLIFTING ★

WOMEN	CATEGORY	WEIGHT	NAME & NATIONALITY
48 kg	Snatch	98 kg	Yang Lian (China)
	○ Clean & jerk	121 kg	Nurcan Taylan (Turkey)
	Total	217 kg	Yang Lian (China)
53 kg	○ Snatch	103 kg	Li Ping (China)
	Clean & jerk	129 kg	Li Ping (China)
	○ Total	230 kg	Li Ping (China)
58 kg	Snatch	111 kg	Chen Yanqing (China)
	Clean & jerk	141 kg	Qiu Hongmei (China)
	Total	251 kg	Chen Yanqing (China)
63 kg	Snatch	116 kg	Pawina Thongsuk (Thailand)
	○ Clean & jerk	143 kg	Maiya Maneza (Kazakhstan)
	Total	257 kg	Liu Haixia (China)
69 kg	Snatch	128 kg	Liu Chunhong (China)
	Clean & jerk	158 kg	Liu Chunhong (China)
	Total	286 kg	Liu Chunhong (China)
75 kg	○ Snatch	134 kg	Svetlana Podobedova (Kazakhstan)
	○ Clean & jerk	161 kg	Svetlana Podobedova (Kazakhstan)
	○ Total	295 kg	Svetlana Podobedova (Kazakhstan)
75+ kg	○ Snatch	145 kg	Tatiana Kashirina (Russia)
	Clean & jerk	187 kg	Jang Mi-Ran (South Korea)
	Total	326 kg	Jang Mi-Ran (South Korea)

★ LONGEST SPORTS MARATHONS ★

SPORT	TIME	NAME & NATIONALITY
○ Aerobics	29 hr. 5 min.	Julian Hitch (UK)
Baseball	48 hr. 9 min. 27 sec.	Jonny G Foundation Cardinals and Edward Jones Browns (U.S.A.)
○ Basketball	107 hours	György Boronkay Technical and Grammar School (Hungary)
Basketball (wheelchair)	26 hr. 3 min.	University of Omaha students and staff (U.S.A.)
○ Bowling (tenpin)	134 hr. 57 min.	Stephen Shanabrook (U.S.A.)
Bowls (indoor)	36 hours	Arnos Bowling Club (UK)
Bowls (outdoor)	170 hr. 3 min.	Goulburn Railway Bowling Club (Australia)
○ Cricket	105 hours	Blunham Cricket Club (UK)
Curling	54 hr. 1 min.	The Burlington Golf and Country Club (Canada)

LOCATION	DATE
Santo Domingo, Dominican Republic	Oct. 1, 2006
Antalya, Turkey	Sep. 17, 2010
Santo Domingo, Dominican Republic	Oct. 1, 2006
Guangzhou, China	Nov. 14, 2010
Taian City, China	Apr. 22, 2007
Guangzhou, China	Nov. 14, 2010
Doha, Qatar	Dec. 3, 2006
Taian City, China	Apr. 23, 2007
Doha, Qatar	Dec. 3, 2006
Doha, Qatar	Nov. 12, 2005
Antalya, Turkey	Sep. 20, 2010
Chiang Mai, Thailand	Sep. 23, 2007
Beijing, China	Aug. 13, 2008
Beijing, China	Aug. 13, 2008
Beijing, China	Aug. 13, 2008
Antalya, Turkey	Sep. 23, 2010
Antalya, Turkey	Sep. 23, 2010
Antalya, Turkey	Sep. 23, 2010
Antalya, Turkey	Sep. 23, 2010
Goyang, South Korea	Nov. 28, 2009
Beijing, China	Aug. 16, 2008

○WOMEN'S 75 KG: SNATCH, CLEAN & JERK, TOTAL On September 23, 2010, at the World Championships in Antalya, Turkey, Svetlana Podobedova (Kazakhstan) swept the board in the women's 75 kg competition, achieving new world records in snatch (134 kg), clean & jerk (161 kg), and total (295 kg).

LOCATION	DATE
London, UK	Apr. 24–25, 2010
St. Louis, Missouri, U.S.A.	Oct. 9–11, 2009
Vác, Hungary	Jul. 1–5, 2010
Omaha, Nebraska, U.S.A.	Sep. 24–25, 2004
Plano, Texas, U.S.A.	Jun. 14–19, 2010
Southgate, London, UK	Apr. 20–21, 2002
Goulburn, NSW, Australia	Jan. 19–26, 2009
Blunham, Bedfordshire, UK	Aug. 26–30, 2010
Burlington, Ontario, Canada	Mar. 12–14, 2010

★ LONGEST SPORTS MARATHONS ★

SPORT	TIME	NAME & NATIONALITY
○ Darts (doubles)	32 hr. 4 min.	Scott Maynard, Nathanael Hubbard, Chris Taylor, Shane Rose (Australia)
○ Darts (singles)	32 hr. 25 min.	Joanne and Danielle Tonks (UK)
○ Floorball	25 hr. 13 min.	London Sharks and friends (UK)
○ Soccer	60 hours	Pink Panthers and Black Eagles (UK)
○ Soccer (five-a-side)	33 hr. 30 min.	Youghal United AFC (Ireland)
Hockey (ice)	241 hr. 21 min.	Brent Saik and friends (Canada)
Hockey (indoor)	50 hours	Bert & Macs and Mid-Town Certigard teams (Canada)
○ Hockey (inline/roller)	25 hr. 20 min.	Roller Hockey Guernerin (France)
Hockey (street)	105 hr. 17 min.	Molson Canadian and Canadian Tire teams (Canada)
Korfball	30 hr. 2 min.	Kingfisher Korfball Club (UK)
Netball	58 hours	Sleaford Netball Club (UK)
Pétanque (boules)	52 hours	Gilles de B'Heinsch (Belgium)
Pool (singles)	53 hr. 25 min.	Brian Lilley and Daniel Maloney (U.S.A.)
Skiing	202 hr. 1 min.	Nick Willey (Australia)
Snowboarding	180 hr. 34 min.	Bernhard Mair (Austria)
Table soccer	51 hr. 52 min.	Alexander Gruber, Roman Schelling, Enrico Lechtaler, Christian Nägele (Austria)
Table tennis (doubles)	101 hr. 1 min. 11 sec.	Lance, Phil, and Mark Warren, Bill Weir (U.S.A.)
Table tennis (singles)	132 hr. 31 min.	Danny Price and Randy Nunes (U.S.A.)
○ Tennis (doubles)	56 hr. 37 min. 13 sec.	Gavin White, Jeganathan Ramasamy, Simon Burk, David Sears (Australia)
○ Tennis (singles)	55 hr. 55 min. 55 sec.	Christian Masurenko and Denis Heitmann (Germany)
○ Volleyball (beach)	25 hr. 39 min.	Mateusz Baca, Sebastian Lüdke, Tomasz Olszak, Wojciech Kurczynski (Germany)
Volleyball (indoor)	76 hr. 30 min.	Zespól Szkól Ekonomicznych students (Poland)

Measuring around 400 ft. (120 m) tall, the Jetavanarama Dagoba in the ancient city of Anuradhapura, Sri Lanka, is the **largest Buddhist brick monument**.

LOCATION	DATE
Chapel Hill, Queensland, Australia	May 22, 2010
Stafford, Staffordshire, UK	Apr. 30–May 1, 2010
Haywards Head, West Sussex, UK	May 29–30, 2010
Loughborough, Leicestershire, UK	Oct. 22–24, 2010
Youghal, Ireland	Jun. 5–7, 2010
Strathcona, Alberta, Canada	Feb. 8–18, 2008
Lethbridge, Alberta, Canada	Mar. 25–27, 2008
La Guérinière, France	Dec. 3–4, 2010
Lethbridge, Alberta, Canada	Aug. 20–24, 2008
Larkfield, Kent, UK	Jun. 14–15, 2008
Sleaford, Lincolnshire, UK	Jul. 25–27, 2008
Arlon, Belgium	Sep. 18–20, 2009
Spring Lake, North Carolina, U.S.A.	Oct. 10–12, 2008
Thredbo, NSW, Australia	Sep. 2–10, 2005
Bad Kleinkirchheim, Austria	Jan. 9–16, 2004
Bregenz, Austria	Jun. 27–29, 2008
Sacramento, California, U.S.A.	Apr. 9–13, 1979
Cherry Hill, New Jersey, U.S.A.	Aug. 20–26, 1978
Sydney, NSW, Australia	Sep. 10–12, 2010
Herford, Germany	Aug. 6–8, 2010
Görlitz, Germany	Jul. 3–4, 2010
Sosnowiec, Poland	Dec. 4–7, 2009

Our final connection brings us back to China, where we started—in Lushan County, Henan Province, you'll find the O**tallest Buddha statue**, the Zhongyuan Buddha, which measures 418 ft. 76 in. (127.64 m).

★ WATERSKIING ★

MEN	RECORD	NAME & NATIONALITY
O Slalom	2 buoy | 9.75 m line | 58 km/h	Chris Parrish (U.S.A.)
Barefoot slalom	20.6 crossings of wake in 30 seconds	Keith St Onge (U.S.A.)
Tricks	12,400 points	Nicolas Le Forestier (France)
O Barefoot tricks	12,150 points	David Small (GB)
Jump	75.2 m (246 ft. 8 in.)	Freddy Krueger (U.S.A.)
O Barefoot jump	29.9 m (98 ft. 1 in.)	David Small (GB)
Ski fly	91.1 m (298 ft. 10 in.)	Jaret Llewellyn (Canada)
Overall	2,818.01 points*	Jaret Llewellyn (Canada)

WOMEN	RECORD	NAME & NATIONALITY
O Slalom	1.5 buoy | 10.25 m line | 55 km/h	Regina Jaquess (U.S.A.)
Barefoot slalom	17.0 crossings of wake in 30 seconds	Nadine de Villiers (South Africa)
O Tricks	9,690 points	Natallia Berdnikava (Belarus)
Barefoot tricks	4,400 points	Nadine de Villiers (South Africa)
O Jump	57.1 m (187 ft. 4 in.)	June Fladborg (Denmark)
O Barefoot jump	21 m (69 ft.)	Elaine Heller (U.S.A.)
Ski fly	69.4 m (227 ft. 8.2 in.)	Elena Milakova (Russia)
O Overall	2,945.85 points**	Regina Jaquess (U.S.A.)

*5@11.25 m, 10,730 tricks, 71.7 m jump

**4@10.75 m, 7,920 tricks, 53.6 m jump; calculated with the 2006 scoring method

LOCATION	DATE
Covington, U.S.A.	Jun. 13, 2010
Bronkhorstspruit, South Africa	Jan. 6, 2006
Lac de Joux, Switzerland	Sep. 4, 2005
Adna, U.S.A.	Jun. 12, 2010
Seffner, U.S.A.	Nov. 2, 2008
Brandenburg, Germany	Aug. 11, 2010
Orlando, U.S.A.	May 14, 2000
Seffner, U.S.A.	Sep. 29, 2002

LOCATION	DATE
Santa Rosa, U.S.A.	Oct. 24, 2010
Witbank, South Africa	Jan. 5, 2001
Winter Garden, U.S.A.	Oct. 26, 2010
Witbank, South Africa	Jan. 5, 2001
Lincoln, UK	Aug. 24, 2010
Brandenburg, Germany	Aug. 12, 2010
Pine Mountain, U.S.A.	May 26, 2002
Santa Rosa, U.S.A.	Jun. 20, 2010

○ WOMEN'S BAREFOOT JUMP
Elaine Heller (U.S.A.), pictured at the 2009 Barefoot Ski Nationals at Mystic Lakes in Maize, Kansas, U.S.A., jumped a record 69 ft. (21 m) in the same event in Brandenburg, Germany, on August 12, 2010.

ACKNOWLEDGMENTS

Guinness World Records would like to thank the following individuals, organizations, groups, websites, schools, colleges, and universities for their help and advice in compiling this year's edition:

3Run; Academy of Motion Picture Arts & Sciences; Shabir Ahluwalia; *Airboating Magazine* LLC (Matt Hartman); Carmen Alfonzo Portillo; Alfons Andresson Gidlöf; Vilgot Andresson Gidlöf; Ulla Anlander; Paulina Amaya; Arctic Kingdom; Ascent Media; Attenda (Charlotte, Phil, Mark, and team); Bender Helper Impact (Eric Kanner, Alyson Hagert, Mark Karges, Brian Reinert); Back-to-back worldwide competition; BBC Radio 3; Bender Media (Susan and Sally); Maud Bissier; Baby Boatface; Joseph Boatfield; Luke Boatfield; Box Office Mojo; British Airways; British Film Institute; The Bronx Zoo (Linda Wied); Sarah Brown; Bureau of Indian Affairs, United States Department of the Interior (Dr. Richard Meyers, Ms. Teddi Penland); CAN Networks (Paul, Damaris, and team); Angelo Carbone; Clara Chambers; Camille Chambers; Georgina Charles; Mark Chisnell; Christie's–London (Meg Ford); Simone Ciancotti; Vincenzo Di Cillo; Adam Cloke; Antonia Coffman; Collaboration (Mr. Suzuki, Miho, Masumi, and all our friends); Comic Relief; Connection Cars (Tracey Dunkerley, Rob Dunkerley); Consumer Electronics Association (Carolyn Slater); *Coronation Street* (ITV); Council on Tall Buildings and Urban Habitat (Marshall Gerometta); CYCLO IMAGE Co. Ltd. (Ken Arai); Deep Metal Piercing, Dortmund, Germany; Denmaur Independent Papers Limited; East Looe Town Trust, Cornwall, UK; The Eden Project, London; Louis Epstein; Kate Ereira; Europroduzione/Veralia (Marco, Stefano, Gabriel, Renato, Carlo, and all our friends); Amelia Ewen; Toby Ewen; Explorersweb (Tom and Tina Sjögren); Eyeworks Australia and New Zealand (Julie, Alison, and all); Eyeworks Germany (Kaethe, Andi, Michael, and all); Rebecca Fall; Benjamin Fall; Joanna Fells; Rebecca Fells; Simon Fells; *First Drop* magazine, European Coaster Club (Justin Garvanovic); F.J.T. Logistics Limited (Ray Harper, Gavin Hennessey); Alexis Forcada Zamora; *Forbes;* Formulation Inc. (Marcus, Ayako, Kei, and all our friends); Fuji Television Network, Inc. (Ryu Utsui); Gerontology Research Group; Thomasina Gibson; Gobierno Delegacional de Iztapalapa; Green Events, Llanwrtyd Wells, UK; Brandon Greenwood; Jordan Greenwood; Ryan Greenwood; Victoria Grimsell; Grover Cleveland Birthplace (Sharon Farrell); Hampshire Sports and Prestige Cars (Richard Johnston); High Noon Entertainment (Pam, Jim, Adam, Ian, Mark, Jeremy, and all); Hikone Castle, Shiga, Japan; Lorena Hinojosa; Tamsin Holman; Marsha Hoover; Hunter College of The City University of New York (Dr. Richard Belsky); ICM (Michael and Greg); IGFA (Jack Vitek); IMDB.com; INP Media (Bryn Downing);

Integrated Colour Editions Europe (Roger Hawkins, Susie Hawkins, Clare Merryfield); Intelligent Textiles; International Jugglers' Association; International Sport Juggling Federation; Anita Ives; Dominique Jando; Dr. Lewis Jones; Juggling Information Service; Lambiek (Amsterdam); Orla Langton; Thea Langton; The Leigh Bureau (Jennifer Bird Bowen); London Cocktail Club, Goodge St., London; Sean Macaulay; Lourdes Mangas; Luke Meloy; Metropolis Collectibles, Inc. & ComicConnect, Corp. (Ben Smith); Miditech (Niret, Nivedith, Vidyuth, Tarun, Niraja, Komal, Nischint, Alphi, Mazin, Sunil, Denzil, Monil, Nikita, and all the production team); Harriet Molloy; Joshua Molloy; Sophie Molloy; Matilda Morales; Dora Morales; Moulin Rouge (Fanny Rabasse); Adrian Muscari; NASA; National Geographic Society (Michael Fry); National Oceanic and Atmospheric Administration; National TV Awards; New Jersey State History Fair (Beverly Weaver); *New York Times* (John Noble Wilford); Caroline Newby; Matilda Nieberg; Saúl Nuñez Sanchez; Shaun Opperman; Andrew Peacock; Charlotte Peacock; Stefano Perni; Clara Piccirillo; Robert Pullar; Queens College of The City University of New York (Dr. Morris Rossabi); R&G Productions (Stephane, Jerome, David, Eric, and all our friends); Lauren Randolph; Elizabeth Rayner; Re:fine Group (Alex); David Rea; Restaurante Bismark; Martyn Richards; Ritz-Carlton Hotel, Bachelor Gulch, U.S.A.; Fabián Rojas y familia; Roller Coaster Database (Duane Marden); Rosa Romero Vélez; Royal Geographic Society (Dr. Steven Toole, Lis Parham); Pablo Rubio; MTG Rummery Esq.; James Rushmere; Elley Rushmere; Scarborough Book Festival; Christopher W. Schneider; *The Scottish Sun;* Abdulla Shareef; Mauro Di Sí; Richard Sisson; Society for American Baseball Research (Lyle Spatz); Sotheby's–London (Catherine Slowther, Peter Selley); Sotheby's–New York (Elizabeth R. Muller, Selby Kiffer, Justin Caldwell); Ian Starr; Nick Steel; Stora Enso Veitsiluoto; *The Sun* newspaper (Caroline Iggulden); Holly Taylor; Charlie Taylor; Kevin Thompson; Spencer Thrower; TomTom (Rosie Tickner); Top 8 Magic (Brian David-Marshall, Matthew Wang); TNR; truTV (Marissa, Robyn, Angel, Mark, Stephen, Michael, and all); UNESCO; University of Cambridge (Dr. Lisa Maher, Dr. Jay T. Stock); Majorie Vallee; Andres Vallejo; Donna Vano; Lorenzo Veltri; Viacom18 (Vivek, Rmil, Ashvini, Smitha, Shivani, Sachin, Tanushree, and all); Visit Britain (Charlotte Tuffin); Screech Washington; The Water Rocket Achievement World Record Association; David White; Wildlife Conservation Society (Madeleine Thompson); Wildlife Conservation Society Library (Kerry Prendergast); Beverley Williams; Adam Wilson; Lydia Wood; Barry Woods; Dan Woods; World Juggling Federation; World Sailing Speed Record Council (John Reed); Xara Computers (Adnaan, Muzahir, and team); X Games; Yale University (Dr. Jonathan D. Spence); YouTube; Preity Zinta; Zippy Production (Mitsue).

PICTURE CREDITS

xii, xv Getty Images/Getty Images/Mykel Nicolaou/GWR; **xiii, xv, xvi** Getty Images/Nick Obank/Getty Images/Paul Michael Hughes/GWR/Drew Gardner/GWR; **xviii, xix, xx** (U.S.A.) Brian Palmer/GWR; **xvii, xviii, xxi, xxii, xxiv, xxv** (U.S.A.) Paul Drinkwater/NBC; **xxii** (U.S.A.) Scott Gries; **xxiii, xxiv** (U.S.A.) Brian Brantley/GWR/Kevork Djansezian/Getty Images/Tom Donoghue/David M. Russell/Watershed Visual Media; **xxvi–xxix, xxxiii** Getty Images/Miguel Medina/GWR/Tim Anderson/GWR/Matt May/GWR/Luca Di Tommaso/GWR; **xxviii, xxx, xxxi, xxxii** Jay Williams/GWR; **xxxiv, xxxv, xxxvi, xxxvii, xxxix** Paul Michael Hughes/GWR/Paul Michael Hughes/GWR/Edwin Koo/GWR; **xxxvii, xxxviii** Paul Michael Hughes/GWR; **xl, xli** Photolibrary/Awashima Marine Park/Getty Images; **xlii, xliii, xliv** Gerry Penny/Corbis/NASA/Martin Ruegner/Getty Images; **3** ESA/Herschel; **4, 5** Mountain High/Getty Images/NASA/NASA; **4, 5, 6** NASA/NASA/NASA/Casey Reed/Penn State/NASA; **7, 8** Getty Images/Science Photo Library/NASA; **10** NASA/NASA; **11, 15** NASA; **12, 14, 16** NASA/NASA/NASA/NASA/NASA; **16, 17** NASA/NASA/Ho New/Reuters; **19, 20** NASA/NASA/NASA/John Foster/Science Photo Library; **21, 22** NASA/Getty Images/Getty Images/Getty Images; **21, 22, 23** NASA/NASA/Getty Images/Getty Images; **24, 25, 26** NASA/NASA/Getty Images/NASA/Laurent Hamels/Getty Images; **27, 28** Dr. Scott Lieberman/AP/PA/Getty Images/Alamy/Ralph Morse/Getty Images/Getty Images; **31** Sean Heavey/Barcroft Media; **32** Mark A. Garlick/space-art.co.uk; **33, 34** Alamy/Alamy/smart-elements.com/Getty Images/Getty Images/Warut Roonguthai/Element Photo Gallery/Getty Images/smart-elements.com/David Wall/Alamy/Getty Images; **36, 37** Thomas Kunz/Alamy/Getty Images/Gavin Hellier/Getty Images; **38, 39** Charles O. Cecil/Alamy/Getty Images/George Steinmetz/Corbis/Survival International/Reuters; **39, 40** AFP/Alamy/Getty Images/Daniel Garcia/Getty Images/Russ Widstrand/Getty Images; **40, 41, 42** Alamy/NOAA/Alamy/Hannah Johnston/Getty Images/Getty Images/Alamy; **43, 44, 46** Getty Images/B. O'Kane/Alamy/Philippe Bourseiller/Getty Images; **45, 46** Gary Corbett/Alamy/Robert Frerck/Getty Images/Steve Bloom/Barcroft Media; **47, 48, 49** Getty Images/Getty Images/Getty Images; **49, 50** Getty Images/Getty Images/Alamy; **52, 53, 55** Nati Harnik/AP/PA/Gerard Fritz/Getty Images/Arnar Thorisson/AP/PA; **51, 54, 56** Peter Caton/Artyom Korotayev/Getty Images/WENN; **59, 61** Bruce Davidson/Nature PL/Gunther Michel/Still Pictures/Science Photo Library/Alamy; **60, 61, 62** Photolibrary/Stephen Dalton/NHPA/Pete Oxford/FLPA/Louise Murray/Science Photo Library; **62, 63, 64** Joseph Brown/University of Kansas/AFP/Durrell Wildlife Conservation Trust/Getty Images; **64, 65** Robin Moore/iLCP/Robin Moore/iLCP/Russell A. Mittermeier/Javier Garcí/Conservation International; **66, 67, 69** Robbin

Thorp/AP/PA/Getty Images/Yeshey Dorji; **67, 68** Adnan Moussalli and Devi Stuart-Fox/Bryson Voirin/Getty Images; **71, 73** C & M Fallows/SeaPics/Photolibrary/Alamy; **70, 72** Getty Images/Annie Katz/Getty Images; **75, 76** Thomas Marent/Getty Images/Suzy Bennett/Alamy/FLPA/Alamy; **74, 76, 77** Photolibrary/Alamy/Photolibrary/Michael Giannechini/Science Photo Library; **79, 80, 81** Joel Sartore/National Geographic/Genevieve Vallee/Alamy/Martin Harvey/Corbis; **79, 81, 82** Alamy/FLPA/Tui De Roy/National Geographic; **83, 84, 85** Dr. Jeremy Burgess/Science Photo Library/Science Photo Library/Photolibrary/Photolibrary; **83, 85, 86, 87** Steve Gschmeissner/Science Photo Library/Photolibrary/Steve Gschmeissner/Science Photo Library/David Scharf/Science Photo Library; **87, 88** Eric Vandeville/Getty Images/Photolibrary/Pink Tentacle; **89, 90** Mark Bowler/Nature PL/Ezzal/Ifremer/A. Fifis/Ken Catania/Visuals Unlimited; **93, 95, 96** Tom Gardner/Alamy/City & County of Honolulu/Walt Anderson/Getty Images/Howard Rice/Photolibrary; **92, 93, 94** Daniel J. Cox/Alamy/Alamy/Getty Images/Getty Images; **99** Peter Horree/Alamy; **102, 103** Getty Images/Getty Images/Alisdair Macdonald/Rex Features/Getty Images/Getty Images; **100, 101, 102, 104** Getty Images/Getty Images/Getty Images/Getty Images/Getty Images/Getty Images; **105, 106** Eric Vandeville/Getty Images/Getty Images; **106, 107, 108** Ray Tang/Rex Features/Getty Images/Stan Tess/Alamy/Timm Schamberger/Getty Images; **109, 110, 111** Davit Hakobyan/Getty Images/The Art Archive/Getty Images/Alamy/Erich Lessing/AKG/Erich Lessing/AKG; **109, 110, 111, 112** Getty Images/AKG/Alamy/AKG/Davies and Starr/Getty Images/Alamy/John Cartwright/Alamy; **113, 115** AKG/AKG/Art Archive/AKG/Getty Images; **114, 115** Bridgeman Art Library/Art Archive/British Museum/Alamy; **116, 117, 119, 120** Getty Images/Seth Joel/Corbis/Mary Evans Picture Library/Getty Images; **117, 118, 119, 120** Danita Delimont/Getty Images/Alamy/NASA/Ted Soqui/Corbis/Ian Sanders/Alamy/Alamy; **123** Ranald Mackechnie/GWR; **125, 127** Ranald Mackechnie/GWR/Thomas Mukoya/Reuters/Adrees Latif/Reuters; **124, 125, 126** Chris Lewington/Alamy/Ranald Mackechnie/GWR/John Wright/GWR/John Wright/GWR; **129, 130** Ryan Schude/GWR/Paul Michael Hughes/GWR; **128, 129, 131** Ryan Schude/GWR/John Wright/GWR/Ranald Mackechnie/GWR; **133, 134, 135** Paul Michael Hughes/GWR/John Wright/GWR/Charlie Saceda/Getty Images/Gary Parker; **136** Ryan Schude/GWR/Barcroft Media; **137, 138** Getty Images/Monica M. Davey/Getty Images; **139, 141** Rex Features; **142, 143, 145** Rex Features/John Wright/GWR/John Wright/GWR; **144, 146** Richard Bradbury/GWR/Chris Granger/GWR; **149, 150, 151** Ranald Mackechnie/GWR/Ranald Mackechnie/GWR; **152, 153** John Wright/GWR/Amy Sancetta/AP/PA; **152, 153, 154, 155** Wong Maye-E/AP/PA/Ralph Crane/Getty Images/Alamy; **155, 157, 158** Nick Hannes/GWR/John Wright/GWR; **156, 158, 159** Ranald Mackechnie/GWR/John Wright/GWR; **160, 161, 162** Ranald Mackechnie/GWR/Mike Marsland/GWR; **164, 165, 167, 168** K. K. Najeeb/Ranald Mackechnie/GWR; **165, 166, 168, 169** David M. Russell/Disney ABC/Ranald Mackechnie/GWR/Ranald Mackechnie/GWR; **169, 170, 171, 173** AFP/Aman Sharma/AP/PA; **170, 172** Franz Neumayr/MMV; **174, 176** Toby Melville/Reuters/Ismael Mohamad/Eyevine; **174, 175, 176, 178** Mark

Ralston/Getty Images; **180** John Wright/GWR; **178, 179, 181, 182** Paul Michael Hughes/GWR/John Wright/GWR/John Wright/GWR/John Wright/GWR; **185, 186** Ranald Mackechnie/GWR/Paul Michael Hughes/GWR; **183, 184** Ranald Mackechnie/GWR; **187, 189, 190** John Wright/GWR; **188, 191** John Wright/GWR/John Wright/GWR; **192, 194, 195** Getty Images/Brian Thompson/Shinsuke Kamioka/GWR; **197, 198, 199** Ranald Mackechnie/GWR/Tim Anderson/GWR/John Wright/GWR; **200, 201, 202** Paul Michael Hughes/GWR; **200, 203, 204** Craig Lenihan/AP/PA/Craig Lenihan/AP/PA; **207** Adam Moore/GWR; **208, 210** Nicholas DeVore/Getty Images/PA/PA; **210, 211, 212** Bill Janscha/AP/PA/AFP/Getty Images/Getty Images/AP/PA/AP/PA/Getty Images; **214, 216** Keith Ducatel/Keith Ducatel/Andy Sillaber; **213, 215** Shinsuke Kamioka/GWR; **217, 219, 221** Galen Rowell/Corbis; **218, 220** Namgyal Sherpa/Getty Images/Ryan Schude/GWR; **223, 224, 226** Richard Bradbury/GWR; **227, 228** Rex Features; **226, 227** Tony Cheng/AP/PA/Richard Bradbury/GWR; **229, 230, 232** Corbis/Vincent Yu/AP/PA; **231, 232** Cate Gillon/Getty Images/Richard Bradbury/GWR; **233, 235, 236** U.S.A.F./Jay Williams/GWR/Reuters; **234, 235** Carl De Souza/Getty Images/Thierry Boccon-Gibod-Pool/Getty Images/U.S.A.F./Ryan Schude/GWR; **239** Reuters; **239, 240, 242** World-mapper.org/Getty Images; **240** Getty Images/Getty Images; **244, 246, 247** Reuters/Rodrigo Arangua/Getty Images/David Greedy/Getty Images/Jaime Saldarriaga/Reuters; **245, 246, 247** Larry W. Smith/Getty Images/Maya Vidon/Getty Images/Getty Images/Veronique de Viguerie/Getty Images; **247, 248** Mahmoud Ahmadinejad/Getty Images/Vitaly Armand/Getty Images; **248, 249, 250, 251** Alexander Nemenov/Getty Images/Ben Stansall/Getty Images/Manpreet Romana/Getty Images/Chung Sung-Jun/Getty Images; **252, 254** Paul Michael Hughes/GWR; **255, 256** Ryan Schude/GWR; **257, 258** Anwar Amro/Getty Images/Umit Bektas/Reuters/Paul Michael Hughes/GWR; **260, 262** Paul Michael Hughes/GWR; **259, 261** Geoffrey Swaine/Rex Features/Rex Features/Rex Features; **263, 264** Paul Michael Hughes/GWR/Ryan Schude/GWR; **265, 266** Lu Liang/Paul Michael Hughes/GWR/Jacob Chinn/GWR; **268, 269** Ryan Schude/GWR/Ryan Schude/GWR; **268, 269, 270** Rex Features; **271, 273** Ranald Mackechnie/GWR; **272** Ryan Schude/GWR; **276, 278** Shinsuke Kamioka/GWR/Ranald Mackechnie/GWR; **275, 277** Ranald Mackechnie/GWR/Stuart Hendry/GWR; **280, 281, 283** Geoff Pugh/Rex Features/Amit Dave/Reuters/Divya Bhaskar/Barcroft Media; **285, 288** Paula Bronstein/Getty Images/Rex Features/Sukree Sukplang/Reuters/Getty Images; **286, 287, 288** Alastair Muir/Rex Features/Miramax/Kobal/Nils Jorgensen/Rex Features/Fox TV/Getty Images/Fred Duval/Getty Images/Paul Grover/Getty Images; **289, 290, 291** Alamy/Alamy/Getty Images/Betsie Van der Meer/Getty Images; **292, 293** AP/PA/Scott J. Ferrel/Getty Images; **297** Stuart Hendry/GWR; **297, 298, 299, 300** AFP/Getty Images/Alamy/Alamy/Los Alamos National Laboratory/SPL; **298, 300, 301** PA/Getty Images/Getty Images/Los Alamos National Laboratory/PA/Kevin Murrell/Getty Images; **303** Colorado State University/Steve Allen/AFP/Ho New/Reuters; **304, 305** CERN/CERN/ESA/Alexander Nemenov/Getty Images; **305, 306, 309** SII Nanotechnology Inc./M. Fuchsle/AFP/Hari Manoharan/Stanford University/Periodic

Videos/Periodic Videos/D. Carr and H. Craighead/Cornell University; **307, 308, 309** Advanced Materials/Science/AAAS/NIST/CU; **314, 315, 316, 318** Alexa Reach/Getty Images/Getty Images/Ian Dagnall/Alamy; **315, 317, 318** zynga/youtube.com/Judson Laipply; **319, 320, 321** Vanderbilt Cup Races/Getty Images/E. Bacon/Getty Images/Corbis/Getty Images/Corbis/Corbis/Troxx/AP/PA; **319, 323** Nathan Allred; **324, 325, 327** John Gaps/AP/PA/Ho New/Reuters/NASA; **326, 327** Rajan Chaughule/Getty Images/AP/PA/Alamy; **328, 329, 331** Alamy/Joao Abreu Miranda/Getty Images; **329, 330** PA; **332, 333, 334** Charlie Magee/Sean Gallup/Getty Images/Tim Wallace/Newspress; **334, 335, 336** Getty Images; **337, 338** Miniatur Wunderland/Yoshikazu Tsuno/Getty Images/Getty Images; **339, 340** Getty Images/Photolibrary/K. K. Arora/Reuters; **341, 344** WENN/Patrik Stollarz/Getty Images/Geoffrey Robinson/Rex Features; **343, 344** Richard Bradbury/GWR/David Torrence/GWR; **346, 347, 348** Jack Guez/Getty Images; **345, 347, 348** Todd Reichert/Todd Reichert/Laurent Gillieron/Getty Images; **350, 352** U.S. Navy/U.S. Navy; **349** Getty Images/Getty Images; **353, 355** Patrick H. Corkery/Unitel Launch Alliance; **352, 354** Jo Yong/Reuters/David Silverman/Getty Images; **356, 357, 358** Photolibrary/WENN; **357, 359** Mitchell Funk/Getty Images; **361, 362, 364** Chris Cheadle/Alamy/Getty Images/Mosab Omar/Reuters/Ho New/Reuters; **363, 364** Michael James Brown/Alamy/Phil Roche/MDC; **365, 366** Getty Images; **365, 367, 368** Getty Images; **369, 370, 371** WENN/Ranald Mackechnie/GWR; **373, 374** Tim Anderson/GWR; **374, 375** Ranald Mackechnie/GWR; **379** Disney/Pixar; **379, 380, 381** George Doyle/Getty Images/Lucasfilm Ltd./Ronald Grant Archive/20th Century Fox/Rex Features/Chelsea Lauren/Getty Images; **381, 382** Daniel Sakow/PA; **383, 384, 386** Shinsuke Kamioka/GWR; **384, 385** Ryan Schude/GWR; **387, 388, 389** Wizards of the Coast/Sonny Meddle/Rex Features; **387, 389, 390** Wizards of the Coast/Wizards of the Coast; **391, 393, 394** Getty Images; **393, 394** Timothy A. Clary/AFP/Alamy; **395, 396** Warner Bros./Warner Bros./Warner Bros./Disney; **397, 398** 20th Century Fox/Warner Bros.; **399, 400, 401, 402, 403** Getty Images/Globo Films/Kobal Collection/Melampo/Kobal Collection/Touhoku Shinsha/Kobal Collection/Kobal Collection/Getty Images; **400, 401, 402, 403** Kobal Collection/Rex Features/Paramount/Rex Features/Kobal Collection/Kobal Collection/Yogen Shah/Getty Images; **404, 406, 407** Michael Tran/Getty Images/Kevin Winter/Getty Images/Rex Features; **405, 408** Tom Watkins/Rex Features; **411, 412, 413** Carlos R. Alvarez/Getty Images/Kevin Winter/Getty Images; **409, 410, 412** Ian West/PA/Kevin Winter/Getty Images/Charlie Gray; **413, 416** Marjorie Curty; **414** Ranald Mackechnie/GWR; **417, 418, 420** CBS/HBO/ITV/HBO; **419, 420, 421** NBC/Rex Features/Rex Features/Rex Features; **422, 425, 426** Kobal Collection/Rex Features; **422, 423, 424** Popperfoto/Getty Images/BBC; **427, 428, 429** Alamy/Rex Features/Roger Bamber/Rex Features/Getty Images/Rex Features; **429, 430** ITV/Rex Features/BBC/CBS; **431, 432** Getty Images/Peter Macdiarmid/Getty Images; **432, 433, 434** Gjon Mili/Getty Images/Peter Macdiarmid/Getty Images/Julian Andrews/Getty Images/Getty Images/Getty Images/Getty Images/Getty Images/Getty Images; **437** Red Bull; **438, 439, 441** Getty Images/Getty Images/Andy Lyons/Getty Images/

Reuters/Mike Blake/Reuters/Philippe Huguen/Getty Images/Getty Images; **439, 440, 441** Rex Features/Christopher Lee/Getty Images; **441, 442, 443, 444** Alamy/British Museum Images/Getty Images/Getty Images/Getty Images/Getty Images; **444, 445, 446** Getty Images/Getty Images/Phil Walter/Getty Images/Getty Images/Jason Lee/Reuters; **447, 448** Getty Images/Stuart Franklin/Action Images/Adam Pretty/Getty Images; **449, 450** Ron Kuntz/Getty Images/Daniel Garcia/Getty Images/Jerry Cooke/Getty Images; **454, 455** Mark Ralston/Getty Images/Frederic J. Brown/Getty Images; **452, 453, 455** Bob Thomas/Getty Images/Scott Barbour/Getty Images/Ng Han Guan/AP/PA; **458, 460, 461** Dennis Flaherty/Getty Images/Joe Robbins/Getty Images/Nick Laham/Getty Images/Victor Decolongon/Getty Images/Donald Miralle/Getty Images; **465, 464, 467** Al Bello/Getty Images/Jamie Squire/Getty Images/Jonathan Nackstrand/Getty Images/Ethan Miller/Getty Images/Jed Jacobsohn/Getty Images/Robyn Beck/Getty Images; **465, 464, 467** Allen Einstein/Getty Images/Lee Warren/Getty Images/Reuters/Rex Features; **464, 465, 466, 467** Getty Images/Morry GashAP/PA/Hamish Blair/Getty Images/Tim Wimborne/Reuters; **468, 469** Phil Walter/Getty Images/Shaun Botterill/Getty Images/Clive Mason/Getty Images/Jewel Samad/Getty Images; **470, 471** John MacDougall/Getty Images/Doug Pensinger/Getty Images/Getty Images/Gerard Julien/Getty Images; **472, 473, 476** Aizar Raldes/Getty Images/Matthew Stockman/Getty/Damien Meyer/Getty Images; **473, 474, 475** Don Emmert/Getty Images/Patin Carrera/Brian Bahr/Getty Images; **477, 478, 479** Timothy A. Clary/Getty Images/Jose Jordan/Getty Images/Guillaume Baptiste/Getty Images; **477, 479, 480** Patrik Stollarz/Getty Images/Fred Dufour/Getty Images/David Cannon/Getty Images; **482, 483, 484** Torsten Blackwood/Getty Images/PA/Nancy Lane/AP/PA/Stanko Gruden/Getty Images; **482, 484** Adam Nurkiewicz/Getty Images/Matthew Peters/Getty Images/Getty Images/Robert Riger/Getty Images; **485, 486, 488, 489** Gerry Penny/Getty Images/Getty Images/Getty Images/Walter Iooss Jr./Getty Images; **487, 488** Clive Mason/Getty Images/Brendan McDermid/Reuters/Getty Images/Getty Images; **490, 491, 493** Julian Finney/Getty Images/Shaun Curry/Getty Images; **494, 495** Rogan Ward/Reuters/Josh Hedges/Getty Images/Peter Jones/Reuters/Richard Bouhet/Getty Images; **496, 497** Stefano Rellandini/Reuters; **499, 501** Albert Gea/Reuters/Julian Herbert/Getty Images/Alan Crowhurst/Getty Images; **498, 500** Vincent Jannink/Getty Images/Paul Gilham/Getty Images/Al Bello/Getty Images/Jesse D. Garrabrant/Getty Images; **502, 503, 504** Christian Petersen/Getty Images/Mark Dadswell/Getty Images/Shuji Kajiyama/AP/PA/AP/PA; **502, 504** David Ramos/Getty Images/Graham Stewart/Getty Images/Sankei/Getty Images; **505, 507, 508** Shaun Botterill/Getty Images/Emmanuel Dunand/Getty Images/Paul Kane/Getty Images; **506, 507** Alexander Joe/Getty Images/Getty Images/David E. Klutho/Getty Images; **509, 510** Tom Lovelock/AP/PA; **512, 513** Richard Bradbury/GWR/Images of Life; **514, 515, 516** Miguel Villagran/Getty Images/Emma Wood/Shinsuke Kamioka/GWR/Paul Michael Hughes/GWR; **516, 517, 520** Terje Bendiksby/Getty Images/PA/Robert Brown/Billabong XXL .com; **517, 518, 519** Heinz Kluetmeier/Getty Images/Alamy/Andy Hooper/Rex Features; **523, 527** Tiziana Fabi/Getty Images; **527** Esko Anttila; **529,**

IN MEMORIAM

A. Alexander (**longest magic show**), Walter Breuning (**oldest man**), Herbert Fischer (**one-half of the oldest living married couple**), Fluffy (**longest snake in captivity**), James Fuchs (**most shot-put competitions won**), Oscar (**oldest ever pig**), Eunice Sanborn (**oldest woman**), Valerio De Simoni (**longest journey by ATV**), Jack Stepham (**highest combined age for four siblings**), Grete Waitz (**most wins of the New York Marathon, female**), Samuel Wanjiru (**fastest London and Chicago Marathons**).

INDEX

This year's index is organized into two parts: by subject and by superlative. **Bold entries** in the subject index indicate a main entry on a topic, and **BOLD CAPITALS** indicate an entire chapter. Neither index lists personal names.

SUBJECT INDEX

death-dives, 154
deaths, 176; Everest, 210; Isle of Man
    TT, 519; lightning, 230, 231; natural
    disasters, 382; by robot, 305; space,
    24–28; in war, 119
Deepwater Horizon, 325
density, xii
department stores, 249
depths of space, 6–10
deserts, xliv, 40, 94, 132
detectives, TV, 423, 424, 425
diamonds, 4
dirndls, 173
disasters: space, 24–28; nuclear reactor, 419
discus, 447, 532
distance & duration, 481–85
diving: board, 447, 498, 511, 512; cliff,
    437; death-dive, 154; freediving, 520,
    535; scuba, 140, 173, 274, 275, 521
diving suits, 172
diving watches, 314
divorce, 100
Djoser Step Pyramid, Egypt, 109
DJs, 413
DNA, 243
Do Not Disturb signs, 275
dodgeball, 175
dogs, 109, 186, **263–67;** bark, 265;
    collections, 271; fancy dress, xxviii;
    search dogs, 355; skipping, 192; sled
    dogs, 495, 521; in space, 28; walking,
    266; wild, 71
dolls, voodoo, 371
dolphins, 50, 64
dominoes, 280; human, 175
Donald Duck, 271
donkeys, 271
drag racing, 475, 500
dragons, 271
Dreadnought, HMS, 351
dreams, 234
dressing up: dogs, xxviii; marathon runners,
    492; mass participation, 176, 177, 536
drinks, 255, 258
driving, 475, 476
drugs, 244, 247, 250
drums, 415
ducks, rubber, 274
duct tape, 191
DVDs, 418

E

eagles, 72
ear: hair, 142; wax, 434

early civilizations, 111
earnings, 458–62; fashion designer, 172;
    models, 171; sportsmen, 458–62
ears, 90, 264
Earth, 31–34; population, 239–43
earthquakes, 303
eating, 256, 259, 261, 448; animals, 71, 89
echidna, 68
egg-and-spoon race, 513
eggs, 89, 159, 186, 262; balancing, 183,
    259; dyeing, 592; throwing, 189
Egypt, ancient, 109
Eisner comic awards, 382
electric: aircraft, 345; railroad, 336;
    vehicles, 329, 332
electricity, 183, 443
electronics, consumer, 310–314
elephants, 154, 155, 243, 272
Elvis costumes, 177
Emmy Awards, 427
empires, 112–16
encryption, 289
endangered species, 66–70, 96
energy, 32, 33, 329; alternative, 328–32
English Channel, 235
ENIAC computer, 297
Enterprise, USS, 350
epic architecture, 360–64
Estonia, 400
Europa, 14
Everest Marathon, 518
Everest, Mount, xxxix, **209–12,** 218, 219,
    220; flights over, 236
executions, 243, 246
Explorers' Grand Slam, 220
exploring the poles, 221–25
eyebrows, 142
eyes, 90, 593

F

Facebook, 316, 318, 591
falafels, 258
fantastic voyages, 212–17
fashion, 169–73, 412
fastest on wheels, 472–76
fasting, 84
feet, 131
fencing, 447
ferrets, 513
fertility rate, 38
festivals, 80
fiddles, 413
FIFA World Cup, xxxiv, xxxv, 467, 468,
    480, 498, 506

Index

running: endurance, 495, 497; in high
heels, 191, 514; man vs horse, 513;
transcontinental, 213, 481; wall
running, 150; *see also* track & field;
marathons
runs (cricket), 466
Russia, 402
Ryder Cup (golf), 508

S

sailing, xliii, 231
salads, 257
Salamis, Battle of, 112
saliva, 256
salt, 518
salt & pepper shakers, 277
Salyut 1 space station, 28
sandcastles, 161
sandwiches, 256, 388
sat-navs, 108
satellites, 353
sausages, 255
saxophones, 415
scales, 309
scarification, 125
SCI-TECH & ENGINEERING,
295–376
science, 302–05, 427, 428
scooters, 163
scorpions, 61
scrapbooks, 279
scratchcards, 376
screens, 311, 312, 593
screws, xxvi
scuba-diving, 173, 274, 275, 521
sculpture, 434; balloon, xv; coat hangers,
434
Sedna, 8
seeds, 112, 302
Seven Summits, 217, 218, 221
shafts, 188
Shark Bay, Australia, 50
sharks, xli, 72
ships, 246; **warships, 349–52**
Shoemaker-Levy 9 comet, 11
shoes, xxx, 110, 151, 165, 170, 224, 367
shooting, 447, 457
shopping carts, 373
shops, 248, 249
shrimps, 90
siblings, 135, 139
Sid Meier's Civilization, 386
sideflips, 150
simulators, spaceflight, 305

singing, 416, 417
singlets, 177
Sirius Star, 327
Six Nations (rugby), 467, 497
skateboarding, 163, 200, 488, 515;
journeys, 215
skateboards, 371
skating, 366; inline, 473, 476, 510; limbo,
591; *see also* ice skating
ski jumping, 482, 516
skiing, 10, 11; kite-ski, 216; marathons,
548–51; Nordic, 301; polar, 255; sand
dune, 300; speed, 470, 499
SKILLS & TALENTS, 147–204
skin, 124, 125, 161
skipping, 176; dogs, 192; Double Dutch,
xxx; Texas, 158
skuas, 70
skydiving, 154, 471, 510
Skyrunner World Series, 495, 497
skyscrapers, 119
sled dog racing, 495, 521
sloths, 68
smiley faces, 178
smoothies, 258
snails, 274
snakes, 70, 73
sneezing, 303, 510
sniper detectors, 353
snooker, 460, 465, 472, 480, 485
snow, 55, 182
snowballs, 250, 376
snowboarding, 550–51
snow-kiting, 224
snow leopard, 72
snowmobiles, 342, 511
soap bubbles, xiii
soap operas, 421
soccer, 157, 471, 485, 498, 501, 502;
Australian, 507; Canadian, 503;
earnings, 460; European, 467, 481,
498, 501, 502, 505, 506; five-a-side,
550–51; goals, xxxiv, 453, 467, 468,
471, 487, 489, 498, 501, 502, 503;
managers, 484; marathons, 550–51;
tournaments, 452, 483, 498, 501;
video games, 383; World Cup, xxxiv,
xxxv, 468, 480, 481, 506
soccer balls, 368; balanced on head, 187;
juggling, 197, 399; keepy uppy,
174
social networks, 314, 316, 317, 318
SOCIETY, 237–94
socks, 170, 183, 186
solar power: aircraft, 347; automobile,

V

vacations, 79, 215
vampires, 177
VARIETY OF LIFE, 57–96
Vatican City, 66
vaults, 150, 160
vegetables, 251–53
vehicles, 341–44; alternative power, 329–32
video gaming, 337, **383–85**, 427; arcade games, 336; consoles, 311, 313; 383; dance games, 166, 386; marathons, 277, 383; peripherals, 313
village Earth, 239–43
violins, 413, 416
Vogue magazine, 170
voice, human, xv
volcanoes, 14, 15, 42, 45, 46, 53, 396, 481; lava, 397, 480
volleyball, 444, 550–51
vomit, 227
voting, 119, 165
Voyager spacecraft, 7, 12
voyages, 212–17
vuvuzelas, 374

W

waistlines, 126
walking: cable, 207; circumnavigation, 231; journeys, 213, 214, 216; Nordic, 216
wallets, 376
wars, 119, 248, 249, 250, 251
warships, 349–52
washing machines, 185
washing up, 185
wasps, 61, 78
waste containers, 343
watches, 116, 314
water, 33, 34, 47–51, 249; walking on, 88
watercress, 261
waterfalls, 51
watering cans, 374
water lilies, 95
watermelons, 158, 179
waterskiing, 366, 552–53
water slides, xxviii
water world, 47–51
waves, 329, 520
waxing, 160
wedding chapels, 344
weddings, 305, 355
weight: holding, 178; lifting, 178, 496, 546–47; 593

whales, 43, 82
what's on TV, 417–21
wheel skills, 200–04
wheelchairs: basketball, 453, 457; marathon, 457; 474, 475; Paralympics, 452; rugby, 453
wheelies: bicycle, 201, 204; motorcycle, 192, 324
whips, 159, 194
whiskers, 268
whistling, 416
whoopee cushions, xv
wickets (cricket), 463
Wikileaks, 314
wildebeest, 80
Wimbledon, 464, 477, 484, 487
wind, xiii
wind power, 329, 331
windows, 180, 186
windsurfing, 521
wine, 46, 47, 465
wine labels, 464
wing suits, xii
wing walking, xxx, 233
winning ways, 497–501
Wizard of Oz, The, xxxii
WNBA (Women's National Basketball Association), 462, 467, 500, 504
wombat, 77
women's suffrage, 119
world championships: *air guitar,* xiv; wacky sports, 513–16; *see also specific sports*
world cinema, 399–403
World Heritage sites, 43–51
World of Warcraft, 337, 384
world of wonders, 43–47
world wide web, 119
world's fastest . . . , 467–71
worms, xlii, 86
wrestling: finger, 514; mashed potato, 516; sumo, 176, 496, 504
writing, 112, 322

X Y Z

X Games, 499
Yellowstone National Park, U.S.A., 47
yo-yos, 159, 283, 371, 513
yoga, 140, 595
youngest & oldest, 476–81
YouTube, 286, 317
Yukon Quest, 495
zooplankton, 78
zoos, 108

SUPERLATIVE INDEX

STOP PRESS

●**Longest time without a government in peacetime** As of May 16, 2011, Belgium had gone 337 days without a government, following elections in June 2010. The record (which may have been beaten by the time you read this) is 354 days—on July 27, 2003, the National Assembly elections in Cambodia failed to give any one party the two-thirds majority of seats required to form a government, a stalemate that was not resolved until July 15, 2004.

○**Longest journey on an ATV** At the time of going to press, the Expedition Squad—Valerio De Simoni, Kristopher Davant, and James Kenyon (all Australia)—had exceeded the previous record distance of 16,864 miles (27,141 km) to register the longest journey on an ATV. The group continued their tour, hoping to complete an estimated 31,070 miles (50,000 km).

○**Most downloaded podcast** The Adam Carolla Show (U.S.A.) received 59,574,843 unique downloads from March 2009 to March 16, 2011.

●**Farthest distance limbo skating under automobiles** Rohan Ajit Kokane (India) limbo-skated for a distance of 126 ft. 11 in. (38.68 m) under automobiles for *Guinness World Records—Ab India Todega* at the Juhu Aerodrome in Mumbai, India, on February 17, 2011.

●**Most comments on a Facebook post** A post on the Facebook page for Roberto Esposito (Italy) on January 10, 2011, drew 389,141 comments.

○**LONGEST RIDE THROUGH A TUNNEL OF FIRE** Shabir Ahluwalia (India) took his motorcycle on a death-defying ride through a 224-ft. 8-in. (68.49-m) tunnel of fire on the set of *Guinness World Records—Ab India Todega* in Mumbai, India, on March 13, 2011. Even more impressively, he went through the tunnel twice.

●FASTEST TIME TO CLIMB THE BURJ KHALIFA TOWER SOLO Alain Robert (France) took 6 hr. 13 min. 55 sec. to top the Burj Khalifa tower, the world's **tallest building**, in Dubai, UAE, completing his task at 12:17 a.m. on March 29, 2011.

Alain had not climbed the building before and sought permission from real-estate developer Emaar Properties, who convinced him to wear safety equipment during the attempt. Alain did so, but chose his own method of climbing, using only his bare hands and rubber shoes.

TALL STORY Alain's daredevil climbs have seen him clash with the authorities, and he has been arrested and imprisoned many times. He has used his climbs to raise thousands of dollars for charities, though.

●**Most people dyeing eggs** A group of 317 people dyed eggs together at Carowinds (U.S.A.) in Charlotte, North Carolina, U.S.A., on April 23, 2011. The Easter-themed record attempt launched a summer 2011 partnership between Guinness World Records and Cedar Fair Entertainment Company.

●**Most espressos made in one hour (team)** The Coffee Club Aspley (Australia) brewed up 5,061 espressos in Brisbane, Australia, on October 7, 2010. Five espresso machines were used, with four team members to each machine.

●**LOUDEST CAT PURR** Smokey, owned by Lucinda Ruth Adams (UK), produced a purr that peaked at 67.7 dB—measured from a distance of 3 ft. 3 in. (1 m)—the loudest by a domestic cat, on March 25, 2011. This purr-fect achievement took place at Spring Hill farm, Pitsford, Northampton, UK.

●**Heaviest weight lifted with both eye sockets** On April 28, 2011, Yang Guang He (China) lifted an eye-watering 51 lb. 12.96 oz. (23.5 kg)—in the form of two buckets of water—using only his orbits on the set of *Lo Show dei Record*, in Milan, Italy.

GWR iPad challenges Following the launch of the *Guinness World Records at Your Fingertips* app, three individuals set new iPad world records: ●**fastest time to type the alphabet backward**: "Neurojc," 2.03 seconds (January 31, 2011); ●**fastest 100 meters**: "Kenny!," 6.28 seconds (April 23, 2011); ●**most color sequences memorized**: "ilyas.isk," 67 (March 29, 2011).

●**Largest 3D-movie screen** LG Electronics (South Korea) unveiled a supersized 3,196.87-ft.² (297-m²) 3D-movie screen at the Grand Palais in Paris, France, on April 21, 2011. The screen was created to showcase their latest 3D technology and was 88 ft. 6 in. (27 m) long and 36 ft. 1 in. (11 m) wide.

At the same event, the company also assembled the ●**largest attendance at a 3D-film screening**. An audience of 1,148 watched the animated film *Rio* (U.S.A., 2011) in stereoscopic 3D.

●**Fastest time to pull an aircraft 25 m** On April 21, 2011, Žydrūnas Savickas (Lithuania) pulled an aircraft 82 ft. 0.2 in. (25 m) in 48.97 seconds on the set of *Lo Show dei Record*, in Milan, Italy. For this record, the aircraft, including the pilot, must weigh more than 11.02 tons (10 metric tons).

○**LONGEST GLOW-IN-THE-DARK NECKLACE** At the Edinburgh Science Festival in Scotland, UK, on April 9, 2011, mad scientist Dr. Bunhead—aka Tom Pringle (UK)—and The Glow Company created a chemiluminescent necklace measuring an incredible 1,071 ft. (326 m) long. It was worn by 100 volunteers simultaneously.

○**KAZOO ENSEMBLE** A 5,190-strong kazoo ensemble appeared on March 14, 2011, at the "Big Red Nose Show" in the Royal Albert Hall, London, UK. Backed by the BBC Concert Orchestra, and led by comedienne Sue Perkins, they performed Richard Wagner's "Ride of the Valkyries" and Eric Coates's "Dambusters March."

WHAT A BUZZ! Pictured are BBC Radio 3 presenter Katie Derham and funny fox Basil Brush contributing to the kazoo collective. No formal kazoo training is required—just pop it in your mouth and hum!

○**Fastest guitar player** Vanny Tonon (Italy) played "The Flight of the Bumblebee," by Nikolai Rimsky-Korsakov, at a speed of 340 beats per minute (BPM) on the set of *Lo Show dei Record,* in Milan, Italy, on April 21, 2011.

○**Longest time to hold the breath underwater (male)** Ricardo da Gama Bahia (Brazil) held his breath for a lung-bursting 20 min. 21 sec. while submerged at Estilo Swimming School in Rio de Janeiro, Brazil, on September 16, 2010.

GWR GOES TO INDIA

As we go to press, we are delighted to announce the launch of our new TV show in India: *Guinness World Records—Ab India Todega*. Below are just a few of the highlights that have already featured on the show. We look forward to many more exciting new records from India in the year to come!

●**MOST CONSECUTIVE YOGA POSITIONS ON A MOTORCYCLE** Yogaraj C. P. (India) held 23 consecutive yoga poses while riding a motorcycle in Mumbai, India, on February 17, 2011.

The ●**most balloons released by an airplane ribbon-cut** are 5,734, by Anil Thapar, with the help of Preity Zinta (both India), in Baramati, India, on February 24, 2011.

●**FASTEST HOT-WATER BOTTLE BURST (FEMALE)** Shobha S. Tipnis (India) blew up and burst a standard hot-water bottle in 41.20 seconds in Mumbai, India, on March 17, 2011.

The ●**fastest 20 m wife-carrying backwards** is 9.82 seconds, by Manav Gohil and Shweta Kawaatra (both India) in Jogeshwari, Mumbai, on March 18, 2011.

●**MOST LAYERED BED-OF-NAILS SANDWICH**
Vispi and his team (all India)—five people altogether—created a record-breaking bed-of-nails sandwich in Mumbai, India, on February 23, 2011. They held the position for 26 seconds.